رجال حول الرسول

Men Around The Messenger

Khalid Muhammed Khalid

Islamic Book Service

Men Around The Messenger

by Khalid Muhammed Khalid

ISBN: 81-7231-399-3

Reprint Edition- 2004

Published by ***Abdul Naeem*** for
Islamic Book Service
2241, Kucha Chelan, Darya Ganj, New Delhi-110 002
Ph.: 23253514, 23265380, 23286551, Fax: 23277913
E-mail: ibsdelhi@del2.vsnl.net.in
islamic@eth.net
Website:www.islamic-india.com

Printed at: ***Noida Printing Press,*** C-31, Sector-7, Noida (Ghaziabad) U.P.

CONTENTS

TRANSLATOR'S PREFAÇE

While reading this book, we cannot help but be moved by the lives of the Companions herein depicted. How we long to have their awe and reverence for Allah! How we long to spend the same hours in worship as they! How we long to be as brave as they were in the face of danger! How we long to be as patient as they were under torture!

Narrated 'Abd Allah (May Allah be pleased with him): The Prophet (PBUH) said, "The best people are those living in my generation, and then those who will follow them, and then those who will follow the latter. Then there will come some people who will bear witness before taking oaths, and take oaths before bearing witness." (Bukhaarii)

It is our hope that this book will fulfill a need for the English speaking Muslim to learn more about that first generation of Muslims. Indeed the Companions - those men and women who were contemporaneous with the Prophet Mubammad (PBUH) -- inspire and encourage us. Read these stories and share them with your children, for these Companions are a part of our Islamic heritage that will, Allah willing, strengthen us as a nation if we try to follow their examples.

Enough said for the reason for choosing this book to translate, for the book stands on its own merit. Let us explain our reasons for some choices within the translation.

The translator is always faced with the question of how to transliterate. Arabic names and whether to translate or transliterate Islamic terms. The reader may find the spelling of names in this book different than he or she is accustomed to. That is because we have chosen to transliterate as closely to the Arabic pronunciation as possible, believing that the English-speaking Muslim should make an effort to pronounce the names correctly. Lacking diacritic marks, we have transliterated the long vowels with double vowels, which should not confuse the reader. Please refer to the notes on transliteration which follow.

An exception to this is the spelling of some places names. If there is an English form of a name available, this has been used instead of a transliterated Arabic name.

As for Islamic terms, we felt that most of the terms left in the Arabic would be familiar to the Muslim reader, and they have not been italicized as foreign terms although, as noted above, their spelling may not be the usual one. Many of these words have been incorporated into the English language and may be found in many dictionaries, although the Muslim reader is not always satisfied with the dictionary's definition. Therefore, a glossary has been provided for those words which may not be familiar to all readers.

Numbers within parentheses refer to surah and verse of the Holy Qur'aan.

May Almighty Allah accept this work, and may we and all those who participated in the preparation of this text be accepted into the presence of the Most High on the day when nothing, neither wealth nor children, will be useful.

NOTES ON TRANSLITERATION

Arabic	English
ء	' (omitted in initial position)
ب	b
ت	t
ة	h or t (when followed by another Arabic word)
ث	th
ج	j
ح	h
خ	kh
د	d
ذ	dh
ر	r
ز	z
س	s
ش	sh
ص	s
ض	d
ط	t
ظ	dh
ع	

غ	gh
ف	f
ق	q
ك	k
ل	l
م	m
ن	n
هـ	h
و	w (consonant or dipthong) uu (long vowel)
ي	y (consonant) ii (long vowel)
ا	aa (long vowel)
اَ	fatḫah a
اِ	Kasrah i
اُ	ḏummah u
ّ	shiddah double letter

IN THE NAME OF ALLAH,
THE MOST BENEFICENT, THE MOST MERCIFUL

INTRODUCTION

It was neither invented discourse nor false rumor that was recorded in history about the great company of men who came into the world of belief and faith. That is because the entirety of human history has never witnessed such accurate documentation, honesty, and investigation of facts as did that epoch of Islamic history and its men. An extraordinary human effort has been exerted to study and pursue its tidings. Successive generations of able and brilliant scholars have not left unexamined even the smallest details nor minutest explanations concerning that early epoch without putting them under microscopic investigation, scrutiny, and criticism.

The spectacular magnitude we encounter on the pages of this book of those colossal men of the Companions of the Messenger (PBUH) is not something legendary, even though they may seem like legends due to their miraculous nature! These are facts characteristic of the personality and life of the Prophet's Companions. They soar high and are exalted and ennobled, not because of the author or, depicter, but because of what the Companions themselves desired and the extraordinary and righteous effort they exerted for the sake of excelling and attaining perfection.

This book does not claim the power to present this immaculate and extraordinary magnitude to the reader. Suffice it to refer to its characteristics and to approach its horizon.

Surely history has not witnessed men who set their intentions and will to achieve a totally lofty and just goal and then devoted their entire lives to it in such an extremely fearless manner, with personal sacrifice and exertion, as it has witnessed in these men around the Messenger (PBUH).

They came to life at their appointed time and their promised day. When life was craving for someone to rejuvenate its spiritual values, those Companions came with their noble Messenger (PBUH) as heralds and sincere believers. When life was craving for someone to remove the shackles of troubled humanity and to liberate its existence and destiny, they came and stood by their great Messenger as revolutionaries and liberators. When life was craving for someone to, present human civilization with new and sound inclination, they came as pioneers and luminaries.

How could those righteous men achieve what they did in a few years! How did they triumph over the ancient world, with all its empires and sovereignties, and turn it into a ruinous mount! How could they build with Allah's Qur'aan and His Words a new world reverberating with freshness, glittering with glory and surpassing in capability! Above all, how were they able, with the speed of light, to illuminate human conscience with the truth of monotheism and sweep away forever the paganism of ancient centuries! This was their real miracle!

Moreover, their real miracle resides in that remarkable psychological power with which they shaped their virtues and adhered to their faith in a manner that defies comparison.

However, all their achieved miracles were nothing but a modest reflection of the greater miracle that enlightened the world on the day Allah willed His noble Qur'aan to be sent down, His honorable Messenger to deliver the message, and the procession of Islam to start its paces on the road of enlightenment.

In this book, which was previously published in five separate parts and is issued now in a complete new edition, we present sixty personalities of the Prophet's Companions, (May Allah have peace upon them all). As mentioned at the conclusion of this book, these sixty men represent several thousand others of their brethren who were contemporaneous with the Messenger (PBUH) and who believed in him and supported him. In their reflection we see the images of all the Companions. We see their faith, their constancy, their heroism and their loyalty to Allah and His Messenger (PBUH). We see the effort they exerted, the calamities they endured, and the victory they achieved. We also see the eminent role they played in liberating all humanity from the paganism of conscience and the loss of destiny.

However, the reader will not encounter among these sixty the four Companions who were to become the Messenger's successors : Abu Bakr, 'Umar, 'Uthmaan, and 'Aliy. Allah has enabled us to devote a separate book for each one of them. The four books appeared as: Then Came Abu Bakr Between the Hands o 'Umar - In The Presence of 'Aliy, and Farewell 'Uthmaan.

Now let us approach in awe and delight those righteous men, to welcome the best human examples, the most graceful and most virtuous. Let us see under their humble garments the most sublime and lofty in greatness and wisdom known to the whole world. Let us witness the legion of truth treading the ancient world in piety, filling the sky with standards of new truth in which they announced the religion of monotheism and the liberation of mankind.

Khaalid Muhammad Khaalid

THE LIGHT THEY FOLLOWED

What a teacher he was, and what a man! He was filled with greatness, honesty, and sublimity! Truly, those overwhelmed with his greatness have their excuse, and those who sacrificed their lives for his sake are the most triumphant.

Muhammad Ibn 'Abd Allah was Allah's Messenger to the people in the midsummer of life. What mystery was available to him that made him a man to honor among human beings! And what grand hands did he extend towards heaven to let all the gates of mercy, blessing, and guidance open widely! What faith, what chastity, and what purity! What modesty, what love and what loyalty! What devotion to truth and what reverence to life and the living?

Allah bestowed upon him the amount of blessing to qualify him to carry His standard and speak for Him, and made him capable of being the last of His messengers. Therefore, Allah's bounty towards him was great. But however the brains, inspiration, and pens compete to talk about him or to sing hymns of praise to reveal his greatness, they all seem insignificant due to his superior traits.

If the introductory pages of this book need to start with a talk about the Messenger (PBUH), they cannot hope to give him his due of praise nor claim that they are really introducing the great Messenger to the readers. It is only a mere reference to his eminence and some of his superior qualities which make people cherish him and which drew him an unprecedented loyalty by some of the figures mentioned in the book - whether they were Muhaajiruun or Ansaar or from the Quraish.

No sooner had life emerged than Allah made all its breeze hail his coming, and sent messengers to all men everywhere, carrying the principles of the divine call and the fragrance of the caller, the truth of the teachings, the eminence of the master, the enlightenment of the message and the compassion of the Messenger (PBUH).

That is true. This was the main objective, no more. It is to perceive in the light of one of his beams some of the traits of his rare eminence that brought about the believers' loyalty and made them perceive in him the goal and the way, the teacher and the friend.

What made the nobles of his people hasten to his words and his religion! Abu Bakr, Talhah, Az-Zubair, 'Uthmaan Ibn 'Affaan, 'Abd ArRahman Ibn 'Awf, and Sa'd Ibn Abi Waqqaas, all abandoned in haste the wealth and glory of their community which surrounded them, receiving at the same time heavy burdens in life, full of cares, troubles, and conflict.

What made the weak of his community seek his protection, hasten to his standard and his call, when they saw him without wealth or weapon, with harm inflicted upon him and evil following him in a terrifying way, without his being able to avoid it!

What made the pre-Islamic tyrant 'Umar Ibn Al-Khattaab, who went to cut off his noble head with his sword, return to cut off with the same sword - made sharper through faith - the heads of the Prophet's enemies and his persecutors !

What made the city's elite and noble men go to him and promise to be his companions, voluntarily embracing a set of trouble and terror, knowing that the struggle between them and the

Quraish would be more horrifying than terror itself!

What made those who believed in him increase and not decrease, though he declared day and night, "I hold no good or harm for you. I do not know what will become of me or you"!

What made them believe that the world would open its countries to them and that their feet would be wading in the gold and crowns of the world ! And that the Qur'aan they were reciting in secret would reverberate in strong tones and ringing voice, not only in their own generation or in their own peninsula but throughout the ages and everywhere

What made them believe the prophecy told them by the Messenger, though when they turned right and left they found nothing except heat, barren land, and stones emitting boiling vapor, their pointed heads looking like devils' heads !

What filled their hearts with certainty and will-power !

It was Ibn 'Abd Allah, who else could have done that !

They saw themselves with their own eyes all his virtues and all that distinguished him. They saw his chastity, his purity, his honesty, his straightforwardness, and his courage. They saw his superiority and his compassion. They saw his intellect and his eloquence. They saw the sun shining the way his truth and eminence shone.

They heard the growth of life running in his veins when Muhammad started to bestow upon them his daily revelation and his past contemplation. They saw all these and more, not through a mask but face to face and in practice, through their own vision and perception.

When an Arab of those days saw something, he would talk as an expert. The Arabs were people of perception and intuition. If one of them saw some footprints on the road, he would tell you, "These are the footprints of such-and-such a person." He would smell the breath of the one talking to him and realize what truth or falsity was inherent.

These men saw Muhammad and were his contemporaries since his coming into existence as a newborn babe. Nothing was concealed from them in his life. The stage of childhood which is unperceived by other than the child's people and close relations was, in the case of Muhammad, seen and perceived by all the people of Makkah. That was because his childhood was not like any other. It drew attention to itself for its early signs of manliness and initiative, and for rejecting the usual play of children for the seriousness of men.

As an example, the Quraish used to talk about 'Abd Al-Mttialib's grandson who kept away from the children's playgrounds and their celebrations, and used to say whenever he was invited to them, "I was not created for that."

Moreover, when his wet-nurse Haliimah took him back to his people, she told them her observations, her experience with the child, and what she saw in him to convince them he was not an ordinary child. She believed there was a hidden secret in him, unknown except to Allah, which might be revealed one day.

As to his youth, what chastity! He was clearer and more translucent. His people's preoccupation with him and their talk about him were more constant and praising. As to his manhood, it was fully perceived by every eye, ear, and heart. Above all, it was his community's conscience, measuring through his conduct and behavior all their visions of truth, goodness, and beauty.

It was, then, a transparent and comprehended life from cradle to grave. All his visions, his steps, his words, his movements, even his dreams, his hopes, and his remembrances were the right of all the people from the first day he was born. It was as if Almighty Allah wished it to be like that to tell the people, "That is My Messenger to you; his way is through reason and intellect, and that is his whole life since he was a baby."

Therefore, with all you possess of reason and intellect, examine his life and judge. Do you perceive any sense of suspicion? Do you see any false matter? Did he ever tell a lie or betray anyone? Did he ever treat anyone unjustly? Did he ever expose a defect? Did he ever abandon his kinship relations? Did he neglect a duty or leave a noble action? Did he insult anyone or worship an idol? Peruse well and meticulously and investigate, as there is no stage of his life that is hidden or veiled.

If his life as you see and perceive is nothing but purity, truth, and eminence, does it appeal to reason or logic that a man of such traits would tell lies after the age of forty? About whom would he lie? About Allah in order to claim he was His Messenger (PBUH), chosen, selected, and inspired by Him?

No, this is the answer of feeling and intuition. What is your way of thinking and what right do you have to tell lies?

This, we believe, was the attitude of the early believers towards Allah's Messenger (PBUH), the Muhaajiruun as well as those who sheltered and supported him.

it was a firm and swift attitude that did not leave any place for hesitation or idleness. A man who had such a pure and enlightened life could not play false with Allah. With such sharp insight, the believers saw the light of Allah and they followed.

They would thank their insight when they saw later how Allah's Messenger (PBUH) was supported by Allah and how the whole peninsula was obliged to him. Many unperceived blessings and spoils were bestowed upon them while he became more modest, more austere, and more pious, until he met Allah at the appointed time, lying down on a mat that left its impressions on his body.

And when they saw him, the Messenger whose standards victoriously and proudly filled the horizon, descended the pulpit and received the people, saying while he wept, "Whoever's back I whipped, here is my back, let him take his revenge; whoever's money I took, here is my money, let him take of it."

The believers saw him, while his uncle Al-'Abbaas was asking him to offer him one of the jobs obtained by ordinary Muslims, and he gently apologized, saying, "Truly, uncle, we do not offer that job to someone who asks or someone who cares for it."

They saw him not only sharing the trouble and hunger that befell people, but establishing for himself and his folk an unforsaken principle which was, "To be the first to feel hunger if people go hungry, and the last to satisfy his hunger when people were starving."

Yes, the early believers would be more thankful for their insight which perceived things well even before they came, thanking Allah Who had guided them to faith.

They would also see that life which was the best proof of the truth of the Messenger (PBUH) when he said to them: "I am Allah's Messenger unto you." His life was truly eminent. Its eminence and purity are the best evidence of the truth of the great teacher and noble Messenger (PBUH). Its level of excellence and eminence never declined nor fell, but remained steadfast from cradle to grave.

Throughout life and after reaching his prime, it was as clear as day that the man who led that life and conveyed such a message was not seeking wealth, money or sovereignty. When these were offered him on a golden platter associated with his triumphant leadership, he rejected them all and lived his life till the last breath devoting himself to Allah, repentant and chaste.

He never deviated from the purposes of his great life the breadth of a hair, and never broke a promise to Allah in worship or in jihaad.

No sooner would the latter part of the night begin than he would get up, make his ablution and remain as he was accustomed to do, invoking Allah, praying, and crying.

Mountains of wealth and money were accumulated in his possession, yet he did not change and never took of it except as the poorest and lowest of Muslims did. Then he died leaving only his armour in mortgage.

All the countries of the world came closer due to his call, and most of the kings of the earth stood before his message, in which he called them to Islam, in awe and supplication. Yet, not an atom of boasting or arrogance crossed his way even at a great distance. When he saw people approaching him troubled and disturbed out of awe and reverence, he said to them, "Be easy, my mother used to eat dried meat in Makkah."

When all the enemies of his faith put down their weapons and bowed their heads waiting for him to pass judgment and while

10,000 swords of the Muslims were glittering on the Day of Conquest over the hills of Makkah, he merely said to his enemies, "Disperse, you are free!"

Even at the height of the victory for which he devoted his life, he deprived himself of it. He walked in the victory procession on the Day of the Conquest bowing his head down until people could not see his face and repeated hymns of thanks to Allah in low tones, wet with tears, humbly raising his words to Allah until he reached the Ka'bah. He then confronted the idols and did what he did to them and said, <*Truth has come and falsehood has vanished, indeed, falsehood is bound to vanish* > *(17: 81).*

Is there any more doubt about his message? He was a man who dedicated his whole life to a call in which he had no personal gain of wealth, position, sovereignty, or power. Biographical immortality was not even considered by him because he believed solely in the immorality of the second life when one is in the hands of Allah.

He was a man who spent his life from childhood till the age of forty in purity and contemplation. Then he spent the rest of it in worship, guidance, jihaad and struggle, and when the world was brightened to him he rejected all its false glory and adhered to his way, his worship, and his message. How could such a man be a liar?

Why should he tell lies? Surely, such a man and such a messenger was above that !

We have mentioned that logic and reason were - and still are - the best proof of the truth of Muhammad (PBUH) when he said, "I am Allah's Messenger." It does not appeal to good logic or to sound reason that a man who lived such a good life, lies about Allah. Early believers who hastened to believe in his message, and whom we are honored to know something about through the pages of this book, had such a relation with him after their guidance from Allah, which is the best evidence of logic and reason.

We see Muhammad (PBUH) before his message, and we see him after his message. We see him in his cradle, and we see him shrouded by death. But, have we seen any contradiction or inconsistency in all his life? Never !

Let us now approach the first years of his message. Those were years one rarely finds an equal to in the annals of history for the constancy, truth, and eminence. Those were the years which revealed, more than any others, all the facets of the teacher and guide of all humanity. Those were years that opened the living book of his life and heroism and, more than any other years, represented the cradle of his miracles.

Throughout those years, the Messenger of Allah was alone. He left all he possessed of comfort, security, and settled life. He approached the people with what they were not familiar, or rather with what they detested. He approached them and directed his words to their reasons, and it is a difficult task for a person who directs his speech to the minds of people instead of their feelings. The Messenger of Allah, Muhammad (PBUH) did not only do that, since the consequence of addressing the mind might be bearable if you are standing within the circle of common conventions and common aspirations. But when you call them towards a distant future which you perceive but they do not, which you live in and they are not aware of, it is a difficult task. Indeed, when you address their mind and rise to destroy the essence of their lives from the base, though you do that in a sincere, honest way and not urged by a certain purpose or glory, it is a risk which cannot be taken except by the leaders of the righteous people and messengers.

The Messenger (PBUH) was the hero and great master of that situation. The form of worship at that time was worshiping idols, whose rites were observed as a religion. The Messenger (PBUH) did not turn to any maneuvers or intrigues. The unpaved road and the heavy burden would have been good excuses if he had used his brilliant mind to prepare them for the word "monotheism" instead of surprising them with it. He was able and it was his right to prepare to isolate the community from its idol-gods which had been handed down from generation to generation for centuries. He could have started by going around the issue to avoid as much as possible a direct confrontation he knew would bestir all the envy of his people and draw upon them all their weapons against him.

Yet, he did not. This illustrates that he was a Messenger (PBUH). He heard a divine voice within him telling him to rise, and he did, and telling him to deliver the message, and he did so without the force of weapons and without fleeing! He confronted them from the first instant with the essence of the message and the core of the case: "O people, I am the Messenger of Allah unto you, to worship Him and not to set partners with Him. These idols are intellectual falsehood. They are of no harm or benefit to you."

From the very beginning he faced them with such clear and plain words, and from the very beginning he faced the severe struggle, which he had to undergo until his departure from life!

Or were the early believers in need of a prompting power to support the Prophet (PBUH)!

What awakened conscience would not be stirred by such a rare and unique scene! It was the scene of a man known to the people to have full intellectual power and immaculate behavior, standing alone, facing his people with a call which could bring mountains down. Words were issuing forth from his heart and lips, obedient and superb, as if in them lay all the power, will, and design of the future, as if it were fate announcing its proclamation!

But perhaps this was the prompting of a good spirit, after which Muhammad (PBUH) would worship his Lord as he liked, leaving the deities of his people in their place and leaving his community's religion alone.

If such a thought occurred to some minds at that time, Muhammed (PBUH) soon dissipated it. He made it quite clear to the people that he was a Messenger and had to convey the message, that he could not be silent nor turn into himself after being guided by the truth and enlightenment. All the powers of the world and nature could not have silenced him or stopped him because it was Allah Who made him speak and move and Who guided his footsteps.

The Quraish's reaction came as swift as flames stirred by a violent wind. Troubles began to be wrecked upon a soul unaccustomed to anything but absolute grace. The Messenger (PBUH) then began to teach his first lessons with utmost mastery and amazing loyalty. The image of this scene is paramount in all places and at all times, as well as in history. Those with an awakened conscience in Makkah were pleased, filled with admiration, and came closer. They beheld a lofty and majestic man. They did not know whether his neck had become longer until it was able to touch the sky or the sky had come down to crown his head. They beheld loyalty, steadfastness and eminence.

However, the best scene they beheld was on the day when the noblemen of the Quraish went to Abu Taalib saying, "Verily, we cannot tolerate a person who insults our fathers, mocks our dreams, and finds fault with our deities. You either stop him or we fight both of you until one of the parties is destroyed."

Abu Taalib sent a message to his nephew saying, "My nephew, your people have approached me and talked about your affairs. You have to think of me and yourself and not burden me with what I cannot endure."

What then was the attitude of the Messenger of Allah (PBUH)? The only man who had stood with him seemed to be abandoning him or rather seemed unable to confront the Quraish who sharpened all their teeth. The Messenger (PBUH) did not hesitate in his reply, and his determination did not waver. No! He did not even search for the words to show his tenacity. It was already there, efficiently rising to deliver one of his most significant lessons to the whole of humanity and to dictate its highest principles.

Thus he spoke: "O uncle, by Allah, if they put the sun on my right and the moon on my left in order to abandon this matter until it is manifested by Allah or I perish by it, I would never abandon it!"

Peace be upon you, O Prophet of Islam, you who were colossal among men, and your words were colossal.

AbuTaalib there upon restored his courage and the courage of his forefathers at once, clasped the right hand of his nephew with his two hands, and said, "Say what you like, for, by Allah,

I will never force you to do anything at all."

Muhammad (PBUH) then did not depend on his uncle for protection and security, though his uncle was capable of that, but he was the one bestowing security, protection and steadfastness on people around him.

Any honest person who beholds a scene like that cannot but hasten to love, be loyal to, and believe in that Messenger (PBUH).

His persistence regarding truth, his perseverence with the message, and his patience during great troubles were all for the sake of Allah and not for personal benefit. All these were bound to attract brilliant minds and to awaken the conscientious people to follow the light beckoning to them and hasten to the honest and true Messenger (PBUH) who came to purify our souls and guide us. People beheld him while harm was reaching him from every corner. The condolence he had sought in his uncle Abu -Taalib and his wife Khadiijah was denied him because they both died within days of each other.

Whoever desires to imagine the extent of persecution and war launched by the Quraish against the unarmed Messenger, suffice it to know that Abu Lahab himself, who was his most bitter rival and enemy, was so conscience-stricken one day by what he beheld that he announced he would protect the Messenger, help him, and stand against any aggression against him. But the Messenger refused his protection and remained lofty, raising his head and remaining loyal to his message. Nobody could avert harm from him because nobody dared to do so! Even the eminent Abu - Bakr could do nothing but weep.

One day, the Messenger (PBUH) went to the Ka'bah and, while

he was circumambulating it, the nobles of the Quraish who were waiting for him suddenly ran and surrounded him, saying, "Is it you that say such-and-such a thing about our deities?" And he calmly answered them, "Yes, I say that." They held him by the end of his clothes while Abu Bakr pleaded for his release, saying with tears pouring, "Are you going to kill a man for saying, Allah is my Lord?"

Who ever saw the Messenger on the day of At-Taa'if was sure to see some example of his truth and loyalty worthy of him. He turned his face towards the tribe of Thaqiif, calling them to Allah, the One and the Vanquisher.

Was not what he was encountering from his clan and his folk enough? Did it not warn him of an increasing harm when it comes from people he had no blood relations with? Absolutely not, because these harmful consequences were not considered by him. Almighty Allah had commanded him to deliver the message, and that was enough. He remembered the day when the intransigence of his community increased and he went home covering himself in bed in sorrow. He heard the voice of heaven reaching his heart, and immediately he heard the voice of revelation casting the same matter as on the day of the cave: < O *you encovered --- Arise and warn* > (74: 1-2).

Then he had to deliver the message and warn. Therefore, he was a Messenger who did not care about harm and did not search for comfort. Let him go then to At-Taa'if to convey the word of Allah to its people.

There, however, the nobles of the community surrounded him and were more cunning than their mates in Makkah. They set children and hooligans against him, and they abandoned the most sacred of the customs of the Arabs, which is hospitality to guests and protection of the one who asks for help.

They set their hooligans and their young boys after the Messenger (PBUH), throwing stones at him. This was the one for whom the Quraish offered to collect money to make him the richest among them and to be their leader and king! Yet, he refused saying, "I am but the slave of Allah and His Messenger."

Now we behold him in At-Taa'if where he retired to an orchard to be protected by its walls from the pursuit of the hooligans. His right hand was stretched towards heaven praying to Allah while his left hand was protecting his face from the stones thrown at him. He was calling to his Creator and Lord, saying, "If You are not angry with me, I do not care for other things, but granting me Your mercy is too generous of You."

Indeed, he was a Messenger who knew how to address his Lord with courtesy! When he declared that he did not care about harm for the sake of Allah, he also declared that he was in dire need for mercy granted by Allah. In a situation like this, he did not feel proud about his endurance and courage, nor did he boast. Boasting in such a situation might suggest bestowing favor on Allah, and this fact could not be hidden from Muhammad. Therefore, the best way to express his courage and endurance in such a situation was his pleading and his invocation.

So he went on asking Allah's pardon and invoking Him, "0 Allah, to You I complain of the weakness of my strength, my inability to find a way, and my humiliation by the people. 0 the Most Compassionate, You are the Lord of the weak, and You are my Lord. To whom do You entrust me? To a distant relation who ignores me or to an enemy who has power over me? If You are not angry with me, I do not care about other things, but granting me Your mercy is too generous of You. I seek refuge in the light of Your face that brightens the darkness and amends the affairs of this world and the next. Do not be angry or dissatisfied with me. I beg Your favor until You are satisfied with me. There is no strength or power except through You."

What loyalty the Prophet (PBUH) had to his call! He was an unarmed person faced with plots everywhere he went. He had nothing in life to strengthen him, yet he carried all that persistence, all that steadfastness and loyalty!

People beheld him returning from At-Taa'if to Makkah without any sense of despair or defeat, but more hopeful, optimistic, and dedicated. Moreover, he presented himself to the tribes, reaching them in their own localities and districts. One day he went to Bani Kindah, another day to Bani Haniifah, then to Bani 'Aamir, and thus from one tribe to another. He said to them all, "I am the Messenger of Allah to you. He commands you to worship Allah and not to take partners with Him, and to abandon what you worship of idols." At the houses of the close-by tribes, Abu Lahab used to follow him, saying to the people, "Do not believe him, for he is calling you to what is false."

People beheld the Messenger of Allah in such a critical situation seeking believers and assistants, but he was met with ingratitude and enmity. They saw him refusing any bargains and refusing to have a worldly price for faith.

In those scorching days, he presented himself to Bani 'Aamir Ibn Sa'sa'ah and sat with them speaking about Allah and reciting some of His words. They inquired, "Do you believe that if we supported you in your affair and then Allah raised you above those who opposed you, we would take the matter after you?" He (PBUH) answered saying, "This matter is in the hands of Allah. He puts it wherever He wishes." There and then they dispersed, saying, "We need not your affair." The Messenger (PBUH) left them, looking for believers who do not buy a little worth with their faith.

People beheld him, but few believed in him. Despite their number, he found in them comfort and company. But the Quraish decided that each tribe should be in charge of giving lessons to the believers among them. So, suddenly, persecution descended like a mad storm and hit all the Muslims. The polytheists did not know a crime but committed it against the Muslims. However, here an unexpected surprise took place. Muhammad (PBUH) gave orders to all the Muslims to emigrate to Abyssinia and decided to remain alone to face the aggression!

Why did he not emigrate to convey the word of Allah in another place, for Allah is the Lord of All the Worlds and not the Lord of the Quraish alone? Or why did he not let them stay with him, since in their staying there was confirmed benefit? Surely their stay in Makkah, in spite of their small number, would have induced others to embrace Islam, the religion of Allah.

Furthermore, there were among them a good number of the noblest families of the Quraish, the strongest and the most powerful. From the tribe of Bani Umaiyah there were 'Uthmaan Ibn 'Affaan, 'Amr Ibn Sa'iid Ibn Al-'Aa,s, and Khaalid Ibn Sa'iid Ibn Al-'Aa,s. From Bani Asad there were Az-Zubair Ibn Al-'Awaam, Al-Aswad Ibn Nawfal, Yaziid Ibn Zam'ah and 'Amr Ibn Umaiyah. From the tribe of Bani Zahrah there were 'Abd Ar-Rahman Ibn 'Awf, 'Aamir Ibn Abi Waqqaas Maalik Ibn Ahyab, and Al-Muttalib Ibn Azhar. There were these and others whose families would not be patient for long with their persecution and infliction of harm upon them. Why, then, did the Messenger (PBUH) not let them stay with him to support him and to be a sign of possible power in his hands?

Here the eminence of Muhammad (PBUH), the Messenger of Allah shines. He did not want commotion or civil war, even if the probability of his success was there, or even if he was sure of his success! Here the Messenger's humanity and compassion are illustrated, for he could not bear to see people persecuted because of him, although he was well aware that sacrifice was the price paid in every noble struggle and in every great mission. Sacrifice should be made whenever it was inevitable. But now, when it is possible to avoid suffering, let the Muslims turn that way. Why, then, did he not join them?

He was not commanded to depart. His place was there where idols were. He would keep uttering the name of Allah, the One. He would keep receiving pain and harm without anxiety or disquietude since it was he who was harmed and not those weak people who believed in him and followed him and not even those noble men who also believed in him and followed him! Whoever knows examples of such cases of steadfastness and nobility of sacrifice, let him come up with them. It is a lofty matter capable only of leading messengers and chosen ones.

The man and the Messenger came together in Muhammad (PBUH) in such a magnificent and well-knit encounter. Those who had doubts in his message did not have any doubt in his eminence, the purity of his quintessence, or the purity of his humanity. Allah, Who knew where to place His Message, had chosen such a man who was the best humanity could achieve in elevation, loftiness, and honesty. People heard him reprimanding them for any exaggeration in glorifying him or even when they merely stated his eminence without any exaggeration. He prohibited them even from standing up in his presence when he came upon them when they were seated. He said, "Do not stand as non-Arabs do when they glorify one another."

When the sun eclipsed on the day of the death of his beloved son Ibraahiim, the Muslims mentioned that it was an eclipse out of sadness for the loss of Ibraahiim. But the great and honest Messenger (PBUH) hastened to refute and negate this assumption before it turned into a legend. He stood among the Muslims, addressing them as follows: "The sun and the moon are two of the signs of Allah. They never eclipse for the death or life of anybody."

He was the one trusted with the minds of people and their thinking, and so accomplishing what was entrusted to him was more worthy than the glory of all the world. He was certain that he came to humanity to change their way of life and that he was not a Messenger to the Quraish alone, or to the Arabs only, but was Allah's Messenger to all the people on earth!

Almighty Allah directed his vision to how far his mission would reach and his banner flutter. He perceived the truth of the faith he announced, the living immortality it would have until Allah inherits the earth and those upon it. Nevertheless, he did not see in himself, or his religion or his unprecedented success more than a brick in the construction! This great man stood to proclaim this idea in one of his best statements, saying, "The relation between prophets who came before me and myself is like a man who built a house and constructed it well and decorated it, except for a brick in one of its corners. This made people go round it and express their astonishment, saying. Won't this brick be placed? I am such a brick, and I am the last of the Prophets."

All that long life he lived, all his struggles and heroism, all his glory and purity, all the victory achieved in his life for his religion and the victory he knew would be achieved after his death were nothing but a brick, a mere brick in a lofty and deeply founded building. He was the one who proclaimed this and reiterated it. In addition, he did not make up such a speech out of assumed modesty, to nourish a hunger for glory. He emphasized the situation as a fact. Its delivery and transmission he considered part of the quintessence of his message. Though modesty was one of the essential characteristics of Muhammad (PBUH), it was not the only sign of his greatness, which reached an unrivaled level of excellence and superiority to be a sign and a symbol itself.

That was the teacher of mankind and the last of the prophets. He was the light seen by the people, and he lived among them as a human being, and then after his departure from this world, he was seen by the whole world as a truth and a memory.

Now, while we meet a number of his noble Companions on the following pages of this book - where we will be astonished by their faith, their sacrifices, and the good cause they set for their lives, which was unprecedented - the reason for their marvelous lives will be clear before us.

This reason was nothing but the light they followed who was Muhammad, the Messenger of Allah (PBUH). Almighty Allah had combined in him the vision of truth and self-dignity, which honored life and illuminated the destiny of mankind.

(1)
MUS'AB IBN -UMAIR
The First Envoy of Islam

This man among the Companions of the Prophet Muhammad (PBUH), how good it is for us to start with him. He was the flower of the Quraish, the most handsome and youthful! Historians and narrators describe him as "the most charming of the Makkans".

He was born and brought up in wealth, and he grew up with its luxuries. Perhaps there was no boy in Makkah who was pampered by his parents like Mus'ab Ibn 'Umair. This mirthful youth, caressed and pampered, the talk of the ladies of Makkah, the jewel of its clubs and assemblies: is it possible for him to be one of the legends of faith?

By Allah, how interesting a tale, the story of Mus'ab Ibn 'Umair or Mus'ab the Good, as he was nicknamed among the Muslims! He was one of those made by Islam and fostered by the Prophet Muhammad (PBUH).

But who was he? His story is a pride of all mankind. The youth heard one day what the people of Makkah had begun to hear about Muhammad the Truthful, that Allah had sent him as bearer of glad tidings and a warner to call them to the worship of Allah the One God. When Makkah slept and awoke there was no other talk but the Prophet Muhammad (PBUH) and his religion, and this spoiled boy was one of the most attentive listeners.

That was because, although he was young, the flower of clubs and assemblies, the outward appearance of wisdom and common sense were among the traits of Mus'ab.

He heard that the Prophet (PBUH) and those who believed in him, were meeting far away from the dignitaries and great men of the Quraish at As-Safaa in the house of Al-Arqam Ibn Al-Arqam (Daar Al-Arqam). He wasted no time. He went one night to the Daar Al-Arqam, yearning and anxious. There, the Prophet (PBUH) was meeting his Companions, reciting the Qur'aan to them and praying with them to Allah the Most Exalted. Mus'ab had hardly taken his seat and contemplated the verses of Qur'aan recited by the Prophet (PBUH) when his heart became the promised heart that night.

The pleasure almost flung him from his seat as he was filled with a wild ecstasy. But the Prophet (PBUH) patted his throbbing heart with his blessed right hand, and the silence of the ocean's depth filled his heart. In the twinkling of an eye, the youth who had just become Muslim appeared to have more wisdom than his age and a determination that would change the course of time!

Mus'ab's mother was Khunaas Bint Maalik, and people feared her almost to the point of terror because she possessed a strong personality. When Mus'ab became a Muslim, he was neither careful before nor afraid of anyone on the face of the earth except his mother. Even if Makkah, with all its idols, nobles, and deserts were to challenge him, he would stand up to it. As for a dispute with his mother, this was an impossible horror, so he thought quickly and decided to keep his Islam secret until Allah willed. He continued to frequent Daar Al-Arqam and take lessons from the Prophet (PBUH). He was satisfied with his faith and avoided the anger of his mother, who had no knowledge of his embracing Islam.

However, Makkah at that time kept no secret, for the eyes and ears of the Quraish were everywhere, very alert and checking every footprint in its hot sands. Once, 'Uthmaan Ibn Talhah saw him steadily entering Al-Arqam's house, then he saw him a second time praying the prayer like Muhammad. No sooner had he seen him than he ran quickly with the news to Mus'ab's mother, who was astonished by it.

Mus'ab stood before his mother, the people, and the nobles of Makkah who assembled around him, telling them the irrefutable truth and reciting the Qur'aan with which the Prophet (PBUH) cleansed their hearts and filled them with honor, wisdom, justice, and piety.

His mother aimed a heavy blow at him, but the hand which was meant as an arrow soon succumbed to the powerful light which increased the radiance of his face with innocent glory because it demanded respect with its quiet confidence. However, his mother, under the pressure of her motherliness, spared him the beating and the pain, although it was within her power to avenge her gods whom he had abandoned. Instead she took him to a rough corner of her house and shut him in it. She put shackles on him and imprisoned him there until he heard the news of the emigration (hijrah) of some of the believers to Abyssinia. He thought to himself and was able to delude his mother and his guards, and so escaped to Abyssinia.

There he stayed in Abyssinia with his fellow emigrants and then returned with them to Makkah. He also emigrated to Abyssinia for the second time with the Companions whom the Prophet (PBUH) advised to emigrate and they obeyed. But whether Mus'ab was in Abyssinia or Makkah, the experience of his faith proclaimed itself in all places and at all times.

Mus'ab became confident that his life had become good enough to be offered as a sacrifice to the Supreme Originator and great Creator. He went out one day to some Muslims while they were sitting around the Prophet (PBUH), and no sooner did they see him than they lowered their heads and shed some tears because they saw him wearing worn out garments. They were accustomed to his former appearance before he had become a Muslim, when his clothes had been like garden flowers, elegant and fragrant.

The Prophet (PBUH) saw him with the eyes of wisdom, thankful and loving, and his lips smiled gracefully as he said, "I saw Mus'ab here, and there was no youth in Makkah more petted by his parents than he. Then he abandoned all that for the love of Allah and His Prophet!"

His mother had withheld from him all the luxury he had been overwhelmed by, when she could not return him to her religion. She refused to let anyone who had abandoned their gods eat of her food, even if he was her son. Her last connection with him was when she tried to imprison him for a second time after his return from Abyssinia, and he swore that if she did that, he would kill all those who came to her aid to lock him up. She knew the truth of his determination when he was intent and decided to do something, and so she bade him goodbye weeping.

The parting moment revealed a strange adherence to infidelity on the part of his mother, and the greater adherence to faith on the part of her son. When she said to him, while turning him out of her house, "Go away, I am no longer your mother," he went close to her and said, "O mother, I am advising you and my heart is with you, please bear witness that there is no god but Allah and that Muhammad is His servant and messenger." She replied to him, angrily raging, "By the stars, I will never enter your religion, to degrade my status and weaken my senses!"

So Mus'ab left the great luxury in which he had been living. He became satisfied with a hard life he had never seen before, wearing the roughest clothes, eating one day and going hungry another. This spirit, which was grounded in the strongest faith, adorned with the light of Allah, made him another man, one who appeals to the eyes of other great souls.

While he was in this state, the Prophet (PBUH) commissioned him with the greatest mission of his life, which was to be his envoy to Al-Madiinah. His mission was to instruct the Ansaar who believed in the Prophet (PBUH) and had pledged their allegiance to him at "Aqabah, to call others to Islam, and to prepare Al-Madiinah for the day of the great Hijrah. There were among the Companions of the Prophet (PBUH) at that time others who were older than Mus`ab and more prominent and nearer to the Prophet (PBUH) by family relations. But the Prophet (PBUH) chose Mus`ab the Good, knowing that he was entrusting to him the most important task of that time, putting into his hands the destiny of Islam at Al-Madiinah. The radiant city of Al-Madiinah was destined to be the home of Hijrah, the springboard of Islamic preachers and the liberators of the future.

Mus'ab was equal to the task and trust, which Allah had given him and he was equipped with an excellent mind and noble character. He won the hearts of the Madinites with his piety, uprightness and sincerity. And so they embraced the religion of Allah in flocks. At the time the Prophet (PBUH) sent him there, only twelve Muslims had pledged allegiance to the Prophet (PBUH) at the Pledge of 'Aqabah. He had hardly completed a few months when they answered to the call of Allah and the Prophet (PBUH). During the next pilgrimage season, the Madinite Muslims sent a delegation of 70 believing men and women to Makkah to meet the Prophet (PBUH).

They came with their teacher and their Prophet's envoy, Mus'ab Ibn 'Umair. Mus'ab had proven, by his good sense and excellence, that the Prophet (PBUH) knew well how to choose his envoys and teachers.

Mus'ab had understood his mission well. He knew that he was a caller to Allah and preacher of His religion, which calls people to right guidance and the straight path. Like the Prophet (PBUH) in whom he believed, he was no more than a deliverer of the message. There he stood fast, with As'ad Ibn Zoraarah as host, and both of them used to visit the tribes, dwellings, and assemblies, reciting to the people what he had of the Book of Allah, instilling in them that Allah is no more than One God.

He had confronted certain instances, which could have put an end to his life and that of those with him but for his active, intelligent, great mind. One day, he was taken by surprise while preaching to the people to find Usaid Ibn Hudair,, leader of the 'Abd Al-Ashhal tribe, at Al-Madiinah confronting him with a drawn arrow.

He was raging with anger and animosity against the one who had come to corrupt the religion of his people by telling them to abandon their gods and talking to them about the idea of only One God Whom they did not know before and had never heard of. Their gods were to them the center of their worship. Whenever any of them needed them, he knew their places. They would invoke them for help. That was how they thought and imagined!

As for the God of Muhammad, to whom this envoy was calling, nobody knew His place, nor could anybody see Him! When the Muslims who were sitting around Mus'ab saw Usaid Ibn Hudair advancing in his unbridled anger, they were frightened, but

Mus'ab the Good stood firm. Usaid stood before him and As'ad Ibn Zoraarah shouting, "What brought you here? Are you coming to corrupt our faith? Go away if you wish to be saved !"

And like the calmness of the sea and its force, Mus'ab started his fine speech saying, "Won't you sit down and listen? If you like our cause, you can accept; and if you dislike it, we will spare you of what you hate."

Allah is the Greatest! How grand an opening whose ending would be pleasant! Usaid was a thoughtful and clever man, and here he saw Mus'ab inviting him to listen and no more. If he was convinced he would accept it, and if he was not convinced, then Mus'ab would leave his neighborhood and his clan, and move to another neighborhood without harm, nor being harmed. There and then Usaid answered him saying, "Well, that is fair," and he dropped his arrow to the ground and sat down listening.

Mus'ab had hardly read the Qur'aan, explaining the mission with which Muhammad Ibn 'Abd Allah (PBUH) came, when the conscience of Usaid began to clear and brighten and change with the effectiveness of the words. He became overwhelmed by its beauty. When Mus'ab finished speaking, Usaid Ibn Hudair exclaimed to him and those with him, "How beautiful is this speech, and how true! How can one enter this religion?" Mus'ab told him to purify his body and clothes and say, "I bear witness that there is no god but Allah."

Usaid retired for some time and then returned pouring clean water on his head and standing there proclaiming, "I bear witness that there is no god but Allah, and that Muhammad is the Messenger of Allah."

The news spread like lightning and then Sa'd lbn Mu'aadh came and listened to Mus'ab, and he was convinced and embraced Islam. Then came Sa'd lbn 'Ubaadah.

There and then blessings came with their entering Islam. The people of AI-Madiinah came together asking one another, if Usaid lbn Hudair, Sa'd lbn Mu'aadh and Sa-d lbn 'Ubaadah have embraced Islam, what are we waiting for? Go straight to Mus'ab and believe. By Allah, he is calling us to the truth and the straight path!"

The first envoy of the Prophet (PBUH) succeeded without comparison. It was a success, which he deserved and to which he was equal.

The days and years passed by. The Prophet (PBUH) and his Companions emigrated to AI-Madiinah, and the Quraish were raging with envy and their ungodly pursuit after the pious worshippers. So the Battle of Badr took place, in which they were taught a lesson and lost their strong hold. After that they prepared themselves for revenge, and thus came the Battle of Uhud. The Muslims mobilized themselves, and the Prophet (PBUH) stood in their midst to sort out among their faithful faces and to choose one to bear the standard. He then called for Mus'ab the Good, and he advanced and carried the standard.

The terrible battle was raging, the fighting furious. The archers disregarded the orders of the Prophet (PBUH) by leaving their positions on the mountain when they saw the polytheists withdrawing as if defeated. But this act of theirs soon turned the victory of the Muslims to defeat. The Muslims were taken at unawares by the cavalry of the Quraish at the mountain top, and many Muslims were killed by the swords of the polytheists as a consequence.

When they saw the confusion and horror splitting the ranks of the Muslims, the polytheists concentrated on the Prophet of Allah to finish him off. Mus'ab saw the impending threat, so he raised the standard high, shouting, "Allahu Akbar! Allah is the Greatest!" like the roar of a lion. He turned and jumped left and right, fighting and killing the foe. All he wanted was to draw the attention of the enemy to himself in order to turn their attention away from the Prophet (PBUH). He thus became as a whole army in himself. Nay, Mus'ab went alone to fight as if he were an army of giants raising the standard in sanctity with one hand, striking with his sword with the other. But the enemies were multiplying on him. They wanted to step on his corpse so that they could find the Prophet (PBUH)..

Let us allow a living witness to describe for us the last scene of Mus'ab the Great. Ibn Sa'd said: Ibraahiim Ibn Muhammad Ibn Sharhabiil Al-'Abdriy related from his father, who said: Mus'ab Ibn 'Umair carried the standard on the Day of Uhud. When the Muslims were scattered, he stood fast until he met Ibn Quma'ah who was a knight. He struck him on his right hand and cut it off, but Mus'ab said, *"<And Muhammad is but a Messenger. Messengers have passed away before him >" (3:144).* He carried the standard with his left hand and leaned on it. He struck his left hand and cut it off, and so he leaned on the standard and held it with his upper arms to his chest, all the while saying, *"<And Muhammad is but a Messenger. Messengers have passed away before him. >"*. Then a third one struck him with his spear, and the spear went through him. Mus'ab fell and then the standard.

Nay, the cream of martyrdom had fallen! He fell after he had struggled for the sake of Allah in the great battle of sacrifice and faith. He had thought that if he fell, he would be a stepping stone to the death of the Prophet (PBUH) because he would be without defense and protection. But he put himself in harm's way for the sake of the Prophet (PBUH). Overpowered by his fear for and love of him, he continued to say with every sword stroke that fell on him from the foe, "*<And Muhammad is but a Messenger. Messengers have passed away before him >"(3:144)*. This verse was revealed later, after he had spoken it.

After the bitter battle, they found the corpse of the upright martyr lying with his face in the dust, as if he feared to look while harm fell on the Prophet (PBUH). So he hid his face so that he would avoid the scene. Or perhaps, he was shy when he fell as a martyr, before making sure of the safety of the Prophet of Allah, and before serving to the very end, guarding and protecting him.

Allah is with you, O' Mus"ab ! What a great life story!

The Prophet (PBUH) and his Companions came to inspect the scene of the battle and bid farewell to its martyrs. Pausing at Mus'ab's body, many tears dripped from the Prophet's eyes.

Khabbaab Ibn Al-Arat narrated: "We emigrated with the Prophet (PBUH) for Allah's cause, so our reward became due with Allah. Some of us passed away without enjoying anything in this life of His reward, and one of them was Mus`ab Ibn 'Umair, who was martyred on the Day of Uhud. He did not leave behind anything except a sheet of shredded woolen cloth. If we covered his head with it, his feet were uncovered, and if we covered his feet with it, his head was uncovered. The Prophet (PBUH) said to us, "Cover his head with it and put lemon grass over his feet."

Despite the deep, sad pain which the Prophet (PBUH) suffered over the loss of his uncle Hamzah and the mutilation of his corpse by the polytheists in a manner that drew tears from the Prophet (PBUH) and broke his heart; despite the fact that the field of battle was littered with the corpses of his Companions, all of whom represented the peak of truth, piety and enlightenment; despite all this, he stood at the corpse of his first envoy, bidding him farewell and weeping bitterly. Nay, the Prophet (PBUH) stood at the remains of Mus'ab lbn 'Umair saying, while his eyes were flowing with tears, love and loyalty, "*<Among the believers are men who have been true to their covenant with Allah >*" (33:23).

Then he gave a sad look at the garment in which he was shrouded and said, "I saw you at Makkah; and there was not a more precious jewel, nor more distinguished one than you, and here you are bare-headed in a garment!" Then the Prophet (PBUH) looked at all the martyrs in the battlefield and said, "The Prophet of Allah witnesses that you are martyrs to Allah on the Day of Resurrection." Then he gathered his living Companions around him and said, "O people, visit them, come to them, anc salute them. By Allah, no Muslim will salute them but that they will salute him in return."

Peace be on you, O' Mus'ab. Peace be on you, O' Martyrs. Peace and blessings of Allah be upon you!

(2) SALMAAN AL-FAARISIY
The Seeker after Truth

From Persia comes our hero this time, and from Persia many came to embrace Islam in the long run, and it made some of them extraordinary, unsurpassable in faith and knowledge in religion and worldly affairs.

It is one of the wonders of Islam and its greatness that it never enters a country on Allah's earth but that it exerts invaluable influence on all its potentialities and forces, bringing forth the latent genius of its people and followers. From there came forth Muslim philosophers, physicians, jurists, astronomers, inventors, and mathematicians.

Behold, they reached all heights, broke all frontiers, until the first era of Islam flourished with great geniuses in all fields of intellectual activity such as administration and science. Verily, they came from various nations, but their religion remained one.

The Prophet (PBUH) had prophesied this blessed spread of his religion. Indeed, he had been so promised by his Almighty Lord. He had pointed to the time, place, and day, and he had seen in his mind's eye the banner of Islam fluttering in all corners of the earth and over the palaces of its earthly rulers.

Salmaan Al-Faarisiy (The Persian) bore witness to this and was firmly connected with what happened. That was on the Day of Al-Khandaq (The Trench) in the year A.H. 5, when the leaders of the Jews approached Makkah to stir up the polytheists and form an alliance against the Prophet (PBUH) and the Muslims, asking the polytheists to enter upon a treaty for decisive battle to eradicate the new religion.

The ungodly war was planned: the Quraish army and allies would attack Al-Madiinah from outside, while the Bani Quraidhah would attack from within, behind the ranks of the Muslims, who would then fall prey and be crushed. One day the Prophet (PBUH) and the Muslims were taken unaware by a huge well-armed army marching on Al-Madiinah. The Qur'aan depicts the scene thus:*<When they came against you from above you and from below you and your eyes turned away and your hearts reached to your throats, and you imagined vain thoughts about GOD; in that place the believers were tried and shaken most severely > (33:10-11).*

Twenty-four thousand fighters under the command of Abu Sufyaan and 'Uyainah Ibn Hisn were advancing on Al-Madiinah to storm it and to lay siege to it in order to get rid of Muhammad, his religion, and his Companions. This army did not represent the Quraish alone, for they were in alliance with all the tribes, and all had vested interests that were threatened by Islam. It was a last and decisive attempt embarked on by all the enemies of the Prophet (PBUH), based upon individual, collective, and tribal interests.

The Muslims found themselves in a precarious situation. The Prophet (PBUH) assembled his Companions for consultation. Certainly they were gathered to reach a decision on defense and battle, but how could they put up a defense? And then a long-legged man with flowing hair for whom the Prophet (PBUH) bore great love, Salmaan Al-Faarisiy, held up his head and took a look at Al-Madiinah, which was surrounded by hills, mountains, and exposed open country which could be easily broken through by the enemy.

Salmaan had much experience, in warfare and its tactics in his native Persia. So he proposed to the Prophet (PBUH) something which the Arabs had never seen before in warfare. It was the digging of a trench in the exposed places around Al-Madiinah.

And Allah knows what could have been the position of the Muslims in that battle had they not dug the trench, which was no sooner seen by the Quraish than they were stunned by despair. The forces of the enemy still remained in their tents for a month, unable to take Al-Madiinah, until Allah sent them one night a storm which devastated their tents and tore them asunder.

Then Abu Sufyaan announced to his forces that they should return to where they had come from. They were despondent and frustrated.

During the excavation of the trench, Salmaan took his place among the Muslims while they dug and removed the sand. The Prophet (PBUH) was also taking part in digging where Salmaan was working in a group. Their pickaxes could not smash a stubborn rock, in spite of the fact that Salmaan was of strong build and hardworking. A single stroke of his would break a rock to pieces, but he stood in front of this stubborn one. He let all those around him try to break it, but in vain. Salmaan went to the Prophet (PBUH) to ask him to divert the trench around that stubborn and challenging rock.

The Prophet (PBUHJ returned with Salmaan to see the rock himself. When he saw it, he called for a pickax and asked the Companions to keep back from the splinters. He said, "In the name of Allah," and then raised his blessed, firm hands gripping the pickaxe and let it fall.

The rock broke, making a great light. Salmaan said that he himself saw that light shining upon Al-Madiinah. The Prophet (PBUH) raised the pickaxe and gave a second blow and the rock broke more. At that moment the Prophet (PBUH) said loudly, "Allahu Akbar" - Allah is the Greatest - I have been given the keys to Rome; its red palaces have been lit for me and my nation has vanquished it."

The Prophet (PBUH) struck his third blow. Then the rock shattered and its glittering light was seen! The Prophet (PBUH) told them that he was now looking at the palaces of Syria, San'aa' and others like them, and the cities of the world over which the banner of Islam would flutter one day. The Muslims shouted in deep faith, "This is what Allah and His Prophet have promised us!"

Salmaan was the originator of the project to dig the trench, and he was associated with the rock out of which poured some secrets of the unseen and of destiny. When he called the Prophet (PBUH) to break it, he stood by the side of the Prophet (PBUH), saw the light, and heard the glad omen, and he lived to see the prophecy fulfilled and abided in its living reality. He saw the great capitals of Persia and Rome (Byzantium), the palaces of San'aa', Syria, Egypt, and Iraq. He saw every place trembling with the blessed ecstasy which was issuing forth from the high minarets in all parts of the world, spreading the light of guidance and goodness.

And here he is sitting there in the shade of a tree before his house in Al-Madiinah telling his guests about his great adventures in the quest for truth, explaining to them how he abandoned the religion of his Persian people for Christianity and then for Islam. How he abandoned his father's wealth and estate and threw himself into the arms of the wilderness in the quest for the release of his tension and soul. How he was sold in a slave market on his way to search for truth. How he met with the Prophet (PBUH) and how he came to believe in him.

Now let us approach his great court and listen to his grand tale, which he is recounting.

I come from Isfahan, from a place called Jai, and I was the most beloved son of my father, who was a figure of high esteem among his people. We used to worship fire. I devoted myself to fire worship until I became custodian of the fire, which we lit and never allowed to be extinguished.

My father had an estate. One day, he sent me there. I passed by a Christian church and heard them praying. I went in and saw what they were doing. I was impressed by what I saw in their prayers. I said, "This is better than our religion." I did not leave them until sunset, nor did I go to my father's estate, nor did I return to my father until he sent people to search for me.

I asked the Christians about their affair and prayers, which impressed me, and about the origin of their religion. They answered, "In Syria." I said to my father when I returned to him, "I passed by people praying in a church of theirs, and I was impressed by their prayer, and I could see that their religion is better than ours." He questioned me and I questioned him, and then he put fetters on my feet and locked me up.

Then I sent to the Christians saying I had entered their religion, and I requested that whenever a caravan came from Syria, they should tell me before its return in order for me to travel with them, and so they did.

I broke loose from the iron fetters and went away. I set out with them for Syria. While I was there, I asked about their learned man, and I was told that he was the bishop, leader of the church. I went to him and told him my story. I lived with him, serving, praying, and learning.

But this bishop was not faithful in his religion, because he used to gather money from the people to distribute it, but he would keep it for himself. Then he died.

They appointed a new leader in his place. I have never seen a man more godly, than he in his religion, nor more active in his bid for the Hereafter, nor more pious in the world, nor more punctual at worship. I loved him more than I had ever loved any other person before.

When his fate came, I asked him, "To whom would you recommend me? And to whom would you leave me?" He said, "O my son, I do not know anyone who is on the path I am and who leads the kind of life I lead, except a certain man in Mosul."

When he died, I went to that man in Mosul, and told him the story, and I stayed with him as long as Allah wished me to stay. Then death approached him. So I asked him, "To whom would you advise me to go to?" He directed me to a pious man in Nisiibiin." So I went to him and told him my story. I stayed with him as long as Allah wished me to stay. When death overtook him, I asked him as before. He told me to meet a person at 'Amuriah in Byzantium. So, to Byzantium I went and stayed with that man, earning my living there by rearing cattle and sheep.

Then death approached him, and I asked him, "To whom should I go?" He said, "O my son, I know no one anywhere who is on the path we have been on so that I can tell you to go to him. But you have been overtaken by an epoch in which there will appear a prophet in the pure creed of Ibraahiim (Abraham). He will migrate to the place of palm trees. If you can be sincere to him, then do so. He has signs, which will be manifested: he does not eat of charity, yet he accepts gifts, and between his shoulders is the seal of Prophethood. When you see him, you will know him."

A caravan passed by me on that day. I asked them where they had come from and learned that they were from the Arabian Peninsula. So I told them, "I give you these cattle and sheep of mine in return for your taking me to your land." They agreed. So they took me in their company until they brought me to Wadi Al-Quraa and there they wronged me. They sold me to a Jew. I saw many palm trees and cherished the hope that it was the land that had been described to me and which would be the future place of the advent of the prophet, but it was not.

I stayed with this Jew who bought me until another from Bani Quraidhah came to him one day and bought me from him. I stayed with him until we came to Al-Madiinah. By Allah, I had hardly seen it when I knew that it was the land described to me.

I stayed with the Jew, working for him on his plantation in Bani Quraidhah until Allah sent His Prophet, who later emigrated to Al Madiinah and dismounted at Qubaa' among the Bani 'Amr Ibn "Awf. Indeed, one day, I was at the top of a palm tree with my master sitting below it when a Jewish man came. He was a cousin of his and said to him, "May Allah destroy Bani Qubaa'. They are spreading a rumor about a man at Qubaa' who came from Makkah claiming that he is a prophet." By Allah, he had hardly said it, when I was seized by a tremor, and the palm tree shook until I almost fell on my master. I climbed down quickly saying, "What are you saying? What news?" My master gave me a nasty slap and said; "What have you got to do with this? Return to your work!"

So, I returned to work. At nightfall I gathered what I had and went out until I came to the Prophet (PBUH) at Qubaa'. I entered and found him sitting with some of his Companions.

Then I said, "You are in need and a stranger. I have some food, which I intend to give out as charity. When they showed me your lodgings, I thought you most deserve it, so I have come to you with it." I put the food down. The Prophet (PBUH) said to his Companions, "Eat in the name of Allah." He abstained and never took of it. I said to myself, "This, by Allah, is one sign. He does not eat of charity!"

I returned to meet the Prophet (PBUH) again the next day, carrying some food, and said to him (PBUH), "I can see that you do not partake of charity. I have something which I want to give to you as a present." I placed it before him. He said to his Companions, "Eat in the name of Allah" and he ate with them. So I said to myself, "This indeed is the second sign. He eats of presents." I returned and stayed away for a while. Then I came to him, and I saw him sitting, having returned from a burial, and surrounded by his Companions. He had two garments, carrying one on his shoulder and wearing the other. I greeted him, then bent to see the upper part of his back. He knew what I was looking for, so he threw aside his garment off his shoulder and, behold, the sign between his shoulders, the seal of Prophethood, was clear just as the Christian monk had described."

At once, I staggered towards him, kissing him and weeping. He called to me to come forward and I sat before him. I told him my story as you have already heard me describe the events.

When I became a Muslim, slavery prevented me from taking part in the battles of Badr and Uhud. Therefore the Prophet (PBUH) advised me, "Go into terms with your master for him to free you," and so I did. The Prophet (PBUH) told the Companions to assist me, and Allah freed me from bondage. I became a free Muslim, taking part with the Prophet (PBUH) in the Battle of Al-Khandaq and others.

With these simple clear words, Salmaan spoke of his great, noble, and sacrificial adventure for the sake of Allah, seeking after the reality of religion that led him to Allah and helped him to find his role in this life.

What kind of a noble person was this man? What great superiority was achieved by his aspiring spirit, that restless spirit that withstood difficulties and defeated them, confronted the impossible and it gave way! What devotion to the truth, and what sincerity that led its owner voluntarily away from the estate of his father, with all its wealth and luxury, to the wilderness, with all its difficulties and suffering. He moved from land to land, town to town, seeking acquaintances, persevering, worshiping and searching for his destiny among people, sects, and different ways of life. And adhering all the way to the truth with all its noble sacrifices, for the sake of guidance until he was sold into slavery. He was then rewarded by Allah, the best of rewards, making him reach the truth and come into the presence of His Prophet. And then He granted him longevity, enough for him to see the banner of Islam fluttering in all parts of the world and His Muslim worshippers filling its space and corners with guidance, progress and justice!

What do you expect of the Islam of a man with such a noble character but to be a man of such truth! It was an Islam of the Godfearing and innocent. In his devotion he was intelligent, pious, and the person nearest to "Umar lbn Al-Khattaab.

He once stayed with Abu Ad-Dardaa', under the same roof. Abu Ad-Dardaa' used to pray all night and fast all day. Salmaan blamed him for this excessive worship. One day, Salmaan wanted to stop him from fasting and to say it was supererogatory. Abu Ad-Dardaa' asked him, "Would you prevent me from fasting for my Lord and from praying to

Him?" Salmaan replied, "No, your eyes have a claim upon you, your family has a claim upon you, so fast intermittently, then pray and sleep."

This reached the Prophet (PBUH) who said, "Salmaan is, indeed, full of knowledge." The Prophet (PBUH) was often impressed by his wisdom and knowledge, just as he was impressed by his character and religion. On the Day of Al-Khandaq, the Ansaar stood up and said, "Salmaan is of us," the Muhaajiruun stood up also and said, "Salmaan is of us." The Prophet called to them saying, "Salmaan is of us, O People of the House (Prophet's house)."

Indeed, he deserved this honor! 'Aliy Ibn Abi Taalib, (May Allah honor his face) nicknamed him "Luqmaan the Wise". He was asked about after his death: "There was a man who was of the People of the House. Who among you is like Luqmaan the Wise? He was a man of knowledge who absorbed all the scriptures of the People of the Book. He was like a sea that was never exhausted!"

He was held in the minds of Prophet's Companions with all highest regards and in the greatest position and respect. During the Caliphate of 'Umar, he came to Al-Madiinah on a visit and 'Umar accorded him what he had never accorded to anyone before when he assembled his Companions and said, "Come, let us go out and welcome Salmaan!" They received him at the border of Al-Madiinah.

Salmaan had lived with the Prophet (PBUH) ever since he met him, and believed in him as a free Muslim, and worshiped with him. He lived during the Caliphate of Abu Bakr, "Umar and 'Uthmaan, in whose era he met his Lord. In most of these years, the banner of Islam spread everywhere, and the treasures of Islam were carried to Al-Madiinah in floods and distributed to the people in the form of regular allowance and fixed salaries. The responsibilities of ruling increased on all fronts, as well as duties and the overwhelming burden of holding official posts. So where did Salmaan stand in this respect? Where do we see him in the time of splendor, plenty, and enjoyment?

Open wide your eyes. Do you see that humble man sitting there in the shade making baskets and utensils out of palm fronds?

That is Salmaan. Take a good look at him. Look at his short garment, which is so short that it is only down to his knees. That was him in grand old age. His grant was 4,000 to 6,000 Dirhams a year, but he distributed all of it, refusing to take a Dirham of it, and he used to say, "I would buy palm fronds with one dirham to work on and then sell it for three dirhams. I retained one dirham of it as capital, spent one dirham on my family, and gave away one dirham, and if 'Umar Ibn Al-Khattaab prevented me from that, I would not stop."

What next, O'followers of Muhammad? What next, O' noblest of mankind in all ages? Some of us used to think, whenever we heard the conduct of the Companions and their piety - for example, Abu Bakr, 'Umar, Abu Dhar and their brethren — that it was based on the life of the Arabian Peninsula, where the Arabs find pleasure in simplicity. And here we are before a man from Persia, the land of pleasure, luxury, and civilization, and he was not of the poor but of its upper class. What about him now refusing property, wealth, and enjoyment, and insisting that he live on one dirham a day from the work of his hands? How about his refusing leadership and position except for something relating to jihaad and only if none but he were suitable for it, and it was forced upon him, and he accepted it weeping and shy? How about when he accepted leadership, which was forced upon him but he refused to take his lawful dues? Hishaam Ibn Hasaan relates from Al-Hassan: The allowance of Salmaan was 5,000. He lived among 30,000 people and used to dress in a garment cut into halves. He wore one and sat on the other half. Whenever his allowance was due him, he distributed it to the needy and lived on the earnings of his hands!

Why do you think he was doing all this work and worshiping with all this devotion, and yet he was a Persian child of luxury, the upbringing of civilization? You can hear the reply from him. While he was on his deathbed, the great spirit mounting forth to meet his Lord, Exalted and Merciful, Sa'd Ibn Abi Waqaas went to greet him, and Salmaan wept! Sa'd said, "What makes you weep, O' Abu 'Abd Allah? The Prophet of Allah died pleased with you!" Salmaan replied, "By Allah, I am not weeping in fear of death, nor for love of the world. But the Prophet of Allah put me on an oath. He said, 'Let any of you have in this world like the provision of the traveler,' and here I have owned many things around me". Sa'd said: "I looked around and I saw nothing but a water-pot and vessel to eat in!" Then I said to him, "O' Abu 'Abd Allah, give us a parting word of advice for us to follow." He said, O Sa'd, remember Allah for your cares, if you have any. Remember Allah in your judgment, if you judge. Remember Allah when you distribute the share." This was the man who filled his spirit with riches just as it filled him with renunciation of the pleasures of this world, its riches, and pride. The oath, which he and the rest of the Companions had taken before the Prophet of Allah was that they must not let the world possess them and that they should take nothing from it but the provision of the traveler in his bag.

Salmaan had kept the oath, yet still his tears ran when he saw his soul preparing for departure, fearing that he had gone beyond the limits. There was nothing around him except a vessel to eat in and a water-pot, and yet still he considered himself lavish! Did I not tell you that he was the nearest in resemblance to 'Umar? During the days of his rule over the Madiinah area, he never changed his way. He had refused, as we have seen, to receive his salary as a ruler, but went on making baskets to earn his living. His dress was no more than a gown, resembling his old clothes in simplicity.

One day while on the road, he met a man arriving from Syria, carrying a load of figs and dates. The load was too heavy for him and made him weary. No sooner did the Syrian see the man in front of him, who appeared to be one of the common people and poor than he thought of putting the load on his shoulders and when he reached his destination he would give him something for his labor. So he beckoned to the man (Salmaan, the governor), and he came up to him. The Syrian said to him, "Relieve me of this load." He carried it, and they walked together.

While on their way, they met a group of people. He greeted them and they stood up in obeisance, replying, "And unto the governor be peace!" "Who is the governor?" The Syrian asked himself. His surprise increased when he saw some of them rushing towards Salmaan to take the load off his shoulders. "Let us carry it, O' governor". When the Syrian knew that he was the governor of Al-Madiinah, he was astonished. Words of apology and regret fell from his lips, and he went forward to grab the load. But Salmaan shook his head in refusal, saying, "No, not until I take you to your destination."

He was asked one day, "What troubles you in the leadership?" He replied, "The pleasure of nurturing it and the bitterness of meaning!"

A friend of his came to him one day at his house and found him kneading dough. He asked him, "Where is your servant? " He replied, "We have sent her on an errand and we hate to charge her with two duties."

When we say "his house" let us remember what kind of house it was. When Salmaan thought of building it, he asked the mason, "How are you going to build it?" The mason was courteous and yet witty. He knew the piety and devotion of Salmaan, so he replied to him saying, "Fear not. It is a house for you to protect yourself against the heat of the sun and dwell in the cold weather. When you stand erect in it, it touches your head." Salmaan said to him, "Yes! That is it, so go on and build it."

There was nothing of the goods of this world which could attract Salmaan for a moment, nor did they leave any traces in his heart except one thing, which he was particularly mindful of and had entrusted to his wife, requesting her to keep it far away in a safe place. In his last sickness, and in the morning on which he gave up his soul, he called her, "Bring me the trust which I left in safe keeping!" She brought it and behold! it was a bottle of musk. He had gained it on the day of liberating the city of Jalwalaa' and kept it to be his perfume on the day of his death. Then he called for a pot of water, sprinkled the musk into it, stirred it with his hand and then said to his wife, "Sprinkle it on me, for there will now come to me creatures from the creatures of Allah. They do not eat food and what they like is perfume."

Having done so he said to her, "Shut the door and go down."

She did what he bade her to do. After a while she went up to him and saw his blessed soul had departed his body and his frame. It was gone to the Supreme Master, and it ascended with the desire to meet Him as he had an appointment there with the Prophet Muhammad (PBUH) and his two Companions Abu Bakr and 'Umar and the noble circle of martyrs!

Long had the burning desire stirred Salmaan. The time had come for him to rest in peace.

(3)

ABU DHAR AL-GHIFAARIY

The Leader of Opposition and an Enemy of Wealth

Cheerfully and happily did he turn toward Makkah, Indeed, the difficulty of his journey and the hard, burning desert sand made him suffer pain. However, the goal he was striving to reach made him forget his pain and filled his soul with joy and delight.

He entered Makkah disguised as one of those who came to circumambulate the great idols of the Sacred House of the Ka'bah or as a passer-by who had lost his way or who had traveled far and sought provision and shelter.

If the inhabitants of Makkah knew that he had come to search for Muhammad (PBUH) and to listen to him, they would cut him into pieces. He did not fear being cut up piece by piece, but not before meeting the person he had crossed the hot burning deserts to see and for whose sake afterwards he was willing to risk his life because he believed in him and was convinced of his honesty and the truth of his message.

He went about secretly gathering information and whenever he heard someone speaking about Muhammad (PBUH), he carefully approached him until he was finally able to compile all the scattered pieces of information which he had heard here and there. Finally, he was guided to the place where he was able to see Muhammad (PBUH).

One morning he went there and found the Prophet (PBUH) sitting alone. He approached him and said, "O, my Arab brother, good morning." Thereupon the Prophet replied, "And may peace be upon you, my brother." Abu Dhar then said, "Sing to me some of what you are saying." The Prophet (PBUH) answered, "It isn't a poem to be sung, but a Holy Qur'aan." Abu Dhar said, "Then recite for me."

The Prophet (PBUH) recited to him while he listened. It was not long until Abu Dhar shouted, "I bear witness that there is no god but Allah and that Muhammad is His Prophet (PBUH) and Messenger." The Prophet (PBUH) asked him, "Where are you from, my Arab brother?" Abu Dhar answered, "From Ghifaar." A broad smile appeared on the Prophet's lips (PBUH) and his face was filled with wonder and astonishment.

However, Abu Dhar was also smiling, for he knew well that the reason behind the Prophet's astonishment was because the man who had just embraced Islam in front of him was from Ghifaar. Ghifaar was a tribe with a notorious reputation for highway robbery. Its people were famous for theft and were known as allies of darkness and night. Woe to him who fell into their hands on a dark night!

Was it possible that one of them would embrace Islam while it was still a new, secret religion?

Narrating the story himself, Abu Dhar said: The Prophet (PBUH) lifted his eyes out of astonishment, due to Ghifaar's reputation. Then he said, "Allah guides whom He wills." Indeed, Allah guides whom He wills.

Abu Dhar (May Allah be pleased with him) was one of those whom Allah wanted to be rightly guided and for whom He wanted the best. His insight was always directed towards truth.

It has been narrated that he worshiped Allah during the period of Jaahiliyah, which means that he revolted against the worship of idols and turned towards the belief in One Great Creator.

Therefore, he had hardly heard about the appearance of a prophet rejecting idols and their worship and calling to the worship of Allah, the One, the Sublime, the Vanquisher, when he immediately set out and quickened his steps to meet this new Messenger of Allah (PBUH).

Immediately, without hesitation, he embraced Islam. His order among the converts was fifth or sixth, which means that he converted during the first days, if not the first hours, of Islam. His conversion was indeed very early.

When he embraced Islam the Prophet (PBUH) was till secretly whispering the call to Islam to himself and to the five who believed in him. Abu Dhar could not do anything except carry his faith within his heart, secretly leaving Makkah and returning to his people.

However, Abu Dhar — his real name was Jundub Ibn Janaadah - had a restless and agitated temper. He had been created to revolt against falsehood wherever it existed. Now he saw falsehood with his own eyes as lifeless rocks piled upon each other. The birth of their worship was long before his existence: minds and foreheads bowed down in front of them and people calling to them saying, "At your service, at your service!"

It is true that he saw the Prophet's preference to whisper in those days, but he wished that a loud shout declaring Islam publicly be made by the venerable and honorable followers before his departure.

Immediately after embracing Islam, he turned to the Prophet (PBUH) with the following question: "O' Messenger of Allah, what is it that you order me?" The Prophet (PBUH) replied, "Go back to your kin until my order reaches you." Abu Dhar said, "In the name of the One, Who owns my soul between His hands, I am not going back until I cry out loudly declaring Islam within the mosque!"

Did I not tell you? His temper was restless and agitated. At the same moment when, Abu Dhar discovered a totally new world, a wonderful new world represented by the Prophet (PBUH) whom he believed in and by the call which he became acquainted with by the Prophet's tongue, at that same moment he was asked to return silently to his kin. Was that possible? It was beyond his ability.

Hereupon, he entered the Sacred House and cried out as loud as he could, "I bear witness that there is no god but Allah and that Muhammad is His Messenger!"

As far as we know, it was the first public pronouncement declaring Islam and challenging the arrogance of the Quraish, which reached their ears. It was cried out by a stranger, who did not have any relatives, reputation, or protection in Makkah.

He acted out of his own dedication and courage even though he knew what was going to happen. He was surrounded by the polytheists, who hit him till he fell down.

This news reached Al 'Abbaas, the Prophet's uncle. He came quickly but could not rescue Abu Dhar except by a clever trick. Thus he told them, "O' you Quraish! You are merchants and your route crosses over Ghifaar and this man here is one of their tribesmen. Beware, he may incite his kin against you, provoking them to rob your caravans while passing by." They came back to their senses and left him alone.

Having tasted the sweetness of being hurt in the cause of Allah, Abu Dhar did not want to leave Makkah without being given more.

So, on the next day, or perhaps on the same day, Abu Dhar encountered two women circling around two idols (Usaaf and Naa'ilah) and calling upon them. He stood in front of them rudely disgracing their idols. The women shouted loudly, and men hastened as fast as lightening, immediately hitting him until he fell down unconscious.

When he regained consciousness he shouted again that there is no god but Allah and Muhammed (PBUH) is His Messenger.

The Prophet (PBUH) realized the nature of his new disciple and his amazing ability to encounter falsehood. However, the time for public declaration of the message had not yet come, so again he ordered Abu Dhar to go back to his kin and whenever he heard the announcement of the new religion, he would play his role.

Abu Dhar returned to his kin and tribe, telling them about the Prophet (PBUH) who called people to worship only Allah and who guided them to noble manners. His people embraced Islam one by one. Bani Ghifaar alone did not suffice him; he turned to Bani Aslim, to spread his lights there.

Time passed and the Prophet (PBUH) emigrated to Al-Madiinah and there, together with Muslims, he settled down.

One day the city welcomed long lines of people on horseback and on foot. Their feet made a great noise. Were it not for their loud shout "Allah is the Greatest", the viewer would have thought it was an attacking polytheist army. The great parade approached and entered Al-Madiinah. Their destination was the Prophet's (PBUH) Mosque. The parade consisted of two tribes, Bani Ghifaar and Bani Aslim. Abu Dhar made them come as Muslims, all of them: men, women, elderly, youth, and even the children!

No doubt, the Prophet's wonder and astonishment increased. In the distant past he had been very astonished when he witnessed one of the tribe of Ghifaar announce his embracement of Islam, and he had expressed on that day his wonder saying, "Allah guides whom He wills."

But now, the whole tribe had come after already becoming Muslim. It had lived several years under the banner of Islam since Allah guided it by means of Abu Dhar. Now it had come together with Bani Aslim.

The former allies of the devil, the notorious highwaymen, had become the allies of truth and great men of good deeds.

Is it not true that Allah guides whom He pleases? The Prophet (PBUH) looked at their kind faces with eyes full of joy, tenderness, and love. He looked at Bani Ghifaar and said, "May Allah forgive Ghifaar." 'Then he turned to Bani Aslim and said, "May Allah make peace with Aslim."

Abu Dhar, this magnificent propogator of Islam who was obstinate, unyielding, and difficult to be defeated: was the Prophet (PBUH) not going to salute him with a special greeting?

Indeed, his reward was going to be abundant and his greeting blessed. He was going to carry on his chest- but also his history was going to carry - the highest, most honorable, and most respectable medals. Generations and centuries will pass away, but the Prophet's opinion about Abu Dhar will always stay alive in people's memory: "The earth never carried above it, nor did the sky ever shade under it a more truthful tongue than Abu Dhar's".

The Prophet (PBUH) determined his Companion's future and

summed up his whole life in those simple words.

Bold and daring truthfulness was the essence of Abu Dhar's whole life. Truthfulness of his inner soul as well as his appearance. Truthfulness of his faith as well as his tongue. All his life he was truthful. Neither deceiving himself or anyone else, nor allowing anyone to deceive him.

His truthfulness was not mute merit. According to Abu Dhar, truthfulness is never silent. Truthfulness is equivalent to openness and publicity, publicity of truth and challenge to falsehood, support of right and refutation of wrong. Truthfulness is a reasonable ally to truth and a courageous expression of it; both quicken their pace.

The Prophet (PBUH) could see with his unmistaken insight— across remote distances and the far unknown future — all the different difficulties Abu Dhar had to face due to his truthfulness and firmness. He therefore was always ordering him to let patience and deliberateness be his manner.

The Prophet once asked him, "O' Abu Dhar! What would you do if you witnessed a time when commanders monopolize the war booty?" He replied, "I swear by Allah, Who sent you with the truth, I would strike them with my sword!" The Prophet (PBUH) said to him, "Shall I guide you to what is better? Be patient till you meet me."

Why did the Prophet (PBUH) ask him this specific question? Commanders, money? It was the cause Abu Dhar was going to devote his life to and the problem he was to encounter with society in the future.

The Prophet (PBUH) knew it; therefore he asked him this

question in order to provide him with this precious advice: "Be patient till you meet me."

Abu Dhar kept his teacher and Prophet's instruction unforgotten. Therefore, he did not carry a sword against those commanders who enriched themselves by taking what was the public money. But also, he did not keep silent, and he did not let them rest.

Indeed, although the Prophet (PBUH) had forbidden him to carry his sword against them, he did not forbid him to carry a sharp truthful tongue. And that is what he did.

The era of the Prophet (PBUH) and of Abu Bakr and 'Umar passed with its complete transcendence over all worldly temptations. Even the tempted desirous and greedy souls could not find a paved and open way for their devious desires. In those days there were no deviations to be oppossed loudly by Abu Dhar's sharp words. As long as the Commander of the Faithful 'Umar lived, Muslim governors, rulers, and even the wealthy, were forced to live a humble, modest, aesthetic and just life, almost beyond human capacity. No governor of the Caliph, whether in Iraq, Syria, Yemen, or anywhere else in the region, could ever eat a kind of sweet unaffordable by ordinary people, without such a piece of information soon reaching 'Umar, who would immediately order that governor to return to Al-Madiinah, where he would face a severe punishment.

Therefore, Abu Dhar lived without trouble and happily, with much inward peace, as long as 'Umar was Commander of the Faithful. Nothing ever annoyed Abu Dhar more than the abuse of power and the monopoly of wealth. 'Umar's firm control over power and his fair distribution of wealth allowed him tranquility and satisfaction.

It was because of this that he was able to devote himself to Allah's worship and jihaad in the cause of Allah, never keeping silent if any infringement was seen here or there, which rarely happened.

However, the greatest, most just and most magnificent ruler that human beings were ever to experience left our world one day, leaving behind a tremendous gap, causing inevitable reactions beyond human expectations.

The Islamic campaigns continued, thus bringing under control more regions. At the same time, desires and longing for ambition to enjoy the comforts and luxury of life started to float to the surface. In these events, Abu Dhar saw the impending danger. The banners of personal glory were about to tempt those, whose role in life was to lift the standard of Allah. Life with its false embellishments and its wild arrogance was about to tempt those, whose role was to make out of life a plantation of good deeds.

Money — created by Allah to be obedient to His servants for the benefit of mankind — was about to turn into a tyrant master. A master of whom? The Prophet's Companions.

The Prophet (PBUH) died with a pawned shield, although piles of war booty were under his service. The excellence of the earth — created by Allah for all human beings and with their rights upon it mutually corresponding — was about to turn into a monopoly and privilege.

Power — a responsibility that pious people tremble at when thinking about its horrible charge in the Hereafter — turned into a means of authority, wealth, and destructive luxury.

Abu Dhar realized all that. He did not search for his duties or responsibilities, but rather took his sword, waved it in the air and set out to face his society with his unbeatable sword. But soon the echo of the Prophet's (PBUH) advice struck his heart, so he returned it to its scabbard. He remembered the Prophet (PBUH) had said he should not lift it in the face of a Muslim.

< *It is not lawful for a believer to kill another believer except by error* > *(4:92).*

His role was not to fight but to oppose. The sword was not a means of change and reformation, but the truthful, sincere, and brave word was. The fair word does not lose its path, and its consequences are not terrifying. The Prophet (PBUH) once said, while surrounded by his Companions, that the earth never carried above it, nor did the sky ever shade a more truthful tongue than Abu Dhar's.

Why should someone who owns such a truthful tongue and truthful conviction need a sword ?

A single word by him hit the target more than uncountable swords. Therefore, Abu Dhar was to encounter all the governors, the wealthy, and all those who worshipped the worldly life and relied upon it, thereby representing an even greater danger to the religion which came to be a guide, not a tax collector; prophethood, not dominion; mercy, not afflication; humbleness, not superiority; equality, not differentiation; satisfaction, not greed; sufficiency, not luxury; and a life of ease full of temptation, with this life the only goal.

So Abu Dhar went out to face all those challenges, and Allah will judge truthfully between him and them, and Allah is the Most Just of Judges.

Abu Dhar went out to the strongholds of power and wealth, attacking them one after the other. Within a short time he became the standard around which the laborers of Islam and the masses gathered. Even in the remote districts, where people had not yet met him, word about him got around and he became well known until he hardly passed through a land in which his name had not reached the ears of some of the people and without crucial questions being raised which threatened the welfare and worldly interests of the powerful and wealthy.

If this honorable, rebellious Companion was to select an appropriate standard for himself and his movement, he would not find a better one than an iron, a glowing, hot, and flaming iron. Thus he turned the following words into his chant and earnest appeal, repeating them every time and every place he went. People repeated them after him as if they were an anthem:

Announce to those who hoard up gold and silver, the warning of branding irons with which their foreheads and bodies will be branded in the hereafter.

He never ascended a mountain or descended a valley or entered a city or faced a ruler without repeating the same words, so much so that people would always welcome him when he approached them by repeating, "*Announce to those who hoard up gold and silver, the warning of branding irons..*" .

This statement turned into "signature time" for his message to which he devoted his life. That was because he saw wealth being accumulated and monopolized for power and being turned into a means of supremacy and abuse. He saw an overwhelming passion for life which was about to erase all beauty, piety, devotion, and sincerity built up during the previous years of the great mission of the Messenger of Allah.

When he began his attack, he started with the most authoritative and horrible stronghold: there in Syria, where Mu'aawiyah Ibn Abi Sufyaan was ruling one of the most fertile lands in the world of Islam, granting and distributing money carelessly, thereby bestowing undeserved privileges upon people of power and rank in order to guarantee his future, a future he aspired to promote.

There in Syria, the country of overwhelming palaces, country estates and fortunes which tempted the remnants of the carriers of the Islamic message, he began his attack. Abu Dhar wanted to confront the center of danger before it ruined and destroyed all Muslims.

The leader of the opposition to corrupt worldly power wore his humble gown and hastened as fast as lightning towards Syria. Ordinary people hardly heard about his arrival before they hurried to welcome him with great enthusiasm and longing desire, surrounding him wherever he would go or stay. "O' Abu Dhar, please tell us . . ." "O' Companion of the Prophet (PBUH) please tell us . . ."

Sharp-eyed, he would take a glance at the multitude around him, seeing the majority of them suffering from poverty and need. He then directed his eyes to a place not too far away where he saw many palaces and landed estates. Then he shouted to those around him, "I wonder why those who don't find something to eat don't go out holding their swords ready to fight?"

Then he immediately remembered the Prophet's admonition to replace opposition and rebellion with patience, and to replace the sword with brave and daring words, abandoning the language of war and returning to logic, reason, and conviction; teaching people that they are all equal like the teeth of a comb; that they are all partners as far as the means of living are concerned; that no one is superior to another except in piety; and that their ruler should be the first to starve if the people suffer hunger and the last to satisfy his appetite if they become sated.

He decided to create by means of his words and bravery a public opinion all over the Muslim countries which would represent, through its intelligence, indomitability, and strength, a hindering force to the deviations of the rulers and the rich and wealthy, in order to hinder the appearance and spread of a power and wealth monopolizing class.

Within a few days, the whole of Syria turned into what resembled a bee-hive which had found its queen. If Abu Dhar would have given the slightest passing gesture of revolt, the whole of Syria would have been set on fire. But, as mentioned before, he focused his interest on creating a respectable public opinion. His words turned into the subject of conversation everywhere, inside mosques, during meetings, and even on roads.

Danger increased and reached its peak for Abu Dhar, speaking about the newly acquired privileges of the rich and powerful, on the day in which be argued with Mu'aawiyah in front of the masses.

Every witness of that debate told those who missed it, so that its news spread as fast as wildfire.

Abu Dhar, who possessed the most truthful tongue on earth, as the Prophet (PBUH) described him, stood up. He asked Mu'aawiyah about his wealth before and after being in power, about the house in which he was living in Makkah, and the castles he owned in Syria. Then he raised the question to the Companions who had accompanied Mu'aawiyah to Syria and were now owners of estates and castles.

After that he cried to them, "Is it you among whom the Prophet lived when the Qur'aan was being revealed?" Then he answered himself, "Yes, it is you! The Qur'aan was revealed among you. It is you who experienced with the Prophet (PBUH) all the different scenes.

Then he asked them again, "Can't you find this verse in the Book of Allah? <*. . . and those who hoard up gold and silver, and do not expend it in the cause of GOD, announce to them a painful chastisment - On the Day when it shall be heated in the Fire of Hell, and with it their foreheads, and their bodies, and their backs shall be branded, "This is what you treasured for yourselves, so taste the evil of what you were treasuring ."* > *(9: 34-35).*

However, Mu'aawiyah wanted to end the whole dispute by arguing that this verse was mentioned regarding the People of the Book (i.e. the Jews and Christians). Here upon cried Abu Dhar, "No, it has been revealed for us all."

Abu Dhar then continued his talk, advising Mu'aawiyah and his followers to give up their landed estates, castles, money, and all their possessions, and to abstain from saving for themselves more than their daily need.

Through the people's assemblies, congregations, and meetings, the news of the debate spread and reached everyone's ears.

Louder and louder was Abu Dhar's anthem to be heard everywhere: "Announce to those who hoard up gold and silver the warning of branding irons." Mu'aawiyah felt the danger of the words of the great, honorable, and rebellious Companion who terrified him. Yet Mu'aawiyah appreciated his value and did not harm him, but he immediately wrote to the Caliph 'Uthmaan (May Allah be pleased with him), "Abu Dhar spoils the people in Syria."

'Uthmaan sent for Abu Dhar, asking him to come to Al Madiinah. Abu Dhar set off from Syria with kindness, affection, and honor. His farewell day was celebrated in Syria in a manner Damascus had never witnessed the like of.

"I don't need your world!" That is what Abu Dhar said to the Caliph 'Uthmaan after he reached Al-Madiinah and a prolonged conversation took place between them.

After this conversation and after having heard the news coming from all different regions of the Muslim world, it was confirmed that Abu Dhar's opinions had actually agitated the multitudes, who began to crystallize around them. It was at that time that 'Uthmaan began to truly realize the actual danger of Abu Dhar's opinion and its strength. He therefore decided to keep him beside him at Al Madiinah.

'Uthmaan presented to him his decision in a very kind and friendly way. He said to him, "Stay here beside me. You will be endowed with blessings day and night." Abu Dhar then answered, "I don't need your world."

Indeed, he did not need people's world. He was one of those saints who searched for the enrichment of their soul, dedicating his life to giving, not to receiving!

He asked the Caliph 'Uthmaan (May Allah be pleased with him) to allow him to go out to Ar-Rabadhah, and he allowed him.

Despite his fierce opposition, he stayed close to Allah and His Prophet (PBUH) in a very honest way, always keeping within his soul the Prophet's advice never to carry a sword. It was as if the Prophet had seen the whole of Abu Dhar's destiny and future, so he bestowed upon him this precious advice.

Abu Dhar never hid his annoyance when seeing those who liked to ignite the flames of civil strife by using his words and opinions as a means to satisfy their passionate desire and cunning deceits.

One day, while in Ar-Rabadhah, a delegation from Kufa came to ask him to raise the flag of revolution against the caliph. He drove them back with decisive words: "By Allah, if 'Uthmaan was to crucify me on the longest board or on a mountain, I would patiently obey, for Allah's reward would be waiting for me, and I see it to be the best for me. And if he was to force me to walk from one end of the horizon to the other, I would patiently obey, for Allah's reward would be waiting for me, and I see it to be the best for me. And if he was to force me back to my home I would patiently obey, for Allah's reward would be waiting for me, and I see it to be the best for me."

He was a man who was not interested in any worldly gain; thus he was blessed with insight by Allah. He realized again the tremendous danger involved in armed civil strife; therefore, he abstained from it. But he also realized the tremendous danger involved in silence; therefore, he abstained from it. That is why he raised his voice, not his sword, and raised the word of truth and sincerity.

He was not tempted by greedy desires nor hindered by worldly obstacles.

Abu Dhar kept himself busy with and devoted himself to sincere, honest opposition.

He spent his whole life focusing on the faults of power and the faults of money. Thus power and money possessed the temptation. Abu Dhar was afraid his brethren would fall into their traps — his same brethren who had carried the standard of Islam with the Prophet (PBUH) and whom he wanted to remain the carriers of the Prophet's message (PBUH).

Power and money were, furthermore, the backbone of societies and communities. If misused, the destiny of people would encounter serious and imminent danger.

Abu Dhar wished so much that the Prophet's Companions would not be appointed as governors and would not collect fortunes, but would rather stay as they always had been: as spiritual guides to the right path for Allah's worshipers.

He knew well the voracity of life and the voracity of money, and he knew that the example of Abu Dhar and 'Umar was never going to be repeated! How often did he hear the Prophet (PBUH) asking his Companions to be aware of the temptation of authority saying, "It's a deposition in trust, and on the Day of Resurrection, it will be a shame and regret except to the one who was endowed with it justly and accomplished his duty."

Abu Dhar went so far that he avoided his brethren if he did not boycott them, for no other reason than that they had become rulers and, of course, had become wealthier.

Abu Muusaa Al-Ash'ariy once met him. He had hardly seen him when he stretched his arms with joy and delight shouting, "Welcome Abu Dhar! Welcome my brother!" But Abu Dhar held himself back saying, "I am not your brother; I was so before you became an administrator and governor."

In the same way, Abu Hurairah once met and embraced him in welcome, but Abu Dhar pushed him back and said, "Isn't it you who became governor, then extended your buildings and possessed plantations and cattle?" Abu Hurairah defended himself, trying to prove his innocence and refute those rumors.

It may seem that Abu Dhar had an exaggerated position towards power and wealth, but he had a logic, which was shaped by his sincerity to himself and his faith. Thus, Abu Dhar stood with his dreams, deeds, behavior, and viewpoints according to the same standard the Prophet (PBUH) and his two Companions Abu Bakr and 'Umar had left behind.

If some people saw that standard to be an out-of-reach ideal, Abu Dhar saw it to be an example charting the path of life and toil, especially for those who had actually experienced the Prophet (PBUH), prayed behind him, taken part in jihaad with him, and sworn the oath of allegiance to him.

In addition to that- as mentioned before-his inspired intellect knew the decisive influence of power and property in determining people's destiny. Therefore, any disturbance, which might afflict the trustworthiness of power or the fairness of wealth, represents an imminent danger which must be resisted and opposed.

As long as he lived, Abu Dhar upheld the standard of the Prophet (PBUH) and his two Companions' good example. He was a great figure in the art of predominance over the temptation of power and wealth. The governorship of Iraq was once offered to him, but he said, "By Allah, you will never tempt me with your world."

Once, one of his companions saw him wearing an old gown and asked him, "Don't you have another one? I saw you a couple of days ago with two other gowns in your hands." Abu Dhar replied, "O cousin! I gave them to someone who needed them more than I do." He said to him, " By Allah, you need them!" Abu Dhar then answered, "May Allah forgive us. You glorify this life! Can't you see that I am wearing a gown? And I own another one for the congregational Friday prayer. Moreover, I own a goat, which I milk and a donkey, which I ride. Is there a better blessing?"

He once sat down talking to people and said, "My friend advised me to do seven things:

- He asked me to love the poor and to get closer to them.
- He asked me to look to those who are inferior and not to those who are superior.
- He asked me never to ask anyone for anything (i.e. to abstain from begging).
- He asked me to be kind to my relatives.
- He asked me to say the truth, no matter how sour it may be.
- He asked me never to be afraid of a critic's censure.
- And he asked me to frequently say, "There is no power nor might except Allah's."

He lived according to this advice until he became a living conscience moving among his people.

Imam Aliy once said, "There is no one nowadays who is nonchalant about people's criticism — as far as Allah and His rules are concerned — except Abu Dhar."

He lived opposing the abuse of power and the monopoly of property. He lived insisting all that was wrong and building all that was right. He lived devoted to the responsibility of good advice and warning.

When he was hindered from spelling out his Fatwaa (Formal legal opinion in Islamic law), he raised his voice and said to those hindering him, "By the name of the One in Whose hands my soul is, if you put the sword to my neck and I still thought that I could carry out a word I've heard from the Prophet (PBUH) before you cut, I would carry it out."

Had the Muslims listened on that day to his advice, a lot of civil strife and turmoil would have been prevented — turmoil that reached its peak and dangers that became grave, serious, and imminent. The state, society and Muslim nation had to face all that rebellion and aggrevated, alarming danger.

But then Abu Dhar was suffering the agony of death in Ar-Rabadhah, the place he chose to stay in after his disagreement with 'Uthmaan (May Allah be pleased with him). Let us go to him to give him farewell and let us see how the last scene of his admirable life is.

This slim dark-skinned woman sitting crying beside him is his wife. He is asking her, "Why do you cry and death is true?" She answers crying, "You are dying and I don't have a gown which suffices to be a winding sheet!" He smiles like a passing evening glow and says to her "Calm down. Don't cry. I heard the Prophet (PBUH) once saying while I was sitting among a number of Companions, "One of you will die in a desert land, and a group of the faithful will witness him." All those who were sitting with me at that assembly have died, whether in a village or among a congregation. No one is left except me, and now I am dying in a desert land. Watch out, a group of the faithful will soon show up. By Allah, I didn't lie in my life." He passed away. Blessed was he.

There is a caravan which sets off on a journey across the desert. It consists of a group of the faithful with 'Abd Allah Ibn Mas'uud, the Prophet's Companion, at their head. Ibn Mas'uud visualized the scene before he reached it: a scene of an outstretched body like that of a dead person and beside him a crying woman and boy.

He redirects his camel's bridle and the whole caravan follows him towards the scene. He has hardly taken a look at the dead body, when he realizes that it is his companion and brother in Islam, Abu Dhar.

His tears roll down abundantly while he stands in front of this virtuous body saying, "The Messenger of Allah was truthful. You will walk alone, die alone, and resurrect alone."

Ibn Mas'uud (May Allah be pleased with him) narrated the interpretation of the statement "You will walk alone, die alone, and resurrect alone," to his companions:

That was in the ninth year after Hijrah, during the Battle of Tabuuk, when the Prophet (PBUH) had ordered full preparation to meet the Romans, who had begun to carry out their conspiracies and cunning tricks against Islam.

The days in which people were asked to go out for jihaad were very hot, distressful, and hard. The destination was far away and the enemy terrifying.

A group of Muslims refrained from going forth, justifying their position with different apologies. The Prophet (PBUH) and his Companions went forth. The farther they went, the more exhausted and tired they became. Whenever a man stayed behind people said, "O' Prophet! So-and-so stayed behind." He then said, "Let him! If he's any good, he will reach you. If he's something else, then Allah will save you his trouble."

One day the people turned around. They could not find Abu

Dhar. They told the Prophet (PBUH) that Abu Dhar had stayed behind and his camel had slowed down. It is here that the Prophet (PBUH) repeated his first statement. Abu Dhar's camel became weaker under the severe pressure of hunger, thirst, and hot weather. It stumbled due to weakness and fatigue. Abu Dhar tried by all means to force it to move forward, but the burden of the camel's exhaustion was too heavy.

Finally, Abu Dhar felt that he would be left behind, losing the caravan's traces. Therefore, he dismounted from his camel, took his belongings, carried them on his back, and continued his route on foot over the burning desert sand, hurrying in order to rejoin the Prophet (PBUH) and his Companions.

In the early morning, while the Muslims were stopped for a while to rest, one of them saw a cloud of dust and sand behind which the shadow of a man could be seen. The one who saw that said to the Prophet (PBUH), "O' Messenger of Allah, there is someone walking alone." The Prophet (PBUH) said, "It is Abu Dhar."

The Muslims continued their talk until the man crossed the remaining distance between them. Only then were they able to know who he was.

The respectful traveler approached little by little. Although he could only with great effort pull his feet out of the burning sand and with a lot of pain carry the heavy burden on his back, he was very delighted to have finally reached the blessed caravan without straying behind and abandoning the Prophet (PBUH) and his Companions.

When he at last reached the caravan, someone shouted, "O' Prophet, it's Abu Dhar." Abu Dhar headed towards the Prophet

(PBUH). The Prophet (PBUH) had hardly seen him, when he tenderly, kindly, and sadly smiled and said, "Allah will have mercy upon Abu Dhar. He walks alone, dies alone, and resurrects alone."

Twenty years or more had passed since then. Abu Dhar died alone in the desert of Ar-Rabadhah, having walked on a path no one else had passed over so gloriously.

He is also remembered alone by history for his brave resistance and his great asceticism. Allah will also resurrect him alone, because the multitude of his various merits will not enable anyone else to find a place near him.

(4)
BILAAL IBN RABAAH
Sneering at Horror!

Whenever 'Umar Ibn Al Khattaab mentioned Abu Bakr he would say,"Abu Bakr is our master and the emancipator of our master."That is to say, Bilaal.

Indeed, the man to whom 'Umar would give the agnomen "Our Master" must be a great and fortunate man. However, this man — who was very dark in complexion, slender, very tall, thick-haired and with a sparse beard, as described by the narrators — would hardly hear words of praise and commendation directed at him and bestowed bountifully upon him without bending his head, lowering his eyelids and saying with tears flowing down his two cheeks, "Indeed, I am an Abyssinian. Yesterday, I was only a slave!"

So who is this Abyssinian who was yesterday only a slave? He is Bilaal Ibn Rabaab the announcer of the time of Muslim prayer and the troublemaker to the idols. He was one of the miracles of faith and truthfulness, one of Islam's great miracles. For out of every ten Muslims, from the beginning of Islam until today and until Allah wills, we will meet seven, at least, who know Bilaal. That is, there are hundreds of millions of people throughout the centuries and generations who know Bilaal, remember his name, and know his role just as they know the two greatest Caliphs in Islam, Abu Bakr and 'Umar!

Even if you ask a child who is still in his first years of primary school in India, Egypt, Pakistan, Malaysia, or China, in the two Americas, Europe, or Russia, in Iraq, Syria, Turkey, Iran, or Sudan, in Tunis, Algeria, or Morocco, in the depth of Africa and in the mountains of Asia, in every place on the earth where Muslims reside, you can ask any Muslim child, "Who is Bilaal, child?" He will answer you, "He was the muezzin of the Messenger (PBUH) and he was the slave whose master used to torture him with hot burning stones to make him apostatize. But instead he said, 'One, One.' "

Whenever you consider this enduring fame that Islam bestowed upon Bilaal, you should know that before Islam this Bilaal was no more than a slave who tended herds of camels for his master for a handful of dates. Had it not been for Islam, it would have been his fate to remain a slave, wandering among the crowd until death brought an end to his life and caused him to perish in the profoundest depths of forgetfulness.

However, his faith proved to be true, and the magnificence of the religion which he believed in gave him, during his lifetime and in history, an elevated place among the great and holy men of Islam. Indeed, many human beings of distinction, prestige, or wealth have not obtained even one-tenth of the immortality which Bilaal, the Abyssinian slave, gained. Indeed, many historical figures were not conferred even a portion of the fame which has been bestowed upon Bilaal.

Indeed, the black color of his complexion, his modest lineage, and his contemptible position among people as a slave did not deprive him, when he chose to embrace Islam, of occupying the high place which his truthfulness, certainty, purity, and self-sacrifice qualified him for. For him, all this would not have been on the scale of estimation and honor except as an astonishing occurrence when greatness is found where it could not possibly be.

People thought that a slave like Bilaal-who descended from

strange roots, who had neither kinfolk nor power, who did not possess any control over his life but was himself a possession of his master who had bought him with his money, who came and went amid the sheep, camels, and other livestock of his master — they thought that such a human creature would neither have power over anything, nor become anything. But he went beyond all expectations and possessed great faith that no one like him could possess! He was the first muezzin of the Messenger and of Isl'am, a position which was aspired to by all the masters and nobles of the Quraish who embraced Islam and followed the Messenger. Yes, Bilaal lbn Rabaah.

Oh what valor and greatness are expressed by these three words — Bilaal lbn Rabaah!

He was an Abyssinian from the black race. His destiny made him a slave of some people of the tribe of Jumah in Makkah, where his mother was one of their slave girls. He led the life of a slave whose bleak days were alike and who had no right over his day and no hope for his tomorrow.

The news of Muhammad's (PBUH) call began and reached his ears when people in Makkah began to talk about it and when he began listening to the discussions of his master and his guests, especially Umayah lbn Khalaf, one of the elders of the Bani Jumah, of which Bilaal was one of the slaves. How often did he hear Umayah talking to his friends for some time and to some persons of his tribe. Many times they talked about the Messenger with words that were overflowing with anxiety, rage, and malice!

Bilaal, on the other hand, was receiving between those words of insane fury and rage the attributes of this new religion. He began to feel that they were new qualities for the environment, which he lived in. He was also able to receive during their threatening, thunderous talks their acknowledgement of Muhammad's nobility, truthfulness, and loyalty. Yes indeed, he heard them wondering and amazed at what Muhammad came with. They said to one another, "Muhammad was never a liar, magician, or mad, but we have to describe him this way until we turn away from him those who rush to his religion."

He heard them talking about his honesty and loyalty, about his manliness and nobility, and about his purity and composure of his intelligence. He heard them whispering about the reasons, which caused them to challenge and antagonize him: first, their allegiance to the religion of their fathers; second, their fear over the glory of the Quraish which was bestowed upon them because of their religious status as a center of idol worship and resort in the whole of the Arabian Peninsula; third, the envy of the tribe of Bani Haashim that anyone from them should claim to be a prophet or messenger.

One day Bilaal Ibn Rabaah recognized the light of Allah and heard His resonance in the depths of his good soul. So he went to the Messenger of Allah and converted to Islam. It did not take long before the news of his embracing Islam was spread. It was a shock to the chiefs of the Bani Jumah, who were very proud and conceited. The devils of the earth sat couched over the breast of Umayah Ibn Khalaf, who considered the acceptance of Islam by one of their slaves a blow that overwhelmed them with shame and disgrace.

Their Abyssinian slave converted to Islam and followed Muhammad. Umayah said to himself, "It does not matter. Indeed the sun this day shall not set but with the Islam of this stray slave." However, the sun never did set with the Islam of Bilaal, but it set one day with all the idols of the Quraish and the patrons of paganism among them.

As for Bilaal, he adopted an attitude that would honor not only Islam, even though Islam was more worthy of it, but also all humanity. He resisted the harshest kind of torture like all pious great men. Allah made him an example of the fact that blackness of skin and bondage would not decry the greatness of the soul if it found its faith, adhered to its Creator, and clung to its right.

Bilaal gave a profound lesson to those of his age and every age, for those of his religion and every religion, a lesson which embraced the idea that freedom and supremacy of conscience could not be bartered either for gold or punishment, even if it filled the earth. He was stripped naked and laid on hot coals to make him renounce his religion, but he refused.

The Messenger (PBUH) and Islam made this weak Abyssinian slave, a teacher to all humanity in the art of respecting conscience and defending its freedom and supremacy. They used to take him out in the midday heat when the desert turned to a fatal hell. Then they would throw him naked on its scorching rocks and bring a burning hot rock, which took several men to lift from its place, and throw it onto his body and chest. This savage torture was repeated every day until the hearts of some of his executioners took pity on him. Finally, they agreed to set him free on condition that he would speak well of their gods, even with only one word that would allow them to keep their pride so that the Quraish would not say they had been defeated and humiliated by the resistance of their persevering slave.

But even this one word, which he could eject from outside his heart and with it buy his life and soul without losing his faith or abandoning his conviction, Bilaal refused to say. Yes, he refused to say it and began to repeat his lasting chant instead: "One! One!"

His torturers shouted at him, imploring him, " Mention the name of Al-Laat and Al-'Uzzaa." But he answered, "One! One!" They said to him, "Say as we say." But he answered them with remarkable mockery and caustic irony, "Indeed my tongue is not good at that."

So Bilaal remained in the melting heat and under the weight of the heavy rock, and by sunset they raised him up and put a rope around his neck. Then they ordered their boys to take him around the mountains and streets of Makkah. And Bilaal's tongue did not mention anything other than his holy chant, "One! One!"

When the night overtook them, they began bargaining with him, 'Tomorrow, speak well of our gods, say, 'My lord is Al-Laat and Al'Uzzaa,' and we'll leave you alone. We are tired of torturing you as if we are the tortured ones." But he shook his head and said, "One! One!" So, Umayah Ibn Khalaf kicked him and exploded with exasperating fury, and shouted, "What bad luck has thrown you upon us, O slave of evil? By Al-Laat and Al-'Uzzaa, I'll make you an example for slaves and masters." But Bilaal answered with the holy greatness and certainty of a believer, "One! One!"

And he who was assigned to play the role of a sympathizer, returned to talking and bargaining. He said, "Take it easy, Umayah. By Al-Laat, he will not be tortured again. Indeed Bilaal is one of us, his mother is our slave girl. He will not be pleased to talk about and ridicule us because of his Islam." But Bilaal gazed at their lying cunning faces and his mouth slackened like the light of dawn. He said with calmness that shook them violently, "One! One!"

It was the next day and midday approached. Bilaal was taken to the sun-baked ground. He was patient, brave, firm, and expecting the reward in the Hereafter.

Abu Bakr As-Siddiiq went to them while they were torturing him and shouted at them, "Are you killing a man because he says, 'Allah is my Lord?" Then he shouted at Umayah lbn Khalaf, "Take more than his price and set him free." It was as if Umayah were drowning and had caught a lifeboat. It was to his liking and he was very much pleased when he heard Abu Bakr offering the price of his freedom, since they had despaired of subjugating Bilaal. And as they were merchants, they realized that selling him was more profitable to them than his death.

They sold him to Abu-Bakr, and then he emancipated him immediately, and Bilaal took his place among free men. When As Siddiiq put his arm round Bilaal, rushing with him to freedom, Umayah said to him, "Take him, for by Al-Laat and Al-'Uzzaa, if you had refused to buy him except for one ounce of gold, I would have sold him to you." Abu Bakr realized the bitterness of despair and disappointment hidden in these words. It was appropriate not to answer, but because they violated the dignity of this man who had become his brother and his equal, he answered Umayah saying, "By Allah, if you had refused to sell him except for a hundred ounces, I would have paid it." He departed with his companion to the Messenger of Allah, giving him news of his liberation, and there was a great celebration.

After the Hijrah of the Messenger (PBUH) and the Muslims to Al-Madiinah and their settling there, the Messenger instituted the Adhaan. So who would become the muezzin five times a day? Who would call across distant lands, "Allah is the Greatest" and "There is no god but Allah"?

It was Bilaal, who had shouted thirteen years before while the torture was destroying him, "Allah is One! One!" He was chosen by the Messenger that day to be the first muezzin in Islam.

With his melodious soul-stirring voice, he filled the hearts with faith and the ears with awe when he called:

Allah is the Greatest, Allah is the Greatest.
Allah is the Greatest, Allah is the Greatest.
I bear witness that there is no god but Allah.
I bear witness that there is no god but Allah.
I bear witness that Muhammad is the Messenger of Allah.
I bear witness that Muhammad is the Messenger of Allah.
Come to Prayer, Come to Prayer.
Come to Success, Come to Success.
Allah is the Greatest, Allah is the Greatest.
There is no god but Allah.

Fighting broke out between the Muslims and the army of the Quraish who came to invade Al-Madiinah. The war raged fiercely and terribly while Bilaal was there attacking and moving about in the first battle. Islam was plunged into the Battle of Badr, whose motto the Messenger (PBUH) ordered to be, "One! One!"

In this battle, the Quraish sacrificed their youth and all their noblemen to their destruction. Umayah Ibn Khalaf, who had been Bilaal's master and who used to torture him with deadly brutality, was about to retreat from fighting. But his friend 'Uqbah Ibn Abu Mu'iit went to him when he heard the news of his withdrawal, carrying a censer in his right hand. When he arrived he was sitting among his people. He threw the censer between his hands and said to him, "O'Abu 'Aliy, use this. You are one of the women." But Umayah shouted at him saying, "May Allah make you and what you came with ugly!" And he did not find a way out, so he went out to fight.

What other secrets does destiny conceal and unfold? 'Uqbah

Ibn Abu Mu'iit had been the greatest supporter of Umayah in the torture of Bilaal and other weak Muslims. And on that day, he himself was the one who urged him to go to the Battle of Badr where he would die, just as it would be the place where Uqbah would die! Umayah had been one of the shirkers from war. Had it not been for what Uqbah did to him, he would not have gone out fighting.

But Allah executes His command. So let Umayah go out, because there was an old account between him and one of the slaves of Allah. It was time to settle it. The Judge never dies. As you owe, you shall be owed to.

Indeed destiny would be very much pleased to mock the tyrants. Uqbah, whose provocations Umayah used to listen to and follow his desire to torture the innocent believers, was the same person who would lead Umayah to his death. By the hand of whom? By the hand of Bilaal himself and Bilaal alone! The same hands that Umayah used to chain and whose owner he beat and tortured. Those very hands were on that day, in the Battle of Badr, on a rendezvous that destiny had set the best time for, with the torture of the Quraish who had humiliated the believers unjustly and aggressively. That is what really happened.

When the fighting began between the two sides, and the side of the Muslims shouted the motto, "One! One!" the heart of Umayah was startled, and a warning came to him. The word, which his slave used to repeat yesterday under torture and horror, became today the motto of a whole religion and of a whole new nation.

"One! One!" Is it so? With this quickness? And with this rapid growth?

The swords dashed in the battle and the fighting became severe.

As the battle neared its end, Umayah lbn Khalaf noticed 'Abd Ar Rahman lbn 'Awf, the Companion of the Messenger of Allah. He sought refuge with him and asked to be his captive, hoping to save his life. "Abd Ar-Rahman accepted his supplication and granted him refuge. Then he took him and walked with him amidst the battle to the place where captives were held.

On the way Bilaal noticed him and shouted, "The head of *kufr* (disbelief), Umayah lbn Khalaf! May I not be saved if he is saved!" He lifted up his sword to cut off the head, which was all the time full or pride and arrogance. But "Abd Ar-Rahman lbn "Awf shouted at him, "O'Bilaal, he is my captive!" A captive while the war was still raging? A captive while his sword was still dripping blood because of what he had been doing just moments before to the bodies of the Muslims? No! In Bilaal's opinion, this was an irony and abuse of the mind, and Umayah had scoffed and abused the mind enough. He scoffed until there was no irony remaining for such a day, such a dilemma, and such a fate!

Bilaal realized that he would not be able alone to storm the sanctuary of his brother in faith, 'Abd Ar-Rahman lbn 'Awf. So he shouted at the top of his voice to the Muslims, "O' helpers of Allah! The head of Kufr, Umayah lbn Khalaf! May I not be saved if he is saved!" A band of Muslims approached with swords dripping blood. They surrounded Umayah and his son, who was fighting with the Quraish. 'Abd Ar-Rahman lbn 'Awf could not do anything. He could not even protect his armor, which the crowd removed. Bilaal gazed long at the body of Umayah, who fell beneath the smashing swords. Then he hastened away from him shouting, "One! One!"

I do not think it is our right to examine the virtue of leniency in Bilaal on this occasion. If the meeting between Bilaal and

Umayah had taken place in other circumstances, we would have been allowed to ask Bilaal for leniency, and a man like him in faith and piety would not have withheld it. But the meeting, which took place between them was in a war, where each party came to destroy its enemy.

The swords were blazing, the killed were falling. Then Bilaal saw Umayah, who had not left even a small place on his body free of the traces of his torture. Where and how did he see him? He saw him in the arena of battle and fighting, mowing down with his sword all of the heads of Muslims he could. If he had reached the head of Bilaal then, he would have cut it off. In such circumstances as the two men met, it is not fair to ask Bilaal: Why did you not forgive him gently?

The days went by and Makkah was conquered. The Messenger (PBUH) entered it, thankful and saying, "Allah is the Greatest," at the head of 10,000 Muslims. He headed for the Ka'bah immediately, this holy place which the Quraish had crowded with idols amounting to the number of days of the year. "The truth has come and falsehood has vanished."

Ever since that day, there has been no 'Uzzaa, no Laat and no Hubal. Man will not bow to a rock or idol after today. People will worship no one with all his conscience but Allah, Who has no likeness, the One, Most Great, Most High. The Messenger entered the Ka'bah accompanied by Bilaal. He had hardly entered it when he faced a carved idol representing Ibraahiim (Abraham) (PBUH) prophesying with sticks.

The Messenger (PBUH) was angry and said, "May Allah kill them. Our ancestor never did prophesy with sticks, Ibraahiim was not a Jew or Christian, but he was a true Muslim and was never a polytheist." Then he ordered Bilaal to ascend to the top of the mosque and call to Prayer, and Bilaal called the Adhaan. How magnificent was the time, place, and occasion!

Life came to a standstill in Makkah, and thousands of Muslims stood like motionless air, repeating in submissiveness and whispering the words of the Adhaan after Bilaal while the polytheists were in their homes hardly believing what was happening.

Is this Muhammad (PBUH) and his poor followers, who were expelled yesterday from their homes? Is this really he, with 10,000 of his believers? Is this really he, whom we chased away, fought and killed his most beloved kin and relations? Is this really he, who was speaking to us a few minutes ago while our necks were at his mercy, saying, "Go, you are free!"?

But three nobles of the Quraish were sitting in the open space in front of the Ka'bah, as if they were touched by the scene of Bilaal treading their idols with his feet and sending above its heaped wreckage his voice with the Adhaan, spreading to all the horizons of Makkah, like a passing spring. These three were Abu Sufyaan lbn Harb, who had embraced Islam only hours ago, and 'Attaab lbn Usaid and Al-Haarith lbn Hishaam, who had not yet embraced Islam.

'Attaab, with his eyes on Bilaal crying out the Adhaan, said, "Allah has honored Usaid in that he did not hear this, or else he would have heard what would infuriate him." Al-Haarith said, "By Allah, if I were sure that Muhammad (PBUH) is telling the truth, I would follow him" Abu Sufyaan, the old fox, commented on their speech saying, "I am not saying a word, for if I do, these pebbles will inform about me."

When the Prophet left the Ka'bah he saw them, read their faces instantly, and said with his eyes shining with the light of Allah and the joy of victory, "I know what you've said," and he told them what they had said.

Al-Haarith and'Attaab shouted, "We bear witness that you are the Messenger of Allah. By Allah, no one heard us, so we can't say somebody informed you!"

And they welcomed Bilaal with new hearts, which enclosed the echo of the words, which they had heard in the Messenger's speech just after he entered Makkah. "O' people of the Quraish, Allah has removed from you the arrogance of pre-Islamic paganism, and its boasting about forefathers. People are descended from Adam, and Adam was from dust."

Bilaal lived with the Messenger of Allah (PBUH), witnessing all the battles with him, calling to Prayer and observing the rites of this great religion that took him out of darkness to light and from servitude to freedom. The stature of Islam along with the stature of Muslims was elevated. Every day, Bilaal was getting closer to the heart of the Messenger of Allah, who used to describe him as "one of the inhabitants of Paradise."

But Bilaal remained just as he was, noble and humble, always considering himself "the Abyssinian who only yesterday was a slave." One day he was proposing to two girls for himself and his brother, so he said to their father, " I am Bilaal and this is my brother, two slaves from Abyssinia. We were astray and Allah guided us. We were two slaves and Allah emancipated us. If you agree on us marrying your daughters, all praise is to Allah; if you refuse, then Allah is the Greatest."

The Messenger passed away to Allah, well pleased and well pleasing, and Abu Bakr As-Siddiiq took the command of the

Muslims after him. Bilaal went to the caliph (successor) of the Messenger of Allah and said to him, "O' Caliph of the Messenger of Allah, I heard the Messenger of Allah (PBUH) say, "The best deed of a believer is jihaad in the cause of Allah.""

Abu Bakr said to him, "So what do you want, Bilaal?" He said, I want to defend in the cause of Allah until I die." Abu Bakr said, "And who will call the Adhaan for us?" Bilaal said, with his eyes overflowing with tears, "I will not call the Adhaan for anyone after the Messenger of Allah." Abu Bakr said, "Stay and call to Prayer for us, Bilaal." Bilaal said, "If you emancipated me to be for you, I will do what you want, but if you emancipated me for Allah, leave me to Whom I was emancipated for." Abu Bakr said, "I emancipated you for Allah, Bilaal."

The narrators differ. Some of them believe that he traveled and remained fighting and defending. Some others narrate that he accepted Abu Bakr's request to stay with him in Madiinah. When Abu Bakr died and 'Umar succeeded him, Bilaal asked his permission and went to Syria.

Anyhow, Bilaal vowed the remaining part of his life to fight in the cause of Islam, determined to meet Allah and His Messenger having done the best deed they love.

His melodious, welcoming, awe-inspiring voice did not call the Adhaan any more, because whenever he uttered in his Adhaan, "I bear witness that Muhammad (PBUH) is the Messenger of Allah," memories would stir him, and his voice would vanish under his sadness while the tears cried out the words.

His last Adhaan was during the days 'Umar, the Commander of

the Faithful, when he visited Syria. The Muslims entreated him to persuade Bilaal to call one Adhaan for them. The Commander of the Faithful called Bilaal when it was time for Prayer and pleaded with him to make the Adhaan. Bilaal ascended and did so. The Companions of the Messenger of Allah (PBUH) who were with the Commander of the Faithful while Bilaal was calling the Adhaan, wept as they never did before, and "Umar the most strongly.

Bilaal died in Syria, fighting in the cause of Allah just as he had wanted. Beneath the dust of Damascus, today there lies the body of one of the greatest men of humankind in standing up for the creed of Islam with conviction.

(5)
'ABD ALLAH IBN 'UMAR
The Persistent and Repentant to Allah

When he was at the peak of his long life he said, "I swore the oath of allegiance to the Prophet (PBUH). I never broke my oath, nor have I turned to something else to this day. I never swore allegiance to those in civil strife, nor did I awake a sleeping Muslim."

These words are a summary of the life of that virtuous man who lived past the age of 80. His relationship with Islam and the Prophet began when he was only 13 years old, when he accompanied his father to the battle of Badr, hoping to have a place among the Mujaahiduun, but he was sent back by the Prophet due to his young age. Since that day-and even before that when he accompanied his father on his Hijrah to Al-Madiinah-that young boy who possessed premature manly merits began his relation with the Prophet of Islam (PBUH).

From that day till the day he passed away at the age of 85, we will always find him persistent, repentant, never deviating from his path, not even by a hairbreadth, never breaking the oath of allegiance which he had sworn, nor breaking a pledge he had made. The merits of 'Abd Allah Ibn 'Umar, which dazzle people's vision, are abundant. Among these are his knowledge, modesty, the straightness of his conscience and path, his generosity, piety, persistence in worship, and his sincere adherence to the Prophet's model. By means of all these merits and qualities did Ibn "Umar shape his unique personality, his sincere and truthful life.

He learned a lot of good manners from his father, "Umar Ibn

Al-Khattaab, and together with him, they learned from the Prophet (PBUH) all the good manners and all that can be described as noble virtues.

Like his father, his belief in Allah and His Prophet was perfect; therefore, the way he pursued the Prophet's steps was admirable. He was always looking at what the Prophet was doing in every matter and then humbly imitating his deeds to the finest detail. For example, wherever the Prophet prayed, there also would lbn 'Umar pray, and on the same spot. If the Prophet invoked Allah while standing, then lbn 'Umar would invoke Allah while standing. If the Prophet invoked Allah while sitting, so also would lbn 'Umar invoke Allah while sitting. On the same particular route where the Prophet once dismounted from his camel and prayed two rak'ahs, so would lbn "Umar do the same while traveling to the same place.

Moreover, he remembered that the Prophet's camel turned twice at a certain spot in Makkah before the Prophet dismounted and before his two rak'ahs of prayer. The camel may have done that spontaneously to prepare itself a suitable halting place, but lbn 'Umar would reach that spot, turn his camel in a circle, then allow it to kneel down. After that he would pray two rak'ahs in exactly the same manner he had seen the Prophet (PBUH) do. Such exaggerated imitation once provoked the Mother of the Believers 'Aa'ishah (May Allah be pleased with her) to say, "No one followed the Prophet's steps in his coming and going as lbn 'Umar did."

He spent his long, blessed life and his firm loyalty adhering to the Prophet's Sunnah to the extent that a time came when the virtuous Muslims were asking Allah, "O' Allah, save lbn 'Umar as long as I live so that I can follow him. I don't know anyone still adhering to the early traditions except him."

Similar to that strong and firm adherence to each of the Prophet's steps and practice (Sunnah) was Ibn 'Umar's respect for the Prophetic traditions (Hadith). He never related a hadith unless he remembered it to the letter. His contemporaries said, "None of the Companions of the Prophet was more cautious not to add or subtract something from a hadith than "Abd Allah Ibn 'Umar."

In the same way he was very cautious when giving a *fatwah* (Legal formal opinion in Islamic Law). One day somebody came to ask him a *fatwah.* When he put forward his question, Ibn 'Umar answered, "I have no knowledge concerning what you are asking about." The man went his way. He had hardly left the place when Ibn "Umar rubbed his hands happily saying to himself, "Ibn "Umar has been asked about what he doesn't know, so he said, ' I don't know!' "

He was very much afraid to perform *ijtihaad* (Independent judgement in a legal question) in his *fatwah,* although he was living according to the instructions of a great religion, a religion which grants a reward to the one who makes a mistake and two rewards to the one who comes out with a correct righteous *fatwah.* However, Ibn 'Umar's piety deprived him of the courage to make any *fatwahs.*

In the same way he refrained from the post of judge. The position of a judge was one of the highest positions of state and society, guaranteeing the one engaged in its wealth, prestige, and glory. But why should the pious Ibn 'Umar need money, prestige, and glory? The Caliph 'Uthmaan once sent for him and asked him to hold the position of Judge but he apologized. 'Uthmaan asked him, "Do you disobey me?" Ibn "Umar answered, "No, but it came to my knowledge that judges are of three kinds: one who judges ignorantly: he is in hell; one who judges according to his desire: he is in hell; one who involves himself in making *ijtihaad* and is unerring in his judgment. That one will turn empty-handed, no sin committed and no reward to be granted. I ask you by Allah to exempt me." 'Uthmaan exempted him after he pledged him never to tell anyone about that, for 'Uthmaan knew Ibn 'Umar's place in people's hearts and he was afraid that if the pious and virtuous knew his refraining from holding the position of judge, they would follow him and do the same, and then the Caliph would not find a pious person to be judge.

It may seem as if Ibn 'Umar's stance was a passive one. However, it was not so. Ibn 'Umar did not abstain from accepting the post when there was no one more suitable to hold it than himself. In fact a lot of the Prophet's pious and virtuous Companions were actually occupied with *fatwah* and judgment.

His restraint and abstention would not paralyze the function of jurisdiction, nor would it cause it to be held by unqualified ones, so Ibn 'Umar preferred to devote his time to purifying his soul with more worship and more obedience. Furthermore, in that stage of Islamic history, life became more comfortable and luxurious, money more abundant, positions and authoritative ranks more available. The temptation of money and authoritative ranks began to enter the hearts of the pious and faithful, which made some of the Prophet's Companions- Ibn 'Umar among them- to lift the banner of resistance to that temptation by means of making themselves models and examples of worship, piety, and abstention, refraining from high ranks in order to defeat their temptation.

Ibn 'Umar made himself a "friend of the night", praying at night, crying, and asking forgiveness during its latter hours before daybreak. He had once, during his youth, seen a dream.

The Prophet interpreted it in a way, which made the night prayer 'Abd Allah's utmost hope and a means of his delight and joy.

Let us listen to him, while he narrates the story of his dream: During the Prophetic era, I saw a dream in which I was riding a piece of brocade which let me fly to any place in Paradise I wished. Then I saw two approaching me, intending to take me to hell, but an angel met them saying, "Don't be afraid," so they left me. My sister Hafsah narrated the dream to the Prophet (PBUH), who said, "What an excellent man 'Abd Allah is. If he is praying at night, then let him pray more."

From that day until he met with Allah, he never stopped performing his night prayer, neither while staying in one place nor while traveling. He was frequently praying, reciting the Qur'aan, and praising Allah. Like his father, his tears rolled down abundantly whenever he heard a warning verse in the Qur'aan.

'Ubaid Ibn 'Umar said: I was once reading to 'Abd Allah Ibn 'Umar this verse: <*How will it be for them when We bring from every nation a witness, and bring you to witness over them all? On that day those who disbelieved and disobeyed the Messenger will wish the earth to be split open and swallow them, but they will never conceal from GOD any of their saying* > *(4:41-42)* Ibn'Umar began to cry till his beard was wet from his tears. One day he was sitting among his brothers reading < *Woe to those who give insufficient measure, who when others measure for them they make full measure, but when they measure out, or weigh out for others, they give less than due. Do such not think that they shall be raised up on a Mighty Day? The Day when all mankind shall stand before the Lord of the Worlds* > *(83:1-6)*. Then he repeated again and again < *The Day when all mankind shall stand before the Lord of the Worlds* > while his tears were rolling down like heavy rain falls from the sky until he fell down because of his tremendous sorrow and crying.

His generosity, asceticism and piety all worked together in complete harmony to shape the most magnificent merits of that great man. He gave out abundantly because he was generous. He granted the fine halaal things because he was pious, never caring if his generosity left him poor because he was ascetic.

lbn 'Umar (May Allah be pleased with him) was one of those who had high incomes. He was a successful, honest merchant for a greater part of his life, and his income from the treasury (Bait Al-Maal) was abundant. However, he never saved that money for himself, but always spent it copiously on the poor, the needy, and beggars.

Ayub lbn Waa'il Ar-Rassiby tells us about one of his generous acts: One day lbn 'Umar was granted 4,000 dirhams and a piece of velvet. The next day Ayub lbn Waa'il saw him in the market buying his camel some fodder on credit, lbn Waa'il went to his house asking his close relatives, "Wasn't Abu 'Abd Ar-Rahman (i.e. 'Abd Allah lbn 'Umar) granted 4,000 dirhams and a piece of velvet yesterday?" They said, "Yes." He then told them that he had seen him in the market buying fodder for his camel and could not find money for it. They told him, "He didn't go to sleep before distributing all of it, then he carried the velvet on his back and went out. When he returned it wasn't with him. We asked him about it, and he said, 1 gave it to a poor person."

lbn Waa'il went out shaking his head until he entered the market. There he climbed to a higher ground and shouted to the people, "O'merchants, what do you do with your life? Here is lbn'Umar who's been granted 4,000 dirhams, so he distributes them, then the next morning he buys fodder for his camel on credit!"

The one to whom Muhammad (PBUH) was tutor and 'Umar his father must be a great man, deserving all that is great.

Ibn "Umar's generosity, asceticism, and piety, these three qualities demonstrate how sincere his imitation of the Prophetic model was and how sincere his worship.

He imitated the Prophet (PBUH) to the extent that he stood with his camel, where the Prophet had once stood saying, "A camel foot may stand over a camel foot." His respect, good behavior, and admiration towards his father reached also to a far extent. 'Umar's personality forced his foes, his relatives, and, above all, his sons to pay him respect. I say, the one who belongs to that Prophet and that kind of father should never be a slave of money. Large amounts of money came to him but soon passed, just crossing his house at that moment.

His generosity was never a means of arrogance. He always dedicated himself to the poor and needy, rarely eating his meal alone: orphans and poor people were always present. He often blamed some of his sons when they invited the rich, and not the poor ones, to their banquets, thereupon saying, "You leave the hungry behind and invite the sated ones." The poor knew his tenderness, felt his kindness and sympathy, so they sat down across his path for him to take them to his house. When he saw them he was like a sweet scented flower surrounded by a drove of bees to suck its nectar.

Money in his hands was a slave, not a master, a means for necessities and not luxury. Money was not his alone. The poor had a right to it, a mutually corresponding right, with no privilege kept to himself. His self-denial helped him to reach such great generosity that he never stored, endeavored, or had a vivid interest toward the worldly life. On the contrary, he never wished to possess more than a gown to cover his body and just enough food to keep him alive.

Once a friend coming from Khurasan presented him with a fine, delicate handsome, embellished and decorated gown, saying to him, "I've brought you this gown from Khurasan. I would be pleased to see you take off this rough gown and wear this nice one." lbn 'Umar said, "Show it to me then. " He touched it asking, "Is it silk?" His friend said, "No, it's cotton." 'Abd Allah looked at it for a while then pushed it away with his right hand saying, "No, I'm afraid to tempt myself. I'm afraid it would turn me into an arrogant, proud man. Allah dislikes the arrogant, proud ones."

On another day, a friend presented him with a container filled with something, lbn 'Umar asked him, "What's that?" He said, "Excellent medicine, which I brought you from Iraq!" lbn 'Umar said, 'What does it cure?" He said, "It digests food." lbn 'Umar smiled and said to his friend, "Digests food? I haven't satisfied my appetite for 40 years."

He who has not satisfied his appetite for 40 years has not curbed his appetite due to need or poverty, but rather due to self-denial and piety, and a trial to imitate the Prophet and his father.

He was afraid to hear on the Day of Judgment: *<You have wasted all your good deeds for the enjoyment in the life of this world > (46:20).* He realized that he was in this life just as a visitor or a passer-by. He described himself saying, "I haven't put a stone upon another (i.e. I haven't built anything) nor planted a palm tree since the Prophet's death."

Maimuun lbn Muhraan once said, "I entered lbn 'Umar's house and tried to evaluate all that was inside such as the bed, the blanket, the mat and so on. Indeed, everything I didn't find it worth even 100 dirhams."

That was not due to selfishness; he was very generous. But it was due to his asceticism, his disdain of luxury, and his adherence to his attitude of sincerity and piety.

lbn 'Umar lived long enough to witness the Umayyid period, when money became abundant, and land and estates spread, and a luxurious life was to be found in most dwellings, let alone most castles.

Despite all that, he stayed like a firm-rooted mountain, persistent and great, not slipping away from his paths and not abandoning his piety and asceticism. If life with its pleasure and prosperity-which he always escaped from-was mentioned, he said, "I've agreed with my companions upon a matter. I'm afraid if I change my stance I won't meet them again." Then he let the others know that he did not turn his back to the worldly life owing to inability, so he lifted his hands to the sky saying, "O'Allah, You know that if it weren't for fear of You, we would have emulated our clan in the Quraish in this life."

Indeed, if it were not for his God-fearing self, he would have rivaled people in this life, and he would have been triumphant. He did not have to rival people. Life was striving towards him and chasing him with its tempting pleasure.

Is there any position more tempting than the caliph's? It was offered to lbn 'Umar several times, but he refused. He was threatened with death if he refused, but he continued his refusal and his shunning.

Al Hassan (May Allah be pleased with him) reported: When 'Uthmaan lbn 'Affaan was killed, it was said to 'Abd Allah lbn `Umar, "You are the people's master and the son of the people's master. Go out so that people swear to you the oath of allegiance." He said, "By Allah, if I could, I would never allow a drop of blood to be shed because of me." They said. You will either go out or we will kill you in your bed." He repeated his first statement. They tried to tempt him by frightening him, but all in vain!

After that, when time passed and civil strife became rampant, lbn 'Umar was always the hope of the people who urged him to accept the caliph's position. They were ready to swear to him the oath of allegiance, but he always and constantly refused.

His refusal may be seen as a reprehensible act. However, he had his logic and argument. After the murder of 'Uthmaan (May Allah be pleased with him) the situation got worse and aggravated in a dangerous and alarming way.

Although he was very humble towards the position of the caliph, he was ready to accept its responsibilities and face its dangers, but only on the condition that he be voluntarily and willingly chosen by all Muslims. However, to force one single Muslim to swear the oath of allegiance by sword was what he opposed, and so he refused the post of caliph.

At that time, however, this was impossible. Despite his merits, and the public consensus of love and respect for him, the expansion into the different regions, the long distances between them, and the disputes which furiously set fire between the Muslims and divided them into sects fighting each other made it impossible to reach such a consensus set by lbn 'Umar as a condition for his acceptance of the caliphate.

A man once met him and said, "No one is more evil in the whole Muslim community than you!" lbn 'Umar said, "Why? By Allah, I've never shed their blood, or divided their community, or sowed dissension." The man replied, "If you had wished it, every single one would have agreed upon you." lbn 'Umar said, "I don't like to see it (the caliphate) being offered to me while one man says no and another one says yes."

The people still loved him even after events changed and the caliphate went to Mu'aawiyah, then to his son Yaziid, then to Mu'aawiyah II, son of Yaziid, who stepped down renouncing its pleasure after a couple of days in office.Even on that day, when lbn 'Umar was an old man, he was still the people's hope and the hope of the caliphate. Thus Marwaan went to him saying, "Give me your hand to swear to you the oath of allegiance. You're the master of the Arabs, and the son of their master." lbn 'Umar asked, "What are we going to do with the people of the east?" Marwaan said, "Beat them until they swear the oath." lbn 'Umar replied, "I don't like to be 70 years old and a man gets killed because of me."

Marwawan went away singing: I can see civil strife boiling in its pots and the kingdom after Abi Laila (i.e.Mu'aawiyah lbn Yaziid) will end in the hands of the victorious.

This refusal to use force and the sword is what made lbn "Umar hold a position of neutrality and isolation during the armed civil strife between the parties of 'Aliy and Mu'aawiyah, reciting these solemn words:

To the one who says, "Come to prayer," I will respond. And to the one who says, "Come to success," I will respond. But to the one who says, "Come to kill your Muslim brother to take his money," I will say, "No."

But while remaining neutral and isolated he never turned to hypocrisy. How often did he confront Mu'aawiyah-while the latter was at the summit of his authority-with challenges which confused and hurt him till he threatened to kill him, and he was the one who said, "If there is only a tiny hair between me and the people, it won't be torn."

One day Al-Hajaaj stood preaching and said, "Ibn Az-Zubair has distorted the Book of Allah!" Hereupon Ibn 'Umar shouted in his face, "You are lying! You are lying! You are lying!" Al-Hajaaj was at a loss, struck by surprise.

Everything and everyone was terrified even by the mention of his name. He promised Ibn 'Umar the worst punishment, but Ibn 'Umar waved his hand in Al-Hajaaj's face and replied, while people were dazzled, "If you do what you just promised, there is no wonder about it, for you are a foolish imposed ruler."

However, despite his strength and bravery, he remained cautious until his last days, never playing a role in the armed civil strife and refusing to lean towards either of the parties.

Abu Al-'Aaliyah Al Barraa' related; I was once walking behind Ibn 'Umar without his realizing it. I heard him saying to himself, "They are holding their swords, raising them high, killing each other, and saying, "O' Ibn 'Umar, give us a hand!"

He was filled with sorrow and pain seeing Muslims' blood shed by their own hands. As mentioned at the very beginning, he never awoke a sleeping Muslim. If he could have stopped the fight and saved the blood he would have done that, but the events were too powerful; therefore he kept to his house.

His heart was with 'Aliy (May Allah be pleased with him, and not only his heart, but it seems his firm belief, based on a narration of what he said in his last days: "I never felt sorry about something that I missed except that I didn't fight on the side of 'Aliy against the unjust party."

However, when he refused to fight with Imam 'Aliy, on whose side truth was, it was not because he sought a safe position, but rather because he refused the whole matter of the dispute and civil strife and refrained from a fight not one, in which Muslims fight disbelievers, but one between Muslims who cut each other into pieces.

He clarified this when Naafi asked him, "O 'Abu 'Abd Rahman, you are the son of 'Umar and the Companion of the Prophet (PBUH) and you are who you are. What hinders you from that matter?" He meant fighting on `Aliy's side. He replied, "What hinders me is that Allah has forbidden us to shed the blood of a Muslim. Allah the Mighty and Powerful said: < *and continue fighting them until there is no more persecution and GOD'S religion prevails* > ***(2:193)*** and we did that. We fought the disbelievers, until Allah's religion prevailed, but now, what is it we are fighting for? I fought when the idols were all over the Sacred House, from the corner to the door, until Allah cleared the land of the Arabs from it (idolatry). Should I now fight those who say. "There is no god but Allah?" That was his logic, argument, and conviction.

Thus he did not refrain from fighting, nor abstain from taking part in battle to escape fighting, nor did he passively refuse to determine the outcome of the civil war within the Ummah of the faithful. Rather he refused to hold a sword in the face of a Muslim brother.

'Abd Allah Ibn 'Umar lived long and witnessed the days in

which life "opened its gates to the Muslims." Money became more abundant, high positions more available, while ambitions and desires spread. But his magnificent psychological capacities changed the rules of his time. He changed the era of ambition, money, and civil strife into an era of asceticism, humility, piety, and peace. He turned persistently to Allah and lived according to his worship, firm belief, and humbleness. Nothing whatsoever could affect his virtuous nature shaped and modeled by Islam during his early years.

The nature of life changed within the beginning of the Umayyid period. This change was inevitable. It was a period of expansion in every aspect of life, in the ambition of the state as well as the ambitions of individuals.

In the midst of the excitement of temptation and the agitation of an era lured by the idea of expansion with its pleasure and booty, stood Ibn'Umar with his merits, occupying himself with his excellent spiritual progress.

He gained from his great excellent life all that he desired, so that his contemporaries described him by saying, "Ibn 'Umar died while being like 'Umar in his merit."

Moreover, dazzled by the glitter of his merits, his contemporaries liked to compare him with his father 'Umar saying, "'Umar lived in a time when similar ones could be found, and Ibn 'Umar lived in a time when there was no one similar to him."

It is an exaggeration which may be forgiveable, because Ibn 'Umar deserved it. But as for 'Umar, no one can be compared to him. It is absolutely out of the question that a similar one is to be found in any period of time.

In the year A.H. 73, the sun sank and the ship of eternity hoisted its sail towards the next life carrying the body of the last representative of the first days of the Revelation in Makkah and Al-Madiinah: 'Abd Allah Ibn 'Umar Ibn Al-Khattaab.*

---

* The last Companion to pass away was Anas Ibn Maalik (May Allah be pleased with him) who died in Al-Basra in the year A.H. 91 or 93.

(6)
SA'D IBN ABI WAQQAAS
The Lion's Claws!

A continuous stream of incoming news worried the Commander of the Faithful 'Umar lbn Al-Khattaab. This news was about the deceitful attacks launched by the Persian forces against the Muslims at the Battle of AI-Jisr which cost the Muslims 4,000 lives in a single day and, moreover, about the Iraqis' renouncement of allegiance and their violation of agreed-upon convenants. Therefore, he decided to personally lead the Muslim troops in a decisive fight against Persia.

In fact, he set out accompanied by some of his companions, leaving 'Aliy lbn Abi Taalib (May Allah be pleased with him) behind to act as his deputy over Al-Madiinah.

However, he had hardly left Al-Madiinah when some of his companions found it wiser to ask him to return and appoint someone else for this task.

This view was adopted by "Abd Ar-Rahman lbn 'Awf, who saw it unwise to risk the caliph's life in such a way while Islam was going through its most decisive days.

'Umar ordered the Muslims to gather for public consultation. Congregational prayer was then announced and 'Aliy lbn Abi Taalib was sent for. He went with some Madinites to where `Umar and his companions were waiting. At last, they accepted 'Abd Ar-Rahman lbn 'Awfs opinion. The assembly decided that 'Umar was to go back to AI-Madiinah and another Muslim leader be chosen to combat the Persians.

'Umar agreed to their decision, then asked his companions, "Whom do you see fit to be sent to Iraq?" They thought silently for a while. Then 'Abd Ar-Rahman lbn 'Awf shouted, "I've found him!" 'Umar said, " Who is it?" 'Abd Ar-Rahman said, "The Lion's Claws: Sa'd lbn Maalik Az-Zuhariy."

The Muslims supported his choice. 'Umar then sent for Sa'd lbn Maalik Az-Zuhariy, also known as Sa'd lbn Abi Waqqaas, and appointed him governor of Iraq and Commander of the Army.

Who is that "Lion's Claws"? It is he who, whenever he turned to the Prophet while sitting among his Companions, was greeted cheerfully by the Prophet saying, "He's my maternal uncle."

Can anyone tell me who his uncle was? He was Sa'd lbn Abi Waqqaas. His grandfather was Uhaib lbn Manaaf, the paternal uncle of Aaminah, the mother of the Prophet (PBUH). He accepted Islam when he was 17 years old. He embraced Islam very early. When he talked about himself, he said, "I witnessed a day in which I was third in Islam," which means that he was the third to embrace Islam.

When the Prophet (PBUH) spoke about the One God and about the new religion whose teachings he was to spread all around, and before using Daar Al-Arqam as a refuge for himself and the Companions in those early days, Sa'd lbn Abi Waqqaas had already sworn the oath of allegiance to the Prophet (PBUH).

Historical and biographical sources inform us that the conversion of Abu Bakr was the reason for Sa'd's embracing Islam. He may have been one of those who announced their belief in Islam after Abu Bakr convinced them. This group included 'Uthmaan lbn 'Affaan, Az-Zubair lbn Al-`Awaam. Abd

Ar- Rahman Ibn 'Awf and Talhah Ibn 'Ubaid Allah. However, that does not omit the possibility that his conversion had taken place secretly and he had believed even earlier.

Sa'd Ibn Abi Waqqaas had many noble qualities, which he could be proud of. However, he never arrogantly mentioned any of these merits, except for two great privileges. First, he was the first to throw a spear in the cause of Allah and the first to be struck by one. Second, he was the only one for whom the Prophet (PBUH) hoped his parents might be his ransom. That happened when the Prophet (PBUH) said to him on the day of Uhud, "Throw, Sa'd. May my father and mother be your ransom." Yes, indeed, he always mentioned proudly these two noble blessings. Thanking Allah, he always said, "By Allah, I am the first Arab to throw a spear in the cause of Allah."

'Aliy Ibn Abi Taalib said, "I have never heard the Prophet (PBUH) hoping that his parents may be made someone's ransom except Sa'd. On the day of Uhud, I heard the Prophet (PBUH) say, "Throw Sa'd. May my father and mother be your ransom."

Sa"d was considered to be one of the most courageous Arab and Muslim horsemen. He possessed two weapons, his lance and his prayer. Whenever he pierced an enemy with his lance he hurt him; whenever he invoked Allah, He answered. He and the Companions always saw that this was due to the Prophet's prayer in favor of him. One day, when the Prophet saw him doing something which made him glad and delighted, he made the following plea: "O' Allah, make his spear hit unerringly and answer his prayer."

It was in this way that he became famous among his companions for his prayer, which was like a sharp sword. He knew that about himself; therefore, he never cursed a person. Sa'd would just trust Allah to do with him as He liked.

An example of that is what 'Aamir Ibn Sa'd once narrated: Sa"d once saw a man insulting 'Aliy, Talhah and Az-Zubair. He forbade him, but he didn't stop. Sa'd then said, " Then I will invoke Allah against you." The man said, "You're threatening me as if you were a Prophet."

Sa'd went away, performed his ablution and prayed two rak'ahs. Then he lifted his hands up and said, "O'Allah, if You know that that man has insulted people who have already been granted by You, that which is the best and his cursing of them has annoyed You, then make an example out of him." Only a short while had passed, when a stray camel went out of a house. Nothing could stay it till it entered a crowd as if searching for something. Then it attacked the man, and he fell between its legs. It continued to kick the man down till he died.

If this phenomenon was to prove something, then it proved primarily the purity of his soul, the honesty of his faith, and the depth of his sincerity. He always sought to support his piety by halaal food; with great insistence he always refused to take doubtful money.

Sa'd lived until he became one of the wealthiest Muslims. When he died, he left a great fortune behind. Although the abundance of money and its legitimacy are rarely to be found together, they certainly were combined in the hands of Sa'd. Thus Allah granted him a great amount of halaal money.

He (May Allah be pleased with him) was a great figure in the act of charity, as much as he was a great figure in the act of righteously choosing the sources of his money. His ability to collect purely halaal money was equal to, if not second to, his ability to donate it in the cause of Allah.

He became ill during the Farewell Pilgrimage, when he was accompanying the Prophet (PBUH), who visited him. Sa'd asked him (PBUH), "O' Messenger of Allah, I own a lot of money and there is nobody to inherit from me except one daughter. May I contribute two thirds of my money as alms?" The Prophet (PBUH) said, "No." Then he said, "Then half of it?" The Prophet (PBUH) said, " No." Then he said, "Then a third?" The Prophet (PBUH) said, " Yes, and the third is too much. To leave your heirs wealthy is better than to leave them having to be dependent on someone. If you spend any money in the cause of Allah you'll be rewarded for it, even the bite you put in your wife's mouth."

Sa'd did not remain the father of one daughter because he was later on blessed with other children.

Sa'd used to cry a lot out of piety. Whenever he listened to the Prophet (PBUH) preaching or advising, his tears rolled down abundantly, so that his tears nearly filled his lap.

He was blessed with success and accomplishment. Once the Prophet (PBUH) was sitting with the Companions when his eyes gazed on the horizon while listening to what was being revealed secretly and whisperingly. Then he looked at his Companions' faces and said, "A man who belongs to Paradise will soon appear." The Companions turned in all directions trying to learn, who, this successful person may be. After a while, Sa'd arrived.

Later on,'Abd-Allah lbn "Amr lbn Al-'Aas asked him persistently to tell him the worship or deed which made him eligible for such a reward. Sa'd told him, "Nothing more than what we all do or worship, except that I don't carry any spite or hatred towards any Muslim."

This is the "Lion's Claws" as 'Abd Ar-Rahman Ibn `Awf had described him. This is the man whom 'Umar chose for the great day of the Battle of Al-Qaadisiyah.

The Commander of the Faithful had insight into all his glittering merits when he chose him for the most difficult task confronting Islam and the Muslims:

-His prayers were heard and answered; if he asked Allah for victory, he would be granted it.

-His food was pure, his tongue was pure, his conscience was pure.

-He was a man who belonged to Paradise, as the Messenger (PBUH) prophesied.

-He was the horseman on the Day of Badr, the horseman on the Day of Uhud and in every battle he experienced with the Prophet (PBUH).

And another thing, which 'Umar would not forget nor underestimate the value and importance among the characteristics which should be present in anyone facing major tasks, was the strength and firmness of his faith.

'Umar did not forget what happened between Sa`d and his mother when he converted to Islam and followed the Prophet (PBUH). At that time, all attempts to hinder and obstruct him from the cause of Allah had failed. His mother used a device, which none doubted would conquer Sa'd's soul and drive him back to his people's idols. She announced her abstention from food and drink until Sa'd returned to his ancestors' and kin's religion. She actually carried on her hunger strike with death defying determination and had almost approached death.

Despite all that, Sa'd did not care. He would not sell his faith and religion for anything, even if it were his mother's life. Hoping that his heart would yield upon seeing her, some relatives took Sa'd to his mother, who was almost dying.

Sa'd went to her. The scene was so impressive, even mountain rocks would yield and melt. However, his belief in Allah and His Messenger proved to be stronger than rocks and iron. He came with his face nearer and shouted so that she could hear him. "You know, by Allah, mother, if you had 100 souls coming out one after the other I wouldn't abandon my faith in return for anything. Then eat if you like or don't eat!"

His mother changed her mind. A divine revelation greeted Sa'd's position and supported it. < *But if they (both) strive with you to make you join in worship with Me others that of which you have no knowledge, then obey them not...*> *(31 : 15).*

Is he not, indeed, the Lion in his claws? Therefore the Commander of the Faithful should hand him the standard of Al-Qaadisiyah and throw him against the Persians, who recruited more than 100,000 trained warriors equipped with the most dangerous weapons the earth had ever witnessed, led on that day by the most intelligent and cunning warlords.

Indeed, all those horrible legions, will Sa'd meet with his mere 30,000 warriors, equipped only with spears, nothing more. However, their hearts were filled with the will of the new faith with all it represents: belief, vigor, and a rare, dazzling, longing aspiration for death and martyrdom.

The two armies met in combat. No, they did not meet yet.

Sa'd is still there waiting for the advice and instructions of the

Commander of the Faithful. Finally 'Umar's message arrives, ordering him to move towards Al-Qaadisiyah, the gate to Persia.

'Umar's words represented light and guidance: O'Sa'd Ibn Wahiib, do not be deluded if it is said. You are the Prophet's uncle and his Companion. Know that there is no relationship between Allah and anyone except through obedience to Him. All people, the noble ones as well as the lowly, all are equal in front of Allah. Allah is their God and they are His servants. The relationship between them is one of rivalry for preference by means of their wellbeing, whereas they can only get what is in Allah's hands by means of obedience to Him. Remember the Prophet's (PBUH) positions, which he stuck to from the time he was sent to us until he left our world. Hold to them; it is an order.

Then he said to him. Send me information about all your circumstances. Where have you reached and how? What is your enemy's position in respect to yours? Let your messages make me as if I am actually seeing you.

Sa'd wrote to the Commander of the Faithful describing everything. He almost showed him each soldier's position and state. Sa'd reached Al-Qaadissiyah. The Persians gathered their army as they never had before and appointed as their leader one of the most famous and dangerous commanders, Rustum.

Sa'd writes to 'Umar the Commander of the Faithful, who replies: Don't be upset by what you hear from them, nor what they show you. Seek Allah's help and put your trust in Him. Send them people of insight, good judgment, and patience to call him to follow Allah's path, and write me every day.

Sa'd writes again to the Commander of the Faithful saying,

Rustum camped with his troops at Saabaat. He has brought his horses and elephants and marched towards us. "Umar replies to calm him.

Sa'd is a smart, brave horseman, the Prophet's uncle, one of the first converts, and hero of different wars and raids. No sword or lance of his ever failed to reach its target. He stands at the head of his army in one of the greatest historical battles as if he were an ordinary soldier, not deluded by power nor acting arrogantly because of leadership. His self-esteem could tempt him to rely completely on his own capacities, but despite that he always turns to the Commander of the Faithful in Al-Madiinah. Although miles and miles separate them, he sends him a message each day, exchanging viewpoints, advice, and opinions while the great battle is still to come.

That was because Sa'd knew that 'Umar in Al-Madiinah never decided alone, but consulted the Muslims and the Prophet's Companions around him. Despite the war circumstances, Sa'd did not want to deprive himself or his army of the blessings and benefits of public consultation, especially if `Umar, a man with great inspiration, was among the consultants.

Sa'd carried out 'Umar's will and sent Rustum, the Persian leader, a number of his companions to call him to follow Islam and Allah's path.

The conversation between them and the Persian leader lasted long. Finally they ended their talk by telling him, "Allah has chosen us to turn whom He chooses of His creatures from paganism to monotheism, from the narrowness of life to its freedom, from ruler's injustice to Islam's fairness. Whoever accepts our offer, we will leave him alone and will refrain from hurting him. Whoever fights us, we will fight him until we fulfil Allah's promise."

Then Rustum asked, "What is Allah's promise which He made to you?"

The Companion answered, "Paradise for our martyrs and victory for the living ones."

The delegation returned to Sa'd, leader of the Muslims, to tell him that it was war. Ṣa'd's eyes were hereby filled with tears. He had wished so much that the war would be delayed for some time. On that day his illness became more severe, and he had to suffer its heavy burden. The abscesses spread all over his body, to the extent that he could not sit, let alone ride his horse to take part in an extremely fierce and violent battle.

If the war had just been waged before his illness or had it been delayed till he was cured and healthy again, then he would have proved himself brave. But now. . . No, the Messenger of Allah (PBUH) had taught them never to say "If" because "If" means weakness. A strong believer is neither helpless nor weak. Thereupon The Lion's Claws stood up to preach to his soldiers. He began his speech citing the following glorious verse: < *And We have written in the Zaboor (given to David) after the Torahe (given to Moses): "My righteous servants shall inherit the earth"> (21:105).*

Having finished his speech Sa'd led his troops in the Dhuhr Prayer, then turned towards his soldiers and proclaimed four times, " Allahu akbar (Allah is the Greatest)' Allahu akbar! Allahu akbar! Allahu akbar!"

The echo was to be heard all over the universe. Then he stretched out his arm like an unerring arrow pointing to the enemy and shouted to his soldiers, "Let's start this battle accompanied by Allah's blessings."

With pains hard to bear, he ascended to the balcony of his residence, which he used as a dwelling and a headquarters.

On the balcony he sat on a pillow and leaned upon his chest. His door was left open, which meant that by the least Persian attack against his residence he would be captured, alive or dead, but he was far from being afraid or terrified.

His abscesses were bleeding and hurting him severely, but he had something else to think about. Sitting on his balcony, he was shouting, calling, and commanding. First to those in one flank to step forward towards the right, and then to those in another flank to fill out the empty spot on the left. . . Mughiirah, look forward! Jurair follow them! Nu'maan. hit! Ash'ath attack and you also, Qa'qaa'. Forward, forward. Prophet's Companions!

His determined and hopeful sound turned each individual soldier into an army of its own. The Persian soldiers fell like flies and with them fell the worship of fire and paganism. After seeing the death of their commander and their best soldiers, the defeated, scattered remnants rapidly escaped.

The Muslim army pursued them until they reached Nahawind then Al-Madaa'in. There they fought to carry with them at the end the emperor's throne and crown as war booty.

At the Battle of Al-Madaa'in, Sa'd could stand the test and prove himself brave. The Battle of Al-Madaa'in took place two years after the Battle of Al-Qaadissiyah, a period during which a lot of continuous armed clashes took place between the Muslims and the Persians. Finally, the scattered remnants of the Persian army gathered at Al-Madaa'in itself, ready for a decisive and final scene.

Sa'd realized that time was on his enemy's side; therefore, he decided to deprive them of this advantage, but how could he do that? The Tigris River in its flood season stood in the middle between him and Al-Madaa'in.

Thereby, an event took place by which Sa'd succeeded to prove that he indeed deserved 'Abd Ar-Rahman Ibn 'Awfs description of him as the Lion's Claws. Sa'd's faith and determination stood glittering in the face of danger, mocking and making fun of the impossible with admirable bravery Sa'd ordered his army to cross the Tigris River. He ordered them to search for a safe, secure ford in the river, which would enable their crossing. Finally they found a place, but the fording was not free of extreme risks.

Before the army started to cross, the leader Sa'd wisely realized the necessity to safeguard their arrival spot on the opposite bank, where the enemy was camping. Therefore he prepared two detachments, the first of which was called The Detachment of Terror. Its leader was 'Aasim Ibn 'Amr. The second was called The Detachment of the Dumb, led by Al Qa'qaa' Ibn 'Amr.

The soldiers of these two detachments had to encounter many horrible situations to clear a safe place on the opposite bank for the army which would Subsequently cross. They fulfilled their task with amazing skill. Sa'd's success on that day will always be a cause for the perplexity of historians.

Sa'd himself was amazed by his own success. It also amazed his companion and escort Salmaan Al-Faarisiy, who shook his head in astonishment and said, " Islam is indeed new. By Allah, seas have been subdued by them and the land has been subdued by them. In the name of the One in Whose hands Salmaan's soul lies, they will leave it in a group, as they entered it in a group."

Indeed, that is exactly what happened. As they penetrated the Tigris River in a group, so they left it in a group without losing one single soldier, nor annoying a single horse.

It happened that a wooden cup fell from one of the warriors, who felt sorry to be the only one to lose something. He called his companions to help to get it out and a high wave pushed it to where someone could pick it up!

Some historical sources described the magnificence of such a scene as the fording of the river: Sa'd ordered the Muslims to say, "Allah is enough for us and He is the best to trust in." Then he penetrated the Tigris with his horse, and the people penetrated behind him. No one stayed behind. They walked as if they were walking on a land surface until they filled the whole area between the two banks. The water surface could not be seen due to the numerous troops of cavalry and infantry. People went on talking while walking in the water as if they were on land, as a result of their feeling of security and tranquility, their trust in Allah's judgment and His victory, His promise and His support.

When 'Umar appointed him to be Iraq's governor, he set out to build Kufa and established the foundations of Islam in wide broad lands.

One day the inhabitants of Kufa complained to the Commander of the Faithful about Sa'd. They lost control over their flimsy, restless temper and made a funny claim saying, "Sa'd can't pray well." Sa'd laughed loudly and said, "By Allah, I prayed with them exactly as the Prophet's prayer was. I prolonged the first two rak'ahs and shortened the last two."

When 'Umar ordered him back to Al-Madiinah, he did not get annoyed. On the contrary, he responded to 'Umar's call immediately. After some time, 'Umar determined to return him to Kufa, but Sa'd responded laughing, "Do you order me to return to people who claim that I don't perform my prayers well?" He preferred to stay in Al-Madiinah.

When the Commander of the Faithful 'Umar (May Allah be pleased with him) was attacked, he chose six of the Prophet's Companions to be responsible for choosing the next caliph. 'Umar said that he chose six of those with whom the Prophet was pleased before he died. Sa'd Ibn Abi Waqqaas was one of them.

But it seems from 'Umar's last words that if he would have chosen one of the Companions for the caliphate, it would have been Sa'd. He said to his companions, advising and commending, "If Sa'd is to become caliph, that's good; but if someone else is to be caliph, then he has to seek Sa'd's help."

Sa'd lived long. He secluded himself during the period of civil strife following the death of the third Caliph, 'Uthmaan. Furthermore, he ordered his whole family and children not to tell him any news about what was happening.

Once, everyone was anxious to know his position, when his nephew Haashim Ibn 'Utbah Ibn Abi Waqqaas, said to him, "O'uncle, here are 100,000 swords which consider you the more entitled to that matter (i.e. the caliphate)." Sa'd responded, "I want out of the 100,000 swords, just one sword that if it hits a believer it won't do anything, but if it hits a disbeliever it cuts through."

His nephew realized what he meant and left him in his isolation and security.

When the dispute ended in favor of Mu'aawiyah, who took over the reins of government, he asked Sa'd, "Why didn't you fight with us?" He answered, "A dark cloud passed over me. I told it, Shoo! Shoo! I stopped my riding camel until it passed away."

Mu'aawiyah said, "Shoo! Shoo! cannot be found in the glorious Book of Allah, but Allah said < *And if two parties or groups among the believers fall into fighting, then make peace between them both, but if one of them rebels against the other, then fight you (all)against the one that which rebels till it complies with the Command of Allah* > *(49 : 9)*. And you did not take anyone's side. You weren't with the unjust against the just, nor were you with the just against the unjust." Hereupon Sa'd responded, "I wouldn't have fought a man (he meant 'Aliy Ibn Abi Taalib) to whom the Prophet (PBUH) said, "You have towards me the same position Haaruun (Aaron) had towards Muusaa (Moses), except that there isn't any Prophet coming after me."

One day in A.H. 54, having exceeded the age of 80, he was at his house in Al-'Aqiiq preparing to meet Allah.

His son spoke of his final moments: His head was upon my lap, he was passing away. I cried, but he said, "What makes you cry, my son? Allah will never torture me. I belong to Paradise!"

The firmness of his faith could not be weakened even by the quaking fear of death. The Prophet (PBUH) had passed him the good news and he believed firmly in the Prophet's honesty; therefore what was there to be afraid of? "Allah will never torture me. I belong to Paradise!"

However, he wanted to meet Allah carrying the most magnificent and most wonderful memory, a memory which joined him with his religion and his Prophet (PBUH). Therefore, he pointed to his coffer. They opened it and got out an old, torn, threadbare gown. He ordered his kin to shroud him in that gown saying, "I met the disbelievers at the Battle of Badr wearing it. I've saved it for this day."

Indeed, this threadbare gown was not just a gown. It was the banner waving over a long great life. Our hero lived it honestly, bravely, and faithfully.

The body of the last Muhaajiruun was buried in Al- Madiinah, safely laid beside a group of great Companions who preceded him to Allah. Their exhausted bodies had finally found a secure shelter in the ground of Al-Baqii'.

Farewell, Sa'd. Farewell Sa'd, the hero of AI-Qaadissiyah, conquerer of Al-Madaa'in, extinguisher forever of the worshipped fire of Persia!

(7)
SUHAIB IBN SINAAN
O Abu Yahia! A Successful Purchase!

He was born surrounded by comfort and luxury. His father was the governor of Al Uballah and its ruler on behalf of the Persian king, and was one of the Arabs who emigrated to Iraq long before Islam. In his palace on the bank of Euphrates, next to Mosul, the child lived happily and comfortably.

One day, the country was attacked by Romans (Byzantines), who captured a large number and enslaved the boy Suhaib lbn Sinaan.

He was taken by slave traders until finally his long journey ended in Makkah. There he was sold to 'Abd Allah lbn Jud'aan, after having spent his childhood and most of his youth in Roman lands, where he adopted their language and dialect.

His master was so amazed by his intelligence, energy, and sincerity that he emancipated him and set him free, giving him the privilege to trade with him.

One day,(Let his friend 'Ammaar lbn Yaasir tell us) what happened on that day :I met Suhaib lbn Sinaan in front of the door of Daar AI-Arqam, when the Prophet (PBUH) was there. I asked, "What do you want?" He answered, "And what do you want?" I said, "I want to meet Muhammad (PBUH) to hear what he is saying." He said, "I want the same." We both entered and met the Prophet (PBUH), who invited us to embrace Islam, and we converted. We stayed there till evening. Secretly he went out.

Thereupon, Suhaib got to know his path to Daar Al- Arqam. He got to know his path to guidance and light, but also to difficult sacrifice and great redemption. Entering through that wooden door, which separated Daar Al-Arqam and what was inside from the outer world, was not just crossing a threshold, but crossing of a whole world of limitations. An old world, with all that represented-religion, manners, customs and life-crossing it towards a new world with all that represented —religion, manners, customs, and life.

Crossing the threshold of Daar Al-Arqam, a threshold not wider than one foot, meant, in reality, to cross an ocean of terror, wide and expanding. Stepping over such an obstacle, such a threshold, meant the beginning of an era full of great responsibilities.

As for the poor, the stranger, the enslaved, stepping over Daar Al-Arqam's threshold meant exceptional, extraordinary sacrifices.

Suhaib, our hero, was a stranger; 'Ammar Ibn Yaasir, his friend whom he met in front of the door, was a poor man. Why did they go voluntarily to face terror and, moreover, do their best when they are with it in combat?

It was the call of faith,which could not be resisted. It was the good character of Muhammad (PBUH), the scent of which filled the hearts of the reverent with love and guidance. It was his new, shining magnificence. Dazzling minds were fed up with the old, its misguidance and bankruptcy. Above all, it was Allah's mercy, bestowed upon whomever He wishes. His guidance and protection bestowed on whomever turns to Him.

Suhaib holds a position in the ranks of the faithful. He held a great and high position among the persecuted and tortured. He held a high position among the generous and self-sacrificing.

He frankly described his great loyalty to his responsibilities as a Muslim, who had pledged allegiance to the Prophet (PBUH) and walked under Islam's standard: "I was present in every situation witnessed by the Prophet (PBUH). I was present at every pledge called by him. I was present in every detachment organized by him. The Prophet (PBUH) never took part in a raid, at the beginning of the period or the end, without my being on his right or left. Whenever the Muslims feared a danger facing them, I was there in the front, and whenever they feared it in the rear, I was there at the back. I never let the Prophet (PBUH) stay in a position between me and the foe until Prophet(PBUH) met Allah."

It was a dazzling image of extraordinary faith and great loyalty. Ever since the first day he received Allah's light and put his hand into the Prophet's, Suhaib (May Allah be pleased with him and with all his Companions) was imbued with such outstanding faith.

From that day, his relationship towards people and the world, let alone himself, acquired a new dimension.

From that day, his character turned into a firm, humble and devoted one, subduing events and braving various types of horror.

He went on—as already mentioned—bravely and courageously shouldering all his responsibilities, never lagging behind, whenever there was danger or a situation to be encountered. His passionate love and ardent desire were not directed towards gains and spoils but rather towards sacrifice and ransom; not towards the greed of life but rather towards the passion of danger and self sacrifice.

He began the days of his noble redemption and great loyalty with the day of his Hijrah. On that day he abandoned all his wealth, all his gold which he had gained by successful trade during the long years he lived in Makkah. He abandoned all his fortune, all that he owned in a split second, the glory of which was never stained by doubt or retreat.

When the Prophet (PBUH) intended to emigrate, Suhaib knew that and he was supposed to be the third one of the three: the Prophet, Abu Bakr, and Suhaib.

However, the Quraish decided to prevent the Prophet's emigration. Suhaib fell into one of their traps and was thereby hindered for some time from emigrating, while the Prophet (PBUH) and his companion set out accompanied by Allah's blessing.

Suhaib disputed, talked, and argued until he got rid of his persecutors. He mounted his camel and sped across the desert. However, the Quraish sent its hunters to follow him. When they reached him, Suhaib had hardly seen them before facing them and shouting from a near distance, "O' people of Quraish, you know that I am the best marksman. By Allah, you cannot reach me before I shoot each of my arrows with my bow, then I will strike you with my sword until it falls down. Come on, if you like to try. Or if you like, I will tell you where my money is, and so leave me alone."

They agreed to take his money saying, "You came to us as a poor wretch. Your money increased in our land and among us you claimed high rank and now you want to escape together with your money?"

He guided them to the place where he had hidden his fortune, then they left him alone and returned to Makkah.

Strangely enough, they believed his words without doubt, without precaution. They did not ask him to prove his honesty, nor did they ask him to swear. This situation granted him a great honor, which he deserves as an honest and truthful man.

Alone but happy, Suhaib continued his journey until he reached the Prophet (PBUH) at Qubaa'.

When Suhaib came into view, the Prophet (PBUH) was sitting surrounded by his Companions. As soon as the Prophet (PBUH) saw him, he called to him cheerfully, "O'Abu Yahia! A profitable sale! A profitable sale!"

Hereupon, the glorious verse was revealed: *<And of mankind is he who would sell himself, seeking the pleasure of Allah. And Allah is Full of kindness to (His) slaves> (2:201).*

Indeed, Suhaib had paid all his fortune — the fortune he spent all his youth to gather — in return for his faithful soul. He never felt it was an unjust bargain. Money, gold, the whole world, nothing of that sort was worth while as long as he kept his faith, the sovereignty of his conscience, and the determination of his fate.

The Prophet loved him very much. Besides being pious and God-fearing, he was a cheerful and jovial person. The Prophet (PBUH) saw him once eating dates when there was an inflammation in one of his eyes. The Prophet (PBUH) asked him cheerfully, "Do you eat dates when there is inflammation in one of your eyes?" He answered, "What's wrong with that? I eat them with the other eye!"

He was a generous donor, spending all his stipend from the treasury (Bait Al-Ma'al) in the cause of Allah, helping the needy, aiding the sorrowful, feeding the needy, the orphans, and the captives with the best food.

His extreme generosity attracted the attention of 'Umar, who said to him, "I can see you feeding people too much, to the extent that you are spending lavishly." Suhaib answered him, "I've heard the Prophet (PBUH)say, The best of you is the one who feeds (others).' "

The life of Suhaib was filled with an abundance of merits and great situations. To be chosen by 'Umar lbn AI-Khattaab to lead the prayer was another merit to be added.

When the Commander of the Faithful was attacked while leading the Muslims in Fajr Prayer and felt his end was coming nearer and nearer, he began to advise his companions. His last words were, "Let Suhaib lead people in prayer."

On that day 'Umar chose six of the Companions and entrusted them with the choice of the new caliph. The Caliph of the Muslims was the one who led the prayers. In those days following the death of the Commander of the Faithful, until the new caliph was chosen, who was to lead the Muslims in prayer?

'Umar would slow down a thousand times before choosing someone especially in these moments, while his pure soul was passing away to meet Allah. If he chose, then there was no one more eligible than the chosen. He chose Suhaib.

He chose him to lead the Muslims in prayer until the next caliph came to carry out his duties.

He chose him, despite the Roman accent obvious in his language. This choice was a divine blessing upon the pious worshipper Suhaib Ibn Sinaan.

(8)
MU'AADH IBN JABAL
The Most Learned of Halaal and Haraam

Among the seventy-man delegation of the Ansaar who took the oath of allegiance to the Prophet in the Second Allegiance of 'Aqabah sat a young man with a bright face, graceful eyes, and a radiant smile. When he was silent, he attracted attention with his profound peacefulness and devoutness. On the other hand, when he talked, he held his people spell-bound. This young man was Mu'aadh Ibn Jabal (May Allah be pleased with him). He belonged to the Ansaar, and he was among the foremost believers who gave the second oath of allegiance to the Prophet. Naturally, a man of such precedence, faith, and certainty would not miss for the world a battle or an expedition. His uppermost quality was his knowledge of fiqh (jurisprudence)the practical aspect of Muhammad's message. He reached the apex in knowledge and fiqh, to the extent that made the Prophet (PBUH) say, "The most learned man of my nation in halaal and haraam is Mu'aadh Ibn Jabal."

He resembled 'Umar Ibn Al-Khattaab in his enlightenment, courage, and intelligence. When the Prophet sent him to Yemen, he asked him, "How will you give a judgment or settle a dispute?" Mu'aadh answered; "I will refer to the Qur'aan." The Prophet then asked, "What will you do if you do not find the decree you are looking for in Qur'aan?" Mu'aadh answered, "I will refer to the Prophet's Sunnah." The Prophet asked, "But what will you do if you do not find a decree even in the Sunnah?" Mu'aadh readily answered, "I will be judge between mankind by resorting to juristic reasoning (ijtihad) to the best of my power." Now, Mu'aadh's staunch commitment to Allah's Book and the Prophet's Sunnah does not mean that he closed his mind to the countless and endless hidden or equivocal facts that await someone to unravel and adjudicate.

Perhaps both Mu'aadh's ability in juristic reasoning and the courageous usage of his intelligence enabled him to master the fiqh, excelling all other scholars. The Prophet justifiably described Mu'aadh as "the most learned man of my nation in halaal and haraam."

History portrays him as a man of remarkably enlightened, resolute, and decisive mind. For instance, 'Aaez Allah lbn 'Abd Allah narrated that one day he entered the mosque with the Companions of the Prophet (PBUH) at the dawn of 'Umar's caliphate. Then he sat among more than thirty men. Let us hear him narrate the story: "I sat with a group of more than thirty men. They were recalling a hadith of the Prophet (PBUH). In this ring sat a dark, swarthy young man who had a sweet voice and a radiant face. Whenever they disputed about a hidden or ambiguous meaning in the hadith, they at once sought his legal instruction or judgment. He seldom, if ever, spoke unless he was asked. When their meeting was over, I approached him and asked him, "Who are you, O' Allah's Slave?" He answered, "I am Mu'aadh lbn Jabal." So I instantly felt close to him.

Also, Shahr lbn Hawshab said, "Whenever Mu'aadh lbn Jabal was present when the Companions of the Prophet (PBUH) were holding a meeting, they looked at him with reverence."

'Umar lbn Al-Khattaab, the Commander of the Faithful, often consulted him. It seemed that Mu'aadh had a highly disciplined mind and a captivating and convincing logic that moved peacefully and knowledgeably. When we look at his historical background, we will always see him at the center of attention. He always sat there surrounded by people. He always maintained a discrete silence that was only broken whenever people were anxious to hear his judgment and whenever they were in dispute. When he spoke he looked, as one of his contemporaries described, "as if light and pearls were emanating from his mouth rather than speech." He reached his high rank in knowledge and reverence when the Prophet (PBUH) was alive and maintained it after his death, not withstanding his youth, for Mu'aadh died during 'Umar's caliphate at the age of thirty-three years.

Mu'aadh was generous, magnanimous, well mannered, and good-natured. If anyone asked him for money, he would readily and gladly give it to him. His generosity made him spend all his money on charity and aid. When the Prophet (PBUH) died, Mu'aadh was still in Yemen, where the Prophet (PBUH) had sent him with the task of teaching Muslims their religion and fiqh.

When Mu'aadh returned from Yemen during Abu Bakr's caliphate, 'Umar Ibn Al Khattaab was informed that Mu'aadh became wealthy, and he suggested to Abu Bakr that the community should have half of Mu'aadh's wealth. 'Umar did not waste much time as he rushed to Mu'aadh's house and told him about what he and Abu Bakr had agreed on. Mu'aadh was an honest and trustworthy man. The fact that he had made a fortune did not make him vulnerable to suspicion or sin; therefore, he turned down 'Umar's suggestion and refuted his viewpoint. Finally, 'Umar left him. The next day, Mu'aadh hurried towards 'Umar's house and no sooner had he laid his eyes on him than he hugged him. His tears flowed as he said, " Last night, I saw in my dream that I was crossing deep water. I nearly drowned were it not for your help, 'Umar." Afterwards, they both went to Abu Bakr's presence where Mu'aadh asked him to take half his money, but Abu Bakr said, " No, I will take nothing from you." 'Umar glanced at Mu'aadh and said, "Now it is halaal and blessed."

First, the pious Abu Bakr would not take from Mu'aadh one penny unless he was absolutely positive that he had earned it in a lawful halaal way. Second, 'Umar was not trying to accuse or cast suspicion on Mu'aadh. In the final analysis, this epitomizes the era of ideals which was filled with people who were in perpetual competition to climb their way up to the apex of perfection allowed to human beings. Thus some of them soared up to the sky with their good deeds. Some were foremost and the rest followed a middle course. Yet, all of them were travelers on a caravan of goodness.

After a while, Mu'aadh emigrated to Syria, where he lived among its people and the expatriates as a teacher and a scholar of fiqh. When Abu 'Ubaidah, the governor of Syria and a close friend of Mu'aadh, died, the Commander of the Faithful 'Umar Ibn Al-Khattaab assigned Mu'aadh to take his place as a ruler. Only a few months had elapsed after his taking over when he died, humble and repentant to Allah, 'Umar (May Allah be pleased with him) used to say, "If I were to grant Mu'aadh Ibn Jabal succession and Allah asked me, "Why did you make him your successor?" I would readily answer, "I heard Your Prophet (PBUH) say that when those who have knowledge, stand before Almighty Allah, Mu'aadh will be among them."

The succession that 'Umar meant here was not merely over a country or a governorship, but over all the Muslim lands. When 'Umar was asked, before his death, "If you choose your successor now, we will give him our allegiance." He answered, "If Mu'aadh Ibn Jabal were alive and I made him my successor to the caliphate, then I died and met Allah Who asked me, "Whom did you assign to rule Muhammad's nation?" I would answer, "I assigned Mu'aadh Ibn Jabal to rule it after I heard the Prophet (PBUH) say Mu'aadh Ibn Jabal is the Imam of those who have knowledge of Judgment Day."

The Prophet (PBUH) said one day, "O' Mu'aadh, by Allah I love you dearly, so do not forget to recite after every prayer, 'Allah help me in remembering You, in offering thanks to You, and in worshiping You properly.'"

Indeed, the Prophet (PBUH) supplicated Allah to help him to remember Him. The Prophet (PBUH) persevered in stressing this great fact that tells people that authority belongs to Allah, He has the power over all, and there is no power or any might except with His permission, for He is Most High and Most Great.

Definitely, Mu'aadh had learned and fully grasped this fact. He did his utmost to cherish and apply this fundamental basis in his life from that moment onwards.

One day, the Prophet (PBUH) ran into him so he asked him, "How are you this morning Mu'aadh?" He answered, "This morning I woke up as a true believer." The Prophet (PBUH) said, "Every truth has its manifestations, so what are the manifestations of your true belief?" Mu'aadh readily answered, "I have never woken up without believing that I might die before nightfall. I have never slept without believing that I might die before the morning and have never taken a step without believing that I might die before taking the next. It always seems to me that I can see each nation humbled to its knees and each nation called to its record of deeds. It always seems to me that I can see the dwellers of Paradise, wherein are delights everlasting, and the dwellers of Hell, wherein they are in disgracing torment." The Prophet (PBUH) commented, "Now you know, so stick to the truth as long as you live." Indeed Mu'aadh had submitted himself and his destiny to Allah, for Allah was all that mattered to him. It was just that Ibn Mas'uud described him as "an ummah, a leader having all the good and righteous qualities, obedient to Allah and *haniifan*, who worshipped none but Allah. We used to liken him to Ibraahiim (Abraham)(PBUH)."

Mu'aadh advocated knowledge and the remembrance of Allah. Moreover, he invited mankind to seek the useful and true knowledge saying, "I warn you against the deviation of wise men. You will know the truth when you see it, for it has a distinctive light!" He believed that worship was an end and a means to reach justice. One day a Muslim asked him, "Teach me." Mu'aadh asked him, "Will you obey me if I teach you?" The man answered, "I will not disobey you in anything." He said then, "Fast, then break your fast. Pray during the night but you must get some sleep. Earn what is halaal and what is rightfully yours and do not earn sin. Die as a true Muslim. Finally, I warn you against the supplication of those who have been wronged or oppressed." He believed that education meant knowledge and practice; therefore, he said, "Learn whatever you like to learn, yet Allah will not make your learning worthwhile unless you practice what you have learned." He believed that belief and remembrance of Allah meant the perpetual calling to mind of His greatness and the perpetual calling of oneself to account for deeds before Allah does so. Al-Aswad Ibn Hilaal reported. As we were walking with Mu'aadh one day, he said, "Let us sit down for a while to meditate on Allah."

Perhaps the reason behind his discrete silence was his unremitting meditation and contemplation.

Likewise, his once telling the Prophet(PBUH) that he never took a step without believing that he might die before taking the next was due to his engrossment in the remembrance of Allah and in calling himself to account for his deeds.

At the end, death summoned Mu'aadh. It was time to meet Allah. When the stupor of death creeps upon someone, his subconscious takes the reins and spurs the tongue —if it is able to — to disclose the reality of all mankind in concise words that summarize his life story. In those blessed moments, Mu'aadh faintly uttered great words that revealed a great believer, for he gazed up into the sky and humbly supplicated Allah, the Most Merciful, saying, "Allah! I used to fear You but now I implore You. Allah, You know that I did not devote my life to travel in the lands or to earn money or property but rather consecrated it to knowledge, faith and obedience, notwithstanding intense heat or hardships."

He stretched his hand as if he were shaking death and went into a coma. His last words were,"O'Death, welcome! You are a long-awaited beloved. "

At last Mu'aadh ascended to Allah's Paradise.

(9)
AL- MIQDAAD IBN 'AMR
The First Muslim Cavalryman

His companions said about him, "The first cavalryman to strive in the way of Allah was Al-Miqdaad Ibn Al-Aswad, our hero, and Al-Miqdaad Ibn 'Amr was one and the same person."

The story behind this was that Al-Miqdaad Ibn 'Amr was in alliance with Al-Aswad Ibn 'Abd Yaghuuth, who therefore adopted Al-Miqdaad. Thus, he was called Al-Miqdaad Ibn Al-Aswad until the glorious verse which abrogated adoption descended, and he restored his father's name, 'Amr Ibn Saad. Al-Miqdaad was one of the foremost Muslims and the seventh of the seven men who announced their Islam openly and in public. Therefore, he had his share of the Quraish's abuse and atrocities. He tolerated them with the courageousness and satisfaction of a devoted disciple.

His attitude during the Battle of Badr will retain its immortal glory. It was an honorable attitude that impressed all those who witnessed it and made each and every one of them wish it were he who had adopted such an attitude. 'Abd Allah Ibn Mas'uud, the Companion of Allah's Prophet (PBUH) said, "I have seen Al-Miqdaad (May Allah be pleased with him) maintain a firm attitude and I was overtaken by a vicarious feeling to be in his place. This feeling enveloped me to the extent that I wished more than anything in the world that it would come true."

The Day of Badr was a crucial one as the Quraish marched with all their might, stubborn persistence, and haughtiness against the Muslims. On that day, the Muslims were not only few, but also untried and inexperienced in jihaad. Their hearts had not been tested in action. Besides, the Battle of Badr was the dawn of their conquests. The Prophet stood there to strengthen the faith of his Companions and test their combat readiness to break through the enemy infantry and cavalry.

Afterwards, the Prophet (PBUH) began to consult them on war tactics. Surely, the Prophet's Companions knew that when he asked their opinion, he demanded their individual free and courageous expression, even if it happened to contradict the majority. He, who expressed his opinion would not be reproached or criticized.

Al-Miqdaad was afraid lest one of the Muslims should have reservations about the imminent battle. Therefore, he was careful to have precedence in speech. His concise and decisive words coined the slogan of the battle, yet before he had the chance to open his mouth, Abu Bakr As-Siddiiq started talking and by the time he finished his words, Al - Miqdaad's apprehensions had vanished, for Abu Bakr spoke with remarkable eloquence. 'Umar Ibn Al-Khattaab spoke next and followed suit. Finally Al-Miqdaad stepped forward and said,"O'Prophet of Allah, go ahead with what Allah has inspired you to do. We will stand by you. By Allah, we will never say as the Children of Israel said, 'So go you and your Lord and fight you two, we are sitting right here,' Instead, we will say, 'Go you and your Lord and we will fight with you.' By Allah, Who has sent you with the truth, if you take us to the end of the world, we will tolerate all hardships until we reach it with you. We will fight on your left, your right, in front of you and behind you until Allah bestows victory on you," His decisive words were like bullets that made the righteous believers with them fired up with enthusiasm.

The Prophet's face brightened as he uttered a pious supplication for Al-Miqdaad, whose words were so strong and decisive that they drew the pattern that would be followed by anyone who spoke afterwards. Indeed, Al-Miqdaad's words left their impact on the hearts of the believers. Consequently, S'ad Ibn Mu'aadh, a leader of the Ansaar, rose and said, "O' Prophet of Allah, we have believed in you and witnessed that what has descended on you is the truth. We gave you our allegiance, so go ahead with what you intend to do, and we will stand by you. By Allah, Who has sent you with the truth, if you attempt to cross the sea, we will cross it hand in hand with you. None of us will lag behind or turn his back on you. We are not afraid to meet our enemy tomorrow, for we are given to terrible warfare and we are faithful in our desire to meet Allah. I pray to Allah, that we do what will make you proud of us. Go ahead with Allah's blessings."

The Prophet (PBUH) was extremely sanguine on hearing this and said to his Companions, "March forward and be cheerful and confident!" After a while the two armies met in fierce combat. The Muslim cavalry on that day were only three: Al-Miqdaad Ibn 'Amr, Marthid Ibn Abi Marthid, and Az-Zubair Ibn Al 'Awaam. The rest of the Mujaahiduun were infantry or riding on camels.

Al-Miqdaad's previous words not only proved his valor but also his preponderant wisdom and profound thought.

Al-Miqdaad was a wise and intelligent man. His wisdom was not expressed in mere words but in empirical principles and a constant unvarying conduct. His experience was the fuel of his wisdom and intelligence.

The Prophet (PBUH) once assigned him to rule one of the governorships, and when he returned the Prophet (PBUH) asked him,

"How does it feel be a governor?" He answered with admirable honesty, "It made me feel as if I were in a silver tower above the rest of the people. By Allah, Who has sent you with the truth, from now on, I will never expose myself to the temptations of governing."

If that was not wisdom, then what else is? If that was not a wise man, then who else is?

This was an honest and straightforward man who was able to detect, unveil, and admit his innermost weakness. His position as a governor made him vulnerable to haughtiness and vainglory. He detected this weakness in himself at once and took a solemn oath to avoid any position or rank that might jeopardize his piety and righteousness. He kept his oath and renounced any influential or controversial situation for the rest of his life.

He cherished and treasured the hadith of Prophet(PBUH): "He who avoids fitnah (trials, afflictions, and error) is indeed a happy man."

He realized that because the governorship awakened latent pride and haughtiness in him and exposed him to Fitnah, it was better to avoid any position that might arouse this weakness. His wisdom was manifested in his deliberateness and perseverance in his judgment of men. This was also a trait that Allah's Prophet (PBUH) instilled in him, for he taught Muslims that the hearts of the children of Adam are incredibly capricious.

Al-Miqdaad was always for delaying his final judgment of a man to the moment of death, so as to be absolutely positive that the man concerned would not alter, for death means finality. His wisdom was most conspicuous in the dialogue that was narrated by one of his companions: "One day, we sat with Al-Miqdaad and a man passed by and addressed Al- Miqdaad saying, "All kinds of happiness are for these eyes which have seen Allah's Prophet (PBUH). By Allah, we wish that we saw what you have seen and witnessed what you have witnessed." Al-Miqdaad approached him and said, "Why should anyone wish to witness a scene that Allah did not wish him to see? He does not know what it would have been like if he had witnessed it or which party he would have been among if he went back in time. By Allah, Allah's Prophet (PBUH) saw people who were thrown right into hell, so you should thank Allah that you were spared such a trial and were honored by firm belief in Allah and His Prophet (PBUH)."

Undoubtedly, it is remarkable wisdom. You hardly ever meet a believer who loves Allah and the Prophet (PBUH) and does not wish to see and live within the Prophet's sight. Yet the insight of the wise and skillful Miqdaad unveiled the missing dimension of this wish. For is it not possible that if this man had lived during those times he might have ended up among the dwellers of Hell? Is it not possible that he might have sided with the disbelievers? Again, is it not far much better for him to thank Allah, Who destined him to live at a time when Islam is deeply-rooted and fully-fledged, awaiting him to quench his thirst from its inexhaustible pure spring?

Al-Miqdaad's viewpoint was subtly wise and intelligent. He always emerged as the wise and clever man in all his actions, deeds, and words.

Al-Miqdaad's love for Islam was not only great but also reasonable and wise. A man who has such great and wise love inside him must be raised to a high station, for he does not find pleasure in this love per se but rather in its responsibilities and obligations. AlMiqdaad definitely was this type of man. His love for the Prophet filled his heart and deepened his feeling of responsibility towards the Prophet's safety. No sooner was a call for an expedition announced than he darted towards the Prophet's house on horseback armed with his sharp sword!

His love for Islam filled his heart with responsibility for its protections, not only from the plots of its enemies, but also from the errors of its allies.

One day, his army unit went on an expedition, but the enemy troops were able to besiege them. Therefore, their commander gave an order to his soldiers not to graze their camels. One of the Muslim soldiers did not hear his order and, in consequence, disobeyed it. The commander punished him severely, more than he actually deserved. In fact, he did not deserve to be punished at all. AlMiqdaad passed by this man and found him in tears, so he asked him what was the matter, and the latter told him what had happened. Al-Miqdaad took the man to the commander, where he argued with him until he was convinced of his error of judgment. Then Al-Miqdaad said, "Now it is the time for retaliation. He must have his *qisas*-the law of equality of punishment!"

The commander yielded to his judgment but the soldier remitted the retaliation. Al-Miqdaad was thrown into ecstasy over the greatness of the religion that made it possible for them to reach this power of courageous judgment, admirable submission, and great forgiveness. He said as if he were singing a song, "I will see Islam triumphant even if I have to die for it." Indeed, it was his utmost wish to see Islam most powerful before he died. His extraordinary effort to make his wish come true made the Prophet(PBUH) say to him, "O'Al-Miqdaad, Allah ordered me to love you and told me that He loves you."

(10)
SA'IID IBN 'AAMIR
Greatness Under Worn-out Garments

Does any of us know this man or have any of us ever heard his name before? Most probably, the majority of us, if not all, have not heard his name mentioned before. I imagine that you wonder, who is Sa'iid lbn 'Aamir? Well, you are about to embark on a journey back in time so as to find out all that there is to be known about this "happy" ("Sa'iid" means "happy ") man, so fasten your seat belts.

In short, Sa'iid was one of the outstanding Companions of the Prophet (PBUH), notwithstanding the fact that his name was seldom, if ever, mentioned. He was one of the most distinguished unknown pious Companions. It was natural that he, like all Muslims, would accompany Prophet (PBUH) in all his expeditions and battles, for as a believer, he could not lag or turn his back on Allah's Prophet (PBUH) in peace or war. Shortly before the Conquest of Khaibar, Sa'iid submitted himself to Islam. Ever since he embraced Islam and gave his allegiance to the Prophet (PBUH)), he consecrated his life, existence, and destiny to the service of Islam. All the great virtues of obedience, asceticism, dignity, humbleness, piety, and pride thrived harmoniously inside this pure and kind man.

In our attempt to unveil his greatness, we must bear in mind that, in most cases, appearance contrasts with reality. If we are to judge him by his outer looks, we will not do him justice, for he was definitely ill favored as regards his appearance. He had dusty uncombed hair. Nothing in his looks or appearance distinguished him from poor Muslims. If we are to judge his reality by his appearance, we will see nothing impressive or breath taking. But if we dive deep into his inner self beyond his outer appearance, we will see greatness in the full meaning of the word. His greatness stood aloof from the splendor and ornament of life. Yet, it lurked there beyond his modest appearance and worn-out garments. Have you ever seen a pearl hidden inside its shell? Well, he was much like this hidden pearl.

When the Commander of the Faithful 'Umar Iban Al- Khattaab dismissed Mu'aawiyah from his position as governor of Homs in Syria, he exerted himself in searching for someone who was qualified to take over his position.

Undoubtedly, 'Umar's standards of choice of governors and assistants were highly cautious, meticulous, and scrutinizing. He believed that if a governor committed a sin, error, or violation, two people would be asked to account for it before Allah: 'Umar and the governor, even if this governor were in the farthest corner of the earth. His standards of estimation and evaluation of governors were highly subtle, alert, and perceiving. Centuries before the advent of Islam, Homs, was a big city that witnessed, one after the other, the dawn and eclipse of many civilizations. Besides, it was a vital trade center. The attractions of the vast city turned it into a place of seduction and temptation. In 'Umar's opinion only an ascetic, devout, and repentant worshiper would be able to resist and renounce its attractions.

'Umar suddenly realized that Sa'iid Ibn 'Aamir was the man he was looking for and cried out, "Sa'iid Ibn 'Aamir is the right man for this mission." He summoned him. Sa'iid was offered the governorship by the Commander of the Faithful, but he refused saying, "Do not expose me to Fitnah (trials and affliction)." 'Umar then cried out, "By Allah, I will not let you turn me down."

"Do you lay the burdens of your trusteeship and the caliphate upon my shoulders, then you refuse to help me out?" Instantly, Sa'iid was convinced of the logic of 'Umar's words. Indeed, it was not fair to abandon or avoid their obligation towards their trusteeship and towards the caliphate and lay them on 'Umar's shoulders. Moreover, if people like Sa'iid Ibn 'Aamir renounced the responsibility of rule, then 'Umar would definitely have a hard time to find a man who was highly pious and righteous enough to be entrusted with such a mission.

Hence, Sa'iid traveled with his wife to Syria. They were newly-wed. Ever since his bride was a little girl, she had been an exquisitely blooming beauty. 'Umar gave him a considerable sum of money at the time of his departure.

When they settled down in Syria, his wife wanted to use this money, so she asked him to buy appropriate garments, upholstery, and furniture, and to save the rest of it. Sa'iid said to her, "I have a better idea. We are in a country with profitable trade and brisk markets, so it would be better to give this money to a merchant so as to invest it." She said, "But if he loses it?" Sa'iid said, "I will make him a guarantee that the amount will be paid notwithstanding." She answered, "All right then."

Of course, Sa'iid went out and bought the necessities for an ascetic life, then gave all his money in voluntary charity in Allah's cause to the poor and those in need. Time went by, and every now and then his wife would ask him about their money and their profits and he would answer, "It is a highly profitable trade."

One day, she asked him the same question before one of his relatives, who knew what he had done with the money. His relative smiled, then he could not help laughing in a way that made Sa'iid's wife suspicious. Therefore, she prevailed on him to tell her the truth. He told her, "Sa'iid on that day gave all his money in voluntary charity in Allah's cause." Sa'iid's wife was broken-hearted, for not only had she lost her last chance to buy what she wanted but also lost all their money. Sa'iid gazed at her sad, meek eyes glistening with tears that only added more charm and grace to her eyes. Yet before he yielded to this fascinating figure, he perceived Paradise inhabited by his late friends and said, "I had companions who preceded me in ascending to Allah and you will not deviate from the path they have taken, not for the world." He was afraid lest her excelling beauty should make her disobey him; therefore he said as if he were talking to himself, "You know that Paradise is filled with Houris, fair females with wide and lovely eyes as wives for the pious, who are extremely lovely. If one of them had a peep at the earth, she would illuminate it with her light that combines the light of both the earth and the moon. So you should not blame me if I chose to sacrifice your love for their love and not vice versa." Throughout his talk, he was calm, pleased, and satisfied. His wife was peaceful, for she realized that she had no choice but to follow Sa'iid's example and adopt herself to his rigid, ascetic, and pious way of life.

Homs, at that time was called the second Kufa. The reason behind this was that its people were easily stirred and swayed to revolt against their governors. Homs was named after Al-Kufa in Iraq, which was notorious for endless mutiny and uprisings.

Although, the people of Homs were given to mutiny, as we have already mentioned, Allah guided their hearts to His righteous slave Sa'iid. Thus, they loved and obeyed him.

One day, 'Umar said to him, "I find it rather strange that the people of Syria love and obey you." Sa'iid answered, "Maybe they love me because I help and sympathize with them."

Despite the love of the people of Homs for Sa'iid, their innate rebellious disposition got the better of them. Hence, sounds of discontent and complaint began to be heard, thus proving that Homs was not called the second Kufa in vain. One day, as the Commander of the Faithful was visiting Homs, he asked its people who gathered around him for their opinion of Sa'iid. Some made complaints against him which were blessings in disguise, for they unveiled an impressively great man.

'Umar asked the criticizing group to state their complaints one by one. The representative of the group stood up and said, "We have four complaints against Sa'iid: First, he doesn't come out of his house until the sun rises high and the day becomes hot. Second, he does not see anyone at night. Third, there are two days in every month in which he doesn't leave his house at all. Fourth, he faints every now and then, and this annoys us although he can't help it." The man sat down and 'Umar was silent for a while for he was secretly supplicating Allah saying, "Allah, I know that he is one of Your best slaves. Allah, I beseech You not to make me disappointed in him." He summoned Sa'iid to defend himself. Sa'iid replied, "As for their complaint that I do not get out of my house before noon, by Allah I hate to explain the reason that made me do that, but I have to do so. The reason is that my wife does not have a servant, so I knead my dough, wait for it to rise, bake my bread, perform ablution and pray Duhar, then I go out of my house." 'Umar's face brightened as he said, " All praises and thanks be to Allah." Then he urged him to refute the rest of the allegations. Sa'iid went on, "As for their complaint that I do not meet anyone at night, by Allah, I hate to say the reason, but you force me to. Anyway, I have devoted the day to them and consecrated the night for Allah. As for the third complaint that they do not see me two days per month, well, I do not have a servant to wash my garment and I have no spare one. Therefore, I wash it and wait for it to dry shortly before sunset, then I go out of my house to meet them. My defense against the last complaint of the fainting fits is that I saw with my own eyes Khubaib Al-Ansaariy being slain in Makkah. The Quraish cut his body into small pieces and said, 'Do you want to save yourself and see Muhammad in your place instead?' He answered, "By Allah, I will not accept your offer of setting me free to return to my family safe and sound, even if you gave me all the splendors and ornaments of life in return for exposing the Prophet (PBUH) to the least annoyance, even if it was a prick of a thorn." Now, every time this scene of me standing there as a disbeliever, watching Khubaib being tortured to death and doing nothing to save him flickers in my mind, I find myself shaking with fear of Allah's punishment and I faint."

These were Sa'iid's words, which left his lips that were already wet from the flow of his pure and pious tears. The overjoyed 'Umar could not help but cry out, "All praises and thanks be to Allah Who would not make me disappointed in you!" He hugged Sa'iid and kissed his graceful and dignified forehead.

What a great guidance must have been bestowed on those outstanding men! What an excellent instructor Allah's Prophet (PBUH) must have been! What a penetrating light must have emanated from Allah's Book! What an inspiring and instructive school Islam must have been! I wonder, if the earth can take in so much of the piety and righteousness of those fortunate men, I presume that if that happened, then we would no longer call it the earth but rather Paradise. Indeed the "Promised Paradise."

Since it is not time for Paradise yet, it is only natural that those glorious superior men who pass by life are but few, very few.

Sa'iid Ibn 'Aamir was definitely one of those superior Muslims. His position allowed him a considerable salary, yet he took only enough money to buy the necessities for himself and his wife and gave the rest in voluntary charity in the way of Allah. One day, he was urged to spend this surplus on his family and relatives, yet he answered, "Why should I give it to my family and relatives? No, by Allah, I will not sell Allah's pleasure to seek my kin folks' pleasure."

He was later urged, "Spend more money on yourself and on your family and try to enjoy the lawful good things." But he always answered, "I will not stay behind the foremost Muslims after I heard the Prophet (PBUH) say, 'When Almighty Allah gathers all people on the Day of Reckoning, the poor believers will step forward in solemn procession. They will be asked to stop for reckoning but they will answer confidently: We have nothing to account for." Allah will say: "My slaves said the truth. Hence, they will enter Paradise before all other people."

In A.H. 20, Sa'iid met Allah with a pure record, pious heart, and honorable history. He yearned for so long to be among the foremost Muslims; in fact, he consecrated his life to fulfil their covenant and follow in their, footsteps. He yearned for so long for his Prophet (PBUH) and instructor and his pure and repentant comrades. He left all the burdens, troubles, and hardships of life behind. He had nothing but his pious, ascetic, awesome, and great inner self. These virtues made the balance of good deeds heavy, rather than light. He impressed the world with his qualities rather than with his conceit.

Peace be upon Sa'iid Ibn 'Aamir. Peace be upon his life and resurrection. Peace be upon the honorable and obedient Companions of the Prophet and blessings and peace be upon him.

(11)
HAMZAH IBN 'ABD AL-MUTTALIB
The Lion of Allah and The Martyr of Martyrs

After a day full of work, worship, and entertainment, the people of Makkah fell into a deep sleep. The people of the Quraish were turning in their beds except for one who forsook his bed of sleep. He used to go to bed early, rest for a few hours, then wake up in great anxiety for the expected appointment with Allah. He went to the praying corner in his room to supplicate to his God. Whenever his wife awakened upon hearing the voice of his long supplications, she shed tears out of warm sympathy and asked him not to take it so hard and to get some sleep. He only answered her in tears, "The time for sleep is over, Khadiijah." At that time Muhammad was not yet a serious problem for the Quraish, although he had started to draw their attention as he started to spread his call secretly; those who believed in him were still quite few.

There were people among the non-believers who loved and respected him. They yearned to declare their belief in him and become one of his followers, but their fear of the prevailing norms and the pressure of inherited traditions prevented them. Among them was Hamzah Ibn 'Abdul Muttalib, the Prophet's paternal uncle who was at the same time his brother through fosterage (i.e. they had been breast-fed by the same woman).

Hamzah was fully aware of the greatness of his nephew and of the truth he came with. He used to know him not only as a nephew, but also as a brother and friend because they both belonged to the same generation. They always played together and walked together on the same road of life step by step. But in their youth, they departed, each one in his own way. Hamzah preferred the life of leisure, trying to take his place among the prominent leaders of the Quraish and Makkah, while Muhammad chose the life of seclusion away from the crowd, immersed in the deep spiritual meditation that prepared him to receive the truth.

Despite the fact that each of them had a different way of living out his own youth, Hamzah was always attentive to the virtues of his friend and nephew. Such virtues helped Muhammad to win a special place in the hearts of people and helped to draw a clear outline for his great future.

The next day, Hamzah went out as usual. At the Ka'bah he found a number of Quraishi noblemen. He sat with them, listening to what they had to say. They were talking about Muhammad. For the first time Hamzah saw them worried about the call his nephew was propagating with a tone of bitterness and rage marking their voices. Before that, they had never paid attention - at least they had pretended not to do so-but on that day their faces looked perplexed, upset, and aggressive.

Hamzah laughed at their talks and accused them of exaggeration. Abu Jahl said to his companions that Hamzah was the best one to know the danger of his nephew's call and that he pretended to underestimate this danger till the Quraish would relax so much that when they awakened it would be after his nephew had complete control over them.

They kept talking and threatening while Hamzah sat, sometimes smiling, sometimes frowning. When they dispersed his head was full of new ideas about the issues of his nephew that they had discussed in his presence.

Days passed and the Quraish's whispering about the Prophet's call increased. Later, whispering turned into provocation and Hamzah watched from a distance. His nephew's composed, steadfast attitude towards their provocation's puzzled him. Such an attitude was quite unfamiliar to the Bani Quraish, who were themselves known to be strong and challenging.

If doubts of the greatness and truth of Muhammad could steal into anyone's heart, they would have never stolen into Hamzah's heart, because he was the best one to know Muhammad from his early childhood to his youth, then to his proud, honest manhood. Hamzah knew Muhammad as he knew himself and maybe, more. Since they had come into life together, grown up together, and attained full strength together, Muhammad's life had been as pure and clear as the sunlight. It never occurred to Hamzah that Muhammad could make an error or a doubtful act in his life. He never saw Muhammad angry, hopeless, greedy, careless, or unstable.

Hamzah was not only physically strong, but was also wise and strong-willed. Therefore, it was natural for him to follow a man in whose honesty and truthfulness he wholeheartedly believed. Thus he kept a secret in his heart that was soon going to be disclosed.

Then came the day. Hamzah went out of his house towards the desert carrying his bow to practice his favorite sport of hunting (in which he was very skilled). He spent most of his day there. On his way home he passed by the Ka'bah as usual, to circumambulate it.

Near the Ka'bah, a female servant of 'Abd Allah Ibn Jud'aan saw him and said, "O'Abu 'Umaarah! You haven't seen what happened to your nephew at the hands of Abu Al-Hakam

Ibn Hishaam. When he saw Muhammad sitting there, he hurt him and called him bad names and treated him in a way that he hated." She went on to explain what Abu Jahl had done to the Prophet of Allah.

Hamzah listened to her carefully and paused for a while, then with his right hand he picked up his bow and put it on his shoulder. He walked with fast, steady steps towards the Ka'bah, hoping to meet Abu Jahl there. He decided that if he did not find him, he would search for him everywhere till he did.

As soon as he reached the Ka'bah, he glanced at Abu Jahl sitting in the yard in the middle of the Quraishi noblemen. Hamzah advanced very calmly towards Abu Jahl and hit him with his bow on the head till it broke the skin and bled. To everybody's surprise, Hamzah shouted, "You dare to insult Muhammad while I follow his religion and I say what he says? Come and retaliate upon me. Hit me if you can." In a moment they all forgot how their leader Abu Jahl had been insulted and they were all thunderstruck by the news that Hamzah had converted to Muhammad's religion and that he saw what Muhammad saw and said what he said. Could Hamzah really have converted to Islam when he was the strongest and most dignified Quraish young man?

Such was the overwhelming disaster to which the Quraish were helpless, because Hamzah's conversion would attract others from the elite to do the same. Thus Muhammad's call would be supported, and he would find enough solidarity that the Quraish might wake up one day to find their idols being pulled down.

Indeed, Hamzah had converted, and he announced what he had kept secret in his heart for so long.

Again Hamzah picked up his bow, put it on his shoulder, and with steady steps and full strength left the place with everyone looking disappointed and Abu Jahl licking the blood flowing from his wounded head.

Hamzah possessed a sharp sight and clear consciousness. He went home, and after he had relaxed from the day's exhaustion he sat down to think over what had happened. He had announced it in a moment of indignation and rage. He hated to see his nephew getting insulted and suffering injustice with no one to help him. Such racial zeal for the honor of Bani Haashim's talk had made him hit Abu Jahl on the head and shout declaring his Islam. But was that the ideal way for anyone to change the religion of his parents and ancestors and to embrace a new religion whose teachings he had not yet become familiar with and whose true reality he had not acquired sufficient knowledge of? It was true that Hamzah had never had any doubts about Muhanunad's integrity, but could anybody embrace a new religion with all its responsibilities just in a moment of rage as Hamzah had done?

It was true that he had always kept in his heart a great respect for the new call his nephew was carrying and its banner, but what should the right time have been to embrace this religion if he was destined to embrace it? Should it be a moment of indignation and anger or a moment of deep reflection? Thus he was inspired by a clear consciousness to reconsider the whole situation in light of strict and meticulous thinking.

Hamzah started thinking. He spent many restless days and sleepless nights. When one tries to attain the truth by the power of mind, uncertainty will become a means of knowledge, and this is what happened to Hamzah. Once he used his mind to search Islam and to weigh between the old religion and the new one, he started to have doubts raised by his innate inherited nostalgia for his father's religion and by the natural fear of anything new. All his memories of the Ka'bah, the idols, the statues and the high religious status these idols bestowed on the Quraish and Makkah were raised.

It appeared to him that denying all this history and the ancient religion was like a big chasm, which had to be crossed. Hamzah was amazed at how a man could depart from the religion of his father that early and that fast. He regretted what he had done but he went on with the journey of reasonable thinking. But at that moment, he realized that his mind was not enough and that he should resort sincerely to the unseen power. At the Ka'bah he prayed and supplicated to heaven, seeking help from every light that existed in the universe to be guided to the right path.

Let us hear him narrating his own story. I regretted having departed from the religion of my father and kin, and I was in a terrible state of uncertainty and could not sleep. I came to the Ka'bah and supplicated to Allah to open my heart to what was right and to eliminate all doubts from it. Allah answered my prayer and filled my heart with faith and certainty. In the morning I went to the Prophet (PBUH) informing him about myself, and he prayed to Allah that He may keep my heart stable in this religion.

In this way Hamzah converted to Islam, the religion of certainty.

Allah supported Islam with Hamzah's conversion. He was strong in defending the Prophet of Allah (PBUH) and the helpless amongst his Companions. When Abu Jahl saw him among the Muslims, he realized that war was inevitably coming. Therefore he began to support the Quraish to ruin the Prophet and his Companions. He wanted to prepare for a civil war to relieve his heart of anger and bitter feelings.

Hamzah was unable, of course, to prevent all the harm alone, but his conversion was a shield that protected the Muslims, and was the first source of attraction to many tribes to embrace Islam. The second source was 'Umar lbn Al-Khattab's conversion, after which people entered Allah's religion in crowds. Since his conversion, Hamzah devoted all his life and power to Allah and His religion till the Prophet (PBUH) honored him with the noble title, "The Lion of Allah and of His Messenger"

The first military raid launched by the Muslims against their enemies was under the command of Hamzah. The first banner that the Prophet handed to any Muslim was to Hamzah. In the battle of Badr, when the two conflicting parties met, the Lion of Allah and of His Messenger was there, performing great wonders.

The defeated remnants of the Quraish army went back to Makkah, stumbling in disappointment. Abu Sufyaan was broken hearted with a bowed head as he left on the battlefield, the dead bodies of the Quraish martyrs, such as Abu Jahl, 'Utbah Ibn Rabii'ah, Shaibah Ibn Rabii'ah, Umaiyah Ibn Khalaf, 'Uqbah Ibn Abi Mu'ait, Al-Aswad Ibn 'Abdul Al-Asad, Al-Makhzumi, Al- Waliid lbn 'Utbah, Al-Nafr lbn Al-Haarith, Al-'Aas lbn Sa'iid, Ta'mah lbn 'Addi and tens of other great Quraishs..

But the Quraish would not accept the defeat easily. They started to prepare the army and to pull together all powers to avenge their honor and their dead. They insisted to continue the war. In the Battle of Uhud, all the Quraish went to war together with their allies from the Arabs, under the leadership of Abu Sufyaan once again.

The Quraish leaders had targeted two persons in the new battle, namely, the Prophet (PBUH) and Hamzah (May Allah be pleased with him). If one had heard them talking and plotting before the war, one would realize that Hamzah was their second main target after the Prophet (PBUH).

Before they went to war, they had already chosen the person in charge of assassinating Hamzah: an Abyssinian slave with extraordinary skill in spear throwing. They planned for him to kill Hamzah, his only role being to hit him with a deadly spear. They warned him not to be busy with any other preoccupation other than Hamzah, regardless of the situation on the battlefield. They promised him the excellent reward of his freedom. The slave, whose name was Wahshiy, was owned by Jubair Ibn Mut`am. Jubair's uncle had been killed in the Battle of Badr. So, Jubair said to Wahshiy, "Go out with the army and if you kill Hamzah, you will be free." Afterwards, the Quraish sent Wahshiy to Hind Bint 'Utbah, Abu Sufyaan's wife, to give him more encouragement to kill Hamzah, because she had lost her father, uncle, brother, and son and it was said that Hamzah had been behind their deaths.

This was the reason why Hind was the most enthusiastic one of all the Quraish to escalate the war. All she wanted was Hamzah's head, whatever the cost might be. She spent days before the battle pouring all her rage into Wahshiy's heart and making the plans for him. She promised him if he killed Hamzah she would give him her most precious trinkets. With her hateful fingers she held her precious pearl earrings and a number of golden necklaces around her neck and gazed at him saying, "All these are yours if you kill Hamzah."

Wahshiy's mouth watered for the offer, and his soul yearned for the battle after which he would win his freedom and cease to be a slave. In addition to all the jewelry, decorating the necks of the leading woman of the Quraish, the wife of its leader, and the daughter of its master. It was clear then that the whole war and the whole conspiracy were decisively seeking Hamzah.

The Battle of Uhud started and the two armies met. Hamzah was in the middle of the battlefield in battle dress and on his bosom he put an ostrich feather that he used to wear while fighting. He was moving everywhere cutting off the head of each polytheist he reached among the army of the Quraish, It seemed that death was at his command. Whenever he ordered it for anyone it reached him in the heart.

The Muslims were about to gain victory and the defeated army of the Quraish started to withdraw in fright, but the Muslim archers left their places on the mountain to collect the spoils of war that the Quraish had left. If they had not left their places, giving the Quraish cavalry the chance to find a way, the battle would have ended as a gigantic grave for all the Quraish, including men, women, horses, and even cattle.

The Quraish attacked the Muslims by surprise from the back and started striking them with thirsty swords. The Muslims tried to pull themselves together, picking up the weapons they had put down upon seeing the Quraish withdrawing, but the attack was too violent. When Hamzah saw what had happened, he doubled his strength and his activity. Hamzah was striking all around him while Wahshiy was observing him, waiting for the right moment. Let us hear Wahshiy himself describe the scene.

I was an Abyssinian man who used to throw the spear in an Abyssinian way that scarcely misses its target. When the armies met I searched for Hamzah till I found him in the middle of the crowd like a huge camel. He was killing every one around him with his sword. Nothing could stop him. By Allah, I prepared for him. I wanted him. I hid behind a tree so that I might attack him or he might come close to me. At that moment Sabaa'u lbn 'Abd Al-'Uzzaa approached him before me. When Hamzah glanced at him he shouted, "Come to me, you son of the one who circumcises!" and he hit him directly in the head. Then I shook my spear till I was in full control over it and threw it. The spear penetrated him from the back and came out from between his legs. He rose to reach me but could not and soon died. I came to his body and took my spear and went back to sit in the camp. I didn't want anything else to do with him. I killed him only to be free.

Let Wahshiy continue his story: When I returned to Makkah, they set me free. I stayed there till the Prophet (PBUH) entered Makkah on the Day of the Conquest. I fled to At-Taa'if. When the delegation of Al-Taa'if went to declare their conversion to Islam, I heard various people say that I should go to Syria or Yemen or any other place. While I was in such distress, a man said to me, "Woe to you! The Prophet (PBUH) never kills anyone entering his religion." I went to Allah's Prophet (PBUH) in Al- Madiinah, and the moment he first saw me I was already giving my true testimony. When he saw me he said, "Is it you, Wahshiy?" I said, "Yes, Messenger of Allah." He said, "Tell me, how did you kill Hamzah?" I told him, and when I finished he told me, "Woe to you! Get out of my sight and never show your face to me." From that time, I always avoided wherever the Prophet (PBUH) went lest he should see me, till he died.

Afterwards, when the Muslims fought Musailamah the Liar in the Battle of Al-Yamaamah, I went with them. I took with me the same spear that I had killed Hamzah with. When the armies met, I saw Musailamah standing with his sword in his hand. I prepared for him, shook my spear till I had full control over it, threw it, and it went into his body. If I killed with this spear the best of people, Hamzah, I wish that Allah may forgive me, as I killed with it the worst of people, Musailamah.

Thus the Lion of Allah and of His Messenger died as a great martyr. His death was as unusual as his life, because it was not enough for his enemies to kill him. They sacrificed all the men and money of the Quraish to a battle only seeking the Prophet (PBUH) and his uncle Hamzah.

Hind Bint 'Utbah, the wife of Abu Sufyaan, ordered Wahshiy to bring her Hamzah's liver, and he responded to her savage desire. When he returned to her, he delivered the liver to her with his right hand, while taking the necklaces with the left as a reward for the accomplished task. Hind, whose father had been killed in the Battle of Badr and whose husband was the leader of the polytheist army, chewed Hamzah's liver hoping to relieve her heart, but the liver was too tough for her teeth so she spat it out and stood up shouting her poem:

For Badr we've paid you better
In a war more flaring than the other.
I was not patient to revenge the murder of
'Utbah, my son, and my brother.
My vow's fulfilled, my heart's relieved forever.

The battle ended and the polytheists mounted their camels and led their horses back to Makkah. The Prophet (PBUH) and his Companions examined the battlefield to see the martyrs. There, in the heart of the valley, the Prophet (PBUH) was examining the faces of his Companions who had offered their souls to their Lord and had given their lives as a precious sacrifice to Him.

The Prophet (PBUH) suddenly stood up and gazed in an upset

manner at what he saw. He ground his teeth and closed his eyes. He never imagined that the Arabic moral code could be that savage so as to cut and disfigure a dead body in the dreadful way that had happened to his uncle, the Lion of Allah, Hamzah Ibn 'Abd Al-Muttalib. The Prophet (PBUH) opened his shining eyes and looked at the dead body of his uncle saying, "I will never have a worse loss in my life than yours. I have never been more outraged than I am now."

Then he turned to his Companions saying, "It is only for the sake of Safiyah [Hamzah's sister] that she should be grieved and that it should be taken as a practice after me. Otherwise, I would have ordered him to be left without burying so that he may be in the stomachs of beasts and in the craws of birds. If Allah destines me to win over the Quraish, I will cut thirty of them into pieces."

Therefore, the Companions shouted, "By Allah, if one day we conquer them, we will cut them in a way that no Arab has done before!" Allah honored Hamzah by making his death a great lesson for the Muslims to learn justice and mercy, even in situations when penalties and retaliation were justified. No sooner had the Prophet finished his threatening words, then a revelation came down to him while he was still standing in his place with the following verse: < *Call mankind to the Way of your Lord with wisdom and sound advice, and reason with them in a well mannered way. Indeed your Lord is well aware of those who have gone astray from His way, and He is well aware of those who are guided. And if you retaliate, let your retaliation be to the extent that you were afflicted, but if you are patient, it will certainly be best for those who are patient; and be patient, yet your patience is only with the help of GOD, and do not sorrow for them, not distress yourself at what they devise. Indeed GOD is with those who are pious, and those who are doers of good* > *(16:125-127).*

The revelation of these verses in this situation was the best honor for Hamzah. As stated before, the Prophet (PBUH) loved him dearly because he was not only an uncle, but also his brother by fosterage, his playmate in childhood, and the best friend in all his life.

The Prophet (PBUH) did not find any better farewell for Hamzah than praying for him among the numerous martyrs. Hamzah's body was carried to the place of prayer on the battlefield, in the same place, which had witnessed his bravery and embraced his blood. The Prophet (PBUH) and his Companions prayed for him, then they brought another martyr and put him beside Hamzah, and prayed for him. Then they took the martyr away and left Hamzah and brought the next martyr and placed him beside Hamzah and prayed for him and so on. They brought all the martyrs, one after the other and prayed for them beside Hamzah, who on that day was prayed for seventy times (the number of martyrs).

On his way from the battlefield, the Prophet (PBUH) heard the women of Bani 'Abd Al- Ashhal lamenting their martyrs and he said, "But Hamzah has no one to lament him." Sa'd lbn Mu'aadh heard this sentence and thought that the Prophet (PBUH) would be satisfied if the women would lament his uncle. He hurried to the women of Bani 'Abd Al-Ashhal and ordered them to lament .Hamzah. When the Prophet (PBUH) heard them doing this he said, "I did not mean this. Go back, may Allah have mercy on you. There will be no crying anymore." The Prophet's (PBUH) Companions began to say their eulogies for Hamzah in praise of his virtues. The poet Hassaan lbn Thaabit said in the course of a long poem:

Moan for Hamzah, the one
Who won't forget your horse which was old.

He spurs horses when away they run
Like lions in jungles. He's strong and bold,
Whiter than Haashim. He looks in the sun
Except for the night, his tongue never told
Among your swords, in was he done,
Paralyzed be the hands that Wahshiy has sold.

'Abd Allah Ibn Rawaahah also said:
I moaned, but what did moaning do for me?
When they said Hamzah the Lion was killed
Abu Ya'liy, a man with honor was filled
For your death, pillars down were pulled.

Safiyah, Hamzah's sister and the Prophet's (PBUH) aunt said:

To the happy Paradise of Allah he was invited.
Such a destiny for Hamzah was what we wanted,
I won't forget you if I stayed or departed.
I moan for a lion by whom Islam was protected.
0 brother, may Allah for what you did
Make you rewarded.

But the best words said about him were those of the Prophet (PBUH) when he first saw him among the martyrs: "May Allah have mercy on you. You were, as far as I knew, always uniting blood relations and doing all sorts of goodness."

The loss of Hamzah was great and nothing could console the Prophet (PBUH) for it. But to his surprise, Allah offered him the best consolation. When he was walking home from Uhud, he saw a woman from the Bani Diinaar whose husband, father, and brother had been killed in the battle. She asked the returning Muslim soldiers about the battle. When they told her of the death of her father, husband, and brother, she soon asked them anxiously, "What about the Prophet of Allah?" They said, "He is very well as you wish him to be." She said, "Show me, let me look at him." They stayed beside her till the Prophet (PBUH) came and when she saw him she said, "If you are safe, all other disasters will be of no importance."

Yes, this was the best condolence for the Prophet (PBUH). He smiled at this unusual situation which had no similitude in loyalty and devotion. A poor, helpless woman lost in an hour her father, brother, and husband. Her reaction to that news — which if it had fallen on a mountain would have made it collapse —was, "What about the Prophet of Allah?" It was such a well-timed situation that it is evident that Allah planned to console His Prophet (PBUH) for the death of Allah's Lion and martyr of all martyrs.

(12)
'ABD ALLAH IBN MAS'UUD
The First Reciter of Qur'aan

Before the Prophet (PBUH) entered Daar Al-Arqam, Ibn Mas'uud had declared his belief in him. He was the sixth one to embrace Islam and follow the Prophet (PBUH). Thus he was one of the early Muslims.

He narrated his first meeting with the Prophet (PBUH): I was a young shepherd boy responsible for the sheep of 'Uqbah Ibn Abu Mu'ait. The Prophet (PBUH) once came with Abu Bakr and said, "O'boy, do you have milk for us to drink?" and I said, "I can't let you drink their milk." The Prophet (PBUH) said, "Do you have a virgin sheep that has never mated with a male?" I said, "Yes" and brought it to them. The Prophet (PBUH) caught it and stroked its udder and prayed to Allah till the udder filled. Abu Bakr brought him a concave rock into which he milked the sheep. Abu Bakr drank the milk, and then after that the Prophet said to the udder, "Shrink," and it did. I went to the Prophet after this incident and said to him, "Teach me this kind of talk." The Prophet (PBUH) said, "You are already a learned boy."

'Abd Allah Ibn Mas'uud was fascinated to see the pious Servant and Messenger of Allah supplicate Allah and stroke a virgin udder till it gave milk, pure and agreeable to those who drank it. Ibn Mas'uud did not realize that what he had seen was but the least wonderful miracle and that soon he would see at the hands of that honorable Prophet other miracles that would shake the world and fill it with light and faith. He did not realize either that he himself, the poor, weak, hired shepherd boy working for 'Uqbah Ibn Abu Mu'ait, would be one of those miracles when he became, through his Islam, a strong believer capable of defeating the pride of the Quraish and overcoming the oppression of its martyrs.

Before his Islam he never dared to pass by a session attended by any Quraish nobleman except with hastened steps and a bowed head, but after Islam he was capable of going to the Ka'bah, where the elite Quraish congregated and standing among them reading the Qur'aan in a loud, beautiful, impressive voice: < *In the Name of Allah, the Most Merciful, The Most Beneficent! Has taught the Qur'aan. He created man. He taught him eloquent speech. The sun and the moon run on their fixed courses (exactly) calculated with measured out stages for each. And the herbs (or stars) and the trees both prostrate* > *(55: 1-6).*

He went on reciting while the Quraish were thunderstruck, not believing their own eyes or ears. They could not imagine that the one challenging their pride was just one of their hired shepherd boys who was the poor unknown 'Abd Allah Ibn Mas'uud. Let us hear from an eyewitness, Az-Zubair (May Allah be pleased with him), describe the exciting scene: 'Abd Allah Ibn Mas'uud was the first one to recite Qur'aan publicly in Makkah after the Prophet (PBUH). It happened one day that the Prophet's Companions were gathered with the Prophet (PBUH). They said, "By Allah, the Quraish have never heard the Qur'aan being recited to them before. Isn't there any man to recite it so that they may hear it?" Thereupon 'Abd Allah Ibn Mas'uud said, "I." They said, "We are afraid they may harm you." We want a man with a strong family to protect him from those people if they want to harm him." He said, "Let me go, Allah will protect me" Ibn Mas'uud went to the Maqaam at the Ka'bah and recited < *In the Name of Allah, the Most Beneficent, the Most Merciful, The Most Beneficent! Has taught the Qur'aan. . .* > and he went on reciting. The Quraish gazed at him and said, "What does Ibn Umm 'Abd say? He is reciting some of what Muhammad came with." They went to him and began to beat him in the face while he was reciting till he finished whatever Allah wished him to recite from the Surah. He returned to his friends with a wounded face and body, and they told him, "This is what we were afraid would happen to you." He answered them, "Those enemies of Allah have never been more worthless to me than this moment, and if you wish I will go back to them and do the same tomorrow." They said, "No, it is enough for you. You have made them hear what they hated."

Indeed, when Ibn Mas'uud was fascinated by the sheep's udder which was filled with milk before its time, he did not realize that he and his humble friends would be one of the greater miracles of the Prophet (PBUH) on the day they carried the banner of Allah, with which they outshone the sun. He did not realize that such a day was very near. Soon that day came, and the poor, hired boy became a miracle!

He was hardly seen in the crowd of life and not even seen away from that crowd because he was too humble when compared with those who possessed wealth, power, and social status. Financially, he was poor. Physically, he was feeble, and socially, he was a nobody. But Islam compensated him for his poverty with a large share of the treasures of Khosrau and Caesar. Islam also compensated him for his physical weakness, with a strong will that conquered the oppressors and helped to change the whole historical course of events. Again, Islam compensated his humble social status through immortality, knowledge, and honor that gave him an eminent place among the most prominent of historical figures.

The Prophet's prophecy about him which said, "You are a learned boy" was true. Indeed, Allah endowed him with knowledge till he became the most learned of this Ummah and the best one to know Qur'aan by heart, Ibn Mas'uud described himself saying, "I in fact took from the mouth of Allah's Messenger more than seventy Surahs of the Qur'aan. I have a better understanding of the Book of Allah than any one of you."

It could be that Allah wanted to reward him for risking his life when he used to recite Qur'aan everywhere during the years of torture. So, He the Almighty endowed him with a wonderful talent for reciting and understanding Qur'aan to the extent that made the Prophet (PBUH) direct his Companions to follow his example. The Prophet (PBUH) said, "Stick to the method of Ibn Umm'Abd." He recommended that they imitate his way of reciting and learn it from him. The Prophet (PBUH) said, "Whoever wants to hear Qur'aan as fresh as it was revealed, let him hear it from Ibn Umm 'Abd," and said, "Whoever wants to read Qur'aan as fresh as it was revealed, let him read it in the way Ibn Umm 'Abd does."

It was a pleasure for the Prophet (PBUH) to hear Qur'aan being recited from the mouth of Ibn Mas'uud. The Prophet (PBUH) once called on him and said, "Recite to me, 'Abd Allah," and 'Abd Allah said, "How can I recite to you when it was revealed to you?" The Prophet (PBUH) said, "I like to hear it from others." Thereupon Ibn Mas'uud started reading part of Surah An-Nisaa' till he reached the verse: *< How (will it be) then, when We bring from each nation a witness and We bring you as a witness against those people. On that day those who disbelieved and disobeyed the Messenger will wish that they were buried in the earth, but they will never be able to hide a single fact from Allah > (4: 41-42).* Upon hearing this, the Prophet's eyes flooded with tears and he waved to Ibn Mas'uud saying, "Enough, enough, Ibn Mas'uud."

Ibn Mas'uud himself talked proudly about Allah's bounty upon him. "By Allah, there is no Surah in the Book of Allah about which I do not know where and in what context it was revealed. I have a better understanding of the Book of Allah than you do, and if I were to know that someone had a better understanding than I and I could reach him on the back of a mule, I would definitely go to him on a camel's back, but I am not better than you are."

The Prophet's Companions witnessed this for him. The Commander of the Faithful 'Umar lbn Al-Kattaab said about him, "He was filled with knowledge." Also Abu Muusaa Al-Ash'ariy said about him, "Don't ask me about any matter as long as you have this scholar among you." He was not only praised for his knowledge of Qur'aan and jurisprudence, but also for his piety and God-consciousness. Hudhaifah said about him, "I have never seen anyone more like the Prophet(PBUH) in his way of life and characteristics than lbn Mas'uud." He also said, "The lucky Companions of the Prophet (PBUH) realized that lbn Umm 'Abd is the nearest one of them to Allah."

One day a number of Companions were gathered at the house of 'Aliy lbn Abi Taalib and said to him, "O' Commander of the Faithful, we have never seen a man who is more virtuous, more learned, more companionable, friendly, and God-fearing than 'Abd Allah lbn Mas'uud." 'Aliy said, "I beg you by Allah, is this true from your hearts?" They said, "Yes." 'Aliy said, "O' Allah, I testify in front of You that I say about him like what they said and more. He read the Qur'aan and did what is lawful in it and avoided what is forbidden. He was knowledgeable in religion and scholarly in Sunnah."

The Prophet's Companions said about him, "He was admitted to the company of the Prophet (PBUH), whereas we were detained, and he was present in his company, whereas we were absent." This means he used to have more privileges than the others. He used to enter the Prophet's house and sit with him more than anybody else. He was the one, the Prophet (PBUH) entrusted with his secrets to the extent that he was entitled "The Secretary."

Abu Muusaa Al-Ash'ariy (May Allah be pleased with him) said in this context, "I came to Allah's Messenger (PBUH) and thought that Ibn Mas'uud was among the members of his family." This means that the Prophet (PBUH) loved him dearly for his piety and intelligence. He said about him, "If I were to appoint a commander without consulting the Muslims, I would have appointed Ibn Umm 'Abd," and as mentioned before, the Prophet (PBUH) asked his Companions to "Stick to the method of Ibn Umm 'Abd."

He was so near to the Prophet (PBUH) and so trusted by him that he was given more privileges than anyone else was given. The Prophet (PBUH) told him, "My permission to you is that you may raise the curtains." This indicates his being allowed to knock at the Prophet's door at any time during the day or night. This is why the Companions said, "He was admitted to the company of the Prophet (PBUH), whereas we were detained, and he was present in his company, whereas we were absent."

He was really up to this standard. Although such a close relationship could have created some sort of intimacy, Ibn Mas'uud's attitude towards the Prophet (PBUH) was always one of respect and politeness. This was even after the Prophet's death. Although he seldom mentioned the Prophet (PBUH) after his death, in most cases when he did mention him, he began to tremble and shake, and all the signs of worry and perplexity appeared on him. This occurred whenever his lips began to murmur, "I heard the Prophet (PBUH) say..." lest he should forget or change one single letter of what was said.

Let us hear what his brothers in Islam said about such behavior. "Amr lbn Maimuun reported, "I was frequently visited by lbn Mas'uud for about a year, during which time I did not hear him speak about the Prophet (PBUH). But one day he was talking and he uttered, "The Prophet (PBUH) said. . ." At this moment he was badly troubled and started to sweat and corrected himself, "The Prophet (PBUH) said something like that."

'Alqamah lbn Qais reported, "lbn Mas'uud used to speak to people every Thursday night. I never heard him saying, "The Prophet (PBUH) said," but he once said it and he was leaning on a stick that started to shake in his hand.

Also, Masruuq narrated on the authority of 'Abd Allah, "One day lbn Mas'uud was speaking and he said, "I heard the Prophet (PBUH). . ." On this he and his clothes started to shake. Then he corrected himself, 'Something like this."

Thus the veneration of the Prophet (PBUH) in his heart was that great, and this was a sign of his intelligence. Such a man, who accompanied the Prophet (PBUH) more than anybody else, was the best to realize how great the Prophet (PBUH) was. Therefore, he maintained the same manner concerning him during his life and after his death.

lbn Mas'uud never missed the company of the Prophet (PBUH)' either while traveling or at home. He participated in all the battles, and on the Day of Badr his role was significant, especially with Abu Jahl. The Prophet's (PBUH) caliphs, were also fully aware of his proper value. The Commander of the Faithful 'Umar lbn Al-Kattaab appointed him as director of the treasury (Bait Al-Maal) in Kufa and he said to the people there, "By Allah, there is no god but He. You know that I have given you a preference over myself when I sent him to you to learn from him."

The people of Kufa liked him as they never liked anyone before him. It was a real miracle that the whole people of Kufa agreed on liking somebody because they were known to be a people of rebellion and mutiny. They hardly agreed on one kind of food, and they did not tolerate peace and tranquillity. Their love for him was so great that when the Caliph 'Uthmaan (May Allah be pleased with him) wanted to discharge him of his office, they surrounded him and said, "Stay with us and don't go. We will protect you against anything that you don't like." But Ibn Mas'uud gave them an answer that really reflected his greatness and piety. He said, "He has the right of obedience on me. There will be turbulence coming and I hate to be the first to open the door to it."

This wonderful situation discloses to us the nature of the relationship between Ibn Mas'uud and 'Uthmaan. They had an argument and a disagreement between them, which ended with the caliph cutting Ibn Mas'uud's salary from the Bait Al-Maal. In return, Ibn Mas'uud never spoke ill of the caliph. On the contrary, he used to defend him. When he heard about the attempted assassinations on 'Uthmaan, he said his famous words, "If they kill him they will not find anyone like him to succeed." Some of Ibn Mas'uud's friends said, "We never heard him uttering a bad word about 'Uthmaan."

Allah endowed Ibn Mas'uud with wisdom along with his piety. He had an insight that enabled him to see facts beyond the surface, and the capability to express such facts in an intelligent style. For example, he summarized the life of 'Umar Ibn Al-Khattaab in one concise sentence: " 'Umar's Islam was an opening, his Hijrah was a victory, and his rule was a mercy."

He once expressed the idea of the relativity of tune saying, "Your Lord does not have day or night because the light of the earth and the skies is but from the light of His face."

In another context he praised the value of work in raising the social standard of man: "I hate a man living in leisure with nothing to do, either for his worldly life or the life to come." The next is a comprehensive phrase: "The best wealth is the wealth of the soul. The best provision is right conduct. The most major of sins is lying, the most evil earning is usury, and the most evil of what can be eaten is eating up the property of orphans. Whoever excuses others, will be excused by Allah, and whoever forgives others will be forgiven by others."

That was 'Abd Allah Ibn Mas'uud, the Prophet's (PBUH) Companion, and that is but one glimpse of the heroic life he lived in the way of Allah, His Prophet and His religion. That was the man who had been as small as a bird. He was so thin and short that he was the same height as a sitting person. He had very thin legs. He once climbed a tree to pick some arak sticks for the Prophet (PBUH), and when the Companions saw how thin his legs were they laughed. The Prophet (PBUH) said, "Are you laughing at Ibn Mas'uud's legs? On Allah's scales of justice they are heavier than the mountain of Uhud." Indeed that was the poor, weak hired boy who became by faith an Imam (leader) guiding people to the light.

It was Allah's bounty on him that he was counted among the first ten Companions of the Prophet (PBUH) who were promised to enter Paradise while they were still alive. He participated in all the victorious wars with the Prophet (PBUH) and his caliphs. He witnessed how the two greatest empires opened their gates in submission to the banners of Islam. He saw the high positions and lucrative money pouring into the hands of the Muslims, but his mind was never obsessed by such matters. Instead, he was pre-occupied with how to fulfil the pledge he offered to the Prophet (PBUH), and he was also never tempted to give up the life of humbleness and self denial that he used to lead. He had only one wish that he dreamed all his life might come true.

Let us hear him speaking about it: While I was with the Prophet (PBUH) at the Battle of Tabuuk, I woke up at midnight to see a flame of fire near the place of the army. I followed it and found the Prophet (PBUH), Abu Bakr and 'Umar digging a grave to bury 'Abd Allah Dhul Bijaadain Al-Muzaniy, who died at the time. The Prophet (PBUH) was in the grave and asked Abu Bakr and 'Umar, "hand your brother to me," and they did. After he put his body in the grave he said, "O' Allah, in this night I am fully satisfied and pleased with him. So be You pleased with him." I wished I was the one being buried in that hole.

This was his sole wish in his life. It was not related to what people were racing at in this life, such as wealth, social status or glory. It was the wish of a man who possessed a kind heart, a noble soul, and a strong faith. Such a man was guided by Allah, educated by the Prophet (PBUH), and enlightened by Qur'aan.

(13)
HUDHAIFAH IBN AL-YAMMAAN
The Enemy of Hypocrisy, The Friend of Frankness

The people of Madaa'in came out in great numbers to welcome their new governor chosen by their Caliph 'Umar (May Allah be pleased with him). They came out preceded by their interest in that graceful Companion. They had heard much about his good conduct, his piety, and more so about his great achievement in the conquest of Iraq.

While they were waiting for the coming procession, they saw before them a bright fellow riding on a donkey with an old saddle. The man was riding with his legs hanging and holding a loaf of bread and some salt in his hands, and eating and chewing his food. When he came in the midst of the people and they discovered he was Hudhaifah Ibn Al-Yammaan, the expected governor, they were about to lose their wits! But why the surprise? Who did they expect the choice of 'Umar would be? In fact, they were not to blame. Their countries had not been accustomed since Persian days or even before to having rulers of with such graceful style.

Hudhaifah was surrounded and welcomed by numerous people. When he saw that they were gazing at him as if expecting a speech, he looked at them closely and said, "Beware of sedition!" They asked, "What is sedition, Abu 'Abd Allah?" "The gates of rulers," he said. "When one of you is admitted to the presence of the ruler or governor and falsely agrees with what he says and commends him for what he has not done."

It was a wonderful start, as much as it was surprising. People at once remembered what they had heard about their new governor and that he did not detest anything in the whole world as much as he detested and scorned hypocrisy. Such a beginning was the truest expression concerning the character of the new governor and his way of ruling and governing.

As a matter of fact, Hudhaifah Ibn Al-Yammaan was a man who came to life equipped with a unique characteristic in detesting hypocrisy and in having the remarkable capability to detect it in its distant, concealed places. He and his brother Safwaan came to the Prophet (PBUH) accompanied by their father and all embraced Islam. He added more sharpness and polish to his inborn qualities from the time he embraced a powerful, clean, brave, and straightforward religion which scorns cowardice, hypocrisy, and lies.

Moreover, he learnt his manners at the hands of the Messenger (PBUH) who was as clear as the glorious morning light. Nothing was hidden in his life nor in his inner self. He was truthful and trustworthy. He liked the strong in righteousness and detested those who were not straightforward, i.e. the hypocrites and deceivers. Therefore, there was no realm where his talent could bloom and blossom more than it did under the guidance of faith, at the hands of the Messenger and among that generation of his great Companions.

Verily, his talent grew and developed, and he specialized in reading faces and probing into the inner selves. At a glance he could easily read faces and know the secret of the hidden depths and concealed inner mysteries. He attained what he wanted in that realm to the extent that the inspired, intelligent, and resourceful Caliph 'Umar (May Allah be pleased with him) used to ask Hudhaifah's opinion and insight in selecting and knowing men.

Hudhaifah possessed the discretion that made him realize that what is good in this world is obvious to whoever seeks it, and that evil is the thing that is disguised and hidden. Therefore, the intelligent person should be discreet in studying evil in its hidden and apparent forms.

Hudhaifah (May Allah be pleased with him) therefore devoted his time to the study of evil and evil doers, as well as hypocrisy and hypocrites. He reported: "People used to ask Allah's Prophet (PBUH) about good, but I used to ask him about evil, for fear that it should overtake me." I said, "O' Messenger of Allah, we were in ignorant and evil times, then Allah presented us with this good. Will there be evil after this good?" He said, "Yes." I said, "And after this evil, will there be good?" He said, "Yes but it would be tainted with evil (literally, smoke)." I asked, "What will this evil be?" He said, "There will be some people who will lead (people) according to principles other than my tradition. You will see their actions and disapprove of them." I said, "Will there be any evil after that good?" He said, "Yes, there will be some people who will invite others to the doors of Hell, and whoever accepts their invitation to it will be thrown in it (by them)." I said, "O Messenger of Allah! Describe those people to us." He said, "They will belong to us and speak our language." I asked, "What do you order me to do if such a thing should take place in my life?" He said, "Adhere to the group of Muslims and their chief." I asked, "If there is neither a group (of Muslims) nor a chief, what shall I do?" He said, "Keep away from all those different sects, even if you have to eat the roots of a tree, till you meet Allah while you are still in that state."

Note his statement, "People used to ask Allah's Prophet (PBUH) about good, but I used to ask him about evil, for fear that it should overtake me." Hudhaifah lbn Al-Yammaan lived open- eyed and insightful with regards to temptations and the paths of evil so that he might avoid them and warn people of them. This gave him insight of the world, experience with people, and knowledge of the times. He would contemplate matters in his mind as a philosopher would and with the sound judgment of a wise man.

He said (May Allah be pleased with him): " Almighty Allah sent Muhammad (PBUH) to call people from misguidance to the right path, and from disbelief to belief in Allah. Some responded to his call, following the right way. Those who were dead were raised to life and those who were alive died because of their evil doing. When the period of Prophethood was over, caliphates followed the same methods. Then there appeared a detested monarchy. There were people who disavowed with their hearts, hands, and tongues, and who responded to the path of justice. There were those who disavowed with their hearts and tongues but abstained from using their hands. Thus they left out an area of justice. There were also those who disavowed with their hearts, abstaining to use their hands or tongues. Thus they left out two areas of justice. There were those who did not disavow, neither with their hearts, nor with their hands or tongues, and those were the dead in life!

He talked about hearts and a life of guidance or misguidance according to the heart. He said: There are four kinds of hearts: a locked heart, which is the heart of the disbeliever; a duplicitous heart, which is the heart of the hypocrite; a pure heart full of light, which is the heart of the believer; and a heart filled with hypocrisy and faith. Its faith is like a tree supplied with good water, but like hypocrisy because it is like an ulcer filled with pus and blood. Whichever is made will win.

Hudhaifah's experience of evil and his persistence in resisting and challenging it sharpened his tongue and words. He himself informed us about this in a noble Hadith: I approached the Prophet (PBUH) and said, "O Messenger of Allah, I have an abusing tongue towards my people, and I am afraid it might lead me to the fire of Hell." The Prophet (PBUH) said to me, "Do you ask Allah's forgiveness? I repent to Allah a hundred times a day."

That was Hudhaifah, the enemy of hyprocrisy and the friend of frankness. For a man of this character, his faith had to be strong and his loyalty intense. That was Hudhaifah's way, in respect to faith and loyalty. He witnessed his father die as a Muslim in the battle of Uhud, killed in error by Muslim hands, mistaking him for one of the unbelievers.

Hudhaifah was looking around when by chance he saw the swords hitting him, so he called to his attackers, "My father! My father! He's my father!" But it was too late. When the Muslims heard about this incident they were grieved, but Hudhaifah looked at them with mercy and forgiveness and said, "May Allah forgive you. He is the Most Merciful." He then went forward with his sword towards the raging battle, doing his best and performing his duty.

When the battle ended and the Prophet (PBUH) heard the news, he ordered that blood money be paid for the death of Hudhaifah's father, Husail Ibnm Jaabir (May Allah be pleased with him). Hudhaifah refused to take the money and gave it as alms to the Muslims, an act which made the Prophet (PBUH) love and appreciate him even more.

Hudhaifah's faith and loyalty refused to acknowledge inability and weakness, or even the impossible. In the Battle of Al-Khandaq and after the failure of the unbelievers of the Quraish and their Jewish allies, the Prophet (PBUH) wanted to know the latest developments in the enemy camp.

The night was black and terrifying, and a storm was raging as if it wanted to uproot the solid mountains of the desert. The whole situation, which included a siege, stubbornness and perseverance -brought about fear and anxiety. In addition, hunger had reached a high level among the Companions of the Prophet. Therefore, who would have the strength to go amidst the dark dangers of the enemy camp and penetrate it to gather intelligence and news?

The Prophet (PBUH) was the one who selected him from among his Companions as the one to perform such a difficult task. Who was that hero? It was Hudhaifah Ibn Al-Yammaan. The Prophet (PBUH) asked him and he obeyed.

He admitted with great candor in relating the incident that he had no choice but to obey, thus implying that he feared the mission being assigned to him. He was afraid of its consequences. His fear was due to performing this mission under the pinch of hunger, cold weather, and extreme exhaustion that resulted from the siege by the disbelievers that had lasted a month or more.

What happened to Hudhaifah that night was amazing. He covered the distance between the two armies and penetrated the surrounding enemy camp of the Quraish. A violent wind had put out the camp's fires, so the place was enveloped in darkness. Hudhaifah took his place amidst the lines of the fighters. The leader of the Quraish, Abu Sufyaan, was afraid that darkness might surprise them with scouts from the Muslim camp. He stood to warn his army, and Hudhaifah heard his loud voice saying, "O people of the Quraish, each one of you should know who is sitting next to him and should know his name."

Hudhaifah reports, "I hastened to the hand of the man next to me, and said to him, 'Who are you?' He said, 'Such and such a person!' "

He therefore secured his being with the army in peace! Abu Sufyaan resumed his talk to the army, saying, "O people of the Quraish, by Allah, you are not in a place to settle. The horses and the camels are exhausted. The tribe of Bani Quraidah has reneged on us and we learnt about them what we hate, and we suffer from the violent wind as you see. No food can be cooked, no fire can blaze for us, and no structure can hold. You have to leave, for I am leaving." He then mounted his camel and started moving, followed by the fighters.

Hudhaifah said, "But for the promise I gave Allah's Messenger(PBUH), who asked me not to do anything until I returned to him, I would have killed him with an arrow," Hudhaifah then returned to the Messenger (PBUH) and gave him the information and happy news.

Whoever saw Hudhaifah and considered his way of thinking, his philosophy, and his devotion to knowledge could hardly expect any heroism from him in the battlefield. Nevertheless, Hudhaifah contradicted all expectations.

The man who used to worship Allah in solitude, the contemplative one, no sooner did he carry his sword and meet the ignorant pagan army than he disclosed a genius that caught the eyes. Suffice it to know that he was one of only three or five who had the great privilege of invading all the cities of Iraq. In Hamdaan, Ar-Raiy Ad-Dainawar, the conquest was accomplished through him.

In the great Battle of Nahaawand, in which the Persians gathered about 150,000 fighters, Caliph 'Umar, the Commander of the Faithful, chose for the leadership of the Muslim armies An-Nu'maan Ibn Muqrin. Then wrote to Hudhaifah to march to him leading an army from Kufa.

'Umar sent his letter to the fighters, saying, "When the Muslims gather, let every commander lead his army, and let An- Nu'maan Ibn Muqrin be the commander-in-chief of all the armies. If An-Nu'maan is martyred, let Hudhaifah be the leader. If he is martyred, let Jarir Ibn 'Abd Allah lead them."

In this way, the Commander of the Faithful went on choosing the leaders of the battle till he named seven of them. Then the two armies met.

The Persians were 150,000, while the Muslims were only 30,000. A battle, which exceeded all others, commenced. It was the fiercest in history, in terms of violence and heroism. The leader of the Muslim army, An-Nu'maan Ibn Muqrin fell in the battle and was martyred, but before the standard of the Muslims fell to the ground, the new leader caught it with his right hand, and with it he led the wind of victory with vigor and great heroism. This leader was none but Hudhaifah Ibn Al-Yammaan.

At once he held the standard and chose not to announce the news of the death of An-Nu'maan until the battle was over. He called Na'iim Ibn Muqrin to be in the place of his brother to honor him.

How he achieved all this in no time, in the heart of the great battle, was through his bright intuition. Then he turned like a violent tempest wind towards the Persian lines shouting, "Allahu akbar! Allah is the greatest! His Promise is fulfilled! Allahu akbar! He led His soldiers to victory!" Then he turned the head of his horse towards the fighters of his army and called, "O' you followers of Muhammad (PBUH), here are Allah's Gardens ready to receive you, do not let them wait long. Come on, men of the Battle of Badr ! Proceed, O' you heroes of the Battle of Al-Khandaq, Uhud, and Tabuuk!"

Hudhaifah kept all the enthusiasm and interest of the battle, if not more. The fighting ended in overwhelming defeat for the Persians, an unmatched defeat!

That was his genius in wisdom when he remained in his rooms and genius in fighting when he stood on the battlefield. He was also a genius in each mission assigned to him and each advice asked of him.

When Sa'd Ibn Abi Waqqaas and the Muslims with him moved from Madaa'in to Kufa and settled there after the great harm that had afflicted the Muslim Arabs due to Madaa'in's climate, 'Umar wrote to Sa'd to leave at once, after the most suitable sites for Muslims to resettle were found. Who was deputed, to choose the site and the place? It was Hudhaifah Ibn Al Yammaan, accompanied by Salmaan Ibn Ziyaad who sought a suitable place for Muslims.

When they reached the land of Kufa, it was a barren, sandy land, full of pebbles, but Hudhaifah smelled the breezes of healing and health. He said to his companion, "This place, Allah willing." That was how Kufa was planned, and the hands of construction turned it into an inhabited city. As soon as the Muslims emigrated there, their sick were cured, their weak became strong, and their veins were filled with the pulse of health.

Hudhaifah was very intelligent and had various experiences. He always used to say to the Muslims, "Your best are not those who neglect this world for the last, nor those who neglect the last for this world. The best are those who take from this and that."

One day in the year A.H. 36, he was called to meet his Lord. While he was getting ready for the last journey, some of his companions came to see him. He asked them, "Have you brought a shroud with you?" They said, "Yes." He said, "Show it to me." When he saw it, he found it was new and too long. One last sarcastic grin was drawn on his lips, and he said, "This is not a shroud for me. Two white wraps without a shirt are sufficient for me. I will not be left in the grave for a long time, but will be offered a better place or a worse one!"

He then murmured a few words which, when they listened to them, they discerned the following: "Welcome O' death! A dear thing coming after longing. The one who repents now prospers not."

One of the best human souls was raised to Allah, one the most pious, illuminating, and humble spirits.

(14)
'AMMAAR IBN YAASIR
A Man of Paradise!

If there were people born in Paradise, reared and brought to maturity there, and then brought to earth to adorn and enlighten it, then 'Ammaar, his mother Sumaiyah and his father Yaasir would be of them!

But why do we say "if" and why do we make that condition when Yaasir's family were really of Paradise? Allah's Messenger (PBUH) was not merely pacifying them when he said, "Patience, O' Yaasir's family. Verily, your meeting place will be in Paradise." He was declaring a fact, which he knew and reiterating an actuality perceived by him.

'Ammaar's father, Yaasir lbn 'Aamir, left his native place in Yemen seeking a brother of his. In Makkah he found an appealing place, so he settled there and was in alliance wit Abu Hudhaifah lbn AI-Mughirah, who married him to one of his slave women, Sumaiyah Bint Khaiyaat. Out of this blessed marriage Allah granted the parents a son, 'Ammaar. Their embracing of Islam was early, like that of the righteous ones guided by Allah. And like the early righteous Muslims as well, they had their good share of the Quraish's persecution and terror.

The Quraish used to waylay the believers to attack them. If the believers were among the honorable and noble people in their community, the Quraish would pursue them with threats and menace. Abu Jahl would meet one of the believers and tell him, " You abandoned your forefathers' religion and they were better than you. We will spoil your character, degrade your honor, reduce your trade, and exhaust your money." They would then launch a heated war of nerves upon him.

If the believers were among the weak, poor, or slaves of Makkah, then the Quraish would burn them with the fire of persecution.

Yaasir's family belonged to that class. The order for their persecution was handed to Bani Makhzuum. They used to take them all — Yaasir, Sumaiyah and 'Ammaar — to the burning desert of Makkah, where they would pour upon them different kinds of the hell of torture.

Sumaiyah's share of that torment was colossal and terrible. We shall not elaborate about her now, since we shall have-Allah willing- another encounter with her and her likes during those immortal days to talk about the grace of sacrifice and the glory of her firmness. Suffice it to mention now, without any exaggeration, that Sumaiyah, the martyred one, maintained a firm stance that day which gives the whole of humanity an everlasting honor and an ever glorious dignity. Her stance made of her a great mother to believers in all ages, and to the honorable people of all times.

The Messenger (PBUH) used to go where he knew Yaasir's family were tortured. He did not have at that time any means of resistance or keeping harm from them. This was Allah's will, because the new faith-the faith of Ibraahiim Al-Haniifan (Abraham the true)-which was revealed to Muhammad was not a casual and passing reform movement. It was a way of life for the whole humanity of believers who had to inherit along with the religion all its history of heroism, sacrifices, and risks. These abundant noble sacrifices are the cement and the foundation that grant an everlasting firmness and immortality to the faith and the creed. It is the fragrance that fills the hearts of believers with loyalty, joy, and happiness. It is the lighthouse that guides the coming generations to the reality of religion, to its truth and greatness.

Therefore, Islam had to make its sacrifices and have its victims, the meaning of which is illustrated and illuminated in more than one verse of the Qur'aan for the Muslims. Allah says: *<Do the people think that they will be left to say: "We believe", and they shall not be tried?" > (29: 2).*

<Do you think that you will enter Paradise before Allah tests those of you who fought (in His Cause) and (also) tests those who remained patient? > (3: 142).

<And we indeed tested those who were before them. And Allah will certainly make (it) known (the truth of) those who are true, and will certainly make (it) known (the falsehood of) those who are liars, (although Allah knows all that before putting them to test) > (29:3).

<Do you think you shall be left alone while Allah has not yet tested those among you who have striven hard. ..> (9:16).

<Allah will not leave the believers in the state in which you are now, until He distinguishes the wicked from the good.~> (3 : 179).

<And what you suffered (of the disaster) on the day (of the Battle of Uhud when) the two armies met, was by the leave of Allah, in order that He might test the believers > (3 : 166).

That is true. This was the way the Qur'aan taught its bearers and descendants that sacrifice is the essence of faith and that resistance of unjust, oppressive challenges is through firmness, patience, and persistence, which form the best and the most superb virtues of faith.

Therefore, this religion of Allah, when it was laying down its foundation, establishing its principles, and giving its models and examples, had to support and purify itself with sacrifice. In carrying out this great mission, a number of its disciples, supporters, and righteous people were chosen to be lofty models and elevated examples for the coming believers.

Sumaiyah, Yaasir and 'Ammaar were of this great and blessed group, chosen by Islam's destiny to make of their sacrifices, firmness, and persistence a document of Islam's greatness and immortality.

We said that Allah's Messenger (PBUH) used to go out every day to Yaasir's family, commending their fortitude and heroism. His big heart was melting out of mercy and kindness to see them so severely tortured. One day while he was looking for them, 'Ammaar called to him, "O' Messenger of Allah, we are suffering from extreme torment." The Messenger called to him saying, "Patience, Abu Yaqdhaan, patience O' Yaasir's family. Verily, your meeting place will be in Paradise."

'Ammaar's companions described the torture that was inflicted upon him in many of their reports. 'Amr Ibn Al-Hakam, for instance, said, '"Ammaar used to be tortured so much that he would not be aware of what he was saying." 'Amr Ibn Maimuun said, "The polytheists scorched 'Ammaar Ibn Yaasir with fire, and Allah's Messenger (PBUH) used to pass by him, pass his hand over Yaasir's head and say, "O' fire, be cool and peaceful on 'Ammaar, as you were cool and peaceful on Ibraahiim."

Despite that overwhelming terror, it did not vanquish

'Ammaar's spirit, though it overburdened his back and strained his strength.

'Ammaar did not feel utterly ruined except on that day when his executioners employed all their devilry in crime and injustice. They burned his skin with fire, laid him on the heated sands of the desert under the burning stones, ducked him in water until he could hardly breathe and until his wounds and gashes were skinned. On that day, when he fell unconscious under the effect of that horror, they said to him, "Say something good about our gods." They kept saying things, which he repeated without being conscious of what he was saying.

When he became slightly conscious after he had fainted due to their torture, he remembered what he had said and was mad about it. This slip became so concrete to him that he saw it as an unforgivable sin, which could not be atoned for. In a few moments his feeling of guilt made him suffer so much that the torture of the polytheists seemed to him a blessing and a balm.

If he had been left to such feelings for a few hours, they would have destroyed him. He was enduring the dreadful anguish of the body because his spirit was lofty, but now when he thought defeat had reached his spirit, he was overburdened with worries and fear of death and destruction. But Almighty Allah willed that the final, exciting scene would come to its dignified end. An angel stretched out its blessed right hand, shook the hand of 'Ammaar and called to him, "Get up, O' hero! There is no blame or embarrassment for you."

When Allah's Messenger (PBUH) met him, he found him crying. He kept wiping his tears and telling 'Ammaar, 'The polytheists took you, ducked your head in water, and you said such and such a thing?" 'Ammaar answered him, still crying,

"Yes, O' Messenger of Allah." Allah's Messenger (PBUH) said then while smiling, "If they repeat it, say the same thing." Then he recited the glorious Qur'aanic verse: <... *except him who is forced thereto and whose heart is at rest with Faith.* > *(16: 106)*

'Ammaar's tranquility was restored, he no longer felt pain when they punished him, and he no longer cared about it. His spirit conquered and his faith conquered. The Qur'aan had included this blessed transaction, so whatever happened, happened.

'Ammaar remained steadfast until his tormenters were exhausted and they retreated, yielding to his determination.

The Muslims settled in Al-Madiinah after the Hijrah of their Messenger (PBUH). The Islamic community there began to take shape very fast and complete itself. Within that group of believers, 'Ammaar was allocated a dignified position. Allah's Messenger loved him greatly and used to boast among his Companions about 'Ammaar's faith and guidance. He said about him, "Verily, 'Ammaar is filled to the bones with faith."

When a slight misunderstanding happened between Khaalid Ibn Al-Waliid and 'Ammaar, the Messenger (PBUH) said, "Whoever antagonizes 'Ammaar is antagonized by Allah, and whoever detests 'Ammaar is detested by Allah," Thereupon, Khaalid Ibn Al-Waliid, Islam's hero, had to hasten to 'Ammaar, apologizing to him and hoping for his sincere forgiveness.

When the Messenger (PBUH) and his Companions were building the mosque in Al-Madiinah, after their arrival there, Imam 'Aliy (May Allah glorify his face) composed a song and kept on repeating it with other Muslims, saying:

He who frequents the mosques,

Remaining there standing and sitting,
Is not equal to the one who keeps away from dust.

'Ammaar was working at the site of the mosque, so he kept repeating the song, raising his voice. One of his companions thought that 'Ammaar was disparaging him. He therefore said some angry words, which angered the Messenger of Allah, and he said, "What is their business with 'Ammaar? He calls them to Heaven and they call him to Hell. To me, 'Ammaar is but a skin between my eyes and my nose

When the Messenger of Allah loves a man that much, this man's faith, his accomplishment, his loyalty, his grace, his conscience, and manner have reached the top and ended at the pinnacle of allowed perfection.

That was 'Ammaar. Allah had granted him abundant blessings and guidance. In the level of guidance and certitude, he reached a great height, which made the Messenger (PBUH) commend his faith and raise him among the Companions as a model and an example. Saying, "Take the examples of the two succeeding me, Abu Bakr and 'Umar, and follow the guidance of "Ammaar." The narrators described him, saying, "He was tall, with bluish-black eyes, broad shouldered, among the most silent of the people and the least talkative."

How did the life of that giant proceed, the silent, bluish-black eyed, broad-shouldered man whose body bore the scars of the horrible torture and, at the same time, the document of his amazing steadfastness and his extraordinary greatness? How did the life of that loyal disciple, the true believer, the overawing sacrificer proceed?

He witnessed with his tutor and messenger all the battles: Badr,

Uhud, Al-Khandaq and Tabuuk and others. When the Messenger of Allah (PBUH) passed away, the outstanding Companion continued his march. At the meeting of Muslims with Persians, with Romans, and, before that, at their meeting with the army of apostates, 'Ammaar was always there in the first line, an honest, brave soldier who did not miss an opportunity.

He was a pious believer. No desire would take him away from Allah. When the Commander of the Faithful 'Umar Ibn Al-Khattaab chose governors for the Muslims meticulously and with reservation, his eyes usually fell on 'Ammaar Ibn Yaasir in complete trust. That was how he hastened to him and made him the governor of Kufa, and made Ibn Mas'uud in charge with him of its treasury (Bait Al-Maal). He then wrote to the people of Kufa heralding the new governor and said, "I send you 'Ammaar Ibn Yaasir as a governor, and Ibn Mas'uud as a teacher and a minister. They are of the distinguished people of Muhammad's Companions, and of the people of Badr."

During his rule, 'Ammaar followed a way which was hard for worldly people to endure, so that they turned against him, or were about to. His rule made him more modest, more pious, and more ascetic.

One of his contemporaries in Kufa, Ibn Abi Hudhail said about him, "I saw 'Ammaar Ibn Yaasir when he was the governor of Kufa buying some vegetables. He tied them with a rope and carried them on his shoulders and went home."

One of the public said to him when he was the governor of Kufa, "O' you whose ear is cut off." He was scorning him because of his ear, which had been cut off by the swords of the apostates during the Yamaamah War. The governor, in whose hands was the power of rule, merely said to his insulter, "You insulted the best part of my ear. It was injured in the cause of Allah."

It is true. It was injured in the cause of Allah on the Day of Yamaamah, which was one of 'Ammaar's glorious days. This giant set out in stormy courage to annihilate the soldiers in the army of Musailamah the Liar, offering death and destruction. When he perceived a lack of enthusiasm among the Muslims, he sent his quaking shouts, which pushed them as shot arrows.

'Abd Allah Ibn 'Umar (May Allah be pleased with him) reported: I saw 'Ammaar Ibn Yaasir on the Day of Yamaamah on a rock shouting, "O' you Muslim people, are you running away from Paradise? I am 'Ammaar Ibn Yaasir, come to me." When I looked at him, I found his ear cut off and swinging while he was fighting fiercely.

If there is anyone who has his doubts concerning Muhammad (PBUH), the truthful Messenger and the perfect teacher, let him halt in front of these examples of his disciples and Companions and ask himself, "Is it possible for anyone to produce that refined style except a noble messenger and a great teacher?" If they were involved in a fight for Allah's cause, they hastened as if they were looking for death, not only for victory. If they were caliphs and rulers, the caliph went himself to milk the orphans' sheep and make their bread, as Abu Bakr and "Umar did. If they were governors, they carried their food on their backs, tied with a rope, as 'Ammaar did, or gave up their pay and set to making baskets and vessels out of plaited palm leaves, as Salmaan did . Should we not bow in salutation and respect to the faith that produced them and to the Messenger who raised them, and before all that to Almighty Allah Who chose them for that, guided them to it, and made them pioneers to the best nation of people on earth?

Hudhaifah lbn Al-Yammaan, the expert in the inner language, the language of the heart, was preparing to meet Allah and suffering from the agony of death when his companions surrounding him asked, "To whom should we go, if people differ?" Hudhaifah answered in his last words, "You should turn to lbn Sumaiyah because he will not part from truth until death."

Yes, 'Ammaar would turn with the truth wherever it went. Now while we trace his blessed direction and follow the landmarks of his great life, let us approach a momentous scene. But before watching that grand and graceful scene in its glory and perfection, in its sincerity and persistence, let us watch another scene preceding, foreshadowing, and preparing for it.

That scene was following the Muslims' settlement in Al-Madiinah. The honest Messenger (PBUH) rose, surrounded by his righteous Companions, with unkempt hair and full of dust. They were establishing Allah's house and building His mosque. Their faithful hearts were filled with joy, glowed with delight, and murmured their thanks to Allah.

All were working in happiness and hope, carrying stone, mixing mortar, and erecting the building. There was a team here, another team over there. The happy horizon echoed the singing with which they raised with overjoyed voices: "If we stayed while the Prophet worked, it would be misguided work of ours." They sang in that manner, then their voices were raised in another song: "O' Allah, living is but in the next world, then have mercy on the Ansaar and the Muhaajiruun!" Then a third song was raised:

He who frequents the mosques,
Remaining there standing and sitting,
Is not equal to the one who keeps away from dust.

They were cells working, Allah's soldiers, carrying His banner and erecting His building. The honest and kind Messenger was with them, carrying the heaviest of the stones and performing the hardest work. Their singing voices reflected the delight of their satisfied souls. Heaven above them filled the earth that bore them with delight, and bright life was witnessing its best celebrations.

'Ammaar lbn Yaasir was there amidst the celebration, carrying the heavy stones from their quarries to their positions. When the guided mercy, Muhammad 'the Messenger of Allah saw him, he sympathized greatly with him. He approached him and removed the dust from his head with his kind hand. With looks filled with the light of Allah, he contemplated his innocent, faithful face and said in front of all the Companions. "Alas for lbn Sumaiyah, killed by the tyrant group."

The foretelling was repeated once again when a wall 'Ammaar was working beneath fell, and some brethren believed he was dead. "They went to offer condolences to the Messenger (PBUH), and the Companions were shocked by the news, but the Messenger (PBUH) said reassuringly and confidently, "'Ammaar is not dead. The tyrant party will kill 'Ammaar."

Who was this party? And where? When?

'Ammaar listened to the prophecy in a way that showed he knew the great Messenger's truth of perception. Yet, he was not horrified. Since becoming a Muslim he had been expecting death and martyrdom every moment of the day and night.

Days and years passed. The Messenger (PBUH) went to the Supreme Companion, followed by Abu Bakr and then 'Umar (May Allah be pleased with them). 'Uthmaan lbn 'Affaan, "The

Man of Two Lights", became caliph. Conspiracies against Islam were doing their best, trying to gain by treachery and sedition what they lost in war. 'Umar's death was the first success achieved by these conspiracies blowing on Al-Madiinah as a breeze of poison from those countries, whose sovereignty and thrones Islam had destroyed. They were tempted by 'Umar's martyrdom to continue their efforts, so they followed and awakened seditions in most Islamic countries.

In addition, 'Uthmaan might not have given the matter the attention, care, and response it deserved, so the incident happened and 'Uthmaan was martyred and the doors of seditions were opened on the Muslims. Mu'aawiyah started fighting the new caliph, 'Aliy (May Allah glorify his face) for his right in the matter and for the caliphate. The Companions had different stances. Some of them washed their hands of the whole matter and went home, making lbn 'Umar's words their motto :

> To the one who says, "Come to prayer," I will respond. To the one who says, "Come to success," I will respond. But to the one who says, "Come to kill your Muslim brother and to take his money," I will say, "No."

Some Muslims were partial to Mu'aawiyah, others were partial to 'Aliy, the one who demanded the pledge of allegiance to him as the Muslims' caliph. Where do you think 'Ammaar would stand? Where should he stand, the man about whom the Messenger of Allah said, "Follow the guidance of 'Ammaar," and, 'Whoever antagonizes 'Ammaar, will be antagonized by Allah"?

The man who, if he approached the house of Allah's Messenger (PBUH), the latter would say, "Welcome the good-scented, kind man, allow him to come in"?

He stood by 'Aliy Ibn Abi Taalib, not as a prejudiced, biased person, but as one complying with the truth and keeping his promise. 'Ally was the Caliph of the Muslims and had the pledge of allegiance to be its leader (Imam). He took the caliphate and he was worthy of it. Above all, 'Aliy had the qualities that made his place to the Messenger of Allah as that of Haaruun (Aaron) to Muusaa (Moses).

'Ammaar, who always turned towards the truth wherever it was to enlighten his insight and loyalty to the possessor of truth in that fight, turned to 'Aliy on that day and stood by him. 'Aliy (May Allah be pleased with him) was overjoyed with 'Ammaar's pledge and trusted that he was right in his demand because the great man of truth, 'Ammaar Ibn Yaasir, approached and went with him.

The terrible Day of Siffiin arrived. Imam 'Aliy came out to face the serious rebellion which he felt he had to curb. 'Ammaar came out with him, and he was 93 years old then. Imagine a man of 93 going to fight! It is true, as long as he believed that fighting was his responsibility and duty. In fact, he fought more strongly and better than a man of 30. He was the man who was constantly silent, who spoke little. When he moved his lips, he moved them to supplicate, "I seek Allah's protection from sedition. I seek Allah's protection from sedition."

And after the passing away of the Messenger of Allah, these words remained his constant supplication. As days passed, he used to seek Allah's protection more, as if his pure heart felt the coming danger as the days went on. When it did happen and the sedition occurred, Ibn Sumaiyah knew his place, so he stood in Siffiin carrying his sword, a man of 93 to support a right, which he believed should be supported.

He declared his opinion about that fighting: O' people, let us be directed to the people who claim they are avenging 'Uthmaan. By Allah, their intention is not revenge, but they have tasted worldly things and are pleased with them. They know that truth keeps them away from what they enjoy of lust and their world. Those people had no precedent in the past to keep Muslims in obedience to them or in their support. Their hearts have not felt awe towards Allah to force them to follow the truth. They deceive the people by claiming they are avenging 'Uthmaan's death. They seek nothing but to be tyrants and kings."

He then took the standard in his hand, raised it high and fluttering above their heads and shouted, "By Allah in Whose hands my soul lies, I fought with this standard with the Messenger of Allah, and here I am fighting with it today. By Allah, if they defeat us until they reach the palm trees of Hajar, I would still believe we are in the right and they are following the wrong." People followed 'Ammaar and trusted his words.

'Abu 'Abd Ar-Rahman As-Sulamiy reported: "We witnessed with 'Aliy (May Allah be pleased with him) the Battle of Siffiin, and I saw 'Ammaar (May Allah be pleased with him) not taking one turn nor one of its valleys but the Companions of Muhammad (PBUH) would follow him as if he were their standard!"

When 'Ammaar was engaged in the battle he knew he was one of its martyrs. The Messenger's prophecy was illuminated in big letters in front of his eyes, "The tyrant party will kill 'Ammaar." For that reason his voice was ringing over the horizon of the battle with the following tune, 'Today, I meet the dear ones, Muhammad and his Companions." He would then rush like a high arrow towards Mu'aawiyah's position and surround him, singing loudly:

We hit you at its first revelation,
Now we hit you again for its interpretation;
A hitting that removes respect from one's eyes,
And distracts the lover from his lass,
Or restores the right to its own place.

He meant by this that the former Companions of the Messenger (PBUH)-'Ammaar was one of them- had fought Umayyids in the past who were headed by Abu Sufyaan bearing the standard of polytheism and leading its army. They had fought them in the past as the glorious Qur'aan was openly commanding Muslims to fight disbelievers. As for today, even though they were Muslims and were not openly commanded by the Qur'aan to fight them, yet 'Ammaar's search for truth and his comprehension of the aims and goals of the Qur'aan persuaded them to fight so that the usurped right would be restored to its people and the fire of rebellion and sedition would be extinguished once and for all. It also signified that in the past they fought Umayyids for their disbelief in faith and in the Qur'aan. Today they were fighting them for deviating from faitl and their turning away from the Qur'aan, their wrong interpretation and explanation, and their attempts to alter its verses and meaning to their aims and greedy wishes.

This man of 93 was involved in the last battle of his noble and brave life. He was giving the last lesson about perseverance in truth, and bequeathing to life the last of his great, honest, and edifying attitudes.

Mu'aawiyah's men attempted to avoid 'Ammaar as much as they could so as not to kill him with their swords and people would say they were the "tyrant party". Yet, 'Ammaar was fighting as if he were a whole army and his bravery made them mad, so some of Mu'aawiyah's soldiers waited for a chance to hit him.

Mu'aawiyah's army had many regular soldiers from among the new Muslims, who had embraced Islam at the beating of the drums in the Islamic conquest in many of the countries liberated by Islam from the power of the Romans and Persians. Most of these soldiers were the fuel of the civil war caused by the rebellion of Mu'aawiyah and his refusal to pledge allegiançe to 'Aliy as Caliph and Imam. They were the fuel and the oil of the battle that enflamed it.

The disagreement, in spite of its seriousness, could have terminated peacefully if the affairs had remained with the early Muslims. However, it was no sooner formed than it was taken by many hands, that did not care about the fate of Islam, and they kept adding fuel to the disagreement. At noon the news of 'Ammaar's death spread, and the Muslims went on repeating to one another the prophecy of Allah's Messenger (PBUH) which had been heard by all the Companions on the day of the festival while building, the mosque: "Alas for Ibn Sumaiyah, killed by the tyrant party."

Now people knew who was the "tyrant party". It was the one that had killed 'Ammaar, no other but Mu'aawiyah's party. 'Aliy's Companions became more and more convinced of this fact. As for Mu'aawiyah's party, their hearts became suspicious, and some prepared to mutiny and turn to 'Aliy.

No sooner did Mu'aawiyah hear of what had happened than he came out announcing to the people that the prophecy was right, and the Messenger (PBUH) really prophesied that 'Ammaar was going to be killed by the tyrant party. But who killed 'Ammaar? Then he shouted to the people of his party, "He was surely killed by those who came with him out of his house and brought him to the battle." Some people who were inclined towards that interpretation were deceived, and the battle continued till the end.

As for 'Ammaar, Imam "Aliy carried him on his chest to where he and the other Muslims prayed, and then he was buried in his own clothes. Yes, in his blood-smeared clothes which had a pure and good smell. No silk material in the whole world could have been more suitable for the shroud of a graceful martyr and a great saint like 'Ammaar.

Muslims stood at his grave wondering. A few hours before, 'Ammaar had been singing over the battlefield, filled with the delight of the tired stranger who was returning happily home. He had been shouting, "Today I meet the dear ones, Muhammad and his Companions." Did he have a meeting time with them, an exact time to wait for him?

Some Companions approached each other, inquiring. One of them asked, "Do you remember the twilight of that day in Al-Madiinah when we were sitting with Allah's Messenger (PBUH) and suddenly his face brightened and he said, "Paradise is longing for 'Ammaar'?" His friend answered, "Yes, on that day he mentioned others, among which were "Aliy, Salmaan and Bilaal."

Paradise then was longing for 'Ammaar. The longing remained for a long time while he was urging it to wait in order to accomplish all his tasks and complete the last of his achievements. He did them all following his conscience and feeling delight for his achievement. Was it not then time to comply with the call of longing coming from Paradise? Sure, it was: good is rewarded by good. That was how he threw aside his lance and went.

When the dust of his grave was being leveled on his body by his companions, his soul was embracing its happy destiny there in the eternity of Paradise that was longing for 'Ammaar!

(15)
'UBAADAH IBN AS- SAAMIT
A Representative in Allah's Party!

As one of the Ansaar, he was mentioned in the Prophet's words "If the Ansaar chose to move in a certain direction, I would follow them. By Allah, if there had been no emigration, I would have chosen to be one of the Ansaar." 'Ubaadah Ibn As-Saamit was not only one of the Ansaar, but also one of their reknown leaders whom the Prophet (PBUH) chose to represent their people and tribes. When the first Ansaar delegation arrived at Makkah to make the oath of allegiance to the Prophet (PBUH), 'Ubaadah (May Allah be pleased with him) was one of the 12 believers who pledged allegiance to the Prophet (PBUH), embraced Islam, and clasped the Prophet's hand in support and loyalty. In the Second Pledge of Al 'Aqabah, 'Ubaadah was one of the leaders of the 70 men and two women and also one of the representatives of the Ansaars, who gave his pledge to the Prophet (PBUH) during the Hajj season.

Ever since, 'Ubaadah never missed a battle or fell short of a sacrifice, as the arena at that time offered a kaleidoscope of self sacrifice, valor, courage, and defiance. Since he chose Allah and His Prophet, he exerted himself to fulfil his obligations towards his religion. Therefore, his loyalty and obedience to Allah and his relationship with his relatives, allies, and enemies were all molded in a way so as to be compatible with the faith and conduct that a Muslim should have.

In the past, 'Ubaadah's family had been tied in alliance with the Jews of Bani Qainuqaa' in Al-Madiinah. Since the Prophet and his Companions emigrated to Al-Madiinah, the Jews pretended to be on good terms with them; but after the Battle of Badr and a little while before the Battle of Uhud, the Jews of Al- Madiinah began to show their true colors. Consequently, one of the Jewish tribes, Bani Qainuqaa', fabricated reasons for commotion and strife against the Muslims.

As soon as 'Ubaadah realized their real intention, he decidedly threw aside their ancient treaty and said, "I take Allah, His Prophet, and those who have believed in Him as my protectors." The Qur'aan descended on the Prophet (PBUH) to support, salute, and praise 'Ubaadah's loyal and steadfast attitude saying, < *And whosoever takes Allah, His Messenger, and those who have believed as Protectors, then the party of Allah will be victorious* > *(5 : 56).*

Thus, the glorious verse announced the establishment of Allah's party, the members of which were the believers who stood firm by the Prophet's side and advocated the banner of right guidance and truth. They were regarded as the blessed blossom of the seed sown by their predecessors, who did their utmost to support their Messenger and invite people to believe in Allah the Ever-Living, the One Who Sustains and Protects all that exists. This newly born party of Allah would not only include the Companions of the Prophet, but also encompass the true believers of all future generations and times until Allah inherits the earth and whatever is with Him.

'Ubaadah, whose loyal and faithful attitude the verse praised, was not only a representative of the Al-Khazraj tribe, but was also one of the leaders of the pious and righteous Muslims who would always be looked upon by future generations throughout the world as a symbol of chivalry and discipline. His immortal history will forever resound throughout the world.

One day 'Ubaadah heard the Prophet talking about the

responsibilities and obligations of commanders and governors and the punishment that awaited any one of them who abused his authority and manipulated the money entrusted to him. His words shook him so severely that he swore never to accept command, even over two people. He kept this oath. When the Commander of the Faithful 'Umar Ibn Al-Khattaab (May Allah be pleased with him) became the caliph, he could not prevail on 'Ubaadah to accept any influential position except educating and instructing people in Islamic religion. Indeed, this was the appropriate field for 'Ubaadah, away from influential positions that might jeopardize his faith with precarious arrogance, power, and wealth.

Therefore, he traveled with Mu'aadh Ibn Jabal and Abu Ad Dardaa' to Syria, where they illuminated the country with knowledge, fiqh, and enlightment. Afterwards, 'Ubaadah traveled to Palestine, where Mu'aawiyah held jurisdiction in the name of the caliph.

When 'Ubaadah Ibn As-Saamit finally settled down in Syria, he always looked to Al-Madiinah as the capital of Islam and as the center of the caliphate where 'Umar Ibn Al-Khattaab, a master- mind and a peerless man, lived. Then he turned around and looked over Palestine, where Mu'aawiyah Ibn Abi Sufyaan, a worldly-minded and a power hungry man, ruled.

'Ubaadah was, indeed, one of those blessed men who lived the best and the most accomplished days of their lives with the Prophet (PBUH). Those men who gained experience through struggle were cast in the same mold of conflict, struggle, and self-sacrifice. 'Ubaadah had embraced Islam out of conviction rather than fear. Indeed, he sold himself and his fortune to Allah. He was one of the men who were brought up and disciplined by Muhammad (PBUH), who infused them with his wisdom, enlightenment, and greatness. To 'Ubaadah, one of the most excellent models of the man in power was 'Umar. Naturally, if 'Ubaadah tried to judge Mu'aawiyah's conduct and character according to those standards, the result would not be in his favor and conflict would be inevitable. And that is exactly what happened.

'Ubaadah used to say, "We have given a pledge to the Prophet (PBUH) never to be afraid of anyone but Allah." 'Ubaadah was a man who kept his pledges; therefore, he never feared Mu'aawiyah. Although Mu'aawiyah was in authority, 'Ubaadah had already taken oath to stand firm and expose his wrong doings.

Consequently, the people of Palestine watched him closely, holding their breath with astonishment, for the news of the fearless opposition led by 'Ubaadah resounded across the world of Islam and was regarded as an outstanding example that should be followed. Notwithstanding the patience and tolerance Mu'aawiyah was famous for, he soon got tired of 'Ubaadah's opposition, for he considered it a direct threat to his authority. Finally, when 'Ubaadah realized that the gap between him and Mu'aawiyah was widening fatally, he addressed Mu'aawiyah saying, "By Allah, I will never live in the same land with a man like you." Consequently, he left Palestine and returned to Al-Madiinah.

Definitely, 'Umar was a man of outstanding perception and insight. He was so careful to surround governors like Mu'aawiyah, who manipulated their cleverness for their own interest, with a group of ascetic, pious, and steadfast Companions and advisers. He aimed at curbing their aspiration and avarice and reminding them of the era of the Prophet and his great feats.

Therefore, no sooner had the Commander of the Faithful 'Umar

Ibn Al Khattaab seen 'Ubaadah in Al-Madiinah than he asked him, "What brought you back to Al-Madiinah?" When 'Ubaadah told him about his dispute with Mu'aawiyah he ordered him, "Go back to where you belong. By Allah, any land that has no one like you living in it is a wasteland." 'Umar immediately sent a message to Mu'aawiyah saying, "You are not to rule over 'Ubaadah." Indeed, 'Ubaadah was a commander of himself. When a man like 'Umar held 'Ubaadah in such high regard, then, undoubtedly, he must be a great and worthy man, 'Ubaadah's greatness was unveiled through his faith, conscientiousness, and discipline.

This sensible representative of the Ansaar and Islam died in A.H. 34, and his memory and history will forever be cherished and honored by all Muslims.

(16)
KHABBAAB IBN AL-ARAT
A Master in the Art of Self-Sacrifice

A group of the Quraish hastened to Khabbaab's house to take the swords they had asked him to make. Khabbaab was a sword maker who sold his wares to the people of Makkah or sent them to its market.

It was not like Khabbaab to leave his house and work; therefore, the Quraish sat there and waited for his return. After a long time, Khabbaab arrived. His face was bright with questions, and his eyes were filled with graceful tears. He immediately greeted his guests and sat down. They asked him in a hurry, "Khabbaab, did you finish making our swords?" There were no more tears in his eyes. Instead, his eyes were filled with bright delight. He spoke as if to himself, "It makes me wonder!"

His clients asked him, "What makes you wonder? We ask you about our swords. Did you finish them?"

Khabbaab gazed at them as if he were hypnotized. Then he asked them, "Did you see him? Did you hear him?" They looked at one another in astonishment. Then one of them asked slyly, "Did you see him Khabbaab?" Khabbaab asked, "Whom do you mean?" turning the tables on him. The man answered, irritatedly, "I mean the same person that you mean!"

Khabbaab answered after he had exhibited his invulnerability to their attempts to wrest information from him. He wanted to prove to them that if he were to confess his faith before them, he would announce it in public and would not be duped or led on. He would announce his Islam because he saw and embraced what was right.

He was still suspended in his ecstasy and spiritual upliftment, when he answered, "Yes, I did see and hear him. As a matter of fact, I have seen him enveloped and illuminated by truth."

Suddenly, the Quraishi clients began to realize what he meant; therefore one of them shouted, "Who are you talking about, you slave of Umm 'Ammaar?" Khabbaab answered with saintly quietude, "Who else but the brother Arab. Who else of your people is enveloped and illuminated by truth?"

Another shouted and jumped in terror, "Do you mean Muhammad?" Khabbaab nodded in satisfaction and said, "Yes, he is the Messenger of Allah to us, to bring us out of the darkness of disbelief into the light of belief."

No sooner had he finished these words than he fell unconscious. The only thing he remembered was waking up after long hours to find his clients gone and his body full of bleeding bruises and wounds! Nevertheless, his wide eyes encompassed his surroundings as if the place was too narrow for his penetrating stare. Despite the pain, he rose and went into the open, limping his way out of his house, leaning on the wall.

His noble eyes embarked on a long, perpetual journey roaming about the horizon. He was not searching for the familiar dimensions of people, but rather for the missing dimension. Indeed, his eyes travelled in search of the missing dimension in his life, in Makkah, and in the life of people everywhere and at all times. He wondered if what he had heard from the Prophet on that day was the light that leads to the missing dimension in the life of all people.

Khabbaab was wrapped in sublime contemplation and deep thought. Then he went home to treat his wounds and prepare himself for a new round of torture and pain.

From that day, Khabbaab occupied a foremost place among the oppressed and tortured who, notwithstanding their poverty and weakness, rose against the Quraish's haughtiness, tyranny, and madness. He was high in rank among those believers who were devoted to the standard of Islam that fluttered on the boundless horizon. It sounded the end of the era of paganism and despotism, to announce the dawn of a new world, the sovereign of which is Allah, Who is worshipped alone by people who obey Him and do righteous deeds sincerely for His sake, and not to show off or set up rivals with Him in worship. Moreover, it announced the glad tidings of the emergence of the weak and oppressed people who would stand up as one man under the standard of Islam and would stand on equal terms with those who used and abused them in the past.

Khabbaab withstood the consequences that ensued after embracing Islam with an outstanding courage that was becoming of a pioneer of Islam. Ash-Sha'biy narrated, "Khabbaab withstood all the horrors that the polytheists exposed him too. They went so far as to place burning stones onto his naked back until his flesh came off."

Indeed, Khabbaab had his share of horrible torture, yet his resistance and patience were extraordinary. For instance, the polytheists of the Quraish turned all the iron they could find in Khabbaab's place-which he had used to make swords-into fetters and chains. They put them under the fire until they blazed, then chained his body, hands, and legs with them.

One day, Khabbaab went with some of his oppressed brethren

to the Prophet (PBUH) and said, "O' Messenger of Allah, please ask Allah to bestow his victory and safety on us." This was an expression of hope in Allah's safety rather than of faint-heartedness and feebleness.

Now, let us hear the story as told by Khabbaab himself: One day, we went to the Prophet and found him laying his head on a garment in the shade of the Ka'bah. So we said to him, "O' Messenger of Allah, we hope that you will ask Allah to bestow His victory and safety on us." Instantly, the Prophet sat up, and his face reddened as he said, "Not a long time ago, men like you who believed in Allah used to be dragged into a ditch where they were sawed from the head downwards, yet this didn't make them turn back from their religion. They also used to comb them with iron combs that split their flesh and bones, yet they didn't turn their backs on their religion. Believe me, Allah will put an end to all your sufferings and grant you victory so much so that one day, a man will travel from San'aa' to Hadramawt and fear no one but Allah and the wolf, lest it should devour his sheep. But you have no patience."

As soon as Khabbaab and his comrades heard these words, they seemed to have reached the apex of certainty and determination. Therefore, they decided to show Allah and the Prophet (PBUH) nothing but will, patience, and self-sacrifice. Khabbaab then walked patiently yet decidedly into the dungeons of hell.

The Quraish were maddened by his steadfastness and endurance; therefore, they decided to seek the help of his former slave mistress, Umm 'Ammaar, who became Khabbaab's principal torturer. For instance, she used to place burning iron on Khabbaab's head, yet Khabbaab deliberately controlled himself so as to deprive his torturer of the joy of hearing him moan. One day, the Prophet (PBUH) saw his head burned and blackened by the hot iron. His heart was full of sympathy and anguish, but there was nothing that he could do at that time but to supplicate Allah to our forth patience on him and strengthen his faith. Thus the Prophet (PBUH) raised his hands and supplicated "Allah, make Khabbaab victorious over the disbelieving people."

Allah brought it about a few days later. Retaliation befell Umm 'Ammaar as if destiny meant it as an ultimatum to the rest of the torturers. She suffered a peculiar, acute rabies attack that made her, according to historians, bark like dogs. At that time, she was told that the only cure for her ordeal was to cauterize her head. Finally, her stubborn head burned day and night with burning iron

All in all, the Quraish fought faith with torture, while the believers fought torture with self-sacrifice. Khabbaab was one of those whom Allah had chosen to take their place among the masters of self-denial and sacrifice.

Not only had Khabbaab (May Allah be pleased with him) devoted his time to the service of the new religion, but also to worshiping, praying, and instructing. He used to visit his brothers who hid their Islam in dread of the Quraish's tyranny and despotism. There, he used to read the Qur'aan and instruct them. He was, truly, a genius in studying every Surah and Verse in the Qur'aan. Even 'Abd Allah Ibn Mas'uud, whom the Prophet praised by saying, "He who wants to read the Qur'aan in exactly the same way it descended on me, should imitate Ibn Umm 'Abd", considered Khabbaab as a reference to all that concerns the Qur'aan, whether as a text or a textbook.

Khabbaab was the one who was teaching the Qur'aan to Faatimah Bint Al-Khattaab and her husband Sa'iid Ibn Zaid, when 'Umar Ibn Al-Khattaab thrust his way right into their house with unsheathed sword so as to settle his account with Islam and the Prophet (PBUH). Allah willed that as soon as 'Umar heard the Verse in the scroll being recited in a slow and pleasant voice by Khabbaab, he cried out, "Tell me where Muhammad is!" When Khabbaab heard 'Umar's words, he came out of his hiding place and said, '"Umar, by Allah, I do hope that Allah chose you to fulfil the Prophet's supplication. For yesterday, I heard the Prophet say, 'Allah, please support Islam with whom You love best, either Abi Al-Hakam Ibn Hishaam or 'Umar Ibn Al-Khattaab.'" 'Umar repeated his question, "Where is Muhammad now?" Khabbaab answered, "At As-Safaa in Daar Al-Arqam Ibn Abi Arqam." At that very moment, 'Umar ascended towards his great fortune and blessed destiny.

Khabbaab witnessed all the battles and wars side by side with the Prophet. He treasured his faith and certainty throughout his life. When the Muslim treasury (Bait Al-Maal) overflowed with money during the caliphates of 'Umar and 'Uthmaan (May Allah be pleased with them both), Khabbaab had a large salary as one of the foremost Muslim Muhaajiruun.

This abundant income enabled Khabbaab to build himself a house in Kufa. He used to put his money where all his friends, visitors, and those in need could find it. Nevertheless, whenever the Prophet (PBUH) and the Companions who sacrificed their lives for Allah and met Him before the Muslims became victorious and wealthy were mentioned, his eyes filled with tears and he became sleepless.

Listen to him talking to his brothers who came to visit him on his deathbed. They said, "Be content, Abu 'Abd Allah; you will meet your brothers tomorrow." His eyes flowed with tears as he answered,"I am not crying out of fear of death, but you reminded me of the brothers who left this life without enjoying any of its splendor or luxury, yet we have lived on until we have sucked in its splendor and wealth to the extent that we placed this wealth on the sand," and he pointed to his newly-built humble house. Then he pointed to the place where he kept his money and exclaimed, "By Allah, I have never refused to give it to anyone who asked me for it, as if the strings were his." Then he looked upon his shroud and said weeping, "Look, this is my shroud." He considered it extravagant and luxurious. He then said, "Yet Hamzah the Prophet's uncle, on the day of his martyrdom had nothing to be used for a shroud but a torn garment which if placed on his head, would show his feet, and if placed on his feet, would show his head."

Khabbaab died in A.H. 37. Alas, the sword maker in paganism died. The master of self-denial and sacrifice in Islam died. He was one of the group of believers in whose defense the Qur'aan descended on the Prophet when the elite of the Quraish pleaded with the Prophet to assign a day for them and another for the poor Muslims like Khabbaab, Suhaib and Bilaal. However, the great Qur'aan embraced those men of Allah to honor and glorify, and these Verses descended on the noble Prophet:
< *And turn not away those who invoke their Lord, morning and afternoon, seeking His Face. You are accountable for them in nothing, and they are accountable for you in nothing, that you may turn them away and thus become of the Zalimun (unjust). Thus We have tried some of them with others, that they might say: "is it these (poor believers) that Allah has favoured from amongst us?" Does not Allah know best those who are grateful? When those who believe in our Ayat (Verses) come to you, say ; "Salamun 'Alaikum" (peace be on you); your Lord has written Mercy for Himself* > *(6 : 52).*

Thus, whenever the Prophet saw them after the descent of these

Verses, he took special care to honor them. So much so that he spread out his garment so that they would sit on it next to him and patted them on their shoulders saying, "I welcome you whom Allah enjoined me to favor."

It was indeed a tragic loss when one of the pious, noble, and legitimate sons of revelation and the generation of sacrifice died.

All in all, perhaps the best farewell to Khabbaab was the words of Imam 'Aliy (May Allah be pleased with him) when he was on his way back from Siffiin and saw a recently dug moist grave and asked about the deceased.They answered, "It is Khabbaab's grave." Then he contemplated in reverence and sorrow, "O' Allah, bestow Your mercy on Khabbaab, for You know that he was a true Muslim, an obedient Muhaajir and a determined Mujaahid who strove hard in the cause of Allah."

(17)
ABU 'UBAIDAH IBN AL-JARRAAH
The Trustworthy of This Nation

Who was the man whose right hand the Prophet (PBUH) held and said, "In every nation there exists a man worthy of all trust and the trustworthy of this nation is Abu 'Ubaidah lbn Al-Jarraah." Who was the man whom the Prophet sent with reinforcements to 'Amr lbn Al-'Aas in the Dhaat As-Salaasil Expedition and made commander of the army that included 'Umar and Abu Bakr? Who was this Companion who was the first to be called the Commander of the Commanders? Who was that tall, slim man with gaunt face? Who was that strong, trustworthy man, about whom 'Umar lbn Al-Khattaab said on his deathbed? "If Abu 'Ubaidah lbn Al-Jarraah were alive, I would have entrusted him with the caliphate. And if Allah asked me about him, I would say, I assigned the caliphate to the trustworthy of Allah and His Prophet, Abu 'Ubaidah lbn Al-Jarraah."

He embraced Islam at the hands of Abu Bakr As-Siddiiq at the dawn of Islam, even before the Prophet walked into Daar Al-Arqam. He emigrated to Abyssinia during the second emigration, then returned to stand by the Prophet at Badr, Uhud, and the rest of the great battles.

Even after the Prophet's death, he continued to be strong and trustworthy in his striving during the caliphates of Abu Bakr and the Commander of the Faithful 'Umar. He renounced the world and endured its hardships. He pursued his Islam with an admirable asceticism, piety, firmness, and trustworthiness. When Abu 'Ubaidah took the oath of allegiance to the Messenger and dedicated his life in the way of Allah, he knew exactly what those words "in the way of Allah" meant. Moreover, he was ready to endure whatever this way required of self-sacrifice and self-denial. From the time he shook hands with the Prophet as a sign of his pledge, he looked upon himself and his life as something that Allah had entrusted to him to seek His pleasure and abandon every desire or fear that might distract away from Him, When Abu 'Ubaidah fulfilled his pledge as other Companions did, the Prophet saw in his conscientiousness and life style that which made him worthy of the epithet he had given him, namely, "The Trustworthy of This Nation".

Abu 'Ubaidah's trustworthiness towards his responsibilities was one of his most outstanding traits. For instance, in the Battle of Uhud, he realized from the way the battle was conducted that the disbelievers' first priority was to kill the great Messenger (PBUH). To them, achieving victory was of secondary importance compared to killing the Prophet. Therefore, he decided to stay very close to where he was.

Abu 'Ubaidah thrust his sword into the army of pagansim that craved to put out the light of Allah once and for all. Whenever the fierce fight led him far away from the Prophet, he fought ferociously while his eyes were fixed on where the Prophet stood, watching him with great concern. Whenever Abu 'Ubaidah saw a potential danger approaching the Prophet, he jumped swiftly to send the enemies of Allah on their heels before they could injure the Prophet.

When the fight reached the height of ferocity, a group of disbelievers closed in upon Abu 'Ubaidah. Still his eyes were fixed on the Prophet like hawk eyes. Abu 'Ubaidah lost his self-control when he saw an arrow hit the Prophet; yet he recollected himself and thrust his sword into those who closed in upon him as if his sword were a magic one. Finally, he managed to disperse them and darted towards the Messenger, who was wiping the noble blood that ran down his face with his right hand, then exclaimed, "How can they succeed after they tinged with blood the face of their Prophet who invites them to the way of Allah?"

When Abu 'Ubaidah saw the two rings of the Prophet's chain mail that had pierced his cheeks, he rushed and held the first one with his front teeth and pulled it out. Yet as it fell, it took out his upper front teeth as well, and the same thing happened to the lower front teeth when he pulled cut the second ring.

Now, Abu Bakr As-Siddiiq will narrate what he saw in a more impressive way. So let us hear what he has to say: When the Battle of Ubud reached the apex of fierceness and ferocity, the Prophet was wounded, and two of the rings of the Prophet's mail penetrated his cheeks. As soon as I realized what had happened, I rushed to him. A man ran swiftly in the same direction and exclaimed, "Dear Allah, accept this deed as a sign of obedience." Then we both reached the Prophet, but Abu 'Ubaidah was there before me, so he pleaded with me, "Please, by Allah, Abu Bakr, let me pull them out of the Prophet's cheeks," so I let him. Abu 'Ubaidah held one of the rings with his front teeth and pulled it out along with his upper front teeth. Then he pulled out the second along with his lower front teeth. Thus, he lost his teeth.

Abu 'Ubaidah, like all the Companions, fulfilled his responsibilities and obligations with great honesty, and trustworthiness. Accordingly, when the Prophet (PBUH) appointed him as a commander in Al-Khabat Expedition, he had no supplies except for a knapsack full of dates. Notwithstanding the difficult mission and long distance, Abu

'Ubaidah withstood this against all odds with tremendous self-denial and joy. He and his soldiers marched for miles with nothing to eat but a few dates daily until they ran out of dates and had to pick up withered leaves with their bows and crush and swallow them with water. Hence, the expedition was called Al-Khabat (i.e. The Struggle). They proceeded regardless of the danger and the risks. They did not worry about starvation or deprivation. The only thing that mattered to them was to accomplish their glorious mission under the leadership of their strong and trustworthy commander.

The Prophet (PBUH) loved this trustworthy one of his nation so much that he gave him preference over everyone else. For instance, when the Najraan delegation arrived from Yemen after they had embraced Islam, they asked the Prophet to send someone to them to teach them the Qur'aan, the Sunnah, and Islam. The Prophet told them, "I will send you a trustworthy man, a very trustworthy man." When the Companions heard this praise, every one of them prayed that the Prophet meant him with this praise and sincere recommendation.

'Umar Ibn Al-Khattaab (May Allah be pleased with him) narrated thus:I have never craved command in my life except on that day, in hope that I would be the man whom the Prophet held in such high esteem. Therefore, I went in intense heat to perform my Dhuhr prayer. When the Prophet finished leading the prayer, he looked to his right, then to his left. I stood on my toes to draw his attention to me, yet he kept on looking round until he saw Abu 'Ubaidah Ibn Al-Jarraah and ordered him, "Go with them and judge in truth between them in the matters in which they dispute." Afterwards, Abu 'Ubaidah traveled with them.

This incident does not mean that Abu 'Ubaidah was the only one whom the Prophet trusted or appreciated. He was one of the Companions who equally shared the Prophet's invaluable trust and generous appreciation. But he was the only one or one of few who was qualified to be absent from Al-Madiinah for this mission of calling people to accept Islamic monotheism, for he was the perfect man for this assignment. He maintained his trustworthiness as a Companion of the Prophet, and even after his death, he upheld his responsibilities with admirable integrity.

He adhered to the standard of Islam wherever he went, as a soldier in command with valor and esteem, and as a soldier under command with modesty and faithfulness.

When Khaalid Ibn Al-Waliid was the commander of the Muslim armies in one of the great decisive battles, the first action of 'Umar Ibn Al-Khattaab, the new caliph at the time, was to dismiss Khaalid and assign Abu 'Ubaidah in his place. When Abu 'Ubaidah received the message from 'Umar he decided to conceal its purport. He pleaded with the messenger to keep it a secret with great admirable asceticism, intelligence, and fidelity. When Khaalid achieved his great victory, and only then, did Abu 'Ubaidah relay to him the message with extraordinary politeness. On reading the message Khaalid asked him, "May Allah bestow His mercy on you, Abu 'Ubaidah. What made you keep that message from me?" The Trustworthy of the Nation answered, "I was afraid lest it should cause any confusion that might affect the army's morale. We do not crave life or its splendor. We are brothers before Allah."

Thus, Abu 'Ubaidah was assigned as the commander-in-chief in Syria. His army was the mightiest and best equipped among the Muslim armies. You could hardly distinguish him from the rank and file of the army. He was always unassuming. When he heard that the people of Syria were infatuated by him and by his new rank, he asked them to assemble, then addressed them saying, "Fellow men, I'm a Muslim from the Quraish tribe. I will follow any of you like his shadow regardless of the color of his skin, if he is more pious and righteous than me."

May Allah greet you, Abu 'Ubaidah. May Allah bless the religion that refined you and the Prophet who instructed you. He said that he was a Muslim from the Quraish. His religion was Islam and his tribe was Quraish. For him, this sufficed as an identification. His being the commander in chief, the leader of the greatest Muslim army in number, equipment, and victory and they obeyed and respected ruler of Syria, were not privileges in themselves. He was not ensared by the web of conceit or haughtiness. As a matter of fact, all these titles and high positions were the means to a sublime ultimate end.

One day, the Commander of the Faithful visited Syria and asked those who were at his reception, "Where is my brother?" They asked, "Who do you mean?" He answered, "Abu 'Ubaidah Ibn Al-Jarraah." Soon Abu 'Ubaidah arrived and hugged 'Umar, then he invited him over to his house, where he had no furniture. In fact, he had nothing but a sword, a shield, and a saddlebag. 'Umar asked him, smiling, "Why don't you furnish your house as people do?" Abu 'Ubaidah readily answered, "O' Commander of the Faithful, as you see, I have a room to sleep in and that is enough for me."

One day as the Commander of the Faithful 'Umar "Al-Faruuq" was conducting the affairs of the vast Muslim world, he received the sad news of Abu 'Ubaidah's death. He tried to control himself, but his sadness got the better of him and his tears flowed. He asked Allah to bestow His mercy on his brother. He recalled his memories with Abu 'Ubaidah (May Allah be pleased with him) with patience and tenderness. He exclaimed,

"If I were to make a wish, I would have wished a house full of men just like Abu 'Ubaidah."

The Trustworthy of This Nation died in the land, which he had purified from the paganism of the Persians and the oppression of the Romans. Today in Jordan lie his noble remains, which once were full of life, goodness, and satisfaction. It does not matter if you know where he is buried or not, for if you want to find his grave, you will need no guide; the fragrance of his remains will lead you to it.

(18)
'UTHMAAN IBN MADH'UUN
A Monk" Whose Hermitage was Life

If you attempt to arrange the Prophet's Companions in the order of the embracing Islam, 'Uthmaan lbn Madh'uun will be number fourteen. Not only was he the first Muhaajir to die in Al-Madiinah, but also the first Muslim to be buried in Al-Baqii'a. This glorious Companion whose life story you are about to hear was a great "monk". By "monk" here I mean a worshiper throughout life, not a monk sequestered in his hermitage, for life with all its commotion, turmoil, burdens, and virtues was his "hermitage". Life to him meant perseverance in the way of truth and unremitting self-denial good and righteousness.

When we go back in time, when the fresh early rays of Islam were emanating from the Prophet's heart (PBUH) and from his words said in secret and seclusion, 'Uthmaan lbn Madh'uun was there. He was one of the few who rushed to the way of Allah and supported the Prophet. When the Prophet (PBUH) ordered the few oppressed believers to emigrate to Abyssinia, he wanted to save them from the Quraish's oppression, while he chose to be left behind to face it alone. 'Uthmaan, who was at the head of the first group of fugitives, was accompanied by his son, As-Saa'ib. They set their faces towards a far-away land fleeing the plots of Abu Jahl, Allah's enemy, and the Quraish's atrocities.

The emigration of 'Uthmaan lbn Madh'uun — and likewise for the rest of the emigrants to Abyssinia in the first and second emigrations — only made him hold more firmly to his Islam. Definitely, the two emigrations to Abyssinia represented a unique and glorious phenomenon in the cause of Islam, for those who believed in Muhammad (PBUH) and followed the light that had been sent down to him had had enough of paganism, error, and ignorance. Their common sense shunned the idolatry of statues made of rocks and clay. When these fugitives emigrated to Abyssinia, they found an already prevalent and highly disciplined religion with an established clerical hierarchy of bishops and priests. Notwithstanding their attitude towards this religion, it was definitely remote from both the familiar paganism practiced back home and the usual idolatrous rites they had left behind. Undoubtedly, the clergy in Abyssinia exerted much effort to lure those emigrants to apostatize and embrace Christianity.

In spite of all this, those emigrants stood steadfast in their profound loyalty to Islam and to the Prophet Muhammad (PBUH). They anxiously yearned for the day when they would return to their beloved country so as to worship Allah and support the great Prophet (PBUH) in the mosque in peacetime and in the battlefield when the power of disbelief forced them to take up arms. Thus, those emigrants who lived in Abyssinia felt secure and peaceful. 'Uthmaan Ibn Madh'uun was one of them, yet his expatriation did not make him forget his cousin Umaiyah Ibn Khalafs plots and the abuse he dealt him and other Muslims. Hence, he used to amuse himself by rehearsing threats to him, saying, " I hope that all the arrows you aim will miss their target and strike back at you. You fought against generous and noble people and tortured them to death. You will soon be punished, and the common people you used to despise will get back at you."

While the emigrants were, despite their exile, wrapped up in their worship of Allah and the study of the Qur'aan, news spread that the Quraish had submitted themselves to Islam and prostrated themselves to Allah, the One, the Irresistible.

Hurriedly, driven by their nostalgic feelings, the emigrants packed up their belongings and hastened to Makkah. However, no sooner had they reached Makkah's outskirts than they realized that the news about the Quraish's submission to Islam was only the bait to lure them to return. Suddenly, they realized that their excessive credulity had led them right into this trap, yet there was nothing they could do, for Makkah was in sight and there was no escape whatsoever. Makkah's unbelievers were overjoyed to hear that their long-awaited prey was caught in the trap they had laid.

At that time, the right of protection — to be under the assistance, support, refuge, and protection of his patron — was a sacred and honored Arab tradition. Consequently, if a weak man had a claim on a man of high standing, he would instantly enjoy the privileges of the right of protection and would be under an invincible protection and safety. Naturally, not all of those who returned to Makkah had claims on a high-ranking man. Therefore, few enjoyed the protection and safety guaranteed by this right. Among those who did was 'Uthmaan Ibn Madh'uun, who had a claim on Al Waliid Ibn Al-Mughiirah. Hence, he entered Makkah safely and peacefully and attended its councils without being humiliated or harmed.

Yet, every time Ibn Madh'uun — the man who had been refined by the Qur'aan and whom the Prophet (PBUH) had taught and disciplined — looked around, he saw his weak, poor Muslim brothers who had no claim on the right of protection being atrociously abused and unjustly haunted, while he sat safe and sound in his sanctuary away from the least provocation. His free spirit rebelled and his noble compassion got the better of him. Hence, he decided to throw aside Al-Waliid's patronage and take off his shoulders this burdensome sanctuary that deprived him of the bliss of enduring abuse in the way of Allah and of following his Muslim brothers who were the believing vanguard and the glad tidings of the world that would afterwards overflow with faith, monotheism, and light. Let us now call an eyewitness to narrate what occurred.

When 'Uthmaan lbn Madh'uun saw the affliction that had befallen the Prophet's Companions while he was free and safe under AI-Waliid lbn AI-Mughiirah's protection, he said to himself, "By Allah, I realize now that I have a fatal flaw in my character, for here I am sound under the protection of a disbeliever while my brothers and companions are being abused and tortured by disbelievers." Instantly, he hastened to AI-Waliid lbn Al-Mughiirah and spoke. Aby Abd Shams, you have been a dutiful friend, you did your utmost to honor the ties of kinship. But now I must forsake my claim on you." AI-Waliid asked him, "Why, nephew? Did any of my people lay a finger on you?" He answered, "No, but I'm fully satisfied with Allah's protection and sanctuary and I do not want to resort to anyone but Him. So piease come with me to the mosque and withdraw your protection and support in public." They both hastened to the mosque. Then Al-Waliid cried out, '"Uthmaan has asked me to withdraw my protection and support from him." 'Uthmaan said, "He was indeed a loyal, dutiful, and generous patron, but I do not like to resort to the protection and help of anyone but Allah."

As 'Uthmaan was leaving, Lubaid Ibn Rabii'ah was sitting in one of the Quraish's meetings reciting poetry, so he decided to join them and sat down and heard Lubaid recite, "Everything but Allah is falsehood." 'Uthmaan nodded and said, "You spoke the truth." Lubaid continued, "Every blessing is transient." 'Uthmaan objected saying, "You are a liar, for the blessings of Paradise are eternal." Lubaid said, "O' you Quraish, by Allah,

I have not heard before that anyone dared to call a man who was attending your meeting names." A man of Quraish explained, "Do not pay attention to what he says, for he is a fool who has turned apostate." 'Uthmaan objected to the man's insult and both quarrelled until the man lost his temper and punched 'Uthmaan's eye ruthlessly.

Nearby was Al-Waliid Ibn Al-Mughiirah, who saw what had happened and said, "By Allah, nephew, you could have spared yourself the pain if you had stayed under my invulnerable protection." 'Uthmaan answered, "On the contrary, my healthy eye yearns for the pain of my abused eye. I am under the protection of Allah, Who is far better and more capable than you, Abu 'Abd Shams." Al-Waliid urged him saying, "Come on nephew, be sensible and return to my sanctuary and protection." Ibn Madh'uun said firmly, "No." After he left, the pain in his eye was severe yet his spirit was revived, strengthened, and reassured. On his way home he recited, "I don't care if a deluded disbeliever hurt my eye, for it was in the way of Allah. For the Most Merciful will reward me on the Day of Reckoning in compensation for it. My people, if Allah attempts to please someone, then he will be undoubtedly a happy man. Even if you say that I'm a misguided fool, my life will always be consecrated to the Prophet Muhammad's religion (PBUH). I will always do my utmost to please Allah, for our religion is the only truth despite abuse and oppression.

Thus he set an example that was highly becoming of him. In fact, life witnessed the remarkable scene of an excellent man whose graceful, immortal words will resound: "By Allah, my healthy eye yearns to be hurt in the way of Allah. I am under the protection and care of Someone far better and more capable than you." Obviously the scenario of 'Uthmaan's abuse at the hands of the Quraish after he had renounced Al-Waliid's protection was premeditated on his part. He provoked it and was overjoyed by it, for this abuse was to him like the fire that matures, purifies, and ennobles his faith. At last, he followed the footsteps of his believing brothers who did not accept intimidation.

Afterwards, 'Uthmaan decided to emigrate to Al-Madiinah where he would not be haunted or harassed by Abu Jahl, Abu Lahab, Umaiyah, 'Utbah, or any of the other ruthless disbelievers who abused and tormented the Muslims. He traveled to Al-Madiinah with those great Companions who survived the hardships, terror, and horror of the trials with admirable steadfastness and stoutness. They did not emigrate to Al-Madiinah to rest. On the contrary, Al-Madiinah was the springboard that enabled Muslims to strive in the way of Allah all over the world, clinging to Allah's flag and spreading His words, signs, and guidance,

When 'Uthmaan had settled in the illuminated Madiinah, his remarkable, great qualities were unveiled. He ultimately emerged as an ascetic, devout, and repentant worshiper. To sum up, he was the glorious and intelligent "monk" who was not sequestered in his hermitage but rather in life. He spent his life striving in the way of Allah. Indeed, he was the worshiper by night and the fighter by day. In fact, he was the worshipper and the fighter of both night and day.

Although all the Prophet's (PBUH) Companions at that time were inclined to asceticism and devoutness, yet Ibn Madh'uun had a certain strategy in that respect, for he was so remarkably absorbed in his asceticism and devoutness that he turned his life, day and night, into a perpetual blessed prayer and a sweet long glorification. No sooner had he sipped the sweetness of the engrossement in worship than he hastened to abandon all the enticing luxury and splendor of life. Therefore, he wore nothing but coarse clothes and ate nothing but coarse food.

One day, he walked into the mosque in which the Prophet (PBUH) and his Companions were sitting, and he had on a faded, worn-out garment that was patched with a piece of fur. As soon as the Prophet (PBUH) saw him, he sympathized with him, and the Companions' eyes were filled with tears, yet the Prophet (PBUH) said, "Would you like it if you were rich enough to have as many garments as you like and as much food as you like? Would you like your upholstery to be as expensive as the clothes used in covering the Ka'bah." The Companions answered, "We would indeed! We would like to live in luxury surrounded by the splendors of life." The Prophet (PBUH) commented, "You will be wealthy, but you are today far better in your piety and devoutness than you will when you are wealthy." Naturally, when Ibn Madh'uun heard the Prophet's words, he clung more and more to his austere and coarse life. He went so far as to renounce sexual intercourse with his wife, yet when the Prophet (PBUH) heard about this exaggerated attitude, he summoned him and said, "Your wife has the right to have sexual intercourse with you."

The Prophet (PBUH) loved him dearly. When his pure spirit was embarking on its journey towards Heaven, the Prophet (PBUH) was next to him, paying his last farewell to the first Muhaajir to die in Al-Madiinah and the first to be raised to Paradise. He leaned to kiss his forehead and his amiable eyes flowed with tears that wet 'Uthmaan's face, which looked remarkably graceful. The Prophet (PBUH) paid his last farewell to his beloved Companion by saying, "Allah bestow His mercy on you, Abu As-Saa'ib. You are now leaving life that was not able to seduce or mislead you."

The revered Prophet (PBUH) did not forget his Companion after his death; on the contrary, he often mentioned and praised him. For instance, his very last words to his daughter Ruqaiyah on her deathbed were, "Go on, follow in the pious and devout 'Uthmaan Ibn Madh'uun's footsteps up to Paradise."

(19)
ZAID IBN HAARITHAH
The Beloved

In the Battle of Mu'tah, the Prophet (PBUH) stood to pay his farewell to the departing Muslim army on its way to fight the Romans and to announce the name of the three successive commanders of the army. "Zaid lbn Haarithah is your first commander, but in oase he is wounded, Ja'far lbn Abi Taalib will take over the command, and if the latter is wounded then 'Abd Allah lbn Rawaahah will replace him." But who was Zaid lbn Haarithah. Who was the beloved one of the Prophet (PBUH)?

Narrators and historians described his appearance as short, dark, swarthy, and snub-nosed. As for his reality, he was truly a great Muslim.

If we go back in time, we will see Haarithah, Zaid's father, just putting the luggage on the camel that was to carry his wife, Su'dah, to her family. Haarithah paid his farewell to his wife who carried Zaid- at that time a young child-in her arms. But every time he was about to leave his wife and child, who were going with a caravan, to return to his house and work, he was driven by a mysterious and inexplicable urge to keep his wife and son in sight; yet it was time for them to set out on their way and Haarithah had to pay his last farewell to his wife and head back home. His tears flowed as he said goodbye and stood as if pinned to the ground until he lost sight of them. At that moment, he felt broken-hearted.

Su'dah stayed with her family for a while. One day, suddenly her neighborhood was attacked by one of its opposing tribes. Taken by surprise, Bani Ma'n were defeated and Zaid lbn

Haarithah was captured along with other war prisoners. His mother returned home alone. When Haarithah heard the sad news, he was thunderstruck. He traveled everywhere and asked everyone about his beloved Zaid. He recited these lines of poetry on the spur of the moment to lament the loss of his son:

My heart was broken when I lost Zaid. I don't know if he is alive or dead or if I will ever see him again. By Allah, I still do not know if he was killed on the plain or slain on the mountain. His picture comes to the mind's eye whenever the sun rises or sets. Even when the wind blows, it brings along his memory. Alas, I am shrouded by my sadness, grief, and fear for him.

At that time, slavery was a recognized and established social fact that turned into a necessity. This was the case in Athens, which had long enjoyed a flourishing civilization, in Rome, and in the entire ancient world, including the Arab Peninsula. When the opposing tribe attacked the Bani Ma'n, it headed to the market of 'Ukaadh, held at that time, to sell its prisoners of war. The child Zaid, was sold to Hakim Ibn Huzaam, who gave him to his aunt Khadiijah as a gift. At that time, Khadiijah was married to Muhammad Ibn 'Abd Allah but the revelation had not yet descended on him. However, he enjoyed all the promising great qualities of Prophet (PBUH). Khadiijah, on her part, gave her servant Zaid as a gift to her husband, Allah's Prophet. He was very pleased with Zaid and manumitted him at once. His great and compassionate heart overflowed with care and love towards the boy.

Later on, during one of the Hajj seasons, a group of Haarithah's tribe ran into Zaid in Makkah and told him about his parents anguish and grief ever since they had lost him. Zaid asked them to convey his love and longing to his parents. He told them, "Tell my father that I live here with the most generous and loving father." No sooner did his father know his son's whereabouts than he hastened on his way to him, accompanied by his brother.

As soon as they reached Makkah, he asked about the trustworthy Muhammad. When he met him, he said, "O' son of Ibn Abd Al-Muttalib! O' son of the master of his tribe! Your land is one of security and sanctuary and you are famous for helping the distressed and sheltering the captive. We have come here to ask you to give us back our son. So please confer a favor on us and set a reasonable ransom for him." The Prophet knew the great love and attachment Zaid carried in his heart for him, yet at the same time, he respected Haarithah's parental right. Therefore, he told Haarithah, "Ask Zaid to come here and make him choose between you and me. If he chooses you, he is free to go with you, but if he chooses me then, by Allah, I will not leave him for anything in the world." Haarithah's face brightened, for he did not expect such magnanimity; therefore, he said, "You are far more generous than us." Then the Prophet (PBUH) summoned Zaid. When he came he asked him, "Do you recognize these people?" Zaid said, "Yes, this is my father and this is my uncle."

The Prophet (PBUH) told him what he had told Haarithah. Zaid replied, "I will not choose anyone but you, for you are a father and an uncle to me." The Prophet's eyes were full of thankful and compassionate tears. He held Zaid's hand and walked to the Ka'bah, where the Quraish were holding a meeting, and cried out, "I bear witness that Zaid is my son, and in case I die first, he will inherit from me, and in case he dies first, I will inherit from him." Haarithah was overjoyed, for not only had his son been manumitted but he had also become the son of the man who was known by the Quraish as "The Honest and Trustworthy". Moreover, he was a descendant of Bani Haashim and was raised to a high station among his people.

Zaid's father and uncle returned back home leaving their son safe and sound after he had become master of himself and after the Prophet (PBUH) had set to rest their fears concerning his fate.

The Prophet (PBUH) adopted Zaid and from that moment on he was known as Zaid lbn Muhammad.

Suddenly, on a bright morning whose brightness has never been seen before or since, the revelation descended on Muhammad: <*Read! In the name of your Lord who created - created mankind from something, which clings; read! And your Lord is the Most Noble; who taught by the pen; taught mankind what he did not know* > *(96:1-5)*. Then the revelation continued: < *O' you encovered — Arise and warn! And magnify your Lord*> *(74:1-3)*. <*O Messenger'. Proclaim the message, which has been sent down to you from your Lord. And if you do not, then you have not conveyed His message. Allah will protect you from mankind. Verily, Allah guides not the people who disbelieve*> *(5:61)*.

As soon as the Prophet (PBUH) had shouldered the responsibility of his message, Zaid submitted himself to Islam. Narrators said that he was the second man and more probably the first man to embrace Al-lslam.

The Prophet (PBUH) loved Zaid so dearly due to his singular loyalty, greatness of spirit, conscientiousness, honesty, and trustworthiness. All this and more, made Zaid lbn Haarithah or Zaid the Beloved One, as the Companions used to call him, hold a distinguished place in the Prophet's heart (PBUH). 'Aa'ishah (May Allah be pleased with her) said, "The Prophet (PBUH) never sent Zaid on an expedition but as a commander and if his life had not been so short, he would have made him his successor."

Was it possible for anyone to be held in such great esteem by the Prophet? What was Zaid really like?

As we have mentioned, he was that boy who had been kidnapped, sold, and manumitted by the Prophet (PBUH). He was this short, swarthy, snub-nosed man. Above all, he had a compassionate heart and a free soul. Therefore, he was raised to the highest position by his Islam and the Prophet's love for him, for neither Islam nor the Prophet (PBUH) took notice of descent or prestige. Muslims like Bilaal , Suhaib, Khabbaab, 'Ammaar, Usaamah and Zaid were all alike according to this great religion. Each one of them played an important and distinctive role in giving impetus to the rapidly spreading religion. These saintly ones and commanders were the sparkling stars of slam. Islam rectified life values when the glorious Qur'aan said: <*Surely, the most honorable among you in the sight of Allah are the most pious of you* > *(49:13)*. Moreover, it encouraged all promising talents and all pure, trustworthy, and productive potentialities.

The Prophet (PBUH) married his cousin Zainab to Zaid. It seems that Zainab (May Allah be pleased with her) accepted that marriage because her shyness prevented her from turning down the Prophet's intercession. Unfortunately, the gap between them widened every day, and finally their marriage collapsed. The Prophet (PBUH) felt that he was, in a way, responsible for this marriage which ended up in divorce; therefore, he married his cousin and chose a new wife, Umm Kulthuum Bint 'Uqbah for Zaid. The slanderers and the enemies of the Prophet spread doubt concerning the legality of Muhammad's marriage to his son's ex-wife.

The Qur'aan refuted their claims by striking a distinction between sons and adopted sons. It abrogated adoption altogether saying: <*Mohammed is not a father of any man among you, but he is the Messenger of Allah and the last of the Prophets* > *(33:90)*. Hence, Zaid was called after his father's name once again, namely, Zaid lbn Haarithah.

Now, do you see the Muslim troops that marched towards the Battle of Al-Jumuuh? Their commander was Zaid lbn Haarithah. Do you see those Muslims troops that marched to At- Tarf, Al-'lis, and Hismii and other battles? The commander of all those battles was Zaid lbn Haarithah. Truly, as 'Aa'ishah (May Allah be pleased with her) said, "The Prophet never sent Zaid on as expedition but as a commander."

At last, the Battle of Mu'tah took place. It seems that the Romans and their senescent empire were filled with apprehensions and forebodings about the rapid spread of Islam. They saw it as a genuine and fatal threat to their very existence, especially in Syria, which bordered the center of the new, sweeping religion. Therefore, they used Syria as a springboard to the Arab Peninsula and the Muslim nation.

The Prophet (PBUH) realized that the aim of the Roman skirmishes was to test the Muslim combat readiness. Therefore, he decided to take the initiative and exhibit in action Islam's determination to resist and to gain ultimate victory. On 1 Jumaadii A.H. 8, the Muslim army marched towards Al-Balqaa' in Syria until they reached its borders where Heraclius's armies of the Romans and Arabicized tribes residing at the borders were. The Roman army pitched camp at a place called Mashaarif, whereas the Muslim army pitched camp near a town called Mu'tah. Hence, the battle was named Mu'tah.

The Prophet (PBUH) knew how important and crucial this battle was; therefore he chose for its command three of those who were worshippers by night and fighters by day. Those three fighters sold their lives and property to Allah and renounced their needs and desires for the sake of great martyrdom, which would pave their way to win Allah's pleasure and to see Allah, the Generous. These three commanders were in succession: Zaid lbn Haarithah, Ja'far lbn Abi Taalib and 'Abd Allah lbn Rawaahah. (May Allah be pleased with them and they with Him, and may Allah be pleased with all the Companions.) Thus, the Prophet (PBUH) stood to bid farewell to his army and gave them his order saying, "Zaid lbn Haarithah is your first commander, but in case he is wounded, Ja'far lbn Abi Taalib will take over the command, and if he is also wounded, 'Abd Allah lbn Rawaahah will take it over."

Although Ja'far Ibn Abi Taalib was one of the Prophet's closest friends who had valor, fearlessness, and good lineage, yet the Prophet chose him as the second commander after Zaid. Thus, the Prophet (PBUH) stressed the fact that the new religion of Islam came to abolish corrupt human relationships based on false and superficial discrimination. It established new, rational human relationships instead.

It was as if the Prophet foresaw the proceedings of the imminent battle, for he assigned the command of the army to Zaid, Ja'far, and then 'Abd Allah and strangely enough, all of them were raised to Allah in the same order set by him. When the Muslims saw the vanguard of the Roman army, which they had estimated at 200,000 warriors, they were stunned by its enormity that surpassed all expectation. But since when did the battles of faith depend on number?

At that moment,the Muslims flung themselves into the

battlefield regardless of the consequences or jeopardy. Their commander, Zaid, carried the Prophet's standard and fought his way through the enemy's spears, arrows, and swords. He was not so much searching for victory as for concluding his deal with Allah, Who has purchased the lives and properties of Muslims in exchange for Paradise.

Zaid saw neither the sand of Al-Balqaa' nor the Roman forces. The only things that he saw were the hills of Paradise and its green cushions. These images flickered through his mind like the fluttering flags that had announced his wedding day. When he thrust and struck, he not only smote at the necks of his enemies, but also flung the doors open that stood in his way to the vast door through which he would reach the home of peace, the eternal Paradise and Allah's company. Zaid clung to his destiny. His spirit, on its way up to heaven, was overjoyed as it took its last glance at the body of its master that was not covered with soft silk but rather with pure blood shed in the way of Allah. His serene smile widened when he saw the second commander, Ja'far, dart towards the standard and hold it high before it touched the ground.

(20)
JA'FAR IBN ABI TAALIB
You Resemble Your Prophet in Your Looks and Conduct

Notice his majestic youth and blooming vigor, patience, compassion, piety, modesty, and devoutness. Notice his fearlessness, generosity, purity, chastity, honesty, and trustworthiness. Notice his magnificent nature, virtue, and greatness. Do not let the fact that all these excelling traits were found in one man astonish you, for you are looking at a man who resembled the Prophet in his looks and conduct. The Prophet gave him the epithet "Father of the Poor" and the agnomen "The Two Winged". You are about to meet the twittering heavenly sparrow, Ja'far lbn Abii Taalib, one of the great Muslims who contributed much to shaping the conscience of life.

He embraced Islam and was raised to a high station among the early believers. On the same day, his wife, Asmaa' Bint 'Umais, submitted herself to Islam. They had their share of abuse and oppression, which they withstood with courage and joy. When the Prophet (PBUH) advised his Companions to emigrate to Abyssinia, Ja'far and his wife were among those who acted upon his advice. There, they settled for a number of years, during which they had three children: Muhammad, 'Abd Allah and 'Awf.

In Abyssinia, Ja'far lbn Abi Taalib was the eloquent Companion who won through in the way of Allah and His Prophet, for among Allah's graces bestowed on him were his noble heart, alert mind, sagacious spirit, and fluent speech. The Battle of Mu'tah, in which he was martyred, was his most magnificent, glorious and immortal feat. Yet the Day of Al-Mujaawarah, which he executed before An-Najaashii in Abyssinia, was not less in magnificence, glory and grace. In fact, it was a singular battle of words and an impressive scene.

Now, the Muslim emigration to Abyssinia did not set the fears of the Quraish to rest nor lessen their grudges and spite against the Muslims. On the contrary, the Quraish were afraid lest the Muslims should gain momentum there and increase in number and power. If that did not happen, the Quraish's haughtiness and arrogance could not accept the fact that those fugitives had fled their tyranny and ruthlessness and had settled in another country which the Prophet (PBUH) saw as a promising land for Islam. Therefore, the Quraish leaders decided to send delegates to An-Najaashii with expensive gifts and the hope that he would expel those fugitives from his country. The two chosen delegates were 'Abd Allah lbn Abi Rabii'ah and 'Amr lbn Al-Aas before they had embraced Islam.

An-Najaashii, or Negus, the emperor of Abyssinia, was an enlightened believer. Deep inside he embraced a rational and pure Christianity, void of deviation, fanaticism, and narrow-mindedness. He was renowned and highly admired for his justice. Hence, the Prophet (PBUH) chose his country for his Companions' immigration. Now, the Quraish were afraid lest they should not be able to convince him of their viewpoint. Therefore, their two delegates carried many expensive gifts for the bishops and archbishops of the church and were advised not to meet An-Najaashii until they had given those presents to the bishops and convinced them of their viewpoint so that they would support them before An-Najaashii.

As soon as the two delegates arrived in Abyssinia, they met the spiritual leaders and lavished the gifts on them. Then they sent An-Najaashii his presents. Afterwards, they began to incite the priests and bishops against the Muslim immigrants and asked them to support them in their plea to An-Najaashii to expel them. A day was set for the Muslims to meet An-Najaashii and confront, before his eyes, their spiteful and mischevious enemies.

On the appointed day, An-Najaashii sat on the throne in awesome dignity, surrounded by the bishops and his retinue. Right in front of him in the vast hall sat the Muslim immigrants, enveloped by Allah's calmness, tranquility, and mercy, which He had sent down upon them. The two Quraish delegates stood to reiterate their accusation, which they had presented before An-Najaashii in a private meeting right before this huge audience.

They said, "Your Majesty, you well know that a group of fools have turned renegade and have taken asylum in your country. They did not embrace your religion, but rather invented their own religion that neither of us know. We are people of high rank who are related to their fathers, uncles, and tribes, so that you would surrender those wretched renegades to us."

An-Najaashii addressed the Muslims saying, "What is that religion that made you abandon your people's religion and refuse to embrace our religion?" Ja'afar stood to perform the task for which he had been chosen by mutual consultation immediately before this meeting. Ja'far stood up slowly and gracefully, looked with appreciation at the hospitable king and said, "O your Majesty, we used to be a people of ignorance. We worshipped idols, ate dead animals, committed great sin, severed family relations, and acted according to the law of the jungle. We used to believe that survival was only for the fittest until Allah sent from among us a Prophet (PBUH) who was known for his noble descent, honesty, trustworthiness and chastity. He invited us to worship Allah alone and abstain from worshipping stones and idols. He ordered us to speak nothing but the truth and to render back our trusts to those whom they are due. Moreover, he ordered us to keep our ties of kinship intact, be good to our neighbors, and abstain from what is forbidden. He also ordered us not to commit evil, nor to say false statements, nor to eat up the property of orphans, nor to accuse chaste women of wrong doing without proof or witness. Hence, we believed in him and in Allah's message to him. We worshipped Allah alone. We rejected that which we used to associate with Him as His partners. We allowed as lawful what is halaal and prohibited as unlawful what is haraam. Consequently, we were harassed and abused by our people, who tried to turn us away from what Allah had sent down to the Prophet (PBUH) so that we may return to idol worshiping and the evil and unlawful deeds we used to do. We were oppressed, abused and straitened in a way that prevented us from the proper worship of Allah. They even tried to force us to turn apostate. Therefore, we fled to your country and asked for asylum to escape oppression and tyranny."

When Ja'far finished his glorious words which were as clear as daylight, An-Najaashii was gripped by compassion and grace. He addressed Ja'far saying, "Do you have a scroll on which you have written the words of your Prophet?" Ja'far replied, "Yes." An Najaashii ordered, "Read it aloud." Ja'far recited a number of verses from Surat Maryam in such a slow, sweet, subdued, and captivating voice that it made An-Najaashii and all his bishops cry.

When he wiped his tears he swiftly said to the Quraish delegates "These words, of what had descended on 'Iisaa (Jesus), come from the very same source as that of 'Iisaa. You are free men in a free land. By Allah, I will never surrender you to them."

The meeting was over. Allah had helped the Muslims and mad

their feet firm; whereas the Quraish delegates were bitterly defeated. Yet 'Amr Ibn Al-'Aas was a resourceful, crafty man who could neither accept defeat nor despair easily. Therefore, no sooner had he returned to their residence than he sat turning the matter over in his mind. Then he addressed his comrade saying, "By Allah, I will go to An-Najaashii tomorrow and I will pluck the Muslims out from this land once and for all." His comrade replied, "You must not do that, for despite their disobedience, they are still related to us." 'Amr said, "By Allah, I will tell An-Najaashii that they claim that 'Iisaa Ibn Maryam is a slave like the rest of Allah's slaves." Thus the web was spun by the shrewd delegate so as to lead the Muslims unawares right into the trap. The Muslims were put in a tight corner, for if they said that 'Iisaa was Allah's slave, they would incite the king and bishops against them, and if they denied the fact that he was human, then they would turn from their religion.

On the following day, 'Amr hastened to meet the king and said, "Your Majesty, those Muslims utter an awful saying against 'Iisaa." At once, the bishops were agitated by this short but fatal sentence. They asked the Muslims once again to meet the king so as to clarify their religious standpoint concerning 'Iisaa.

When the Muslims found out about the new plot, they discussed the possibilities, then agreed to say nothing but the truth as said by the Prophet (PBUH), regardless of the consequences. Once again, the audience was held and An-Najaashii started it by asking Ja'far, "What does your religion say about 'Iisaa?" Ja'far, stood once again like a gleaming lighthouse and said, "We say what has descended on our Prophet (PBUH): he is Allah's slave, Messenger, His word which, He bestowed, and a spirit created by Him." An-Najaashii cried out in assent and said that the same words had been said by 'Iisaa to describe himself, but the lines of bishops roared in disapproval.

Nevertheless, the enlightened, believing An-Najaashii declared, "You are free to go now. My land is your sanctuary. Anyone who dares to abuse or mistreat you in any way will be severely punished. He addressed his retinue and pointed towards the Quraish delegation declaring, "Give them back their presents, for I do not want them. By Allah, Allah did not take a bribe from me when He restored my kingdom; therefore, I will not be bribed against Him!"

After the Quraish delegates had been utterly disgraced, they headed back to Makkah.

The Muslims headed by Ja'far went on with their secure life in Abyssinia. They settled in the "most hospitable land of the most hospitable people" until Allah gave them permission to return to their Prophet (PBUH), who was celebrating with the Muslims the conquest of Khaibar when Ja'afar and the rest of the emigrants to Abyssinia arrived. The Prophet's (PBUH) heart was filled with joy, happiness, and optimism.

The Prophet (PBUH) hugged him and said, "I do not know which makes me feel happier, Khaibar's conquest or Ja'far's arrival." The Prophet (PBUH) and his Companions traveled to Makkah to perform the 'Umrah to make up for the missed 'Umrah. Then they returned to Al-Madiinah. Ja'far was overjoyed with the news he heard concerning the heroism and valor of his believing brothers who had fought side by side with the Prophet (PBUH) in the Battles of Badr, Uhud and others. His eyes filled with tears over the Companions, who had been true to their covenant with Allah and had fulfilled their obligations as obedient martyrs. Ja'far craved Paradise more than anything in the world. He awaited, impatiently, the glorious moment in which he would win martyrdom.

The Battle of Mu'tah, as we have already mentioned, was

imminent. Ja'far realized that this battle was his lifetime chance to either achieve a glorious victory for Allah's religion or win martyrdom in the way of Allah. Therefore, he pleaded with the Prophet (PBUH) to let him fight in this battle. Ja'far knew beyond doubt that this battle was neither a picnic nor a limited war, but rather an unprecedented crucial war, for it was against the armies of a vast and powerful empire that excelled the Arabs and Muslims in numbers, equipment, expertise, and finance. He yearned to have a role in it.

Thus, he was the second of the three commanders. The two armies met in combat on a distressful day. Ja'far would have been excused if he had been gripped by terror when he saw the 200,000 warriors. Instead, he was gripped by overflowing exaltation, for he felt urged by the pride of the noble believer and the self-confidence of the hero to fight with his equals.

Again, hardly had the standard touched the sand as it slipped from Zaid Ibn Haarithah's right hand, when Ja'far darted and picked it up and broke through the line of the enemy with incredible fearlessness. It was the fearlessness of a man who was not so much craving victory as martyrdom. When the Roman warriors closed in upon him in an encircling move, his horse restricted his movement, so he dismounted and thrust his sword into his enemies. Then he saw one of them approaching his horse so as to mount it. He did not want this impure disbeliever on his horse's back, so he thrust his sword into it and killed it.

He immediately broke through the encircled Roman warriors like a hurricane and recited these vehement lines of poetry:

> How wonderful Paradise is.
> I can see it approaching with its sweet and cool drink.
> The time for the punishment of the Romans is drawing near.

Those unbelievers are not related to us in blood.
I must fight the Romans whenever I see one of their warriors.

The Roman soldiers were stunned by this warrior who fought like a full-armored army. Confounded by his fearlessness, they closed in upon him in a way that left him no escape, for they were determined to slay him. Instantly, they struck with their swords and cut off his right hand. Swiftly he caught the standard with his left hand before it reached the ground. When they struck off his left hand, he caught the standard with his upperarms. At the moment, the only thing that really mattered to him was not to let the standard of the Prophet (PBUH) touch the ground as long as he was alive. Although his pure body was struck down, his upperarm still hugged the standard. The sounds of its fluttering seemed to have summoned 'Abd Allah Ibn Rawaahah, who darted swiftly an' gripped it then galloped towards his great destiny!

Thus, Ja'far died an honorable death. He met Allah, the Most Great, the Most High, enveloped in self-sacrifice and heroism.

When Allah the All-Knower, the All-Aware, inspired His Prophet (PBUH) with the outcome of the battle and Ja'far's martyrdom, his tears flowed as he placed his spirit in Allah's hands. Then he went to his late cousin's house and called his children. He bugged and kissed them while his tears flowed. Then he went back to his meeting surrounded by the Companions. Hassaan Ibn Thaabit, the poet laureate of Islam, lamented the death of Ja'afar and his Companions saying:

At daybreak a man of a blessed nature and graceful face
Commanded the believers to death.
His face was as bright as the moon.
He was a proud man who descended from Al Haashim.
He was a valiant man who rushed to help the oppressed.

He fought until he was martyred
And his reward was Paradise where there are lush green gardens.
Ja'far was loyal and obedient to Muhammad.
If Islam lost one of Al-Haashim,
There are still honorable and pious men of them
Who are the support and pride of Islam.

After Hassaan finished reciting his poem, Ka'b Ibn Maalik recited:

I am griefstricken over the group
Who were struck down in succession in the Battle of Mu'tah.
They strived and fought fiercely and didn't turn their back.
Allah sent His blessings on them
For they were pious and loyal men.
Allah made the heavy rains water their bone,
They stood firm before death in Mu'tah in obedience to Allah
And for fear of His punishment.
They were guided by Ja'far's flag. He was the best Commander.
He broke through the line of the enemy and was struck down
Owing to the fierce and ruthless fight.
Instantly, the bright moon darkened
And the sun eclipsed to lament his death.

At the end, all the poor wept bitterly over the loss of their father, for Ja'afar (May Allah be pleased with him) was the "father of the poor". Abu Hurairah said, "The most generous man towards the poor was Ja'afar Ibn Abi Taalib." Indeed, when he was about to die, he wanted to be the most generous, self-denying and devoted martyr. 'Abd Allah Ibn 'Umar said, "I was with Ja'far in the Battle of Mu'tah and we looked around for him. We found that the enemy had sprayed his body with more than ninety stabs and strikes!"

But those killers did not scratch his invulnerable spirit. No, their swords and spears were the bridge which this glorious martyr crossed to be near Allah, the Most Merciful, the Most High. He was raised to a high station in heaven. His worn-out body was covered all over with the medals of war, namely, the wounds. Now, let us hear what the Prophet (PBUH) said about him: "I have seen him in Paradise. His head and wings — upper arms — were covered with blood!"

(21)
'ABD ALLAH IBN RAWAAHAH
O My Soul, Death Is Inevitable, So It Is Better for You to Be Martyred

When the Prophet (PBUH) met secretly with Al-Madiinah's delegation on the outskirts of Makkah away from the disbelievers of the Quraish, twelve representatives of the Ansaar took an oath of allegiance in the first Pledge of 'Aqabah. 'Abd Allah Ibn Rawaahah was one of those representatives who ushered Islam to Al-Madiinah and who paved the way for the Hijrah, which was considered an excellent springboard for Allah's religion, Islam. 'Abd Allah was also one of the great 73 of the Ansaar who gave the Prophet (PBUH) the Second Pledge of 'Aqabah in the following year. After the Prophet (PBUH) and his Companions emigrated and settled in Al-Madiinah, 'Abd Allah Ibn Rawaahah was the most active Muslim of the Ansaar who strived to support the thriving religion. He was also the most alert Muslim to the plots of 'Abd Allah Ibn Ubaiy whom the people of Al-Madiinah were about to crown king before the Muslims arrived. He never got over the bitterness he felt for losing the chance of his lifetime to become a king. Therefore, he used his craftiness to weave deceitful plots against Islam, while 'Abd Allah Ibn Rawaahah kept on tracing and detecting this craftiness with remarkable insight that frustrated most of Ibn Ubaiy's maneuvers and plots.

Ibn Rawaahah (May Allah be pleased with him) was a scribe at a time in which writing was not prevalent. He was a poet. His poetry flowed with admirable fluency and strength. Ever since his Islam he devoted his poetic genius to its service. The Prophet (PBUH) always admired his poetry, asking him to recite more of it. One day, as he was sitting among his Companions,

'Abd Allah Ibn Rawaahah joined them, so the Prophet (PBUH) asked him, "How do you compose a poem?" 'Abd Allah answered, "First I think about its subject matter, then I recite." He immediately recited:

O the good descendants of Al Haashim
Allah raised you to a high station
Of which you are worthy above all mankind.
My intuition made me realize at once
Your excelling nature,
Contrary to the disbelievers' belief in you.
If you asked some of them for support and help,
They would turn you down.
May Allah establish the good that descends on you firmly
And bestow victory upon you as He did to Muusaa.

The Prophet (PBUH) was elated and said, "I hope that Allah will make your feet firm, too." When the Prophet was circumambulating the Ka'bah in the compensatory 'Umrah, Ibn Rawaahah recited to him:

Were it not for Allah, we would not have been
Guided to the Right path nor charitable
Nor able to perform our prayers.
So descend, peace of mind and reassurance,
On us and establish our feet firmly
When we meet our enemy
In combat. If our oppressors tried to spread
Affliction and trial, unrest, among us
We will not give them way.

Muslims reiterated his graceful lines. The active poet was saddened when the glorious Verse descended saying: <*And for the poets, only the erring people follow them* > *(26:224).*

But soon he was contented to hear another verse saying: <*Except those who believe and do deeds of righteousness, and remember GOD frequently, and defend themselves after being oppressed* > *(26 : 227).*

When Islam rose up in arms in self-defense, lbn Rawaahah saw service in all the battles: Badr, Uhud, Al-Khandaq, Al Hudaibiyyah, and Khaibar, His perpetual slogan was these lines of poetry: "O my soul, death is inevitable, so it is better for you to be martyred."

He shouted at the disbelievers in every battle, "O' disbelievers, get out of my way. My Prophet (PBUH) has all the excellent qualities."

The Battle of Mu'tah started, and, as we have mentioned, he was the third of the Commanders after Zaid and Ja'far. lbn Rawaahah (May Allah be pleased with him) stood there as the army was about to leave Al- Madiinah and recited:

I truly ask the Most Beneficient's forgiveness
and a mortal stroke of a sword
that will strike me down
foaming or a mortal stab
with a spear by a stubborn disbeliever
that will make my liver and intestine
show out of my body. So that
when people pass by my grave,
they will say : By Allah, you are
the most righteous warrior.

Indeed, a stroke or a stab that would convey him into the world of rewarded martyrs was his utmost wish. The army marched towards Mu'tah. When the Muslims saw their enemies, they estimated them at 200,000, for they saw endless waves of warriors. The Muslims glanced back at their small group and were stunned. Some of them suggested, "Let us send a message to the Prophet (PBUH) to tell him of the enormity of the enemy that surpassed all our expectations so he will either order us to wait for reinforcements or to pierce through the enemy lines."

However, Ibn Rawaahah stood amidst the lines of the army and said: "O' my people, by Allah, we do not fight our enemies with numbers, strength or equipment, but rather with this religion which Allah has honored us with. So go right ahead: it is either one of two equally good options, victory or martyrdom." The Muslims, who were lesser in number and greater in faith, cried out, "By Allah, you spoke the truth." The smaller army broke through the mighty host of 200,000 warriors in terrible and cruel fighting.

As we have mentioned, both armies met in fierce combat. The first commander, Zaid Ibn Haarithah, was struck down, he winning glorious martyrdom. The second in command was Ja'far Ibn Abi Taalib, who was overjoyed to be martyred. 'Abd Allah took over the command and grabbed the standard from Ja'far's failing upper arms. The fight reached the peak of ferocity. The smaller army was indistinct amidst the waves of the mighty hosts of Heraclius.

When Ibn Rawaahah was a soldier, he attacked heedlessly and confidently. But now the command placed great responsibilities for the army's safety on his shoulders. It seemed that for a moment he was overtaken by hesitation and dread, yet he instantly shook off those apprehensions, summoned his innate fearlessness and cried out, "O' my soul, you look as if you were afraid to cross the way that leads to Paradise. O' my soul, I took an oath to fight. O' my soul, death is inevitable so you had better be martyred. Now I will experience the inevitability of death. What you have cared for so long is finally yours. So go ahead, for if you follow these two heroes, you will be guided to the way of Paradise." He meant the two heroes who had preceded him in martyrdom, Zaid and Ja'far.

He darted into the Roman armies, fiercely and ruthlessly. Were it not for a previous ordainment from Allah that he was to be martyred on that day, he would have annihilated the fighting hosts. But destiny called and he was martyred. His body was struck down, yet his pure, valiant spirit was raised to the heavens. His most precious wish finally came true, so that "When people pass by my grave, they will say: By Allah you are the most righteous warrior."

The fierce attack in Al-Balqaa' in Syria went on. Back in Al-Madiinah the Prophet (PBUH) was talking peacefully and contentedly with his Companions when he suddenly stopped talking. He closed his eyes a little, then opened them. A gleam flashed from them, yet it was tinged with sadness and compassion. He looked around sadly and said, "Zaid took the standard and fought until he was martyred." He was silent for a while, then continued "Ja'far grasped it and fought until he was marytred. Then 'Abd Allah Ibn Rawaahah grasped it and fought until he was martyred." He was silent for a while, then his eyes sparkled with elation, tranquility, longing, and joy as he said, "They were all raised to Paradise."

What a glorious journey it must have been! What a happy succession! They all marched to conquer, they all were raised up to Paradise. The best salute to immortalize their memory rests in the Prophet's words: "They were raised up to await me in Paradise."

(22)
KHAALID IBN AL-WALIID
A Sleepless Man Who Will Not Let Anyone Sleep

His story is a rather perplexing one. He was the deadly enemy of Muslims in the Battle of Uhud and the deadly enemy of the enemies of Islam in the remaining Muslim battles.

I feel at a loss concerning where to begin and what to begin with. He himself hardly believed that his life had really begun until that day on which he shook hands with the Prophet as a sign of his allegiance to him. If he could have ruled out all the years, even the days that proceeded that day, he would not have thought twice.

Let us then begin with that part of his life, which he himself loved most. Let us begin from that glorious moment when his heart was affected by Allah and his spirit was blessed by the Most Merciful. Thus, it overflowed with devotion to His religion, His Prophet and to a memorable martyrdom in the way of the truth. This martyrdom enabled him to erase the burdens of his advocation of falsehood in the past.

One day, he sat alone in deep thought concerning that new religion that was gaining momentum and gaining ground every day. He wished that Allah, the All-Knower of what is hidden and unseen, would guide him to the right path. His blessed heart was revived by the glad tidings of certainty. Therefore, he said to himself, "By Allah, it is crystal clear now. This man is indeed a Prophet, so how long shall I procrastinate. By Allah, I will go and submit myself to Islam."

Now, let us hear him (May Allah be pleased with him) narrate his blessed visit to the Prophet (PBUH) and his journey from Makkah to Al-Madimah .to join the ranks of the believers: "I hoped to find an escort, and I ran into 'Uthmaan Ibn Talhah and when I told him about my intention, he agreed to escort me. We traveled shortly before daybreak and as we reached the plain, we ran into 'Amr Ibn Al-'Aas.

After we had exchanged greetings, he asked us about our destination, and when we told him, it turned out that he himself was going to the same place to submit himself to Islam. The three of us arrived at Al-Madiinah on the first day of Safar in the eighth year. As soon as I laid my eyes on the Prophet, I said, "Peace be upon the Prophet," so he greeted me with a bright face. Immediately, I submitted myself to Islam and bore witness to the truth. Finally, the Prophet (PBUH) said, "I knew that you have an open mind and I prayed that it would lead you to safety." I took my oath of allegiance to the Prophet then asked him, "Please ask Allah's forgiveness for me for all the wrong doings I have committed to hinder men from the path of Allah." The Prophet said, "Islam erases all the wrong doings committed before it." Yet I pleaded with him, "Please pray for me." Finally, he supplicated Allah, "O' Allah, forgive Khaalid for all the wrong doings he committed before he embraced Islam." Then 'Amr Ibn Al-'Aas and 'Uthmaan Ibn Talhah stepped forward and submitted themselves to Islam and gave their oath of allegiance to the Prophet.

Notice these words "Please ask Allah's forgiveness for me for all the wrong doings I have committed in the past to hinder men from the path of Allah." Now, whoever has the perception and insight to read between the lines will find the true meaning of these words of Khaalid, who became the sword of Allah and the hero of Islam.

When we come across various incidents in the course of his life story, these words are our key to understanding and elucidation.

For the time being, let us accompany Khaalid, who had just embraced Islam, and watch the Quraish's great warrior who had always held the reins of leadership. Let us see the subtlest of Arabs in the art of attack and retreat as he turned his back on the idols of his ancestors and the glory of his people, and welcomed, along with the Prophet and the Muslims, the advent of a new world that Allah had destined to rise under the standard of Muhammad and the slogan of monotheism.

Let us hear the Muslim Khaalid's impressive story. To start with, do you recall the story of the three martyrs of the Battle of Mu'tah? They were Zaid Ibn Haarithah, Ja'far Ibn Abi Taalib and 'Abd Allah Ibn Rawaahah. They were the heroes of the Battle of Mu'tah in Syria, in which the Romans mobilized 200,000 warriors. Nevertheless, the Muslims achieved unprecedented victory.

Do you recall the glorious, sad words with which the Prophet announced the sad news of the death of the three commanders of the battle? "Zaid Ibn Haarithah took the standard and fought holding it until he died as a martyr; then Ja'far took it and fought clinging to it until he won martyrdom; and finally, 'Abd Allah Ibn Rawaahah gripped it and held it fast until he won martyrdom."

This is only part of the Prophet's speech, which I have written before, but now I find it appropriate to write the rest of the story: "Then it was gripped by a sword of the swords of Allah and he fought until he achieved victory."

"Who was that hero? He was Khaalid Ibn Al-Waliid, ho threw

himself into the battlefield as if he were an ordinary soldier under the three commanders whom the Prophet assigned. The first commander was Zaid Ibn Haarithah, the second was Ja'far Ibn Abi Taalib, and the third was 'Abd Allah Ibn Rawaahah. They won martyrdom in the same order on the vicious battlefield.

After the last commander had won martyrdom, Thaabit Ibn Aqram took the standard with his right hand and raised it high amidst the Muslim army. His purpose was to stop any potential disarray inside the lines. Thaabit then carried the standard and hastened towards Khaalid Ibn Al-Waliid and said, "Take the standard, Abu Sulaimaan" Khaalid thought that he did not deserve to take it since he had newly embraced Islam. He had no right to preside over an army that included the Ansaar and Muhaajiruun who had preceded him in embracing Islam.

These qualities of decorum, modesty, and gratitude were becoming of Khaalid's worthiness. He said, "I will not dare to hold it. Go on, hold it, for you deserve it better than me. First, you are older, Second, you witnessed the Battle of Badr." Thaabit answered, "Come on, take it, you know the art of fighting far better than me. By Allah, I only held it to give it to you." Then he called on the Muslims, "Do you vote for Khaalid's command?" They readily answered, "Yes, we do!"

At that moment, the great warrior mounted his horse and thrust the standard forward with his right hand as if he were knocking on closed doors that had been closed for too long and whose time had finally come to be flung wide open. So this act was to lead the hero to a long but passable road on which he would leap during the Prophet's life and after his death until destiny brought his ingenuity to its inevitable end.

Although Khaalid was in charge of the army command, hardly any military expertise could change the already determined outcome of the battle, turning defeat into victory or turning victory into defeat. The only thing that a genius could manage to do was to prevent more casualties or damage in the Muslim army from occurring and end the battle with the remainder of the army intact. Sometimes a great commander must resort to that kind of preventive retreat measure that will prevent the annihilation of the rest of his striking force on the battlefield. However, such a retreat was potentially impossible, yet if the saying, "Nothing stands in the way of a fearless heart" is true, there was no one more fearless and ingenious than Khaalid.

Instantly, The Sword of Allah flung himself into the vast battlefield. His eyes were as sharp as a hawk's. His mind worked quickly, turning over all the potentialities in his mind. While the fierce fight raged, Khaalid quickly split his army into groups, with each assigned a certain task. He used his incredible expertise and outstanding craftiness to open a wide space within the Roman army through which the whole Muslim army retreated intact. This narrow escape was credited to the ingenuity of a Muslim hero. In this battle, the Prophet gave Khaalid the great epithet "The Sword of Allah".

Shortly thereafter, the Quraish violated their treaty with the Prophet (PBUH) and the Muslims marched under Khaalid's command to conquer Makkah. The Prophet assigned the command of the right flank of the army to Khaalid Ibn Al-Waliid.

Khaalid entered Makkah as one of the commanders of the Muslim army and the Muslim nation. He recalled his youth when he galloped across its plains and mountains as one of the commanders of the army of paganism and polytheism. Khaalid stood there recollecting his childhood days playing on its wonderful pastures and his youthful memories of its wild entertainment. These memories of the past weighed down on him, and he was filled with remorse for his wasted life in which he worshipped inanimate and helpless idols.

But before he bit the tips of his fingers in remorse, he was overpowered by the magnificence and spell of this scene of the glorious light that approached Makkah and swept away all that came before it. The astounding scene of the weak and oppressed people, on whose bodies the marks of torture and horror still showed, was magnificent as they returned to the land they had been unjustly driven out of. Only this time, they returned on horseback under the fluttering standard of Islam. Their whispers at Daar Al-Arqam's house yesterday turned today into loud and glorious shouts of "Allahu akhar (Allah is the Greatest)", that shook Makkah and the victorious cry "There is no god but Allah", with which the entire universe seemed to be celebrating a feast day.

How did this miracle come about? What is the explanation of what had happened? Simply, there was no logical or rational explanation whatsoever, but the power of the Verse that the victorious marching soldiers repeated with their "There is no god but Allah" and "Allahu akbar" as they looked with joy at one another and said, < *(It is) a Promise of Allah, and Allah fails not in His Promise* > *(30:6).*

Then Khaalid raised his head and watched in reverence, joy and satisfaction as the standard of Islam fluttered on the horizon. He said to himself, "Indeed, it is a promise of Allah and Allah fails not in His promise." Then he bent his head in gratitude and thanks for Allah's blessing that had guided him to Islam and made him one of those who would usher Islam into Makkah rather than one of those who would be spurred by this conquest to submit themselves to Islam.

Khaalid was always near the Prophet. He devoted his excellent abilities to the service of the religion he firmly believed in and devoted his life to. After the glorious Prophet had died and Abu Bakr became the caliph, the sly and treacherous cyclone of those who apostatized from Islam shrouded the new religion with its deafening roar and devastating outbreak. Abu Bakr, quickly chose the hero of the battlefields and man of the hour, namely Abu Sulaimaan, The Sword of Allah, Khaalid Ibn Al-Waliid. It is true that Abu Bakr himself was at the head of the first army that fought against the apostates; nevertheless, he saved Khaalid for the decisive day and Khaalid was truly the mastermind and inspired hero of the last crucial battle that was considered the most dangerous of all the apostasy battles,

When the apostate armies were taking measures to perfect their large conspiracy, the great Caliph Abu Bakr insisted on taking the lead of the Muslim army. The leaders of the Companions tried desperately to persuade him not to, yet his decision was final. Perhaps he meant to give the cause for which he mobilized and rallied this army a special importance, tinged with sanctity. He could not achieve his aim except by his actual participation in the deadly battle and his direct command of some or all of the Muslim troops. It was a battle between the power of belief against the power of apostasy and darkness.

The outbreak of apostasy posed serious threats, in spite of the fact that it started as an accidental insubordination. Soon, the opportunists and the malicious enemies of Islam, whether from the Arab tribes or from across the borders where the power of Romans and Persians perched, seized their last opportunity to hinder the sweeping tide of Islam. Therefore, they instigated mutiny and chaos from behind the scenes.

Unfortunately, mutiny flowed like an electric current through the Arab tribes, like Asad, Ghatfaan, 'Abs, Tii, Dhubyaan, then Bani 'Aamar, Hawaazin, Sulaim and Bani Tamiim. Hardly had the skirmishes started with limited numbers of soldiers than they were reinforced with enormous armies, often of thousands of warriors. The people of Bahrain, Oman and Al-Mahrah responded to this horrible plot.

Suddenly, Islam was facing a dangerous predicament, and the apostate enemy closed in upon the believers. But Abu Bakr was ready for them. He mobilized the Muslim armies and marched to where the armies of Bani 'Abs, Bani Murah and Bani Dhubyaan gathered.

The battle started and went on for a long time before the Muslims achieved a great victory. No sooner had the victorious Muslim army reached Al-Madiinah than the caliph sent it on another expedition. News spread that the armies of the apostates were increasing in number and weapons by the hour.

Abu Bakr marched at the head of the second army, only this time, the prominent Companions lost their patience and clung to their opinion that the caliph should remain in Al-Madiinah. Accordingly, Imam 'Aliy stood in Abu Bakr's way as he was marching at the head of the army and held the reins of his she camel and asked, "Where to, Caliph of the Prophet? I will tell you the same words that the Prophet told you in the Battle of Uhud: Sheathe your sword, Abu Bakr, and don't expose us to such a tragic loss at this critical time."

The caliph had to comply with this consensus. Therefore, he split the army into eleven divisions and assigned a certain role for each one. Khaalid Ibn Al-Waliid would be the commander over a large division. When the caliph gave every commander his standard, he addressed Khaalid saying, "I heard the Prophet say, 'Khaalid is truly an excellent slave of Allah and a brother of the same tribe. He is a sword of Allah unsheathed against disbelievers and hypocrites.'"

Khaalid and his army fought one battle after another and achieved one victory after another until they reached the crucial battle.

It was in the Battle of Al-Yamaamah that Bani Haniifah and their allies from the Arab tribes organized one of the most dangerous armies of the apostasy, led by Musailamah the Liar. A number of Muslim forces tried to defeat Musailamah's army but failed. Finally the caliph ordered Khaalid to march to where Bani Haniifah was camped.

No sooner had Musailamah heard that Khaalid was on his way to fight him than he reorganized his army, turning it into a devastating and horrible enemy machine. Both armies met in fierce combat. When you read the history of the Prophet (PBUH) a perplexing awe will take hold of you, for you will find yourself watching a battle that resembles our modern battles in its atrocity and horrors, though it differs in weapons and tactics.

Khaalid's army stopped at a sand dune that overlooked Al-Yamaamah. At the same time, Musailamah marched haughtily and with great might followed by endless waves of his soldiers. Khaalid assigned the brigades and standard to the commanders of his army. As the two armies clashed in a terrible, large-scale, devastating war, the Muslim martyrs fell one by one like roses in a garden on which a stubborn tempest blew! Immediately Khaalid realized that the enemy was about to win the battle, so he galloped up a nearby hill and surveyed the battlefield. He realized that his soldiers' morale was waning under the pressure of the blitz of Musailamah's army.

Instantly, he decided to trigger a new feeling of responsibility inside the Muslim army, so he summoned the flanks and reorganized their positions on the battlefield. He cried out victoriously, "Fight together in your own groups and let us see who will surpass the other and win the field." They all obeyed and reorganized themselves in their own groups. Thus, the Muhaajiruun fought under their standard, the Ansaar fought under theirs, and every group fought under its standard. It became fairly easy to determine where defect came from. As a result, the Muslims were charged with admirable enthusiasm, firmness, and determination.

Every now and then, Khaalid was careful to cry out, "Allahu akbar" and "There is no god but Allah." He ordered his army in such a way that he turned the swords of his men into an inevitable victory that no one could escape. It was striking that, in a few minutes, the Muslim army turned the tables on Musailamah's army. Musailamah's soldiers fell in tens of hundreds and thousands like flies that were suffocated by the deadly spray of a pesticide. Khaalid ordered his soldiers with a kind of enthusiasm that flowed into them like an electric current. This was a manifestation of his striking genius. This was the manner in which the most decisive and fierce battle of apostasy was conducted. In the end, Musailamah was slain and the bodies of his men were scattered on the battlefield. Finally, the standard of the liar imposter was buried for ever.

On hearing the good news, the caliph offered the Prayer of Thanksgiving to Allah the Great and Most High for bestowing victory on the hands of this hero.

Abu Bakr had enough discernment and insight to realize the danger of the evil powers that perched on the borders, threatening the promising future of Islam and Muslims. These evil powers were the Persians in Iraq and the Romans in Syria. These two dwindling empires that clung tenaciously to the distorted remnant of their past glory, were not only afflicting the people of Iraq and Syria with horrible torment, but also manipulating them. Notwithstanding the fact that the majority populations were Arabs, they instigated them to fight Muslim Arabs who carried the standard of the new religion, which ought to pull down the vestiges of the ancient world and eradicate the decay and corruption in which it was steeped. The great and blessed caliph sent his orders to Khaalid to march towards Iraq, so the hero did so.

I wish that I were given more space to follow up in detail the proceedings of his magnificent victory.

Upon arriving in Iraq, the first thing that Khaalid did was to dispatch messages to every governor and deputy who ruled the provinces and cities of Iraq in the name of the emperor. These messages were as follows: In the name of Allah, the Most Beneficient, the Most Merciful. Khaalid Ibn Al-Waliid sends this message to the satraps of Persia. Peace will be upon him who follows the guidance. All praises and thanks be to Allah Who dispersed your power and thwarted your deceitful plots. On the one hand, he who performs our prayers directing his face to our Qiblah to face the Sacred Mosque in Makkah and eats our slaughtered animals is a Muslim. He has the same rights and duties that we have. On the other hand, if you do not want to embrace Islam, then as soon as you receive my message, send over the jizyah (tax levied upon non-Muslim people who are under the protection of a Muslim government) and I give you my word that I will respect and honor this covenant. But if you do not agree to either choice, then, by Allah, I will send to you people who crave death as much as you crave life.

Khaalid's scouts whom he planted everywhere warned him against the enormity of the armies that were organized by the commanders of Persia in Iraq. As usual, Khaalid did not waste much time. Therefore, he flung his soldiers against the falsehood of disbelief so as to devastate it.

Victory followed him wherever he went, from Al-Ubullah, to As-Sadiir, An-Najaf, Al-Hiirah, Al-Anbaar then Al-Kaadhimiyah. There was one victory procession after another. The glad tidings of Khaalid's arrival blew like a fresh breeze wherever he went to usher in Islam. The weak and oppressed people found sanctuary in the new religion that saved them from the occupation and oppression of the Persians.

It was impressive that Khaalid's first order to his troops was,' "Do not attack or hurt the peasants. Leave them to work at peace unless some of them attack you. Only then, I permit you to defend yourselves."

He marched on with his victorious army, swept his enemies, and cut through their ranks like a knife cutting through melting butter. The Aadhaan resounded everywhere. I wonder if it had reached the Romans in Syria? Did they realize that cries of "Allah is the Greatest" signaled the end of their deteriorating civilizations? Indeed, they must have heard. In fact, the Aadhaan cast terror into them, yet in a desperate attempt to recapture the phantom of their empire, they decided heedlessly to fight a battle of despair and perdition.

Abu Bakr As-Siddiiq mobilized his armies and chose a group of his prominent commanders such as Abu 'Ubaidah Ibn Al-Jarraah, 'Amr Ibn Al-'Aas, Yaziid Ibn Abi Sufyaan and Mu'aawiyah Ibn Abi Sufyaan to lead them.

When the Roman emperor heard the news of the mobilization of these armies, he advised his ministers and commanders to make peace with the Muslims to avoid inevitable defeat. However, his ministers and commanders insisted on fighting and maintained, "By our Lord, we will make Abu Bakr's hair stand on end before his horses breed in our land." Consequently, they mobilized an army estimated at 240,000 warriors.

The Muslim commanders dispatched this terrifying news to Abu Bakr, who pledged, "By Allah, I will rid them of their doubts through Khaalid." Thus, the antidote of their evil suggestions of mutiny, aggression, and disbelief, namely Khaalid Ibn Al-Waliid, was ordered to go on an expedition to Syria, where he was to command the Muslim armies.

Khaalid promptly acted upon his orders and left Iraq under Al-Muthannaa Ibn Haarithah's supervision and marched with his troops until they reached the Muslim headquarters in Syria. His ingenuity enabled him to organize the Muslim armies and coordinate their different positions in no time. Shortly before the outbreak of war, he addressed his warriors after he had praised and thanked Allah, saying, "This is Allah's day. On this day, we must not give way to pride not let injustice overrule. I advise you to purify your jihaad and your deeds for Allah. Let us take turns in command. Let each and everyone of us take over the command for a day."

"This is Allah's day." What a wonderful onset! "We must not give way to pride nor let injustice overrule." This sentence is even more graceful, adequate, and awesome. On the one hand, the great leader was not lacking in self-denial and cleverness, for inspite of the fact that the caliph had assigned the command of the army to him, he did not want to give Satan a chance to whisper in the breasts of his soldiers. Therefore, he relinquished his absolute hold on the army to every soldier in the ranks even though he was already the commander. Thus, the commander of the army rotated from day to day.

The enormous and well-equipped Roman army was really terrifying. On the other hand, the Roman commander realized that time was in the Muslims' favor, for they were given to protracted battles, which would guarantee their victory. Therefore, he decided to mobilize all their troops for a quick battle to finish off the Arabs once and for all.

Undoubtedly, the courageous Muslims, on that day, were gripped by fear and anxiety. Yet in such predicaments they always resorted to their faith, in which they found hope and victory. Notwithstanding the might of the Roman armies, the experienced Abu Bakr had firm belief in Khaalid's abilities; therefore he said, "Khaalid is the man for it. By Allah, I will rid them of their doubts with Khaalid."

Let the Romans parade their terrifying, enormous forces, for the Muslims had the antidote, Ibn Al-Waliid mobilized and rallied his army, then divided it into brigades. He laid out a new plan for attack and defense that adhered to the Roman war strategy and tactics with which he was well-acquainted from his past experience with the Persians. He was ready for all possibilities. Strangely enough, the battle raged exactly as he had imagined it would, step by step and one fight after another. If he had actually counted the number of strokes of swords, he would not have been much more accurate. Before the two armies clashed, he was worried about the possibility that some of the soldiers, especially those, who had newly embraced Islam, might flee upon seeing the terrifying and enormous Roman army.

Khaalid believed that the ingenuity of victory and firmness were one and the same. He believed that the Muslim army could not afford the loss of even one of its soldiers, for it was enough to spread malignant panic and havoc inside the army, which was something that even the entire Roman army could not succeed in doing. In consequence, he was extremely firm concerning anyone who deserted his post and weapon and ran away. In the Battle of Yarmuuk, in particular, and afterwards, his troops took their positions. He called the Muslim women and, for the first time, gave them swords. He ordered them to stand at the rear of the lines to "Kill anyone who flees." It was the magic touch of a mastermind.

Shortly before the battle erupted, the Roman commander asked Khaalid to show himself, for he wanted a few words with him. Khaalid rode towards him, then they galloped to the area that separated the two armies. Mahan, the Roman commander, addressed Khaalid saying, "We know that nothing but weariness and hunger made you leave your country and go on this expedition. If you wish, we shall give ten dinars, clothes, and food to every one of you, on one condition, that you return to your country and next year we will do the same."

Khaalid gnashed his teeth, as he was provoked by his flagrant lack of manners, yet he repressed himself and answered confidently. "We didn't leave our country out of hunger as you said, but we heard that Roman blood is very delicious and tasty, so we have decided to quench our thirst with it."

Swiftly, the hero rode back to the ranks of his army and raised the Muslim standard to the full length of his arm, then he launched the attack.

Allahu akbar! Let the breeze of Paradise blow!

At once, his army was like a missile as it charged into the battlefield. They met in an extraordinary, monstrous, and deadly combat. The Romans rushed into the battlefield with an enormous number, yet they found that their foes were not an easy prey. The self-sacrifice and firmness that the Muslims displayed on that day were impressive.

In the first place, one of the Muslim soldiers rushed to Abu 'Ubaidah Ibn Al-Jarraah (May Allah be pleased with him) during the battle and said, "I have set my mind on martyrdom. Do you want me to take a message to the Prophet (PBUH) when I meet him?" Abu 'Ubaidah answered, "Yes, tell him we have indeed found true what our Lord had promised us." Immediately, the man darted like an arrow into the horrors of the battlefield. He craved death; therefore, he fought fiercely with one sword while thousands of swords were thrust into him until he won martyrdom.

Secondly, 'Ikramah Ibn Abu Jahl — yes, he was the son of the infamous Abu Jahl. He called out to the Muslims when the Romans were killing anyone who came within the sweep of their swords and said, "I fought against the Prophet before Allah guided me to Islam, so how can I possibly be afraid of fighting Allah's enemy after I submitted myself to Islam?"

Then he cried out, "Who gives me the pledge to death?" He was given the pledge to death by a group of Muslims. Then they broke through the enemy lines. They preferred martyrdom to victory. Allah accepted the bargain they had concluded through their pledge and they won martyrdom.

Thirdly, other Muslims were badly wounded and water was brought so that they might quench their thirst, yet when it was offered to the first one, he pointed to his brother who was lying next to him more seriously wounded and who was more thirsty.

Again, when this brother was offered water, he in his turn pointed to his brother. Finally, the majority of them died thirsty after they had demonstrated an incredible example of self-denial and self-sacrifice. Indeed, the Battle of Al-Yarmuuk witnessed unprecedented and unmatched instances of self-sacrifice.

Among these striking masterpieces of self-sacrifice exhibited by the determined will of the Muslims was the extraordinary portrait of Khaalid lbn Al-Waliid at the head of only 100 soldiers who flung themselves against 40,000 Romans. Khaalid kept calling out to his 100 soldiers saying, "By Allah, the Romans seemed to have lost their patience and courage, therefore I pray to Allah to let you have the upper hand over them."

How could 100 soldiers have the upper hand over 40,000? It is, indeed, incredible! Yet, were not the hearts of these 100 soldiers filled with faith in Allah the Most High, the Most Great? Were they not filled with faith in His trustworthy and honest Prophet (PBUH)? Were they not filled with faith in that cause which represents the most persistent vital issue in life? This cause represents piety and righteousness. And was not their Caliph Abu Bakr As-Siddiiq, (Allah be pleased with him), the man who, while his flags were raised above the whole world, sat there in Al-Madiinah, the new capital of the new world, milking with his own hands the ewes of widows and kneading with his own hands the bread of orphans? Was not their Commander Khaalid lbn Al-Waliid the antidote for the doubts of tyranny, arrogance, oppression, and transgression? Was not the Sword of Allah drawn against the powers of backwardness, decay, and disbelief? Were not all these portraits a depiction of truth, the whole truth, and nothing but the truth?

So let the breeze of victory blow! Let it blow strong, mighty, and victorious!

Khaalid's ingenuity impressed the Roman officers and commanders so much so that Jerjah, a Roman commander, asked Khaalid to show himself during a rest in the fighting. When they met, the Roman commander asked him, "Khaalid, tell me the truth and do not lie, for the freeman doesn't lie. Did Allah send down on your Prophet a heavenly sword and he gave it to you, so that it enables you to kill anyone who comes within its sweep?" Khaalid answered, "No." The man exclaimed, " Then why do they call you the Sword of Allah?" Khaalid explained, "Allah sent His Prophet to us. Some of us believed in him and others disbelieved in him. I was among the disbelievers until Allah guided my heart to Islam and to His Prophet (PBUH) and I gave him my allegiance. Therefore, the Prophet supplicated Allah for me and said, 'You are the Sword of Allah."' The Roman commander asked, "What do you invite people to?" Khaalid answered, "We invite people to monotheism and to Islam." He asked, "Does anyone who submits himself to Islam have the same reward as you?" Khaalid answered, " Yes, and even better." Jerjah exclaimed, "How, when you embraced Islam before he did?"

Khaalid answered, "We lived with the Prophet and saw with our own eyes his signs and miracles. Now anyone who had the chance to see what we saw and hear what we heard was expected to submit himself to Islam sooner or later. As for you who did not see or hear him, if despite this you believe in him and in the unseen, you will find better and greater reward if you purify your conscience and intentions to Allah."

The Roman commander cried out as he urged his horse closer to Khaalid and stood next to him, "Please, Khaalid, teach me Islam!" He submitted himself to Islam and prayed two rak'ahs. Soon, combat erupted and once again, the Roman Jerjah fought, but this time on the Muslim side until he won martyrdom,

Now, let us watch closely how human greatness was manifested in one of its most remarkable scenes. The first version narrated by the historian said that while Khaalid was commanding the Muslim army in this bloody and crucial war and wresting victory out of the claws of the Romans with admirable master strokes, the new caliph, 'Umar Ibn Al-Khattaab, Commander of the Faithful, dispatched a message to him in which he saluted the Muslim army and announced the sad news of Abu Bakr's death (May Allah be pleased with him). Then he ordered Khaalid to give up his command to Abu 'Ubaidah Ibn Al-Jarraah. Khaalid read the message and supplicated Allah to have mercy on Abu Bakr and bestow His guidance on 'Umar. Then he strictly ordered the messenger not to tell anyone about the purport of the message and not to leave his place or communicate with anyone.

Then Khaalid resumed his command of the combat and concealed the news of Abu Bakr's death and 'Umar's orders until they had achieved victory. Finally, the hour of victory came and the Romans were defeated.

It was only then that the hero approached Abu 'Ubaidah and saluted him. At first, Abu 'Ubaidah thought that he did so in jest, yet he soon realized how serious and true this news was. Instantly, he kissed Khaalid between his eyes and praised his greatness.

The second version of the same incident is that the message was sent to Abu 'Ubaidah, who concealed the news from Khaalid until the burden of war was over. Which of the two versions is authentic is not our concern here. The only thing that interests us here is Khaalid's conduct, which was superb in both versions.

I cannot think of a situation in which Khaalid manifested more loyalty and sincerity than this one. It did not matter to him whether he was a commander or a soldier. Both ranks were one and the same to him as long as they enabled him to carry out his duties towards Allah Whom he believed in, the Prophet (PBUH) whom he gave allegiance to, and, finally, towards the religion which he embraced. This great self-control of Khaalid and of other Muslims was not possible without the help and guidance of the unique type of caliphs who were at the head of the Muslim nation at that time. These caliphs were Abu Bakr and 'Umar. The mere mention of either name conjures up all the unique and great traits created in mankind.

Notwithstanding the fact that Khaalid and 'Umar were not exactly best friends, 'Umar's decency, justice, and remarkable greatness were not in the least questioned by Khaalid. Hence, his decisions and judgments were not questioned. The unbiased conscience of the man who issued these orders reached the apex of piety, steadfastness, and veracity.

'Umar, the Commander of the Faithful, had nothing against Khaalid but his overburdening and sharp sword.

He vented these reservations when he suggested to Abu Bakr that Khaalid should be dismissed after the death of Maalik Ibn Nuwairah. He said, "Khaalid's sword is overburdening." He meant that it was swift, sharp, and harsh. The Caliph As--Siddiiq said, "I would not sheathe what Allah had unsheathed against the disbelievers."

Notice that 'Umar did not say that Khaalid was overburdening but used "overburdening" to describe the sword rather than the man. Not only did these words manifest the elevated politeness of the Commander of the Faithful but also his profound appreciation of Khaalid.

Khaalid was a man of war from head to toe. He dedicated his whole life before and after his Islam to becoming a shrewd and daring knight. Even his environment and the way he was brought up were devoted to that ultimate goal.

Whenever he traveled back in time, he saw the wars he waged against the Prophet (PBUH) and his Companions and the strokes of his sword that had slain believers and worshipers. Those memories agitated him and made him conscience- stricken. Therefore, his sword longed to devastate the pillars of disbelief to compensate for his wrong doings in the past.

I think you still remember what went on between Khaalid and the Prophet (PBUH) at the beginning of this chapter, particularly when Khaalid asked the Prophet, "Please ask Allah's forgiveness for me for all the wrong doings I committed to hinder men from Allah's path." You also remember that even when the Prophet told him that Islam erases all the wrong doings committed before it, he pleaded with him until he finally promised him to ask Allah's forgiveness for him for all the mischief he had committed before he submitted himself to Islam.

Surely, when the sword is carried by such an extraordinary knight as Khaalid and thrust upon the commands of a conscience, revived by the warmth of purification, sacrifice, and absolute loyalty to a religion that was surrounded by conspiracy and animosity, it will be impossible for this sword to throw aside its strict principles or its spontaneous sharpness.

For instance, when the Prophet (PBUH) sent him to some Arab tribes after the conquest of Makkah, he said to him, "I am sending you there not as a warrior, but as a Muslim who invites to the way of Allah." Unfortunately, his sword got the better of him and forced him into the role of the warrior, obliterating the role of the Muslim who invites to the way of Allah that the Prophet (PBUH) had ordered him to follow. When the Prophet (PBUH) heard what Khaalid had done, he was stricken with anxiety and pain. Then he turned in the direction of the Qiblah and raised his hands in supplication and apology to Allah and said, "O' Allah, I free myself from blame for what Khaalid has committed." Then he sent 'Aliy to give compensatory blood money to the family of the deceased.

Narrators said that Khaalid absolved himself from blame when he said that 'Abd Allah Ibn Hudhaafah As-Sahmii told him, "The Prophet has ordered you to attack them for their rejection of Islam."

In spite of that, Khaalid possessed superhuman energy. He was overtaken by an irresistible urge to devastate the idolatry of the ancient world. If we had watched him pulling down the 'Uzzaa idol which the Prophet (PBUH) ordered him to destroy, we would see that the resentment and wrath he showed while striking, were so aggressive and violent that he did not seem to be striking at a mass of rock but at a whole army, cutting the throats of its soldiers and spreading death everywhere. For he kept striking with his right hand, then with his left hand, then with his foot. He yelled at the scattered rubble and dust, "Uzzaa, I don't believe in you! Glory is not to be yours! I can see that Allah has humiliated you!"

We will always repeat the words of 'Umar the Commander of the Faithful about Khaalid: "Women who give birth to men like Khaalid are extremely rare," as well as our earnest wish along with 'Umar that his sword would lose its rashness.

On the day of his death, 'Umar cried excessively. Later, people learned that his grief was not only caused by his personal loss, but also by the loss of his last chance to return the command to Khaalid now that people were no longer infatuated with him. The reasons behind his dismissal were now gone. Only this time, unfortunately, the man was gone too.

Indeed, the great hero rushed to take his place in Paradise. For it was about time he caught his breath, considering the fact that no one on earth had been more restless than he. It was really about time his exhausted body would sleep for a while, considering that he was described by his friends and enemies alike as "A sleepless man who would not let anyone sleep."

If it were for him to decide, he would have chosen to live on until he had demolished all the decaying ruins of the ancient world and continued his jihaad in the way of Allah and Islam.

The sweet fragrance of this man's spirit will linger forever more whenever horses neigh and the edge of swords glitter and the standards of monotheism flutter over Muslim armies. He used to say, "Nothing is dearer to me than a frosty night in the company of an infantry of Muhaajiruun when we are to attack the disbelievers in the morning. Not even the night in which I was wedded to a new bride or received the glad tidings of the birth of a new child."

Therefore, the tragedy of his life, in his opinion, was dying in bed after he had spent his entire life on horseback, raising his glittering sword. It was difficult for him to accept that he was to die in bed, after all the battles he had fought next to the Prophet (PBUH). And after he had annihilated the Roman and Persian empires and after he had galloped to Iraq where he achieved one victory after another until he had liberated it. Then he had turned to Syria where he had achieved one victory after another until he had set it free from the bonds of disbelief.

In spite of his position as a commander, he was so modest that if you had seen him you would not have distinguished him from among his soldiers. Yet at the same time, you would have known at once that he must be a commander from the way he shouldered responsibilities and set himself as a good example.

Again, the tragedy of this hero's life was dying in bed. He said as his tears flowed, "All the battles I fought in left my body scarred with wounds and stabs everywhere, yet here I am dying in bed as if I had never witnessed war before. I hope that the cowards will not have a day's rest even after I am dead."

These words were becoming of such a man. When the moment of departure was close, he dictated his will. Can you guess to whom he left all his valuables? It was to "Umar Ibn Al Khattaab himself. Can you guess what were his valuables? They were his horse and his weapon. And what? He had nothing else to bequeath but his horse and weapon.

Thus, his only obsession while he was alive was achieving victory over the enemies of truth. He was not in the least obsessed with life, with all its splendors and luxury. There was one thing that he obsessively cherished and treasured. It was his helmet. He lost it in the Battle of Al-Yannuuk, and he exhausted himself and others in searching for it. When he was criticized for that, he said, "I keep it for luck, for it has some hairs of the Prophet's forehead. It makes me feel optimistic that victory is within reach."

Finally, the body of the hero left his home carried on the shoulders of his companions. The deceased's mother took one last look at the hero, her eyes full of determination tinged with sadness as she commended him to Allah's protection and said, "There are far, far better than a thousand men who flung themselves into the battlefield. Do you ask me about his valor? He was much more courageous than a huge lion that protects its cubs in the time of danger. Do you ask me about his generosity? He was far more generous than an overwhelming torrential rain that slides down from the mountains."

'Umar's heart throbbed and his eyes flowed with tears when he heard her recite these lines of poetry: "You spoke the truth. By Allah, he was everything you said he was."

The hero was buried. His companions stood at his grave inreverence. They felt that the whole universe was so peaceful, humble, and silent that it seemed as if the whole world went into mourning.

I imagine that this awesome stillness was broken only by the neighing of a horse that tugged at its halter and went to its master's grave guided by his scent. As it reached the silent congregation and the moist grave, it shook its head and neighed sharply as it used to do when the hero was on its back, devastating the thrones of Persia and Rome, curing the delusions of paganism and oppression, and eliminating the powers of backwardness and disbelief to pave the way for Islam. As it fixed its eyes on the grave, it kept on raising and lowering its head as if it were bidding its last farewell to its master and hero. Then it stood still with its head raised, yet its eyes flowed with tears. Khaalid bequeathed it along with his weapons to 'Umar in the way of Allah. Yet who is valiant and great enough to deserve to mount it after Khaalid?

Alas, you hero of all victory, the dawn of all nights. You soared with your army above the horrors of war when you said to your soldiers, “The darkest hour is that before dawn.” This became a saying afterwards.

May Allah bless your morning, Abu Sulaimaan. May Allah bestow glory, praise, and eternity on you, Khaalid.

Let us now repeat after ‘ Umar the Commander of the faithful the sweet elegy with which he paid his last farewell to Khaalid: “May Allah have mercy on you, Abu Sulaimaan. What you have now is far better than what you had in life, for you are now with Allah. You were honored in life and content in death.”

(23)
QAIS IBN SA'D IBN 'UBAADAH
The Craftiest of Arabs but for Islam

Although he was young, the Ansaar treated him as a leader. They used to say, "If only we could buy him a beard!" He was not lacking in any of the characteristics that a leader should have except the traditional beard.

But who was this lad for whom his people were willing to spend their money to buy a beard that would make his appearance faultless and becoming of his genuine greatness and astonishing leadership?

This young man was Qais Ibn Sa'd Ibn 'Ubaadah. He belonged to one of the most distinguished and generous Arab houses, on which the Prophet (PBUH) commented, "Generosity is the prevailing trait of this family."

He was a crafty man, and there was no end to his tricks, skillfulness, and cleverness. He spoke the truth when he said, "If it were not for Islam, I would have used my craftiness to outwit all the Arabs."

He was sharp-witted, tricky, and resourceful. In the As-Siffiin Battle, he sided with 'Aliy against Mu'aawiyah. He sat there turning over in his mind the plot that would make Mu'aawiyah and his men the worst losers, but the more he thought about his plot, the more he realized that it came under the heading of dangerous evil plotting. He then repeated Allah's Verse < *But the evil plot encompasses only him who makes it* > *(35:43).* Consequently, he rejected the plot altogether and asked Allah's forgiveness, saying, "By Allah, if Mu'aawiyah is destined to have the upper hand over us, he will not have it because he has outwitted us, but because our piety and fear of Allah have run short."

This man was one of the Ansaar from the Khazraj tribe. He belonged to a great family and inherited all the excellent qualities of his ancestors. He was the son of Sa'd Ibn 'Ubaadah, the Khazraj leader with whom we will be acquainted.

When Sa'd submitted himself to Islam, he held his son Qais's hand and introduced him to the Prophet (PBUH) saying, "This is your servant from now on." The Prophet (PBUH) saw in Qais all the qualities of excellence and righteousness, so he asked him to sit next to him and said, "This place will always be filled by him for the rest of his life." Anas, the Companion of Allah's Prophet (PBUH) said, "Qais Ibn Sa'd Ibn 'Ubaadah was to the Prophet like a chief officer to a commander."

Before his Islam, he was full of craftiness to the extent that no one was able to get the better of him. The people of Al-Madiinah and its surroundings fell short of his cunning. When he embraced Islam, it turned his life and even disposition upside-down as it taught him how to treat people with sincerity rather than with deceit. He was a truly faithful and loyal Muslim. Therefore, he threw aside his cunning and fatal maneuvers. Yet, whenever he faced a difficult situation, his restrained and thwarted craftiness tried to rebel and gain control over him and his actions, and the only thing that made him come to grips with it were these words: "If it were not for Islam I would have used my craftiness to outwit all the Arabs."

His cleverness was surpassed only by his generosity. Generosity was not an accidental behavior on Qais's part, for he belonged to a family renowned for its generosity. It was the custom in those times for all the wealthy and generous people to bid a crier to stand on a high place in the daytime to call guests and passersby to come for food and rest; then, at night, he would light a fire to guide strangers to where food was. People at that time used to say, "He who likes fat and meat must go to Duliim lbn Haarithah's house for food." Now, Duliim lbn Haanthah was Qais's great-grandfather. Thus, Qais was suckled amidst generosity and charity in this high-born family.

One day, both Abu Bakr and 'Umar commented on his generosity saying, "If we let this lad give free rein to his generosity, he would exhaust his father's wealth." When Sa'd lbn 'Ubaadah heard about what they had said, he cried out, "Abu Quhaafah and lbn Al Khattaab should not have tried to encourage my son to become a miser!"

One day, he lent a debtor, who was experiencing hard times a large sum of money. At the appointed time for repayment, this man went to repay his debt to Qais yet he refused saying, "I never take back anything that I have given."

Human nature is unchangeable. Both generosity and courage are inseparable. !ndeed, genuine generosity and courage are like twins: neither is found on its own. If you meet a generous man who is not courageous, then be certain that what you have seen is not real generosity but a mere superficial pretence. On the other hand, if you find someone who is courageous but not generous, then be certain that what you have seen is not courage but a mere impetuous and reckless whim. Qais lbn Sa'd held the reins of generosity with his right hand along with courage and valor. It seems as if he was meant by these lines of poetry:

> If a flag was hoisted in celebration of glory
> Then it must have been held by the right hand of an Arab.

His valor was outstanding in all the battles in which he fought when the Prophet (PBUH) was alive and even after his death.

When courage depends on honesty rather than craftiness, and on straightforwardness and confrontation rather than prevarication and maneuvering, then there must be difficult and endless trouble and intolerable hardships for its possessor. Ever since Qais threw aside his incredible skill of cunning and maneuvering and held onto his straightforward and conspicuous courage, he felt relieved and content, notwithstanding the problems he had to confront and the obligations he had to fulfill.

Genuine courage stems solely out of its possessor's conviction. This conviction is not affected by desire or whim, but rather by truthfulness and honesty with himself.

Hence, when the conflict between 'Aliy and Mu'aawiyah started, Qais sat alone trying to side with the one whom he believed to be in the right. Then as soon as he decided that 'Aliy was right, he did not hesitate to stand by his side with admirable pride, valor, and fearlessness.

Qais was one of the fearless heroes of As-Sifiin, Al-Jamal and An-Nahrawaan. He carried the Ansaar's standard and cried out, "The standard that I'm carrying now is the same one that I used to carry when we marched for war with the Prophet (PBUH) and had Jibriil as our reinforcement. Any man who has no one but the Ansaar on his side is a lucky man."

Imam 'Aliy assigned him to govern Egypt. Now, Mu'aawiyah's eyes were always set on Egypt, as he considered it the most precious stone in his prospective crown. Therefore, no sooner had Mu'aawiyah heard that Qais was to govern Egypt than he lost his self-control and was gripped by apprehensions lest Qais should stand forever in his way to rule Egypt, even if he achieved a decisive victory over Imam 'Aliy. Hence, he used all his cunning methods and unscrupulous tricks to defame Qais before 'Aliy.

Finally, Imam 'Aliy ordered him to leave Egypt. Qais had a legitimate chance to use his cleverness, for he realized that Mu'aawiyah must have incited 'Aliy against him through his sly and crafty tricks, after he had failed to win him over to his side. He aimed at inciting Imam 'Aliy against Qais by casting doubts on his loyalty to him. Therefore, the best answer to Mu'aawiyah's evil plots was to show more loyalty to 'Aliy and what he represented. This loyalty was not a mere pretence or a means to an end on Qais's part, but rather his firm conviction and belief. Therefore, he did not feel for a moment that he was dismissed from his position, for Qais considered the governor ship and all other positions as a means to the ultimate end, namely, to serve his faith and religion. He dedicated himself to the service of the truth. Whether he maintained his governor ship of Egypt or stood by Imam 'Aliy in the battlefield, it was one and the same thing for him, as long as they were a means to attain truth.

When Mu'aawiyah left the Muslims no other way out but to unsheathe their swords against one another, Qais took the command of 5,000 Muslims who shared in mourning for Imam 'Aliy's death.

Al-Hasan thought that it would be best to put an end to the prolonged suffering of Muslims and that deadly horrible conflict.

Therefore he agreed to negotiate with Mu'aawiyah and finally gave him his oath of allegiance. When this happened, Qais pondered the matter in his mind and decided that no matter how right Al Hasan was in his decision, his soldiers had every right to be consulted. Thus, he called them together and addressed them saying, "If you wish, we will keep on fighting to the last breath, or if you wish, I will ask Mu'aawiyah to guarantee your safety and security."

Naturally, Mu'aawiyah was relieved and overjoyed to be rid of one of his most dreaded and dangerous foes.

This man whose craftiness was tamed and subdued by Islam died in A.H. 59 in Al-Madiinah . This was the man who used to say, "If I did not hear the Prophet say, 'Craftiness and deceit reside in hell,' I would have been the craftiest man of the nation." In the end he died, yet the fragrance of this trustworthy and disciplined Muslim still lingers on.

(24)
‘UMAIR IBN WAHB
The Satan of Paganism and Disciple of Islam

On the Day of Badr, he was one of the leaders who took up their swords to put an end to Islam. He was sharp-sighted and a perfect estimator, so his people delegated him to determine the number of Muslims who set forth with the Messenger and to see if the Muslims had ambushers or reinforcements behind them. ‘Umair Ibn Wahb Al-Jamhii galloped on his horse round the camp of the Muslims, then returned to his people and told them that there were about 300 men, and his estimation was right.

They asked him if they had reinforcements behind them. He said, “I found nothing. But O’ you Quraish, I saw horses carrying veritable death. They have neither fortitude nor refuge except their swords. By Allah! I see if one of them is killed, one of you will be killed also. If they killed the same number as you, what would be the benefit of life after that? Think wisely.”

Some of the leaders of the Quraish were affected by his opinion and what he had said and were about to gather their men and return to Makkah without fighting, were it not for Abu Jahl who altered their opinion and ignited the fire of spite and war, in which he was its first victim.

The Quraish gave him the epithet “The Satan of Quraish”. On the Day of Badr, the Satan of Quraish fought fiercely and wildly, but the forces of the Quraish returned to Makkah completely beaten and ‘Umair Ibn Wahb left a part of himself at Al-Madiinah, as the Muslims had taken his son as a prisoner of war.

One day, he joined his cousin Safwaan Ibn Umaiyah, who was

chewing his enemies in deadly bitterness because his father Umaiyah lbn Khalaf had been killed at Badr and his bones buried at Al-Qaliib.

Safwaan and 'Umair sat together ruminating on their enemies. Let 'Urwah lbn Az- Zubair tell us their long dialogue:

Safwaan, mentioning those who were killed at Badr said, "By Allah, there isn't any good in life after them." 'Umair said, "That's true. By Allah, were it not for debts that I'm unable to repay and my children who I fear might be vagabonds after me, I would ride to Muhammad and kill him. I have a plausible reason to give him. I'll say that I have come for the sake of my son, a prisoner of war."

Safwaan seized the chance and said, "I'll repay your debts and maintain your children with mine and comfort them as long as they live." 'Umair agreed and said, "Keep it secret." Then he ordered his sword to be sharpened and poisoned and set out.

When he arrived at Al-Madiinah, 'Umar lbn Al-Khattaab was sitting among some of the Muslims talking about the Day of Badr. 'Umar looked and saw 'Umair lbn Wahb, girded with his sword, making his camel kneel at the door of the mosque. 'Umar said, "That dog, the enemy of Allah, 'Umair lbn Wahb! By Allah, he has come for nothing but evil. It is he who provoked us on the Day of Badr."

'Umar entered and said to the Messenger (PBUH), "O' Prophet of Allah, here is the enemy of Allah, 'Umair lbn Wahb come girded with his sword."

The Prophet (PBUH) said, "Let him in." 'Umar came and took him by the scabbard of his sword round his neck and said to some of the men, "Enter and sit with the Prophet (PBUH) and be cautious of that fellow, he is dishonest." Then 'Umar entered holding the scabbard of his sword round his neck. When the Prophet saw him, he told 'Umar to let him alone and said to 'Umair, "Draw nearer."

Umair approached and said, "Good morning." That was the salutation in the period of Jahiliyah.

The Prophet (PBUH) said, "Allah has honored us with a better salutation than yours. It is As-Salaam, the salutation of the believers in Paradise."

'Umair said, "O'Muhammad, by Allah I have heard it recently."

The Prophet (PBUH) said, "What made you come, 'Umair?" 'Umair said, "I have come for the sake of this captive in your hands." The Prophet (PBUH) said, "Tell the truth, 'Umair, what have you come for?" 'Umair, "I have come for that purpose." The Prophet (PBUH) said, "But you sat with Safwaan lbn Umaiyah at Al-Hijir and mentioned those of Al-Qaliib from the Quraish, then you said, were it not for my debts and my children, I would ride and kill Muhammad. Safwaan promised to repay your debts and maintain your children on condition that you kill me, but Allah prevented you from doing so."

At the moment, 'Umair cried, "I witness that there is no god but Allah and that you are His Prophet. "That matter wasn't attended by anyone except Safwaan and me. By Allah, Allah told it to you. Praise be to Allah who guided me to Islam." The Prophet (PBUH) said to his companions, "Teach your brother the religion and how to read the Qur'aan and set free the prisoner of war."

Thus, 'Umair Ibn Wahb embraced Islam. Thus: the Satan of Quraish was so overwhelmed by the light of the Prophet (PBUH) and the light of Islam that, in a moment, he embraced Islam and turned into the Disciple of Islam.

'Umar Ibn Al-Khattaab, (May Allah be pleased with him) said, "By Allah, I hated him more than I hated a pig, when he appeared. But now, I love him more than I love some of my sons."

'Umair sat thinking deeply about the tolerance of this religion and the greatness of its Prophet. He remembered his previous days in Makkah when he was arguing and fighting against Islam before the Hijrah of the Prophet (PBUH) and his Companions to Al-Madiinah. Then he remembered his fighting on the Day of Badr and his coming on this day to kill the Prophet. All that was abolished in a moment of saying, "There is no god but Allah and Muhammad is His Messenger."

What tolerance! What purity, what self confidence that this great religion carries. At such a moment Islam abolished all his previous sins, Muslims forgave all his crimes and hate, opened their hearts and embraced him. Is not he whose sword is still glimmering in front of their eyes, planning with devilish intention to commit the most ignoble deed? All that was forgotten and nothing was mentioned. 'Umair became in a single moment, one of the Muslims and one of the Prophet's Companions with their rights and duties. Did not he whom 'Umar Ibn Al-Khattaab wanted to kill a short time ago become dearer to him than his sons?

If in one moment of truth, when 'Umair embraced Islam, he deserved all the respect, honor, glory, and splendor of Islam, then Islam is indeed a great religion.

Within a short period of time, 'Umair knew that his duty towards this religion was to serve it as much as he had fought it, to suppor it as much as he had conspired against it and to show Allah anc His Prophet what they liked of truth, struggle, and obedience.

Thus, one day he came to the Prophet and said "O' Prophet o Allah, I had been doing my best to put out the light of Allal and was fond of hurting the Muslims. I would like you to give me permission to go to Makkah to call them to Allah, His Prophet and to Islam. Allah may guide them, otherwise, I'l hurt them in their religion as I used to hurt your companions in their religion."

From the time 'Umair left Makkah for Al-Madiinah, Safwaan Ibn Umaiyah, who had persuaded 'Umair to go and kill the Messenger, walked proudly in the streets of Makkah and dropped into its meetings and clubs joyfully and merrily. And whenever his people and his brothers asked him about the reason for his merriment and ecstasy when the bones of his father were still warm in the sands of Badr, he rubbed his hands proudly and said to the people, "Hurrah ! After a few days, happy new will come and make you forget the Battle of Badr," Every morning he went out of Makkah and asked the caravans, "Hasn' any matter occurred in Al-Madiinah?" Their answers were in the negative, as none of them had heard or seen any importan matter in Al-Madiinah.

Safwaan continued without despair asking caravan after carava until one day he met one and said to them, "Hasn't anything take place in Al-Madiinah?" The traveler said, "Yes, a very importan matter occurred." With a radiant face and at the peak of ecstas Safwaan asked the traveler anxiously, "What happened? Tell me! The man said, '"Umair Ibn Wahb has embraced Islam, and he i there learning the religion and the Qur'aan!"

Safwaan felt giddy, and the good news which he had announced to his people and for which they were waiting to make them forget the Battle of Badr, came to him that day dreadful enough to cause his ruin!

One day the traveler arrived, and 'Umair returned to Makkah holding his sword, ready to fight, and Safwaan Ibn 'Umaiyah was the first who met him. No sooner did Safwaan see 'Umair than he got ready to attack him, but the combat-ready sword in the hand of 'Umair dissuaded him. He was satisfied with some insults vented on 'Umair and went his way.

'Umair entered Makkah as a Muslim, though he had left it a few days earlier as a polytheist. In his memory was the image of 'Umar Ibn Al-Khattaab, when he embraced Islam, and cried, "By Allah! I'll sit as a believer in every place where I sat as a polytheist."

Taking these words as a motto and that situation as a model, 'Umair made up his mind to sacrifice his life for the religion that he had boldly fought against, when he had the force to hurt any Muslim. And thus he began to compensate for what he had missed and to race with time by calling to Islam day and night, secretly and openly. In his heart, faith floods upon him with safety, guidance, and light.

On his tongue are words of truth with which he calls to justice, charity, kindness and good. In this right hand is a sword with which he terrifies the severers, who hinder the believers from the path of Allah and want it crooked. Within a few weeks, those who embraced Islam by the guidance of 'Umair Ibn Wahb were becoming innumerable. 'Umair set forth with them to Al-Madiinah in a delightful, long caravan.

The desert that they crossed during their journey could not hold its astonishment and wonder at that man, who had crossed it a short while ago holding his sword and hurrying towards Al-Madiinah to kill the Prophet (PBUH). Then he had crossed it returning from Al-Madiinah with quite a different face from the first one. He was reciting the Qur'aan on the back of his she-camel. Now, he was crossing the desert for the third time ahead of a long procession of believers filling the desert with the praise of Allah.

Yes, it was a great announcement, that the Satan of the Quraish was turned by the guidance of Allah into a bold Disciple of Islam, who stood beside the Prophet (PBUH) in battles and situations and whose loyalty to the religion of Allah continued to be firm even after the departure of the Prophet from life.

On the day of the Conquest of Makkah, he did not forget his companions and relatives, to call them to Islam, especially after there was no doubt in the truth of the Prophet (PBUH) and his mission.

Safwaan had traveled to Jeddah on his way to Yemen by sea. 'Umair pitied him so much that he decided to deliver him from Satan by all means. He hurried to the Prophet (PBUH) and said, "O' Prophet of Allah, Safwaan Ibn 'Umaiyah is the chief of his people. He set off, escaping from you to throw himself into the sea. Give him safety. Peace be upon you." The Prophet (PBUH) said, "He is safe." 'Umair said "O' Prophet of Allah, give me a token for his safety." The Prophet (PBUH) gave him his turban which he had worn when he entered Makkah.

We let 'Urwah Ibn Az-Zubair complete the story: 'Umair set off till he reached Safwaan, when he was about to sail. 'Umair said, "O' Safwaan, I sacrifice my mother and father for you. Avert perishing yourself. This is the safety of the Prophet of

Allah (PBUH) I came to you with." Safwaan said to him, "Woe to you! Go away, don't speak to me." 'Umair said to him, "O' Safwaan! I sacrifice my mother and father for you. The Prophet of Allah is the best, the most righteous, and the most clement of all people. His glory is yours and his honor is yours." Safwaan said, "I'm afraid." 'Umair said, "He's more clement and more generous than that." He returned with him until they came to the Prophet (PBUH). Safwaan said to the Prophet, "He claims that you have given me safety." The Prophet said, "He speaks the truth." Safwaan said to the Prophet, "Give me the option for two months." The Prophet (PBUH) said, "You have the option for four months."

After a while Safwaan embraced Islam, and 'Umair was extremely happy about his acceptance of Islam.

Ibn Wahb went on his blessed journey to Allah following the great Prophet by whom Allah saved people from straying and took them out of the depth of darkness into light.

(25)
ABU AD-DARDAA
'What a Wise Man Was He!

While the armies of Islam were advancing victoriously, there lived in Al-Madiinah a wonderful philosopher and wise man whose wisdom flowed in his blooming bright words. He kept saying to those around him, "Can I tell you about the best of your deeds, which are more thriving and better than invading your enemies, cutting their throats and cutting yours, and better than dirhams and dinars?"

Those who listened to him craned and hurried to ask him; "And what is that, O'Abu Ad-Dardaa'?" Abu Al-Dardaa' resumed his speech and his face glittered with the light of faith and wisdom, "The remembrance of Allah; the remembrance of Allah is the greatest thing in life."

That wonderful wise man was not preaching an isolationist philosophy by his words. He was not preaching negativism nor the retirement from the responsibilities of the new religion that considers struggle its cornerstone. Yes, Abu Ad-Dardaa' was not that kind of man, but rather he was the man who took up his sword and struggled with the Prophet of Allah (PBUH) since he had embraced Islam till the help and victory of Allah came.

However, he was that type who finds himself in his full lively existence whenever he is alone contemplating under shelter of the sanctuary of wisdom, and he dedicated his life to seeking truth and certitude. Abu Ad-Dardaa', the wise man of those great days (May Allah be pleased with him) was a person who looked forward to His Prophet (PBUH), and he also believed that this faith, with its duties and understanding, was the only ideal way to truth.

Thus, he was engrossed with his faith, dedicating himself to it and forming his life strictly, wisely, and seriously according to it. He walked on that path till he arrived at the truth and took his high position among the truthful ones when communing with his Lord and reciting this verse: < *Truly, my prayer and my devotion, my life and my death are all for GOD, the Lord of the Worlds* > *(6 : 162).*

Yes, the struggle of Abu Ad-Dardaa against and with himself ended in the attainment of this high spiritual position, remote superiority, and personal sacrifice which made him dedicate all his life to Allah, the Cherisher of the Worlds.

Now, let us approach the saint and wise man. Do you observe the light that radiates round his forehead? Do you smell the good perfume coming from his direction? It is the light of wisdom and the perfume of faith. Faith and wisdom have come together happily in this man. His mother was asked about what he liked best; she answered, "Contemplation and consideration. " This is completely in accord with the saying of Allah in more than one *verse* <*Therefore take warning, you, who have eyes to see!* > *(59 : 2).*

When he urged his brothers to contemplate and think, he said to them, "Contemplation for an hour is better than worshipping for the whole night." Worshipping and contemplation and seeking after truth overpowered him and all his life.

On the day he embraced Islam and pledged his allegiance to the Prophet (PBUH) in this glorious religion, he was a successful trader of Al-Madiinah. He spent a part of his life in trade before he embraced Islam and before the Prophet (PBUH) and the Muslims migrated to Al-Madiinah.

He had just embraced Islam a short time before when... But, let him complete the speech for us: I embraced Islam at the hands of the Prophet (PBUH) and I was a trader. I wanted to combine trade and worship, but they would never go together. I abandoned trade and retained worship. Today, it doesn't please me to sell and buy to earn 300 dinars a day, although my shop is at the door of the mosque. I can't say that Allah forbids selling, but I'd like to be of those whom neither traffic nor merchandise can divert from remembrance of Allah.

Do you see how he speaks completely and correctly, while wisdom and truth shine through his words. He hurries before we ask him, "Does Allah forbid trade, O Abu Ad-Dardaa'?" He hurries to sweep away this question from our minds and refers us to the superior goal that he was seeking and for which he left trade, in spite of his success as a trader. He was a man searching for spiritual excellence and superiority and looking for the maximum degree of perfection available to human beings. He wanted worship as a ladder that raises him to the highest level of goodness and approaches right in its glory and truth in its shining origin. If he wanted worship to be merely duties to be done and prohibition to be left, he could manage both his worship and his trade and deeds.

There are many good traders, and there are many good and pious persons working in trade. Among the Companions of the Prophet of Allah (PBUH), there were men whom neither traffic nor merchandise could divert from the remembrance of Allah. But they worked hard to develop their trade and their money by which they served the cause of Islam and satisfied the needs of the Muslims. But the method of those Companions does not diminish the method of Abu Ad-Dardaa', nor does his method diminish theirs, as everyone is fit for what he is created.

And Abu Ad-Dardaa' felt that he was created for what he devoted his life to: excellence in seeking after the truth by practicing the ultimate expression of celibacy according to the faith to which he was guided by Allah, His Prophet and Islam.

Call it mysticism if you wish, but it was the mysticism of a man who had plenty of them keenness of a believer, the capability of a philosopher, the experience of a fighter, and the jurisprudence of the Prophet's Companions. This made his mysticism a lively movement in establishing the soul and not merely shadows of this building.

Yes, that was Abu Ad-Dardaa', the Companion of the Messenger of Allah (PBUH) and his pupil. That was Abu Ad Dardaa', the saint and the wise man, a man who repelled life with both his hands, a man who secluded himself till he burnished and sanctified his soul and it became a clear mirror so that wisdom, rightness, and good reflected in it. That made Abu Ad-Dardaa' a great teacher and an upright wise man.

What happy persons are those who come and listen to him! Come and seek his wisdom, O' people of understanding. Let us begin with his philosophy towards life and towards its delights and vanities. He was influenced to the depths of his soul by the saying of Prophet, "Little and satisfied is better than much and diverted." Allah Almighty said, < *Woe to every taunting slanderer, backbiter, who piles up wealth and counts over it again and again, thinking that his wealth will make him immortal!* > *(104 : 1-3)*

The Messenger of Allah (PBUH) said, "Leave the worries of life as far as possible," and "He who makes life his only aim, Allah will sunder his unity and make poverty between his two eyes. He who makes the Hereafter his only goal, Allah makes riches in his heart and makes every good hurry to him."

Therefore, he lamented over those who fell captive to the ambition of wealth and said, "I seek refuge with the Lord from the dispersion of the heart." He was asked, "What is dispersion of the heart, Abu Ad-Dardaa'?" He answered, " That means I have money everywhere." He called people to possess life by doing without it, that is the real possessing of it. But running after its endless enticements is the worst kind of slavery. Then he said, "He who can not do without life is lifeless."

In his opinion, money is only a means to a mild satisfied living. Thus, people should take it legitimately (in a halaal way) and earn it kindly and mildly and not covet it greedily. He said, "Don't eat anything unless it is good, don't earn any money unless it is good, don't take anything to your house unless it is good."

He wrote to his companions, "After that, any temporary thing you possess in life was possessed by someone else before you, and will be owned by another after you, and you have nothing except what you offered to yourself.

"Give preference over yourself to him, from whom you are collecting money for your sons to inherit. Since you collect money for one of the two: either a good son, who spends the money in obedience to Allah, thus he will be happy with what you earned and free from troubles; or a disobedient son who spends it in sins and disobedience to Allah, and so you will be tortured by what you had collected for him. Entrust their living to the Bounty of Allah and save yourself."

The whole of life from Abu Ad-Dardaa's point of view is merely a loan.

When Cyprus was conquered and the booty was carried to Al-Madiinah, people saw Abu Ad-Dardaa' weep. Astonished, they approached and Jubair Ibn Nufair said to him, "Why are you weeping on the day that Allah supported Islam and the Muslims?" Abu Ad Dardaa' replied with wisdom and deep understanding, "Woe to you, Jubair! What trifling thing creatures are, if they leave the commands of Allah. It was the best nation, having dominion, but it left the commands of Allah, and therefore it came to what you see." Yes, thus he reasoned the quick collapse to the armies of Islam in the conquered countries was caused by the bankruptcy of true spiritualism that protected them and connected them with Allah. So he feared for the Muslims in the coming days, when the ties of faith would decline and the bonds to Allah, truth, and goodness would languish. Consequently, the loan would be taken from their hands as easily as it had been put in their hands before.

As the whole of life was merely a loan in his view, it was also a bridge to an immortal and more magnificent life.

Once his companions went to visit him when he was ill and found him sleeping on a piece of leather. They said to him, "If you wish, you will have better and more comfortable bedding." He replied pointing with his forefinger and looking with his bright eyes at the far distance, "Our home is there. For it, we gather and to it we return. We travel to it and we work for it."

This look at life was not only a point of view but also a way of life. Yaziid Ibn Mu'aawiyah wanted to marry his daughter, Ad-Darda but he refused him and married her to a poor pious Muslim.

People were greatly astonished by that behavior but Abu Ad Dardaa' taught them, saying, "What about Ad-Dardaa' if she had the servants and splendors and she was dazzled by the decorations and pleasures of the palace? What then would happen to her religion?"

This was a wise man of upright morals and clear heart. He refused everything that attracted the brain and fascinated the heart and by doing so he did not escape from happiness but escaped to it.

Real happiness, in his belief, was to possess life, not to be possessed by it. Whenever, the needs of people are limited by contentment and uprightness, they will realize the reality of life as a bridge on which they cross to the home of permanence, return, and immortality. Whenever they do so, their share of real happiness is greater and plentiful. He also said, "It is not better to have much money and many sons, but it is better to have much clemency, much knowledge, and to compete with people in the worship of Allah."

During the caliphate of 'Uthmaan (May Allah be pleased with him), Mu'aawiyah was the governor of Syria and Abu Ad-Dardaa' agreed to occupy the position of the judge according to the caliph's desire. There in Syria, he stood strictly as an example to all those who were tempted by the pleasures of life. He began to remind them of the method of the Prophet (PBUH), his asceticism and that of the early righteous Muslims and martyrs.

Syria at that time, was an urbanized region overflowing with the pleasures and amenities of life, and the inhabitants were greatly annoyed by that person who embittered their lives by his preaching. He gathered them and stood among them preaching, "O'people of Syria, you are brothers in religion, neighbors at home, and supporters against your enemies. But, why aren't you ashamed? You earn what you don't eat, and build what you don't dwell in, and hope for what you can't achieve.

The peoples before you collected cautiously, and hoped confidently, and built firmly, but their gatherings became perdition, their hope became delusion, and their homes became graves.

Those were the people of 'Aad who filled the region from Aden to Oman with wealth and sons. Then a wide sarcastic smile would be drawn on his two lips, and he would wave his arm to the astonished multitude and cry sarcastically, "Who will buy the inheritance of 'Aad people from me for two dirhams?"

He was a brilliant, magnificent, and luminous man. His wisdom was faithful, his feelings were pious, and his logic was perfect and cautious. In his point of view, worship was neither vanity nor pride but a request for good and exposure to the mercy of Allah and continuous supplication that reminded man of his weakness and the favor of his Lord upon him.

He said, "Request the good all your life, and expose yourselves to the mercy of Allah. Allah has fragrance in His mercy, which He ushers upon those whom He pleases among His servants. Ask Allah to hide your defects and make your hearts steady and firm in times of trouble."

This wise man was always open-eyed to vanity in worship, of which he warned people. That vanity makes those who have weak faith worship proudly and boast of their worship to others. Listen to him saying, "An atom's weight of benevolence from a pious man is much better than a mountain's weight of worship from the boaster."

He also said, "Don't charge people with unwanted affairs and don't call them to account as if you are their Lord. Guard your own souls. He who follows up the deeds of people will have his grief increased."

Abu Ad-Dardaa' did not want the worshipper, whatever rank he reaches in worship, to call people to account as if he were the Lord. He should praise Allah for His reconciliation and help by prayer, noble feelings, and good intentions for those who cannot achieve such success. Do you know any better and brighter wisdom than that of this wise man?

His companion, Abu Qalaabah, tells us about him: One day Abu Ad-Dardaa' passed by a man who had committed a sin, and people were insulting him. He prohibited them and said, "If you found him in a ditch, would you not take him out of it?" They said, "Yes." He said to them, "Don't insult him. Praise Allah that He protected you from such an evil." They said to him, "Don't you hate him?" He said, "No, I hate his deed, and if he leaves it, he will be my brother."

If this is one of the two aspects of worship, the second phase is knowledge and learning. Abu Ad-Dardaa' as a wise man and as a worshipper, sanctified knowledge to a great extent and so he said, "None of you can be pious unless he is knowledgeable, and he cannot enjoy knowledge unless he applies it practically."

Yes, knowledge, in his opinion, was understanding, behavior, learning, method, idea, and life. Because this sanctification is of the wise, we find him claiming that the teacher is like the student in favor, recompense, and position. He saw that the greatness of life was dependent on goodness before anything else. He said, "Why do I see your scholars going away and your ignorant people learning nothing? The teacher and the student of goodness are equal in recompense and there is goodness in the other people besides the two." He also said, "People are of three types: a scholar, an educated person, and a savage."

As we have seen before, knowledge was not separate from

following the wisdom of Abu Ad-Dardaa' (May Allah be pleased with him). He said, "The greatest fear of my soul is that it should say to me on the Day of Resurrection, in front of all the creatures, O' owner, did you know? And I would reply Yes. It will say to me, What did you do with what you knew?

He used to respect scholars and honor them very much. Moreover, he used to pray to Allah saying, "O' Lord Almighty, I take refuge in You against the curse of the scholars' hearts.

It was said to him, "How could you be cursed by their hearts?" He said, "Their hearts hate me." Do you see, he believed that the scholars' hate is an unbearable curse; therefore he implored Allah to grant him refuge.

The wisdom of Abu Ad-Dardaa' (May Allah be pleased with him) recommended fraternity and established human relations on the basis of human nature itself. Thus he said, "To admonish your brother is better than to lose him. Give your brother advice and be tender with him, but do not agree with his covetousness lest you should be like him. Tomorrow death comes and you will lose him. And how can you weep over him after death when you did not give him his right while he lived?"

The fear of Allah in His servants is the strongest and hardest basis upon which Abu Ad-Dardaa' established the rights of fraternity. He (May Allah be pleased with him) said, "I hate to wrong anyone but I hate more and more to oppress the person who resorts to Allah, the Most High and the Most Great, for help against my injustice."

Abu Ad-Dardaa', what a great personality and bright soul you are! He warned people against delusion when they thought that unarmed weak people fell easy prey in their hands and power.

He reminded them that those in their weakness have a destructive power when they implore Allah in their disability and offer their plea and the disgrace done to them by people.

This was Abu Ad-Dardaa', the wise man. He was Abu Ad Dardaa' the hermit, the worshipper, ever seeking Allah. When people praised his piety and asked him to implore Allah for them, he replied in humility, "I can't swim well and I fear drowning."

All your wisdom, and you can not swim well, O' Abu Ad Dardaa'? But what an astonishment, and you are nurtured by the Prophet (PBUH), a student of the Qur'aan; son of early Islam, and a companion of Abu Bakr and 'Umar and the rest of those men!

(26)
ZAID IBN AL- KHATTAAB
The Hawk of The Day of Al-Yamaamah

One day, the Prophet (PBUH) sat with a group of Muslims and while they were talking, the Messenger paused, then spoke to those who were sitting around him saying, "Among you there is a man whose molar in Hell is greater than Mount Uhud."

Fright and terror appeared upon the faces of all those present because each one of them was afraid lest he should be the person about whom the Prophet (PBUH) prophesied a dreadful end.

Years passed and all those Companions met their ends as martyrs except Abu Hurairah and Ar-Rajjaal lbn 'Unfuwah, who were still alive. Abu Hurairah was extremely terrified by that prophecy and did not feel comfortable until fate revealed the secret of the unfortunate man: Ar-Rajjaal lbn 'Unfuwah, who apostatized from Islam and joined Musailamah the Liar, and thus witnessed the fulfillment of prophecy upon him.

One day, Ar-Rajjaal lbn 'Unfuwah went to the Messenger of Allah (PBUH) and acknowledged him and learned the teachings of Islam. Then he went to his people and did not return to Al Madiinah till the death of the Prophet and the choice of As-Siddiiq as the Caliph of the Muslims. Ar-Rajjaal told Abu Bakr the news of the inhabitants of Al-Yamaamah and their support for Musailamah and proposed that he be sent to Al-Yamaamah as an envoy in order to confirm Islam among them. The Caliph gave him permission.

Ar-Rajjaal went to Al-Yamaamah, and when he saw the numerous supporters of Musailamah, he believed that they would be victors. His perfidious nature caused him to reserve a place in the prospective state of Musailamah. Consequently he apostatized from Islam and joined Musailamah, wh promised him a prosperous future.

Ar-Rajjaal was more dangerous to Islam than Musailamah himself because he exploited his previous association with Islam and the period he had lived with the Messenger in Al-Madiinah memorizing many verses of the Holy Qur'aan, and hi intercession to Abu Bakr (May Allah be pleased with him), th Caliph of the Muslims. Ar-Rajjaal exploited all those thing for evil purposes and cunningly supported and confirmed th sovereignty of Musailamah and his false prophethood.

He walked among people saying that he heard the Messenge of Allah say that he had taken Musailamah into partnership an when the Messenger (PBUH) died, he was worthy of carryin the banner of prophethood and revelation after him.

The number of Musailamah's supporters increased to a grea extent because of the lies of Ar-Rajjaal and his cunnin exploitation of his previous relationships with Islam and th Messenger (PBUH). When the news of Ar-Rajjaal reached Al Madiinah, the Muslims were exceedingly angry because of th lies of this dangerous apostate who used to mislead people. Hi evil words and deeds expanded the range of the war an intensified the conflict the Muslims had with their enemies an adversaries. The most anxious and the most eager to meet Ar Rajjaal was Zaid Ibn Al-Khattaab, whose heroism and fame wa outstanding in the biographies and books of Islamic history.

I am sure that you have heard about Zaid Ibn Al-Khattaab. H was the brother of 'Umar Ibn Al-Khattaab (May Allah be please with both). Yes! he was his elder brother. He was older tha

'Umar Ibn Al-Khattaab and he embraced Islam and gained the honor of martyrdom before him.

He was the ideal hero whose motto was "Actions speak louder than words." His faith in Allah and His Messenger and His religion was strong and firm. He never stayed away from the Messenger in any setting, and in every battle he sought martyrdom more than he sought victory.

On the Day of Uhud, when the fight between the believers and the polytheists was very fierce, Zaid was fighting boldly. His brother 'Umar Ibn Al-Khattaab (May Allah be pleased with him) saw him as his shield fell down and he was within reach of the enemies. 'Umar cried, "O' Zaid, take my shield and fight with it!" Zaid replied, "I want martyrdom as you want it." He continued fighting without his shield with astonishing heroism.

As we mentioned before, Zaid (May Allah be pleased with him) was longing to meet Ar-Rajjaal, wishing to put an end to his devilish life.

In Zaid's opinion, Ar-Rajjaal was not only an apostate but also a hypocrite and self-seeker. Zaid was, like his brother 'Umar Ibn Al Khattaab, in his abhorrence of hypocrisy and lying, especially when hypocrisy aimed at selfish gain and mean purposes. For those mean purposes Ar-Rajjaal committed his atrocious acts, resulting in the numbers of Musailamah's supporters greatly increasing and causing great numbers of deaths in the Apostate Battles. First he deceived them, and finally he led them to their deaths for the sake of his devilish hopes.

Zaid prepared himself to conclude his faithful life by annihilating that impiety not only in Musailamah's person but also in Ar-Rajjaal, Ibn 'Unfuwah, who was more dangerous and more cunning.

The Day of Al-Yamaamah began gloomy and dim. Khaalid Ibn Al-Waliid gathered the Army of Islam and directed it to its positions and left the leadership of the army to Zaid Ibn Al-Khattaab, who fought Bani Haniifah, the followers of Musailamah, boldly and fiercely. At the beginning, the battle was leaning towards the side of the polytheists, and many of the Muslims fell as martyrs, Zaid saw the feelings of horror in the hearts of some Muslims, so he climbed a hill and cried, "O' people! Grit your teeth, fight your enemy and go straight. By Allah, I'll never speak till Allah beats them or I meet Him and then I give my evidence." Then he descended, gritting his teeth, pressing his lips, never moving his tongue with even a whisper.

His only hope was to kill Ar-Rajjaal, so he began to penetrate the enemy army like an arrow searching for its target, until he saw him. Then he began to attack him from right and left. Whenever the deluge of the battle swallowed Ar-Rajjaal and hid him, Zaid dived towards him until the waves pushed him to the surface again. Zaid approached him and stretched out his sword towards him, but the furious human waves swallowed Ar-Rajjaal again. Then Zaid followed and dived after him so as not to allow him to escape.

At last, Zaid held him by his neck and with the sword, he cut off his head which was full of vanity, lies, and villainy. By the death of the great liar, the ranks of its whole army began to fall. Musailamah and Al-Mahkam Ibn At-Tufail were filled with horror. The killing of Ar-Rajjaal spread in Musailamah's army like a fire on a stormy day.

Musailamah used to promise them inevitable victory and that he, Ar-Rajjaal, and Al-Mahkam Ibn Attufail would promulgate their new religion and establish their state on the day following their victory! Now that Ar-Rajjaal was killed, the whole prophecy of Musailamah was seen as a lie, and tomorrow Al-Mahkam and Musailamah would meet the same fate. Thus the fatal blow of Zaid Ibn Al-Khattaab caused all that destruction in the lines of Musailamah.

No sooner did the Muslims hear the news than they were filled with pride and dignity. The wounded men rose again holding their swords, taking no interest in their wounds. Even for those who were about to die, nothing connected them with life except that very faint light caused by hearing the good news, which was like a very beautiful and rosy dream. They wished, if they had any strength to fight with, they would be able to witness the triumph of the battle in its glorious conclusion. But how could that be? Since the doors of Paradise had opened to welcome them, they were now hearing their names while they were being called to immortality!

Zaid raised his hands towards Heaven supplicating Allah and thanking Him for His blessings. Then he returned to his sword and his silence, as he had sworn by Allah not to utter a word until he had completed the victory or gained the honor of martyrdom.

The battle began to lean to the side of the Muslims and their inevitable victory began to approach rapidly. At that moment Zaid did not desire a better conclusion to his life than praying to Allah to grant him martyrdom on that Day of Yamaamah! The wind of Paradise blew to fill his soul with longing, his eyes with tears, and his determination with firmness. He began to fight as if he was searching for his glorious destiny, and the hero fell! So he died a martyr, magnanimously, gracefully and happily. The Army of Islam returned to Al-Madiinah victorious.

While 'Umar and the Caliph Abu Bakr were welcoming those

who were returning triumphantly, 'Umar began to search for his home coming brother with longing eyes.

Zaid was so tall that he could be easily recognized. But before 'Umar had strained his eyes, one of the returning Muslims approached and consoled him. 'Umar said, "May Allah have mercy upon Zaid, he preceded me in two instances. He embraced Islam before me and gained martyrdom before me, too."

In spite of the victories that Islam won and enjoyed, 'Umar "Al-Faaruuq" never forgot his brother Zaid, and he always said, "When ever the east wind blows, I smell the scent of Zaid."

Yes! The east wind carries the perfume of Zaid (May Allah be pleased with him). But if the caliph gives me permission to add these words to his great expression so as to complete the meaning of his saying, these are the words. "Whenever the winds of triumph blow on Islam since the Day of Al-Yamaamah, Islam finds the scent, the struggles, the heroism, and the greatness of Zaid in these winds!"

Blessings be upon Al-Khattaab under the flag of the Messenger (PBUH). Blessed be they the moment they embraced Islam. Blessed be they when they fought and were martyred. And blessings be upon them in the hereafter.

(27)
TALHAH IBN 'UBAID ALLAH
The Falcon on the Day of Uhud !

< *Of the believers are men, who have been true to their pledge to GOD, from them some have fulfilled their pledges, and some are still in hope of doing so, and they never change at heart* > *(33 : 23).*

The Prophet (PBUH) recited this glorious Verse and then turned to his Companions, pointed to Talhah and said, "Anyone who wants to please himself by looking at a man walking on the earth who has fulfilled his pledge of martyrdom should look at Talhah."

The Prophet's Companions never wished nor did their hearts ever aspire and long for a better announcement than the one the Prophet (PBUH) directed to Talhah Ibn 'Ubaid Allah. By such words he could feel secure towards his destiny and fate. He was going to live and die as one of those who have been true to their pledge so that neither civil strife could affect him, nor any kind of lassitude influence him.

The Prophet (PBUH) announced Paradise to him. How then was the life of such a one who deserved this fine announcement?

He was trading in the land of Basraa, when he met one of the most virtuous monks there. He told him that a Prophet who was going to appear in the Sacred Land and whose appearance was prophesied by all virtuous prophets had risen and his era had already begun, Talhah was very much afraid to miss the procession of guidance, mercy, and salvation.

When Talhah returned to his homeland Makkah after having

spent months in Basraa and traveling around, he found a lot of talk taking place here and there. Whenever he met someone or a group of Makkah inhabitants they would talk to him about Muhammad the Trustworthy, about the angel sent down to him, about the mission he was carrying to the Arabs in particular and all people in general.

The first thing he asked about was Abu Bakr. He learned that Abu Bakr had returned with a caravan and trade not long ago and that he was standing at the side of Muhammad, believing in and defending him.

Talhah said to himself, "Muhammad and Abu Bakr? By Allah, both of them would never join each other and agree upon falsehood " Muhammad had already reached the age of 40. In all these years we've never heard him speak one single lie. Is it possible that he would now lie about Allah and say, 'He sent me as a prophet and He sent me an angel'? It's something hard to believe."

He quickened his steps, directing them towards Abu Bakr's house. They did not talk for long because his long aspiration to meet the Messenger of Allah (PBUH) and to swear to him the oath of allegiance was much faster than his heartbeats.

Abu Bakr accompanied him to the Prophet (PBUH) and he soon embraced Islam, joining there and then the blessed ranks!

That is how Talhah became one of the very early converts.

Despite his honorable rank among his clan, his vast wealth, and his successful trade, he had to taste his own portion of the Quraish's persecution. The task of torturing him and Abu Bakr was given to Nawfal lbn Khuwailid, who was called The Lion of the Quraish. However, their persecution did not last long, as the Quraish soon felt ashamed and began to think about the consequences of their deeds.

Talhah emigrated to Al-Madiinah, when the Prophet (PBUH) ordered the Muslims to emigrate. After that he experienced all the battles together with the Prophet (PBUH) except the Battle of Badr, because the Prophet (PBUH) had sent him and Sa'iid Ibn Zaid on an assignment outside Al-Madiinah.

When they had fulfilled their task and were on their way back to Al Madiinah, the Prophet (PBUH) and his Companions were returning home after the battle. Talhah and his companion felt so sad and tormented for having missed the reward of joining the Prophet (PBUH) in his first jihaad battle.

However, the Prophet (PBUH) accorded them peace of mind when he informed them that their reward was exactly like the warrior's reward; moreover, he gave them a share of the booty exactly like the share he gave to each one who had fought the battle.

Then came the Battle of Uhud, when the Quraish, with all their might and tyranny, came to take blood revenge for the Day of Badr and to restore their dignity by defeating the Muslims once and for all, a defeat which was thought by the Quraish to be a simple matter and a predetermined fate. The fierce battle took place, and soon the battlefield was filled with its awful harvest: calamity overtook the polytheists.

Then when the Muslims saw them retreating, they laid down their weapons and the archers descended from their posts and began to collect their share of booty. Immediately and suddenly the Quraish army turned back to hold the field and tip the balance of the battle in their favor.

The fighting's ferocity, cruelty, and crushing resumed. The surprise attack had the effect of scattering the army.

Talhah saw that the side of the battlefield, where the Prophet (PBUH) was standing had become the target of the polytheists' concentration. He immediately hurried towards the Prophet (PBUH). He (May Allah be pleased with him) traversed a path, a long one, although it was in fact a short distance.

It was a path in which a single inch could not be traversed except by confronting tens of ferocious swords and tens of mad lances.

He could see from a far distance how the Prophet's (PBUH) cheek was bleeding and how he was silently suffering. It was then that Talhah got mad, leaped once or twice over the path of horror to reach the Prophet (PBUH), in front of whom he had to experience what he was afraid of: the swords of the polytheists drawn towards the Prophet (PBUH), surrounding him, wanting to get at him.

Talhah stood there like a raging army, striking with his sword to the left and right. He could see the Prophet (PBUH) bleeding and his pains becoming more and more unbearable. He helped him and carried him away from the hole where his foot had gotten stuck.

He supported the Prophet (PBUH) with his left hand and chest, backing up to a safe, secure place, while his right hand (May Allah bless his right hand) fought the swords of the polytheists who surrounded the Prophet and who swarmed the battlefield like locusts.

Let Abu Bakr As-Siddiiq describe for us the whole scene of battle. 'Aa'ishah once said: Whenever Abu Bakr recalled the

Day of Uhud he used to say. It was the Talhah's day. I was the first who approached the Prophet (PBUH). He said to me and to Abu 'Ubaidah lbn Al-Jarraah, "Watch out, for your brother." We looked at him, and we could see more than 70 stabs. His finger was cut off. We tried to remedy his condition.

In all the different events and battles, Talhah was always to be found in the forefront fighting in the cause of Allah, redeeming the Prophet's standard.

Talhah lived among the Muslim community, worshipping Allah with the worshipers, fighting in the cause of Allah with those who fought for truth, following the basic principles of the new religion which was revealed in order to bring people—all people — out of darkness into light.

After he fulfilled his duties towards Allah, he went on seeking the bounty of Allah, expanding and promoting his successful trade and business. Talhah was one of the wealthiest Muslims. His whole fortune was put in the service of his religion, the standard of which he carried with the Prophet (PBUH). He spent it without measure, and so Allah increased it for him without measure.

The Prophet (PBUH) called him "Talhah, the Excellent", "Talhah the Splendid and 'Talhah the Generous" to demonstrate his bountiful generosity.

How often did he give his whole fortune away. Then Allah the Ever-Generous returned it to him manifold! His wife Su'adaa Bint 'Awf reported: Once I approached Talhah. I saw him worried and asked him, "What's the matter?" He said, "The money which I possess is now so abundant that it worries me and makes me feel distressed." I told him, "Never mind, I'll distribute it." He set out to call people and to divide it among them till there wasn't a single dirham left.

On another occasion, he sold his land for a very high price. When he looked at the pile of money, his tears rolled down and he said, " A man in whose house all that money is to remain for a night and he doesn't know for sure what will happen to him is certainly deceived by Allah."

Then he called some of his companions to carry his money with them and walk through the streets of Al-Madiinah distributing it until in the last part of the night he was without a single dirham of that money.

Jaabir Ibn 'Abd Allah described his wealth saying, "I never saw anybody giving out so much money without being asked as did Talhah Ibn 'Ubaid Allah."

He was one of the kindest toward his relatives and kin. He supported them all, though they were numerous. It was once said about him, "He never left an orphan without supporting him and his dependents. He provided for the marriage of the unmarried ones, he provided service for the disabled ones, and paid the debts of the indebted ones."

As-Saa'I'b Ibn Zaid once said, "I accompanied Talhah during travels and during times of settlement. I never saw anybody more generous in terms of money, clothes, and food than Talhah."

The well known civil strife broke out during the caliphate of 'Uthmaan. Talhah supported the argument of 'Uthmaan's opponents, standing on their side in most of their quests to witness change and reformation.

Did he therefore, in such a position, call for 'Uthmaan's murder, or even feel pleased by it? Never! If he had known that the civil strife would develop in such a way, bursting into mad spite, expressing itself in such cruel crime, the victim of which was "The Man of Two Lights" 'Uthmaan (May Allah be pleased with him). We say, if he had known that the civil strife would in the long run lead to such an end and such a conflict, he would have resisted it, and it would have been resisted by the rest of the Companions, who supported him at the beginning, recognizing it as a movement of opposition and warning, and no more.

However, Talhah's stance turned out to be his "life conflict" after the brutal way in which 'Uthmaan was surrounded and killed. Imam 'Aliy had hardly accepted the oath of allegience from Talhah and Az-Zubair at Al-Madiinah, when they both asked permission to go to Makkah for 'Umrah.

From Makkah they both turned to Al-Basrah, where a great multitude was gathering to avenge 'Uthmaan's death. At last it was the Battle of Al-Jamal, where those calling for revenge met with the party supporting 'Aliy.

Whenever 'Aliy thought about this difficult situation, which Islam and Muslims were confronting in this horrible dispute, he burst into sorrowful tears and his laments grew louder and louder. He was forced into this difficult situation.

Being the Caliph of the Muslims, he could not and it was not his right to be tolerant towards any revolt against the state or any armed opposition to the established authority. To crush a rebellion of that sort then, he had to face his brethren, his companions, friends and the followers of his Prophet and his religion, those with whom he had so often encountered and combated the polytheist armies and with whom he had so often joined under the standard of monotheism in battles that refined their Islamic behavior and melted away all weakness and disgrace, there by turning them into brethren — and indeed brethren — supporting each other.

What a conflicting situation! What a difficult harsh test! In order to find a way out of such a conflict and to save the blood of the Muslims, Imam 'Aliy did his utmost.

Nonetheless, the factors opposing Islam- and they were many - which had met their defeat at the hands of the Muslim state ir the days of its great leader 'Umar, had kindled the civil uprisin and continued to stoke it and follow its events and magnitude

He cried a lot and wept abundantly when he saw The Mother o the Faithful 'Aa'ishah on her camel howdah at the head of th army, which rose to fight him. When he saw Talhah and Az Zubair, the disciples of the Prophet (PBUH), he called to then to come out to meet him, so they did. They approached him til their horses touched each other. He said to Talhah. "O' Talhah Did you come with the wife of the Messenger of Allah to us her in your fight while hiding your wife at home?" Then h said to Az-Zubair, "O'Zubair! I ask you by Allah. Do yo remember the day when the Prophet (PBUH) passed you whe we were in such- and-such a place, then he said to you, O Zubair! Do you love 'Aliy?' You replied, 'Why shouldn't I lov my nephew and cousin and the follower of my religion?' H said to you, "O' Zubair! By Allah, you will fight him, bein unjust to him.' "

Az-Zubair (May Allah be pleased with him) said, "Yes, now remember, I had forgotten that. By Allah, I won't fight you."

Az-Zubair and Talhah abstained from taking part in this civ

war. They abstained as soon as things were clarified. When they saw 'Ammaar Ibn Yaasir fighting on 'Ally's side, they remembered the Prophet's prophecy to 'Ammaar: "You will be killed by the unjust party." If 'Ammaar were killed in that war in which Talhah was taking part, then Talhah was unjust.

Talhah and Az-Zubair retreated from the whole fight and had to pay for that retreat with their lives. But they met Allah pleased and delighted with what they had been endowed by Allah: insight and guidance.

As for Az-Zubair, a man named 'Amr Ibn Jarmuuz, followed him and killed him while he was praying.

As for Talhah he was pierced with a lance by Marwaan Ibn Al - Hakım, which killed him on the spot.

The murder of 'Uthmaan represented in Talhah's conscience his "life conflict", as previously mentioned. Despite the fact that, he did not take part in the murder nor agree to it, he had just supported the opposition against him ('Aliy) at a time when it was not obvious that it would intensify and develop into a more serious conflict, until it turned into a dreadful crime.

When he took his place on the day of Al-Jamal amidst the army fighting against the Ibn Abi Taalib, which sought to take revenge for 'Uthmaan's murder, he wished that his position would be an atonement making him feel at ease towards the pressure of his conscience. Before the start of the battle he was supplicating with a voice choked with tears saying, "O' my Lord, accept me this day in favor of 'Uthmaan until You are pleased."

When they met 'Aliy face to face, he and Az-Zubair, both said they felt illuminated by 'Aliy's words and thereby saw it to be right to leave the battlefield.

However, martyrdom had been reserved for them. Indeed, martyrdom was his fate, and he was to meet it and it was to meet him, wherever he was.

Did not the Prophet (PBUH) once say about him, "He's one of those who passed away. Whoever wants to please himself by seeing a martyr walking on the earth, go let him look at Talhah." Thereby did the martyr meet his inevitable fate, and the Battle of Al-Jamal was over. The Mother of the Believers realized that she had made a hasty decision; therefore she left Al-Basrah for the Sacred House and then Al-Madiinah, keeping aloof from the fighting and dispute. Imam 'Aliy provided her with all means of comfort and respect.

When 'Aliy inspected all the martyrs of the battle, he set out to pray the funeral prayer upon them, those who fought on his side as well as those who fought against him. When he finished burying Talhah and Az-Zubair, he stood saluting them for the last time. He finished his words saying, "I wish to be with Talhah and Az-Zubair and 'Uthmaan among those whom Allah described thus: *<We removed from their hearts any malice therein, as brothers they shall rest upon couches facing each other >*" (15:47).

Then he gazed at their grave with kind, gentle, pure, and sad eyes saying, "I've heard with my two ears the Prophet (PBUH) saying, Talhah and Az-Zubair are my neighbors in Paradise."

(28)
AZ -ZUBAIR IBN AL 'AWAAM
The Prophet's Disciple!

It is almost impossible to mention Talhah without mentioning Az-Zubair, too, and almost impossible to mention Az-Zubair without mentioning Talhah as well.

When the Prophet (PBUH) was fraternizing with his Companions in Makkah before the Hijrah to Al-Madiinah, he fraternized with Talhah and Az-Zubair,

The Prophet (PBUH) often talked about them together, for example, in his statement "Talhah and Az-Zubair are my neighbors in Paradise."

Both of them were linked to the Prophet (PBUH) through relationship and descent. As for Talhah, he is linked to the Prophet (PBUH) through Murah Ibn Ka'b. Zubair's lineage is linked to the Prophet through Qusaii Ibn Kulaab. In addition to that, his mother Safiah is the Prophet's paternal aunt.

Talhah and Az-Zubair resembled each other tremendously in their fates. The similarity between them was enormous in terms of their upbringing, their wealth, their generosity, their religious solidarity, and their magnificent bravery. Both of them were early converts to Islam. Both of them were among the ten to whom Paradise was promised by the Prophet (PBUH) and among the six whom 'Umar entrusted with the duty of choosing the next caliph following him. Even their destiny was one of complete similarity. In fact it was one destiny.

As mentioned, Az-Zubair's embracement of Islam was an early

one. Indeed, he was one of the first seven who quickened thei
steps towards Islam and played a role with the blessed earl
converts at Daar Al-Arqam. At that time he was 15 years old
that is how he was endowed with guidance, light, and all th
good, while still a youth. He was a horseman and a bold warrio
from childhood, to the extent that historians mention that th
first sword lifted in Islam was Az-Zubair's sword.

In the very early days of Islam, while the Muslims were stil
few in number, hiding in Daar Al-Arqam, a rumor spread tha
the Prophet (PBUH) had been killed. Az-Zubair had hardl
heard that when he unsheathed his sword and hurried throug
the streets of Makkah although still so young.

First he went to learn the truth of what had been said
determined that if it were true, he would cut the whole of the
Quraish into pieces until they killed him.

On the high hills of Makkah, the Prophet (PBUH) met him
and asked, "What's the matter?" Az-Zubair told him the
news. The Prophet (PBUH) prayed for him and asked Allah
to bestow mercy and all good upon him, and victory upon
his sword.

Despite Az-Zubair's nobility among his clan, he had to carry
the burden of the Quraish's persecution and torment. It was
his uncle who was in charge of his torture. He wrapped him in
a mat, set it on fire to let him suffocate, and called to him
while he was under the pressure of severe torture, "Disbelieve
in Muhammad's Lord and I will ward off this torture."

Az-Zubair, who was at that time no more than a growing youth,
replied in a horrible challenging way, "No! By Allah, I won't
return to polytheism ever again."

Az-Zubair emigrated to Abyssinia twice, in the first and second nigrations. Then he returned to take part in the battles with he Prophet (PBUH). No raid or battle ever missed him.

Plentiful were the stabs which his body had to receive and preserve even after his wounds had been healed. They were ike medals telling of Az-Zubair's heroism and glory.

Let us listen to one of his companions, who once saw and lescribed these medals, which crowded each other over his body: While accompanying Az- Zubair in one of his journeys, saw his body spotted with sword scars. His chest was like hollow eyes due to the variety of stabs and wounds. I said to him, "I've seen on your body what I've never seen before." He replied, "By Allah, I haven't received one of them except while I was with the Prophet (PBUH) and in the cause of Allah."

During the Battle of Uhud, after the army of the Quraish had etreated towards Makkah, the Prophet (PBUH) assigned him ogether with Abu Bakr to follow the Quraish's army and to chase them so they would realize how strong the Muslim party was and would not think of reattacking Al-Madiinah and ontinuing the fight.

Abu Bakr and Az-Zubair led 70 Muslims. Although they were chasing a victorious army, the military skill used by As-Siddiiq nd Az-Zubair, made the Quraish think that they had verestimated the losses of the Muslim party. They thought hat the powerful front row, whose strength Az-Zubair and As-iddiiq successfully demonstrated, was nothing other than the dvance guard of the Prophet's army, which seemed to pproach in order to launch a horrible pursuit. The Quraish astened away and quickened their pace towards Makkah.

On the Day of Al-Yarmuuk, Az-Zubair was an army in himsel When he saw most of the warriors under his command movin backwards when they saw the huge advancing Roma "mountains", he cried, "Allahu akbar! Allah is the greatest! With a sharp striking sword he burst alone into those advancin "mountains", then he retreated, then penetrated the sam horrible rows with his sword in his right hand, never trippin nor slipping.

May Allah be pleased with him who was so much in love wit martyrdom, full of enthusiasm for dying in the cause of Allah He said, "Talhah gives his sons names of the Prophets and h knows there is no prophet after Muhammad (PBUH). But I giv my sons the names of martyrs, and may they die as martyrs!"

In this way, he named one son 'Abd Allah as a good omen after the martyr Companion 'Abd Allah lbn Jahsh; another h named Al-Mundhir after the martyr Companion Al-Mundhir lb 'Amr; another he named 'Urwah after the martyr Companio 'Urwah lbn 'Amr; another he called Hamzah after the marty Companion Hamzah lbn Abi Taalib; another he called Ja'fa after the martyr Companion Ja'far lbn Abi Taalib; another h called Mus'ab after the martyr Companion Mus`ab lbn 'Umai and another he called Khaalid after the martyr Companio Khaalid lbn Sa'iid.

In this way he chose for his sons the names of martyrs, hopin that they would all die martyrs. It is mentioned in his biograph that he never held a governorship, nor the task of collectin taxes or tribute, but only the task of fighting in the cause o Allah. His merit as a warrior can be seen in his total self-relianc and his complete self-confidence.

Even if 100,000 warriors were to join him in combat, you woul still see him fighting as if standing alone on the battlefield, and as if the responsibility of fighting and for victory rested on him alone.

His merit as a warrior is represented in his firmness and the strength of his nerves. He saw his uncle Hamzah on the Day of Uhud: the polytheists had cut his corpse into pieces in a dreadful way. He stood in front of him like a high firm rooted mountain, gritting his teeth while holding his sword tightly, having nothing in mind except a horrible revenge. Soon, however, a divine revelation prohibited the Prophet (PBUH) and the Muslims from even the slightest thought of such a thing.

When the Bani Quraidhah siege lasted a long period without their surrender, the Prophet (PBUH) sent him with 'Aliy Ibn Abi Taalib. There in front of the unsurmountable fortress he stood and repeated several times, "By Allah ! We will taste what Hamzah tasted or we will open their fortress." Then they two alone threw themselves into the fortress. With admirable strong nerves, they were able to terrify the besieged inside it and to open its gates.

On the Day of Hunain, he could see Maalik Ibn 'Awf, leader of the Hawaazin and of the polytheist army, after his defeat in Hunain, standing in the midst of some of his companions and the remnants of his defeated army. He burst alone into their midst and single handedly scattered them and pushed them away from the place of ambush from which they kept an eye on the Muslim leaders, who were returning from the battle field.

His share of the Prophet's love and appreciation was great, The Prophet (PBUH) was so proud of him that he said, "Every prophet has a disciple, and my disciple is Az-Zubair Ibn Al-Awaam." He was not only his cousin and the husband of Asmaa'

Bint Abu Bakr ("The Lady of the Two Belts") but, moreover, he was the powerful, loyal, brave, bold, generous, and bountiful, who gave away and devoted his life and money for Allah, Lord of all the worlds.

His characteristics were noble, his good qualities great. His bravery and generosity were always parallel to each other. He managed a successful trade, and his fortune was enormous; however, he spent all of that in the cause of Islam until he died in debt. His trust in Allah was the reason behind his generosity, bravery, and redemption.

Even when he generously gave up his soul, he asked his son to pay his debt. "If you're unable to pay it, then seek my Master's help," 'Abd Allah asked him, " Which master do you mean?" He answered, "Allah." He is the best Guardian, the best Helper." 'Abd Allah said afterwards, "By Allah I never fell into trouble because of his debt. I only said, 'O' Master of Zubair, pay his debt,' so He did."

On the Day of Al-Jamal, and in the same way previously mentioned about Talhah, was Az-Zubair's end and fate. After he saw it right to refrain from fighting, a group of those who had been keen to see the flames of civil strife continuously raging and never extinguished followed him. A treacherous murderer stabbed him while he was praying and standing between the hands of Allah.

The murderer went to Imam 'Aliy, thinking that he would be announcing to him good news when telling him about his attack upon Az-Zubair and when putting into his hands the sword which he had stolen from him after committing his crime. When 'Aliy knew that Az-Zubair's murderer was standing at his door asking permission to enter, he shouted ordering that he be expelled and said, "Announce Hell to the murderer of Safiah's son!" When they showed him Az Zubair's sword, Imam 'Aliy kissed it and then cried painfully saying, "A sword whose owner had so long wiped the Prophet's grief."

Is there a better, more wonderful and eloquent salute to be directed to Az-Zubair, at the end of our talk than the words of Imarn `Aliy?

May peace be upon Az-Zubair in death after his life. Peaceful greeting after peaceful greeting upon the Prophet's disciple.

(29)
KHUBAIB IBN 'ADIY
A Hero on the Cross !

And now, pave the way for this hero. Come nearer from all directions, from everywhere. Come in any way you can and strive your utmost, come hurrying and submitting. Approach in order to be taught the lesson of sacrifice, an incomparable lesson. You will say, Were not all the stories you have previously told lessons of incomparable sacrifice?

Indeed, they were lesson of incomparable magnificence. Nothing whatsoever can be similar to it. However, you are now in front of a new master illustrating the art of sacrifice, a figure who, if you miss meeting him, then you have missed a great deal, indeed a great deal. Come to us, all people of faith in every nation and country. Come to us, lovers of exaltedness in every period and era. And you, too, who carry a heavy burden of illusion and you whose belief in creed and religions is one of falsehood and error. Come with your illusion. Come and see how Allah's religion built men. Come and see what glory, what strength, what firmness, what determination, what sacrifice, what loyalty!

To sum up, what extraordinary and amazing greatness has been granted by the belief in truth to its sincere followers. Can you see the crucified body? It is our lesson today to all mankind! Indeed, the crucified body in front of you is our subject, our lesson, our master. His name is Khubaib Ibn 'Adiy. Remember this name well! Remember it, sing it, it is an honor for anyone belonging to any religion, to any sect, belonging to any ethnic group and living in any era!

He belonged to the Aws tribe from Al-Madiinah. He belonged

to the Ansaar.

Since the day of the Prophet's Hijrah to Al-Madiinah and since the day of his belief in Allah, Lord of the Worlds, he frequently visited the Prophet (PBUH). His soul, spirit, and conscience were pure, and his belief was firm. He was described by Hassaan Ibn Thaabit, Islam's poet: "He looked like a falcon among the Ansaar. Allah endowed him with noble character and good morals."

When the standards of the Battle of Badr were lifted, he was there, a bold warrior and a daring fighter. Among the polytheists whom he killed with his sword during the battle was Al-Haarith Ibn 'Aamir Ibn Nawfal, After the battle was over and the defeated remnants of the Quraish had returned to Makkah, the sons of Al-Haarith learned that their father had been killed. They learned the name of his killer very well by heart: Khubaib Ibn 'Adiy.

The Muslims returned from Badr to Al-Madiinah and persistently built their new community. Khubaib was a true worshiper, a pious devotee, carrying the nature of a devotee and the longing aspiration of a worshiper. There he turned to worship with the spirit of a passionate lover, praying at night, fasting during the day, glorifying Allah, Lord of the Worlds.

One day the Prophet (PBUH) wanted to know the Quraish's secrets so as to be fully aware of the target of their movements and any preparations for a new battle. Therefore, he chose ten of his Companions, among whom was Khubaib, and 'Aasim Ibn Thaabit as leader.

The expedition set off towards its destination until they reached a place between 'Asafaan and Makkah. News of them reached an area of Hudhail called Bani Hayaan. They hastened to them with 100 of their most skillful spearmen. They set out to pursue them and to follow their tracks.

They almost lost them but for the fact that one of them found some discarded date pits on the sand. He picked them up and, with the amazing skill Arabs were famous for, glanced at them, then shouted loudly so that the others could hear him, "They are date pits from Yathrib*. Let's follow them and they will surely guide us." They followed the discarded date pits until they could see in the distance what they were searching for.

'Aaasim, the expedition's leader, felt that they were being chased, so he ordered his companions to mount the high peak of a mountain. The 100 spearmen approached and surrounded the foot of the mountain and besieged them thoroughly. They asked them to surrender themselves after giving them their word not to hurt them. The ten turned to their leader, 'Aasim Ibn Thaabit Al-Ansaariy (May Allah be pleased with them all), and waited for his command. He then said, "As for me, by Allah, I will never let myself fall into the protection of a polytheist. May Allah inform our Prophet about us."

The spearmen then began to throw their spears at them. Their leader 'Aasim was wounded and died as a martyr. In the same way seven others were wounded and died as martyrs.

The rest were then called and promised that they would be safe if they came down. The three descended, Khubaib and his two friends. The spearmen approached Khubaib and his companion,. Zaid Ibn Ad-Dithinnah, and tied them up. The third one recognized the beginning of their deceipts, so he decided to die there where 'Aasim and his companions had fallen. He died where he wished. That is how some of the greatest, most faithful, most loyal to Allah and his Prophet (PBUH), and most sincere believers passed away. Khubaib and Zaid tried to untie themselves, but they were tied very thoroughly and tightly.

The deceptive spearmen took them to Makkah where they sold them to the polytheists. The name of Khubaib reached everyone's ear. The sons of Al-Haarith Ibn 'Aamir, who had been killed in Badr, remembered his name very well and were moved by spite and hatred. They hurried to buy him. Most of the inhabitants of Makkah, who had lost their fathers and leaders in the Battle of Badr, competed in purchasing him in order to take revenge. They enjoined each other to take revenge on him and commenced to prepare him for a fate to satisfy their desire for revenge, not directed at him, as such, but at all the Muslims.

Some other people took Khubaib's companion Zaid Ibn Ad Dithinnah and set out to torture him severely.

Khubaib submitted his heart, his whole life, and destiny to Allah, Lord of the Worlds. He turned to His worship with a firm soul, unruffled and fearless, accompanied by a divine tranquility. Even hard, solid mountain rocks and terror itself might melt and simply vanish due to it.

Allah was with him, and he was with Allah. Allah's hand was over him, and he could almost feel His fingers within his chest.

One day, one of Al-Haarith's daughters entered where he was kept as a captive at Al-Haarith's house. She quickly hurried out, calling the people to see an unbelievable thing! "By Allah, I saw him holding a big bunch of grapes, eating from it while being fettered with iron chains — at a time when there isn't a

---

* The old name of Al-Madiinah

single grape in Makkah. I can't think of it except as being a blessing from Allah!"

Indeed, it was a blessing given by Allah to His virtuous worshiper, as He gave to Maryam (Mary, mother of Jesus) daughter of 'Imraan before: < *Whenever Zakariya entered the sanctuary he found her furnished with provision, he said, "O' Mary from where did you get this?" She said. "It is from GOD, surely GOD provides who He pleases without measure (3:37).*

The polytheists brought him the news of the death of his companion Zaid Ibn Ad-Dithinnah (May Allah be pleased with him). They hoped thereby to break down his nerves. However, they did not know that Allah, the Most Merciful, had invited him into His hospitality, blessing him with divine tranquility and mercy.

They set out to bargain with him over his faith, promising to save his life if he disbelieved in Muhammad and his Lord, but they were like children trying to catch the sun by a mere arrow-shot.

Indeed, Khubaib's faith was like the sun in its strength, flame, light, and far-reachedness. He shed light upon those seeking light and warmed those seeking warmth, but the one who approached him to challenge him would be burned and destroyed.

When they lost hope of reaching their desire, they took the hero to face his destiny. They took him to a place called At- Tan'iim, where he would be killed. As soon as they reached this place, Khubaib asked them to allow him to pray two rak'ahs. They allowed him with the hope that he would make up his mind to announce his surrender and disbelief in Allah, His Messenger and His religion.

Solemnly, peacefully and humbly Khubaib prayed two rak'ahs. He felt the sweetness of faith within his soul, so that he wished that he could keep on praying and praying. However, he turned toward his killers and said to them, "By Allah, were it not for your thinking that I'm afraid of death, I would have continued praying." Then he lifted his hands towards the sky and said, "O' Allah! Count them one by one and then perish them all!" Then he scanned their faces intently and set out singing:

When I am being martyred as a Muslim,
I do not care in what way I receive my death
For Allah's sake. If He wishes,
He will bless the cut limbs.

It was perhaps the first time in Arab history to crucify a man then kill him on the cross. They had prepared out of palm tree trunks a huge cross on which they fixed Khubaib, his limbs tied tightly. The polytheists gathered in obvious glee at his suffering while spearmen prepared their lances.

All that cruelty was intentionally performed slowly in front of the crucified hero. He did not close his eyes, and amazing tranquility beamed from his face. Then spears began to skirmish and swords to tear his flesh into pieces.

One of the Quraish leaders approached him saying, "Would you like Muhammad to be in your place and you be healthy and secure among your kin?"

Only then did Khubaib burst like a thunderstorm, shouting to his killers, "By Allah, I would not like to be among my relatives and sons enjoying all the world's health and well-being while even a tiny thorn hurts the Prophet."

They were the same great words spoken by Zaid Ibn Ad Dithinnah when he was being killed! The same amazing dazzling strong words Zaid said one day before they were said by Khubaib. At that, Abu Sufyaan, who had not yet embraced Islam, had to shake his head and say astonished, "By Allah I've never seen anybody love somebody else the way Muhammad's companions love Muhammad."

Khubaib's words were so provocative that the spears and swords began to tear the hero's body to pieces, attacking it with complete madness and cruelty.

Not far away from the scene, birds and buzzards were flying around as if waiting for the butchers to end their task and leave the spot so that they could approach the fresh dead body to have a delicious meal. However, soon they called to one another and gathered, and their beaks moved as if whispering and talking.

Suddenly they flew away in the sky, far, far away. They smelled by their instinct the scent of a pious, repentant man, which spread from his crucified body, so they were ashamed to approach him or to hurt him. The flock of birds flew away, just and pure, into the vastness of space.

The group of malicious polytheists returned to their dens in Makkah while the dead body of the martyr stayed there, guarded by a group of Quraishi spearmen,

When they were lifting Khubaib onto the palm trunk cross and tying him firmly, Khubaib turned his face towards the sky asking his Ever Magnificent Lord, "Allah! We fulfilled the mission of Your Messenger. Inform him in the early morning of what is happening to us.

Allah responded to his prayer. While he was in Al-Madiinah, the Prophet (PBUH) was filled with a strong feeling that his Companions were facing a severe trial, and he could almost see the crucified dead body of one of them,

Immediately the Prophet (PBUH) sent for Al-Miqdaad Ibn 'Amr and Az-Zubair Ibn Al-'Awaam. They mounted their horses and set off to cross the land rapidly. Allah guided them to their desired destination. They lowered Khubaib's body to a pure spot of ground waiting to shelter him under its moist soil

No one knows to this day where Khubaib's grave lies. Maybe that is better and more respectable for him so that he remains in history's memory and in the conscience of life a hero, a hero on the cross.

(30)
'UMAIR IBN SA'D
The Matchless!

Do you remember Sa'iid Ibn 'Aamir? That ascetic and steady worshiper who was forced by the Commander of the Faithful 'Umar to accept the Governor-ship of Syria?

We spoke about him in the first part of this book, and we saw the wonder of wonders while talking about his asceticism, his renouncement of all worldly pleasure, and his piety.

But now we will meet on these pages a brother of his, better to say a twin brother, an identical twin in terms of piety, asceticism, elevation and greatness of soul, which is actually incomparable.

It is "Umair Ibn Sa'd. He was called by the Muslims "The Matchless", What do you think about a man about whom there was a public consensus that he deserved that title, a consensus of the Prophet's Companions, with all the merit, enlightenment, and intellect they possessed?

His father was Sa'd, the reciter (May Allah be pleased with him). He experienced the Battle of Badr with the Messenger of Allah and all the following events and stayed loyal to his oath till he passed away as a martyr in the Battle of Al-Qaadisiyah.*

---

* In Sirat Ibn Hishaam, p.519, Vol. 1. The Halaby Second edition, it was mentioned that sa`ad fathe was someone else, who died while the prophet (PBUH) was still alive before the Battle of Tabuuk. But Ibn Sa`d mentioned in At- Tabaqaat Al-Kubrah, Vol. 4, p. 324. Beruit Edition, That his Father was sa`d the reciter and we hold that opinion.

He brought his son with him to the Prophet (PBUH) to swear the oath of allegiance and to embrace Islam.

From the day 'Umair embraced Islam, he turned into a worshiper dwelling at Allah's mihrab (prayer niche), escaping and running away from the lights of fame, withdrawing to the tranquility and calmness of shadow.

It is absolutely out of the question that you find him in the front rows, except the row of prayer — he stations himself in the front row to be granted the reward of the highest in faith — and the rows of jihaad — he hastens to the front row, hoping to be one of the martyrs.

Other than that, he is dedicated to attaining righteousness, piety, and virtue. He is a returner to Allah, weeping for his sins! He is a devotee to Allah, hoping to be accepted as a faithful returner to Him! He is a traveler to Allah in all journeys and all instances.

Allah blessed him with his companions' love for him. He was the delight of their eyes and the darling of their hearts. That was because of his strong, firm belief, his pure soul, his calm nature, the scent of his good qualities, and his beaming appearance. All that made him the joy and pleasure of all those who met or saw him.

No one and nothing whatsoever was superior to his religion. He once heard Julaas Ibn Suwaid Ibn As-Saamit, one of his close relatives, saying, "If the man is truthful, then we've more evil than mules!" He meant by "the man" the Prophet (PBUH). Julaas was one of those who embraced Islam out of fear.

When 'Umair heard that statement, his calm, quiet spirit burst into anger and confusion. Anger because one of those who pretended to be a Muslim had insulted the Prophet by this wicked language. Confusion because a lot of thoughts came quickly to his mind, all revolving around his responsibility towards what he had just heard and denied.

Should he communicate all that he had heard to the Prophet? How, and what about the trustworthiness of private meetings? Should he keep silent and leave what he had heard within his breast? How? And where was his loyalty to the Prophet (PBUH) who was sent by Allah to guide them after having lived astray and to illuminate them after having lived in darkness?

However, his confusion did not last long. The truthfulness to himself helped him to find a way out. 'Umair immediately behaved like a strong man and a pious believer. He turned to Julaas lbn Suwaid, "O' Julaas, by Allah, you're one of the most beloved to myself and the last one I would like to see afflicted by something he dislikes. You've now said something that if I spread it around, it would harm you; if I keep silent, I would ruin my religion, and the fulfillment of duty towards religion has priority. So I'm going to inform the Messenger of Allah what you've said!"

Here 'Umair pleased his pious conscience completely. First, he fulfilled the duty of preserving the trustworthiness of private talks and elevated his great noble soul away from the role of a slandering listener. Second, he fulfilled his duty towards his religion and shed light on a suspicious hypocrite. Third, he gave Julaas a chance to reconsider his fault and to ask Allah for forgiveness. If he had done that straightforwardly, then his conscience would have found peace, because it would not have been necessary any more to inform the Prophet (PBUH).

However, Julaas's pride made him hold to his falsehood. His lips did not spell out the word "sorry" nor any other apology.

'Umair left him saying, "I will inform the Prophet (PBUH) before a revelation makes me a partner of your sin."

The Prophet (PBUH) sent for Julaas, who denied and moreover swore by Allah that he had not said that! However, a Quraanic Verse demonstrated clearly, the true and the false. <*They swear by GOD, that they said nothing, but they indeed uttered the word of unbelief and disbelieved after they had become Muslims, and they intended a plot but could not accomplish, what they intended and they only showed hostility towards Islam after GOD and His Messenger had enriched them out of His Bounty, so if they repent it will be better for them, so if they turn away, GOD will chastise them with a painful chastisement in this world and the Hereafter, and on earth there will be none to protect or help them* > *(9 : 74).*

Julaas found himself forced to confess his fault and to apologize, especially when he heard the holy Verse which accused him, promising him at the same moment Allah's mercy if he repented and refrained from that: < *So if they repent it will be better for them* >

'Umair's action was a blessing for Julass. Thus Julaas repented and his Islamic conduct turned to be more righteous than before. The Prophet (PBUH) held his ear and praised him, "O' my boy! Your ear was loyal and your Lord believed you."

I was delighted when I met 'Umair for the first time four years ago while composing my book *Between the Hands of 'Umar'*. I was amazed. Nothing could amaze me so much as what happened between him and the Commander of the Faithful. I am going to narrate to you that event for you to enjoy with me "excellence" in its most precious and magnificent form.

You all know that the Commander of the Faithful, 'Umar (May Allah be pleased with him) chose his governors very cautiously as if choosing his destiny. He always chose them from among the ascetic, pious, honest, and truthful: those who escaped from power and authority and would not accept it unless forced by the Commander of the Faithful to do so.

Despite his unerring insight and his overwhelming experience, he was very deliberate when choosing his governors and counselors, dealing scrupulously with his decision.

He never stopped his famous statement: "I need a man who, if among his clan would seem to be their prince while he isn't so in reality, and who, if among them would seem to be an ordinary one while being their prince in reality. I need a governor who won't favor himself above the other people in terms of clothing, food, or dwelling; who will lead them in their prayers, distribute their dues among them fairly, and rule them justly, never shutting his door leaving their needs and wishes unfulfilled.

According to these strict requisites he chose 'Umair Ibn Sa'd to be a governor over Horns. 'Umair tried to free himself of that task and to save himself, but the Commander of the Faithful obligated him and imposed it upon him forcefully. 'Umair asked Allah for proper guidance. Then he went to carry out his duty and task.

In Horns, a whole year passed and no land tax reached Al-Madiinah, nor did a single message reach the Commander of the Faithful. The Commander of the Faithful called his scribe, to whom he said, "Write to 'Umair ordering him to come here."

Will you allow me to tell you about the meeting between 'Umar and 'Umair as it was related in my previous book Between the

Hands of 'Umar" *

One day the roads of Al-Madiinah witnessed a dusty, shaggy man, covered by the hardship of travel and hardly pulling his feet out from the hot sandy ground due to his long suffering and the tremendous effort he spent. On his left shoulder there was a sack and a wooden bowl. On his right shoulder there was a small waterskin filled with water. He supported his thin, weak, tired body with a stick.

He turned to 'Umar's assembly with very slow, heavy steps. "O' Commander of the Faithful, peace be upon you."

'Umar replied. Deeply afflicted by the scene of his weakness and overexertion, he asked him, "What's wrong with you, 'Umair?"

"Can't you see I'm healthy, possessing a pure conscience and possessing the whole world?"

'Umar asked, "What do you have with you?"

'Umair replied, "I've a sack in which I carry my food, a bowl in which I eat, my utensils for my ablution and drink, and a stick to lean on and fight an enemy if he crosses my way. By Allah, the whole world is an obedient slave of my belongings."

"Did you come walking on foot?" "Yes."

"Didn't you find anyone who would give you an animal to ride on?"

---

*The first edition appeared in June 1964

"They didn't offer and I didn't ask them."

"What did you do with what we charged you with?"

"I went to the country to which you sent me. There I gathered all its virtuous inhabitants and made them in charge of levying the taxes, so when they did that I put the money there where it belongs. If anything had remained I would have sent it to you."

"Didn't you bring us anything?" "No."

Hereby 'Umar shouted, amazed and happy, "Reappoint 'Umair." But 'Umair replied with complete composure, 'Those were old days. I won't work for you or for anyone else!"

This scene is not a written drama nor an invented conversation. It is a historical event * witnessed by the soil of Al-Madiinah, the old capital of Islam during great unforgotten days. What kinds of men were those unparalleled elevated ones!

'Umar (May Allah be pleased with him) was always wishing How much do I wish to have men like 'Umair to assist me in ruling the Muslims! That was because 'Umair, who had been fairly described by his companions as being "The Matchless", could prove superiority over all human weakness caused by our material existence and our thorny life.

When this great saint was destined to face the test of power and authority, his piety was not afflicted. It rather became more elevated, raised beaming and bright.

* It was mentioned in Hiliat Al-Awliaa' Vol. I. One of our most fundamental sources

When he was Governor of Horns, he drew a clear picture of the tasks of a Muslim ruler. How often did his words from the pulpit shake the multitude of Muslims: “Islam is a well-fortified wall and a firm gate. As for the wall, that’s justice; and the gate is truth. If the wall is torn down and the gate destroyed, then Islam loses its protective strength. Islam remains well-fortified as long as its reign is mighty. The might of its reign cannot be realized by killing with swords or by slashing with whips; rather by the fulfillment of truth and justice!”

Now we greet ‘Umair for the last time, greeting him with humility and respect. Let us bow our heads for the best tutor, Muhammad, the Imam of all the pious, Muhammad, Allah’s mercy sent to the people in the midst of the heat and drought of life.

May Allah’s peace be upon him, may Allah’s mercy be upon him, may Allah’s salutations be unto him, may Allah’s blessings be upon him, and peace be upon all pious ones and peace be upon all his righteous Companions.

(31)
ZAID IBN THAABIT
The Compiler of Qur'aan !

If you hold the Holy Qur'aan with your right hand and concentrate your eyes upon it, and go on applying yourself eagerly and meticulously to its verdant meadows, chapter by chapter, verse by verse, remember that among those who deserve all gratitude and appreciation for such an accomplishment is a great venerable called Zaid lbn Thaabit.

The event of compiling the Qur'aan into one Holy Book is only mentioned in relation with that great Companion. When roses of honor are scattered on the day of remembrance of all the blessed ones who deserve credit for the compilation and preservation of the Qur'aan and putting it into its right order, lbn Thaabit's share of those roses will be the greatest.

He was an Ansaar from Al-Madiinah. When the Prophet (PBUH) reached Al-Madiinah in his Hijrah, Zaid was eleven years old. The young boy embraced Islam together with the Muslims of his clan and was then blessed by a prophetic supplication of Allah. His father took him to take part in the Battle of Badr, but the Prophet sent him back because of his tender age and body.

On the day of Uhud, Zaid went with a group of veterans to the Prophet (PBUH), begging humbly to be accepted into any of the veteran ranks. Their relatives were more insistent, begging and hoping. The Prophet (PBUH) took a thankful look at the young horseman, seeming as if he was going to apologize for not recruiting them in this battle also. However, one of them, Raafi' lbn Khudaij, approached the Prophet (PBUH) holding a lance, moving it skillfully with his right hand. He then said to the Prophet (PBUH), "As you can see, I am a spearman. I can throw very well. Please let me!"

The Prophet (PBUH) greeted the mature and energetic young man with a delightful smile, then he allowed him. The blood burst into the veins of his peers.

The second who approached was Samurah lbn Jundub, who set off waving with this strong hands, so that some of his relatives said to the Prophet, ''Samurah will kill Raafi'." The Prophet (PBUH) greeted him with a kind smile and allowed him.

Both Samurah and Raafi" were already 15 years old, with strong manly shapes. Six of the young peers were left, among them Zaid lbn Thaabit and 'Abd Allah lbn 'Umar. They set out to do their best, humbly begging the first time, weeping and crying the second time, and flexing their muscles the third time. However, they were too young and their bodies were still unripe, so the Prophet (PBUH) promised them to take part in the next battle.

That is why Zaid lbn Thaabit began to play the role of a warrior in the cause of Allah on the Day of Al-Khandaq, in A.H. 5.

His believing, faithful personality was developing rapidly and amazingly. He was not just proficient as a warrior but also as an intellectual possessing various different merits. He followed up the Qur'aanic revelation, learning it by heart, writing it for the Prophet (PBUH), proving to be exquisite in terms of knowledge and wisdom. When the Prophet (PBUH) began to proclaim his message to the outer world and to send his messages to kings and emperors, he ordered Zaid to get acquainted with some of their languages, which is what he actually did in a very short time.

In this way Zaid Ibn Thaabit's personality became brighter and occupied a high position in the newly built society and became subject to Muslims' respect and honor.

Ash- Sha'biy reported: Zaid Ibn Thaabit set out to ride, so Ibn 'Abbaas held the bridle. Zaid said to him, "O' cousin of the Prophet (PBUH), let me pass." Ibn 'Abbaas replied, "No, it's the way we treat our 'Ulamaa (scholars)."

Qabaisah reported: Zaid was Al-Madiinah's most superiors one in the field of judgment, jurisprudence, reciting, and the knowledge of obligatory duties.

Thaabit Ibn 'Ubaid reported, "I've never seen a more cheerful man at home and a more respectable one at his assembly than Zaid."

Ibn 'Abbas said, "The tutors of Qur'aanic recitation among the Companions of the Prophet knew that Zaid was one of those deeply rooted in knowledge."

All these qualities by which Zaid was described by the Prophet's Companions make us more acquainted with the person. Destiny would endow him with the honor of the assignment considered to be one of the most noble tasks in the entire Islamic history, the task of compiling the Qur'aan.

Since the divine revelation began to be revealed upon the Prophet's heart, he would be one of the warners. The message of the Qur'aan and the call to Allah started with these magnificent verses: <*Read: In the Name of your Lord Who created - created mankind from something which clings; Read! And your Lord is the Most Noble; Who taught by the pen. Taught mankind what he did not know* > *(96: I - 5).*

Since the time the revelation started, the Prophet (PBUH) turned his face towards Allah, asking for his further enlightenment and guidance.

During all the years of the Islamic revelation, when the Prophet ended a battle to begin another one; and when he foiled his enemies' conspiracies and plans only to encounter a new foe and another and then another; when he was seriously building a new world, with all that serious means, the Qur'aan was sent down and the Prophet (PBUH) recited and proclaimed it. While there was a small blessed group moved by its keen interest in the Qur'aan from the very first day, some of them set out to learn what they could by heart, and others, who were talented in writing, set out to preserve the written verses.

During the course of almost 23 years the Qur'aan was sent down verse by verse, or some verses following other verses, responding to various circumstances and instances, while those reciters and scribes went on fulfilling their task with great success.

The Qur'aan was not sent down as a whole; thus it was not a composed book, nor an invented one. It is, rather a guide for a new nation built in reality, step by step, day after day. Its faith is promoted and its heart, mind, and determination are shaped according to a divine will, a will not imposed from above, but rather by means of a total conviction in this divine will. That is how the human conduct of this nation is going to be guided.

Therefore, the revelation of the Qur'aan had to be piecemeal, in order to follow up the growth and advancement of such conduct and its ever changing situations and challenging difficulties.

Reciters as well as scribes competed and turned to recite the Qur'aan and to write it down. Leading them were 'Aliy Ibn Abi

Taalib, Ubaiy Ibn K'ab, 'Abd Allah Ibn Mas'uud, 'Abd Allah Ibn 'Abbaas, and the honorable Companion we are talking about right now, Zaid Ibn Thaabit (May Allah be pleased with them all). After it had been completely revealed and during the last period of revelation, the Prophet (PBUH) recited it to the Muslims with its chapters and verses put in order.

After the Prophet's death (PBUH) the Muslims were busy with the apostate battles. During the Battle of Al-Yamaamah-which was mentioned when we talked about Khaalid Ibn Al-Waliid and Zaid Ibn Al-Khattaab-the number of reciters who died as martyrs was tremendous. The flames of war had hardly died down when 'Umar hurried to Caliph Abu Bakr As-Siddiiq (May Allah be pleased with him) asking him insistingly to compile the Qur'aan quickly before the remaining reciters and scribes of the Qur'aan passed away.

The caliph asked Allah for guidance and consulted his companions, then sent for Zaid Ibn Thaabit and told him, "You're a rational youth, in whom we find no faults." Then he ordered him to begin compiling the Qur'aan, assisted by people of experience in that matter. Zaid carried on his work, upon which the whole destiny of Islam as a religion depended.

He stood the test in accomplishing the most difficult and crucial task. He went on compiling the chapters and verses from the reciters' memories and from the written work comparing, refuting and investigating until he could gather the whole Qur'aan and put it in order.

His success was attested to by the honorable record of the Companions' consensus (May Allah be pleased with them). They, especially the scholars, reciters, and scribes, had heard the Qur'aan being recited by the Prophet (PBUH) during all the different phases of Islam.

Zaid once described the tremendous difficulty which this holy, honorable task represented: "By Allah, if they had asked me to move a whole mountain from its place, it would have been easier than the task of compiling the Qur'aan which they ordered me to fulfil!"

Indeed, to carry a whole mountain, or several mountains, on his back would have pleased Zaid more than to make the slightest error in moving a verse or completing a chapter.

His conscience and religion could withstand any error except a mistake such as this, no matter how tiny or unintentional it may be. However, Allah's guidance accompanied him as well as His promise: < *Indeed! We are the One Who has revealed the Qur'aan, and We will most surely preserve it* > *(15: 9).*

So he succeeded in accomplishing his work, his duty, and responsibility as well as it could be.

This was the first phase of the compilation of the Qur'aan. However, at that time it had been compiled and written down in more than one book. Although the little difference between these books was merely in the pronunciation, experience had proven the necessity of uniting them all in one book.

During the caliphate of 'Uthmaan (May Allah be pleased with him) the Muslims continued their expansions, spreading far from Al-Madiinah. During those days, Islam received each day groups of new converts embracing Islam, one group following the other swearing the oath of allegiance. It was becoming more and more obvious what a danger the variety in the Holy Books might present, especially when different tongues recited the

Qur'aan. Even the dialects of the earlier and later Companions differed.

At that stage, a group of Companions with Hudhaifah lbn Al-Yamaan went to the Caliph 'Uthmaan explaining the necessity to unite the Holy Books into one. The Caliph asked Allah for His guidance and consulted his Companions. As Abu Bakr As-Siddiiq had sought Zaid's aid, so did 'Uthmaan.

So, Zaid brought all his companions and assistants together and they brought all the different verses of the Qur'aan from the house of Hafsah the daughter of 'Umar (May Allah be pleased with them), where they were kept safe. Thereupon Zaid and his comrades started to carry on their great task.

All those who helped Zaid were scribes of the revelation and Qur'aan reciters. Despite that, when they disagreed — which rarely happened — they always considered Zaid's word to be the final decision.

We can only imagine the tremendous difficulties encountered by those destined by Allah to gather and preserve the Qur'aan when we read it so easily or hear it recited.

It is exactly like the horrors they encountered and the souls they willingly gave away while fighting in the cause of Allah, in order to spread a virtuous, precious religion over the earth and to dispel darkness with a clear light.

(32)
KHAALID IBN SA'IID
A Fighter of the Foremost Muslims

Khaalid Ibn Sa'iid was born into a highly wealthy and power oriented family. His family lived in luxury and abundance, and his father was proud of his influential high status among the Quraish. Khaalid descended from Ibn Umaiyah, Ibn 'Abd Shams and Ibn 'Abd Manaaf.

When the first rays of Islam crept in, slowly but surely, over Makkah to announce in whispers that revelation had descended upon Muhammad the Trustworthy in the Cave of Hiraa' with a message from Allah to proclaim to His slaves, Khaalid's heart was revived and he gave an ear to the whispering, which was like a wonderful light, and he was also heedful to it. He was thrilled with joy as if he had been waiting for this news all his life. He kept on following these rays of light wherever they went. Whenever he heard his people talking about the new religion, he would join them and listen carefully with repressed joy. Every now and then, he would participate in the conversation with a word or two that gave impetus to the new religion to achieve publicity, effect, and guidance.

If you had seen him in those days, you would have the impression that he was a quiet young man who kept discrete silence. Yet beyond this calm appearance lurked a commotion of human feeling that was full of movement and joy. You could almost hear sounds of drums, trumpets, prayers, and glorification's. You could almost see the hoisted flags. His inner-self was feasting in the full meaning of the world. You could feel the joy, thrill, and even the clamor and clatter of the feast day.

This young man kept this big feast to himself and concealed it from all people. He knew that if his father found out that he harbored all this love, enthusiasm, and support for Muhammad's invitation to Allah's way, he would offer him as a sacrifice to the gods of 'Abd Manaaf. But when our inner selves are full and saturated with a certain feeling, it is not long before we lose control over it and it overflows freely and excessively. One day. . . No, it was not yet daybreak, and Khaalid was in a state of alert sleepiness when he saw a vision that was highly impressionistic, effective, and telling.

To be more precise, one night, Khaalid lbn Sa'iid saw in his sleep a vision of himself standing on the brink of a great fire. His father stood right behind him. Strangely enough, his father was incessantly pushing him towards the brink. He wanted to throw him right into the burning fire. Then Khaalid saw Allah's Prophet rush to him and pull him with his blessed right hand away from the burning fire.

When Khaalid woke up he knew what he had to do. He hastened to Abu Bakr's house and told him about his vision, which was undoubtedly as clear as broad daylight. Abu Bakr said, "Allah chose you for His Mercy. This is the Prophet (PBUH). Follow him closely, for Islam will keep you away from hell."

Khaalid rushed, looking for the Prophet until he found him. Then he asked the Prophet about his message. He (PBUH) answered him saying, "Worship Allah alone and join none with Him in worhship. Believe in Muhammad, His slave and Prophet; and, finally, abandon the worship of idols which do not hear, see, or have power to either harm or benefit you."

The Prophet expressed his heartiest welcome as he shook Khaalid's hand. Khaalid instantly said, "I bear witness that there is no god but Allah and I bear witness that Muhammad is His Messenger." Simultaneously, the repressed joyful songs within him were set free. In fact, his celebration burst forth, and his father found out about his Islam.

Now, on the day of Khaalid's Islam, only four or five people had already preceded him in embracing Islam. Sa'iid thought that his son's early Islam would expose him to the humiliation and ridicule of the Quraish people. The Islam of one of Sa'iid Ibn Al-'Aas's sons, had sufficed to shake the ground under Sa'iid's feet and throw doubts upon the credibility of his leadership.

Hence, he summoned Khaalid and asked him, "Is it true that you have followed Muhammad, despite his blasphemy against our gods?" Khaalid courageously answered, "By Allah, he speaks the truth. I do believe in him and I will follow and obey him."

No sooner had he finished these words than his father leaped on him and beat him ruthlessly. Then he threw him into a pitch dark room in his house, where he was imprisoned. He tortured him with thirst, hunger, and exhaustion. Yet Khaalid kept on crying out from behind his bars, "By Allah, he speaks the truth and I do believe in him."

Sa'iid realized that this torture was not enough; therefore, he dragged him to the sun-baked ground and dug a ditch for him between its heavy burning rocks and kept him there for three days without shade or cover. He had absolutely nothing to drink during those three days. His father gave up all hope that his son would turn back from his faith, so he dragged him back home and kept on luring him to apostatize from the new religion, then threatened him.

This maneuver of promising and threatening went on for a while, yet Khaalid was solid as a rock as he said to his father, "I will not turn apostate even if you promise me the world. I will live and die as a Muslim, so help me Allah." Sa'iid lost his temper and shouted fiercely, "Get out of my sight, you fool! By Al-Laat, I will not sustain you from now on." Khaalid answered, "Allah is the best of those who make provision."

Thus, he left the luxurious house that was full of food, clothes, and comfort. He left it to experience need and deprivation. But why should he worry when he had his faith by his side? Was he not in full control over his conscience and destiny? Then why should he be bothered by hunger, deprivation, or even torture? If a man found all he was looking for in the great truth that Muhammad was inviting people to believe in, there should be nothing in the whole world that could prove to be more important to him than his inner self, which he would then sell to Allah in a bargain in which Allah was both the owner and purchaser!

Thus, Khaalid Ibn Sa'iid subdued torture with sacrifice and overcame deprivation with faith. When the Prophet (PBUH) ordered his believing Companions to embark on the second emigration to Abyssinia, Khaalid Ibn Sa'iid was one of the muhaajiiruun.

Khaalid settled there for the time destined by Allah. Then he returned to his house with his brethren in A.H. 7. When they arrived, the Muslims had just finished the conquest of Khaibar. Khaalid settled in Al-Madiinah amidst the new Muslim society whose nucleus he was a part of, being one of the five first Muslims who had witnessed its birth and established its foundations.

Khaalid did not miss a war or a battle. He was always the first to go forth during war time. As one of the foremost Muslims, and highly conscientious and disciplined, Khaalid was always loved and honored.

He respected his conviction. Hence, he refused to hide or bargain with it. For instance, before the Prophet (PBUH) died, he assigned Khaalid to the post of Governor of Yemen. When he heard the news concerning Abu Bakr's nomination as caliph and the consensus of allegiance given to him, he left his work and set out for Al-Madiinah. He knew that Abu Bakr was an unmatched, righteous, and pious believer. However, he thought that the caliphate was Bani Haashim's right. He believed that Al-'Abbaas or 'Aliy Ibn Abi Taalib should have been the caliph. He clung to his belief and did not take the oath of allegiance to Abu Bakr. Notwithstanding that, Abu Bakr held no grudge against him. On the contrary, he kept his love and appreciation for him. He did not compel him to give the oath nor hate him for refusing. He was hardly mentioned among the Muslims without the great caliph justly praising him. In time, Khaalid Ibn Sa'iid changed his viewpoint, and one day he broke through the lines of the Muslims in the mosque while Abu Bakr was standing on the pulpit and gave the oath of allegiance to him. It was a true and confident pledge to Abu Bakr.

Abu Bakr marched with his armies to Syria and assigned the command of a regiment to Khaalid Ibn Sa'iid. Thus, he became one of the commanders of the armies. But before the troops left Al-Madiinah, 'Umar objected to Khaalid Ibn Sa'iid's command and prevailed on the caliph until he changed his previous order. Khaalid heard what had happened, yet his only response was, "By Allah, I was not overjoyed with being a commander, nor was I broken-hearted for being dismissed."

As-Siddiiq (May Allah be pleased with him) hastened to Khaalid's house to offer him his sincere apology and to explain his new decision. Then he asked Khaalid which of the commanders of the army he would like to accompany to Syria. He asked him if he would like to be with his cousin, "Amr Ibn

Al-'Aas or with Shurahbiil Ibn Hasanah?

Khaalid's answered was highly revealing of his greatness and inner piety, for he answered, "My cousin is closer to me due to the relation of blood and Shurahbiil is closer to me due to his excellent piety." Then he chose to be a soldier in Shurahbiil Ibn Hasanah's regiment.

Abu Bakr summoned Shurahbiil before the outbreak of the war and told him, "Take care of Khaalid Ibn Sa'iid. Treat him, as you would like to be treated if you were in his position. You well know his high rank in Islam. You know that when the Prophet died, he was already his governor in Yemen. I myself assigned him as a commander, then I rescinded my decision. I hope that this revoked order will make him even more pious and righteous, for I think that command is a trial. I gave him the chance to choose his commander and he preferred you to his cousin. If you need the opinion of a pious and true adviser, you must resort to Abu `Ubaidah Ibn Al-Jarraah first; second, Mu`aadh Ibn Jabal; and third, Khaalid Ibn Sa'iid. You will definitely find good advice with them. I warn you against acting upon your viewpoint alone and without consulting them first."

The pioneer of those martyred and rewarded in the Battle of Marj As-Sufar, where the Muslims and Romans met in terrible and deadly combat, was a glorious martyr who took a course in his life, from his early youth to the moment of his martyrdom, characterized by true belief and courageous action.

When the Muslims were examining their wounded and martyred on the battlefield, he lay there, as he always was, a quiet young man with a discrete silence and strong determination. They all cried out, "May Allah be pleased with Khaalid Ibn Sa'iid."

(33)
ABU AIYUUB AL-ANSAARIY
March Forth, Whether You Are Light or Heavy

The Prophet (PBUH) entered Al-Madiinah and put an end to his successful Hijrah. He began his first blessed days in the place of his immigration which destiny had selected for unprecedented and unmatched feats.

Riding on his camel, the Messenger(PBUH) advanced among the massive crowd which overflowed with enthusiasm, love, and longing. People crowded around the camel's halter in competition with one another to offer Allah's Messenger, their hospitality and accommodation. As soon as the procession reached the neighborhood of Bani Saalim lbn 'Awf, the crowd stood in the way of the procession and addressed the Prophet saying, "O' Messenger of Allah, please do accept our hospitable accommodation, for we are influential people who are great in number and wealth. We can also guarantee your support and protection." The Prophet (PBUH) mildly urged them to loosen its halter and get out of its way, for it had been ordered by Allah to stop at a certain place.

The procession advanced to the neighborhoods of Bani Bayaadah, then Bani Saa"idah, then Bani Al-Haarith lbn Al-Khazraj, then to the Bani 'Adiy, lbn An-Najaar. The people of every tribe tried to stop the camel and pleaded with the Prophet (PBUH) to honor them with his approval of their hospitable accommodation. Yet the Prophet (PBUH) gave them the same answer, smiling thankfully, "Get out of its way, for it has been ordered by Allah to go to a certain place." Thus, the Prophet (PBUH) left the choice of his abode to destiny,

Later, this abode would be of critical and glorious importance, for on this land the mosque out of which the words and light of Allah would emanate, illuminating the entire universe, would be built.

Next to this mosque, a dwelling or rather dwellings made of clay and bricks would be built with nothing inside them but that which is barely sufficient for sustenance and living. These dwellings would be inhabited by an inspired instructor and Prophet (PBUH) who dawned upon this world to revive its waning spirit and to bestow honor and peacefulness upon all those who have said that their Lord is only Allah and thereafter stood firm and straight in the Islamic faith by abstaining from all kinds of sins and evil deeds which Allah has forbidden and by performing all kinds of good deeds which He has ordained. They were those who believed in the Oneness of Allah, worshiped none but Him alone and did not confuse their belief with wrong. They were those who purified their religion to Allah and reformed the land and did not make mischief on the earth. Indeed, the Prophet (PBUH) was very careful to leave the choice of the place of his abode to Allah's determined decree.

Hence, he loosened the reins of his camel and did not pull it. Then he set his heart to Allah and supplicated, "Allah, pick and choose for me a place for my abode."

The camel knelt down in front of the house of Bani Maalik Ibn An-Najaar. Then it got up on its feet, circled around the place, then went back to the same spot again and knelt down, lowered its neck, and was motionless. The Prophet (PBUH) was optimistic and glad as he dismounted. One of the Muslims advanced towards the camel, took the saddlebags and carried them into his house. His face shone with joy and satisfaction as the Prophet (PBUH) who was enveloped with good fortune and blessings followed him right into his house.

Would you like to know who was the happy, lucky man in front of whose house the camel knelt down, and the man in whose house the Prophet was guest, and the man whom all the people of the city envied for his great fortune? He was our hero, Abu Aiyuub Al-Ansaariy, also known as Khaalid Ibn Zaid, the grandson of Maalik Ibn An-Najaar.

It was not the first meeting between the Prophet (PBUH) and Abu Aiyuub Al-Ansaariy. They had met before when the Madiinah delegation journeyed to Makkah to take the oath of allegiance to the Prophet (PBUH) in the famous Second Pledge of Al-'Aqabah. Abu Aiyuub Al-Ansaary was among the 70 believers who shook hands with the Prophet (PBUH) and gave him his support and loyalty. It seems that Abu Aiyuub's great fortune was that his house was chosen for the great Muhaajir and the generous Prophet (PBUH) to live in when the Messenger of Allah entered Al-Madiinah and established it as the capital of Allah's new religion.

The Prophet (PBUH) preferred to live on the first floor. However, no sooner had Abu Aiyuub Al-Ansaary ascended to his room on the upper floor then he shook with regret for yielding to the Prophet's wish and accepting to live and sleep above the Prophet (PBUH). Instantly, he pleaded with the Prophet to move to the upper floor. He prevailed upon him, and the Prophet moved to the upper floor. The Prophet (PBUH) stayed there until the mosque was built and his dwelling was built next to it.

Ever since the Quraish began to fight against Islam, to raid Al-Madiinah, the land of Hijrah, and to instigate tribes and organize armies to put out Allah's light, Abu Aiyuub became a professional in warfare and jihaad. This hero was there in Badr, Uhud, Al-Khandaq and the rest of the battles and wars. He sold himself, his money, and property to Allah, the Lord of All the Worlds.

Even after the Prophet had died, Abu Aiyuub never lagged behind or turned his back on a battle that the Muslims were destined to fight in, notwithstanding the hardships and the atrocities. The slogan that he sang day and night, secretly and openly was Allah's verse < *March forth, whether you are light or heavy> (9 :41).*

He never missed an expedition, but once. He refused to fight in an army whose commander was a young Muslim assigned by the caliph. Abu Aiyuub was against this choice. This one and only mistake shook his inner-most self, and he was always full of regrets as he repeated, "It is none of my concern who was appointed by 'Aliy." Ever since that slip, he never missed a battle, no matter what. It sufficed him to live as a soldier in the Muslim army, fight under its standard, and defend its sanctity.

When conflict erupted between "Aliy and Mu'aawiyah, he sided with 'Aliy without the slightest hesitation. He believed that 'Aliy was the rightful Imam who had been chosen by the Muslims. When 'Aliy died and Mu'aawiyah took over the caliphate, the ascetic, steadfast, and pious Abu Aiyuub held himself aloof. He craved nothing of this world but for a place in the battlefield among the mujaahiduun who strive in the way of Allah. Therefore, no sooner had he seen the Muslim army march forth towards Constantinople, than he mounted his horse, raised his sword, and galloped towards a great and long awaited martyrdom.

In this particular battle, he was wounded. The commander of the army paid him a visit to check up on him. He breathed heavily as if his longing to meet Allah made him impatient with the few minutes left of his life. The commander, Yaziid lbn

Mu'aawiyah, asked him, "What is your last wish, Abu Aiyuub?"

I wonder if any of us can guess or imagine what Abu Aiyuub's last wish was? No, his last wish before he died was inconceivable and beyond the imagination of most human beings.

He asked Yaziid to carry his body to the furthest point inside the enemy lands and bury him there, then to break through the enemy line until he reached his grave so that Abu Aiyuub might hear the sound of the galloping Muslim horses clattering over it and realize that they had achieved victory. Do you think this is poetic verse? No, this is neither poetic verse nor a whim of imagination. No, it really happened. It is a fact that the whole world witnessed one day, and stood there watching, unbelievingly, with its eyes wide open, and listening unbelievingly, with its own ears. Yaziid carried out Abu Aiyuub's will to the fullest extent.

Finally, the body of this very great man was buried in the heart of Constantinople — Istanbul nowadays. Even before Islam enveloped this part of the world with its light, the Romans of Constantinople looked up to Abu Aiyuub as a saint. Strangely enough, all the historians who registered the events that sustain the previous claim say, "The Romans looked after his grave, visited it, and asked Allah to send down rain for his sake during times of drought."

Notwithstanding the quick and regular tempo of the battles that Abu Aiyuub's life was full of, leaving him no time to sheathe his sword and take his breath, his life was tranquil and pure as the early morning breeze.

He heard the Prophet (PBUH) relate a hadith and he always cherished it. The Prophet said, "First, if you perform a prayer, perform it neatly as if it was your last prayer. Second, do not utter a word for which you will have to apologize later on. Third, rid yourself of the hope of having whatever is enjoyed by other people."

Thus, he never spread slander or mischief, he never desired anything, and he spent his life absorbed in spiritual longing as a sincere worshiper and with the aloofness of someone on his deathbed. When it was time for him to die, he desired nothing of this world but for this single wish that represented his heroism and greatness: "Carry my body far inside the Roman lands, then bury me there." He believed in victory. He had enough insight to foresee that those distant parts of the world would soon be one of the oases of Islam and would be illumined by its light.

Hence, he wanted to be interred there at the capital of the country, where the final decisive battle would take place and where he could, from his blessed grave, follow up the proceedings of the war: the sweeping Muslim armies, the fluttering flags, the neighing of the horses, their galloping, and the clash of swords. Today, he is lying over there, although he cannot hear the clash of swords and the neighing of horses any more, for the decree of Allah has been fulfilled upon him. Instead, he hears the magnificent sound of the Aadhaan five times a day, emanating from the high minarets across the horizon:

Alhhu akbar. Allah Is the Greatest.
Allahu akbar. Allah Is the Greatest.

His overjoyed spirit in its eternal and glorious home answers saying, "This is what Allah and His Messenger had promised us and Allah and His Messenger spoke the truth."

(34)
AL -'ABBAAS IBN 'ABD AL-MUTTALIB
The Provider of Water of the Two Harams: The Masjid Al-Haram in Makkah and the Masjid An-Nabawi in Al-Madiinah

In the Year of Drought, the Commander of the Faithful "Umar, along with a great number of Muslims, went out into a vast open area to perform the prayer for rain and supplicate Allah the Most Merciful to send down rain. "Umar (May Allah be pleased with him) held Al-Abbaas's right hand in his right hand and raised it towards the sky and supplicated, "O' Almighty Allah, we used to ask You for rain for the Prophet's sake while he was alive. O' Almighty Allah, today, we ask you for rain for the sake of the Prophet's uncle. So please send down rain on us." The Muslim congregation did not leave until rain poured announcing glad tidings, irrigation, and fertility.

The Companions rushed to embrace Al-'Abbaas and express their affection for his blessed status saying, "Rejoice! You are now the provider of water of the two Harams."

What was the man who was called the provider of water of the two Harams really like? Who was this man for whose sake 'Umar beseeched Allah to send down rain, notwithstanding 'Umar's piety, precedence, and high station well known to Allah, His Prophet and the believers? He was Al-'Abbaas, the Prophet's (PBUH) uncle. The Prophet (PBUH) held him in great esteem. His reverence and love for him were inseparable. He always praised his good nature saying, "He is the only one left of my family."

Al-'Abbaas lbn 'Abd Al-Muttalib was the most generous man

of the Quraish. Moreover, he was good to his relatives and maintained the bond of kinship. Al- 'Abbaas, just like Hamzah (May Allah be pleased with them both), was nearly the same age as the Prophet, being only two or three years older. Thus, Muhammad and his uncle Al-'Abbaas were of the same age and generation as children and as young men. Being relatives was not the only bond that made them close friends. They were tied by the bonds of age and life-time friendship.

In addition, Al-'Abbaas's good nature and excellent manners complemented the Prophet's standards of judgment, for Al-'Abbaas was excessively generous, as if he was the sponsor of good and noble deeds towards humanity. He treasured kinship bonds and cherished his family and relatives. He put himself, his influence, and his money at their disposal.

Moreover, he was an extremely intelligent man. His intelligence was tinged with craftiness. This, along with his high station among the Quraish, enabled him to avert mischief and abuse against the Prophet (PBUH) when he began to invite people openly to embrace Islam,

As we have mentioned before, Hamzah treated the Quraish's oppression and injustice and Abu Jahl's arrogance and hostility with his devastating sword. As for Al-'Abbaas, he treated them with a kind of intelligence and craftiness that benefited Islam in the same way that swords did to protect and defend its existence and victory.

A group of historians mentioned Al-'Abbaas among those who were last in embracing Islam, for his Islam was not announced openly until the year of the Conquest of Makkah. However, others narrated that he was foremost in submitting himself to Islam but that he hid his faith.

Abu Raafi'a, the Prophet's(PBUH) servant, said, "I was Al-Abbaas Ibn 'Abd Al-Muttalib's slave when Islam dawned on the family of the house. Thus, Al-'Abbaas, Umm Al-Fadl and I submitted ourselves to Islam, but Al-'Abbaas hid his Islam." This is Abu Raafi'a's statement in which he witnessed Al-'Abbaas's Islam before the Battle of Badr.

Consequently, Al-'Abbaas was a foremost Muslim. His staying in Makkah despite the Prophet's (PBUH) Hijrah was a premeditated plan, which bore fruit. "The Quraish neither hid their suspicions of Al-'Abbaas's real intentions, nor could they find a reason to show hostility to him, especially when he showed nothing but adherence to their way of life and religion.

When the Battle of Badr took place, the Quraish found their golden opportunity to unveil Al-'Abbaas's real allegiance. Al'-Abbaas was a shrewd man who detected, at once, the evil plots which the Quraish resorted to alleviate their anguish and loss.

If Al-'Abbaas was able to inform the Prophet (PBUH) in Al-Madiinah of the Quraish's plans and preparation, they would still succeed in leading him into a battle which he did not believe in and did not want. However, it would be a temporary success, which would soon turn into a devastating upheaval.

The two armies met in combat in the Battle of Badr. The Prophet (PBUH) called his Companions saying, "There are men of Bani Haashim and of other clans of the tribe who were forced to march forth. They do not really want to fight us. Therefore, if any of you meet one of them during the battle, I order you to spare his life. Do not kiil Abu Al-Bakhtariy Ibn Hishaam Ibn Al-Haarith Ibn Assad. Do not kill Al-'Abbaas Ibn 'Abd Al-Muttalib, for he was forced to go forth in this battle."

Now, the Prophet (PBUH) was not favoring his uncle Al-'Abbaas with a privilege, for it was neither the occasion nor the time for privileges. Muhammad (PBUH) would not intercede on his uncle's behalf-while the battle reached the apex of atrocity and while he saw his companions struck down in the battle of truth - if he knew that his uncle was one of the disbelievers. Indeed, if the Prophet had been ordered not to even ask for Allah's forgiveness for his uncle Abi Taalib, despite his endless support, help, and sacrifice for Islam, then how could he order the Muslims who were killing their own disbelieving fathers and brothers in the Battle of Badr to make an exception for his uncle and spare his life? It certainly does not seem logical or feasible. The only logical explanation is that the Prophet knew his uncle's secret and hidden allegiance and his secret services for Islam. He also knew that he was forced to go forth to the battle. Therefore, it was his duty to save him as far as he was able to.

If Abu Al-Bakhtariy lbn Al-Haarith won the Prophet's intercession although he did not hide his Islam nor support it as Al-'Abbaas did, it was because he refused to take part in the Quraish's abuse and oppression against the Muslims. Second, he went forth to battle out of embarrassment and compulsion. Was not a Muslim who hid his Islam and supported it openly and secretly in many notable situations more worthy of this intercession? Indeed, Al-'Abbaas was that Muslim and that helper. Let us go back in time to prove this statement.

When 73 men and two women from a delegation of the Ansaar came to Makkah during the Hajj season to take the oath of allegiance to the Prophet in the Second Pledge of Al-'Aqabah and to make preparations with the Prophet for the imminent emigration of the Muslims to Al-Madiinah, Prophet (PBUH) informed his uncle Al-'Abbaas concerning all that went on between him and the delegation and about the pledge, for he trusted his uncle and treasured his opinion.

When it was time for the secret meeting, the Prophet (PBUH) and his uncle Al-'Abbaas went to where the Ansaar were waiting for them. Al-'Abbaas wanted to test their loyalty and ability to help and protect the Prophet.

Now, let us hear one of the delegation, Ka b Ibn Maalik (May Allah be pleased with him) narrate the proceedings of this meeting: We sat in the ravine waiting for the Prophet (PBUH) until he arrived accompanied by his uncle. Al-'Abbaas Ibn 'Abd Al- Muttalib said, "O' people of Khazraj, you are well aware of Muhammad's lineage. We have prevented our people from abusing him. He lives here protected and supported by his people and in his own country, yet he prefers to accompany you and emigrate to Al-Madiinah. So, on the one hand, if you are certain that you will be capable of giving him sufficient help, protection, and safety, then fulfil your pledge to the fullest. On the other hand, if you intend to forsake and thwart him after he has emigrated to you, then you had better show him your true colors now before it is too late."

As Al-'Abbaas uttered these decisive words, his eyes were surveying the Ansaar's faces in order to trace and observe their reflexes and reaction to his words. Al-'Abbaas was not satisfied with what he saw, for his great intelligence was a practical one that investigated tangible and solid facts and confronted them from all their angles with the scrutiny of a calculating expert.

Hence, he posed an intelligent question: "Describe to me your combat readiness and war strategy." Al-'Abbaas was astute enough and experienced with the nature and disposition of the Quraish to realize that war between Islam and disbelief was inevitable, for on the one hand there was no way that the Quraish would accept to forsake their religion, glory, and arrogance. On the other hand, Islam would not yield its legitimate rights to the power of falsehood. The question was. Would the people of Al- Madiinah stand firmly behind the Prophet (PBUH) at the outbreak of war? Were they, technically speaking, on the same level of expertise in the tactics of war, attack, and retreat as the Quraish were? That was what Al-`Abbaas had in mind when he asked them to describe their combat readiness and war strategy.

The Ansaar were firm as a mass of mountain as they listened to Al-'Abbaas. No sooner had he finished asking this provocative question than the Ansaar spoke: "By Allah, we are given to warfare. We are men of soldierly bearing. We were raised on the tactics of war and trained to fight. We inherited excellent warfare expertise from our fathers and grandfathers. We have learned to keep on shooting arrows until the last one. We have learned to stab with our spears until they break. We have learned to carry our swords and strike hard until either we or our enemy is vanquished."

Al-'Abbaas was overjoyed as he said, " I can tell from what I have just heard that you are masters of warfare, but do you have armor?" They answered, "Of course, we have armor, shields, and helmets."

Afterwards, a great and magnificent dialogue occurred between the Prophet (PBUH) and the Ansaar, which we will narrate in detail later on. That was Al-'Abbaas's attitude at The Second Pledge of Al-'Aqabah. Whether he had already embraced Islam or had not yet taken his final decision does not change the fact that his great attitude determined his forthcoming role in contributing to the eclipse of the power of darkness and the imminent dawn of Islam. Moreover, it sheds light on his outstanding stout-heartedness.

Finally, the Battle of Hunain took place, offering more evidence of the self-sacrifice of this quiet and compassionate man whose impressive and immortal heroism would be projected on the battlefield only under pressing necessity. Otherwise, this innate heroism would dwell in his innermost self, yet it would always be lurking there.

In A.H. 8 and after Allah had enabled His Prophet and Islam to achieve the Conquest of Makkah, some of the influential tribes in the Arab Peninsula were enraged by the quick victory that this new religion had achieved in such a short time. Therefore, the Hawaazan, Thaqiif, Nasr, Jusham, and other tribes held a meeting and agreed to wage a decisive war against the Prophet (PBUH) and the Muslims.

Now, we should not let the word "tribes" mislead us into underestimating the gravity of the wars that the Prophet (PBUH) fought throughout his life. We must not think that they were small scale skirmishes in the mountains. On the contrary, these tribal wars, fought at the tribes' strongholds, were far more difficult and atrocious than ordinary wars. If we bear this fact in mind, we would not only have an accurate evaluation of the incredible effort exerted by the Prophet (PBUH) and his Companions, but also a correct and trustworthy one of the value of this great victory achieved by Islam and the believers, and an illuminated insight into Allah's guidance that was conspicuous in their success and victory.

As we have said, the tribes gathered in endless waves of fierce warriors. There were 12,000 warriors in the Muslim army. Twelve thousand? Who were these warriors? They were those who, not a long time before, had liberated Makkah, dragging the power of polytheism and idolatry to the last and bottomless abyss, and had raised their flags across the horizon without rivalry or competition.

This was undoubtedly an unprecedented victory that made pride stealthily creep into the victorious Muslims. In the final analysis, the Muslims were only human beings. Their large numbers and great achievement in Makkah made them vulnerable to pride. Consequently they said, "We shall not be overcome by a small group."

Their depending solely on their military power, solely and pride in their military conquest were unrighteous sentiments that they would quickly recover from through a painful yet curing shock which was awaiting them, for heaven was preparing them for a much more glorious and elevated end than war. The curing shock was a sudden large-scale defeat shortly after the two armies met in fierce combat. The Muslims at once supplicated Allah in humiliation and submission. They perceived that there was no fleeing from Allah, no refuge but with Him, and there was no power but His. These supplications flowed throughout the battlefield, turning defeat into victory.

Accordingly, the glorious Qur'aan descended addressing the Muslims: < . . . *on the Day of Hunain when you rejoiced at your great number but it availed you naught and the earth, vast as it is, was straitened for you, then you turned back in flight. Then Allah did send down His tranquility upon the Messenger and on the believers, and sent down forces which you saw not, and punished the disbelievers. Such is the recompense of disbelievers* > *(9:25- 26).*

On that day, Al-'Abbaas's voice and firmness were the most outstanding manifestation of this calmness and tranquility and of self-sacrifice. For while the Muslims joined forces in one of the valleys waiting for the arrival of their enemies, the polytheists were already hidden throughout the ravines with unsheathed swords. They wanted to take the initiative. Suddenly, they flung themselves into the battlefield and attacked the Muslims ruthlessly. This blitzkrieg shook the Muslims and made them turn their backs to the battle and run away without even casting a glance at one another. When the Prophet (PBUH) saw the chaos that this sudden attack brought to the Muslim lines, he at once mounted his white mule and cried out at the top of his voice, 'Where are my people? Come back and fight! I am truly the Prophet! I am the son of 'Abd Al-Muttalib!"

At that moment, the Prophet (PBUH) stood there surrounded by Abu Bakr, 'Umar, 'Aliy Ibn Abi Taalib, Al-'Abbaas Ibn 'Abd Al-Muttalib, his son Al-Fadl Ibn Al-'Abbaas, Ja'far Ibn Al-Haarith, Rabii'ah Ibn Al-Haarith, Usaamah Ibn Zaid, Aiman Ibn 'Ubaid and a few other Companions.

There was also a woman who was raised to a high station among those men and heroes, namely, Umm Suliim Bint Milhaan. When she saw the chaos and confusion that the Muslims had fallen into, she mounted her husband Abi Talbah's camel (May Allah be pleased with them both) and hastened towards the Prophet (PBUH). When her baby moved in her womb, she took off her outer garment and pulled it tight around her belly. As soon as she reached the Prophet (PBUH), she gave him her dagger. The Prophet (PBUH) smiled and asked, "Why do you give the dagger to me, Umm Suliim?" She answered, "You are dearer to me than my own father and mother. Kill those who turned their backs on you as you do your enemies, for they deserve the same punishment." The Prophet's face lit up, for he had strong faith in Allah's promise, and he said, "Allah sufficed us against them and has been good to us."

In those difficult moments, Al-'Abbaas was next to the Prophet (PBUH). In fact, he followed him like his shadow, holding the halter tightly and defying danger and death. The Prophet (PBUH) ordered him to cry out at the top of his voice, for he was a stout and loud voiced man, saying, "Come back and fight, O' Ansaar people! Come back, for you took the oath of allegiance to Allah and His Prophet." His voice sounded throughout the battlefield as if it was both the caller and warner of destiny. As soon as those terrified and dispersed Muslims heard his voice, they answered in one breath, "Here I am at your service. Here I am at your service." They flung themselves into the battlefield like a hurricane. They dismounted the horses and camels which would not move and ran with their shields, swords, and bows as if they were pulled by Al-'Abbaas's voice. Once again, the two armies met in fierce combat. The Prophet (PBUH) cried out, "Now it is time for fierce fighting." It was really a ferocious fight. The bodies of Hawaazan and Thaqiif rolled down the battlefield. Allah's warriors defeated the warriors who worshiped the idol of Al-Laat. Allah had sent down His calmness and tranquility on the Prophet and the believers.

The Prophet (PBUH) loved his uncle Al-'Abbaas dearly, to the extent that he could not sleep when the Battle of Badr lay down its burden and his uncle was captured. The Prophet (PBUH) did not try to hide his feelings. When he was asked about the reason for his sleeplessness, despite his sweeping victory, he said, "I heard Al`Abbaas moan in his fetters." As soon as a group of Muslims heard the Prophet's words, they rushed to where the captives were, untied Al-`Abbaas, and returned to the Prophet and said, "O' Prophet, we loosened Al 'Abbaas's fetters a little." But why should Al-`Abbaas alone enjoy this privilege? Consequently, the Prophet ordered them, "Go and do that to all the prisoners."

Indeed, the Prophet's love for Al-'Abbaas did not mean that he should receive special treatment that distinguished him from other captives. When it was decided that a ransom would be taken in exchange for the captives' freedom, the Prophet (PBUH) asked his uncle, "O' 'Abbaas, pay the ransom for yourself and your nephew 'Aqiil Ibn Abi'Taalib, Nawfal Ibn Al-Haarith and your ally, 'Utbah Ibn 'Amr and the brothers of Bani Al-Haarith Ibn Fahr, for you can afford it." Al-'Abbaas wanted to be set free without paying a ransom, saying, "O' Messenger of Allah, I was a Muslim but my people forced me to go forth in this battle." But the Prophet (PBUH) insisted on it. The glorious Qur'aan descended to comment on this incident saying, < *O' Prophet! Say to the captives that are in your hands: If Allah knows any good in your hearts, He will give something better than what has been taken from you, and He will forgive you, and Allah is Oft-Forgiving, Most Merciful* > *(8:70).*

Hence Al-'Abbaas paid the ransom for himself and his friends and returned to Makkah. From that point onwards the Quraish lost their influence over him and their benefit from his insight and guidance. Therefore, Al-'Abbaas took his money and luggage and joined the Prophet in Khaibar so as to have a place in the ranks of Islam and the believers. The Muslims loved, revered, and honored him, especially when they realized how much the Prophet (PBUH) loved and honored him when he said, "Al-'Abbaas was like a twin brother to my father. Consequently, if anyone annoyed Al-'Abbaas, it would be as though he personally annoyed me."

Al-'Abbaas had blessed offspring. 'Abd 'Allah Ibn 'Abbaas, the learned of the Muslim nation, was one of those blessed sons.

On Friday, the 14th of Rajab, A.H. 32, the people of Al'Awaalii in Al-Madiinah heard a crier calling out, "May Allah have mercy on whoever saw Al-'Abbaas Ibn 'Abd Al-Muttalib." They realized at once that Al-'Abbaas had died.

An unprecedented large congregation of people, such as Al-Madiinah had not experienced before, accompanied the funeral procession to the graveyard. The Commander of the Faithful 'Uthmaan (May Allah be pleased with him) performed the funeral prayer. The body of Abu Al-Fadl was laid in Al-Baqii'. He sleeps comforted and delighted among the faithful who have been true to their covenant with Allah.

(35)
ABU HURAIRAH
The Memory of the Revelation Era

It is true that a person's intelligence reckons against him, and those who own extraordinary gifts often pay the price at a time when they should receive a reward or thanks. The noble Companion Abu Hurairah is one of those. He had an unusual gift, which was his strong memory.

He (May Allah be pleased with him) was good in the art of listening and his memory was good in the art of storing. He used to listen, understand, and memorize; then he hardly forgot one word, no matter how long his life lasted. That is why his gift made him memorize and narrate the Prophetic traditions (Hadiths) more than any of the Companions of the Messenger (PBUH).

During the period of Al-Wada'iin, the writers who were specialized in telling lies about the Messenger of Allah (PBUH) misused Abu Hurairah's wide reputation for narrating about the Messenger of Allah (PBUH), and whenever they fabricated a hadith they used to say, "Abu Hurairah said. . . . " By so doing they were attempting to make Abu Hurairah's reputation and status as a narrator about the Prophet (PBUH) questionable. However, because of the extraordinary efforts exerted by great reverent people, who devoted their lives to serve the Prophetic Hadith and reject every falsehood, Abu Hurairah (May Allah be pleased with him) was saved from the lies and fabrications that the vicious wanted to infiltrate into Islam through him and to make him bear their sins.

Now, when we hear a preacher, lecturer or the one who delivers the Friday sermon saying this transmitted expression, "Narrated by Abu Hurairah (May Allah be pleased with him): The Messenger of Allah (PBUH) said,. . ."

I say when you hear this name in that form, or when you meet it many times in books of hadith, biography, jurisprudence, and religious books generally, you have to know that you are meeting the most interesting personality of the Companions with regard to his ability and talents of listening because of the wonderful traditions and wise instructions that he memorized about the Prophet (PBUH), which was his great fortune and incomparable gift.

Having this gift (May Allah be pleased with him), he was naturally one of the Companions who were most capable of vividly reminding you of those days when the Messenger (PBUH) and his Companions were living and of transporting you to that horizon which witnessed the glorious deeds of the Prophet (PBUH) and his Companions who gave vitality and significance to life and led to the right path.

So if these lines have moved your curiosity to get introduced to Abu Hurairah and hear some things about him, here is what you want.

He was one of those who reflected the Islamic revolution and all the tremendous changes that it brought about. He changed from a workman to a master, from a lost man in the crowd to an Imam and outstanding man, from a worshiper of accumulated stones to a believer in Allah, the One, the Irresistible.

He said: I was brought up as an orphan, and I emigrated as a poor man. I worked for Busrah Bint Ghazwaan for my daily food. I used to serve them when they dismounted, and walked near them when they rode. And now Allah has married her to me. All praise to Allah Who made the religion our support and made Abu Hurairah an Imam.

It was A.H. 7 when he went to the Prophet (PBUH), while the latter was in Khaibar, and embraced Islam. From the time he pledged allegiance to the Prophet (PBUH), he would not part from him except to sleep. Thus were the four years in which he lived with the Messenger of Allah (PBUH) from the time he embraced Islam till the Prophet died. We say that those four years were very long, full of virtuous words, deeds, and listening.

By virtue of his good nature, Abu Hurairah was able to play a prominent role by which he could serve the religion of Allah. There were many war heroes among the Companions. There were many jurisprudents, propagators of the faith, and teachers, but the milieu and people lacked writing and scribes. In that time, mankind — not only Arabs — was not much concerned with writing. It was not a sign of development in any society. It was the same even in Europe not so long ago. Most of its kings, with Charlemagne at the top of the list, could not read or write, although they were intelligent and capable at the same time.

Let us go back to our talk about Abu Hurairah. He realized by his nature the need of the new society that Islam was building for those who would keep its legacy and teachings. There were scribes among the Companions who used to write, but they were few. Besides, some of them had no free time to be able to write every hadith that the Messenger uttered.

Abu Hurairah was not a scribe, but learned by heart, and he had this necessary free time, for he had no land to plant or commerce to take care of. Believing that he had embraced Islam late, he intended to compensate for what he had missed by accompanying and sitting with the Messenger (PBUH). Besides, he himself knew the gift Allah had bestowed on him, which was his broad, retentive memory, which became even broader and stronger after the Messenger (PBUH) had invoked Allah to bless it for him. Then why should he not be one of those who took the burden of keeping this legacy and transmitting it to the coming generations? Yes, this was the role that his talents made possible for him to play, and he had to play it without flagging.

Abu Hurairah was not one of the scribes, but, as we said, he had a strong memory that made him retain things in his mind very quickly. He had neither land to plant nor commerce to keep him busy; hence he used to not part from the presence of the Messenger, neither in travel nor at other times.

Thus, he devoted himself and his precise memory to memorizing the hadiths and instructions of the Messenger of Allah (PBUH). When the Prophet (PBUH) died, Abu Hurairah kept narrating his traditions, which made some Companions wonder how he could know all those hadiths? When did he hear them?

Abu Hurairah (May Allah be pleased with him) shed light on this phenomenon, as if defending himself against the doubts of some of the Companions.

He said: You say that Abu Hurairah narrates much about the Prophet (PBUH) and the Muhaajiruun who preceded him to Islam do not narrate those traditions. But my friends among the Muhaajiruun were busy with their contracts in the market, and my friends among the Ansaar were busy with their lands. I was a poor man, always sitting with the Messenger of Allah, so I was present when they were absent, and I memorized if they forgot. Besides, one day the Prophet (PBUH) said, "Whoever spreads his garment till I finish my speech, then collects it to his chest, will never forget whatever I've said" Therefore, I spread my clothes and he directed his speech to me, then I collected it. By Allah, I did not forget what he said to me later on. By Allah, I would have narrated nothing at all, but for a Verse of Allah's Book: < *Surely those who conceal the manifest Revelations and the guidance which We have revealed, after We have made it clear for the people in the Book, those it is who shall be cursed by GOD and by those who curse* > *(2:159).*

This was the way Abu Hurairah explained the reason for being unique in narrating so many hadiths about the Messenger of Allah (PBUH). First, he had the time to accompany the Prophet more than any one else. Second, he had a strong memory blessed by the Messenger so it became stronger. Third, he did not narrate because he was fond of narrating but because spreading those traditions was the responsibility of his religion and life; otherwise he would be a concealer of the good and right, negligent of his duties, and would deserve the punishment of the negligent.

For these reasons he kept narrating, and nothing could stop or hinder him, even when "Umar, the Commander of the Faithful, told him, "Stop narrating about the Messenger of Allah, or I'll send you to the land of the Daws" — the land of his people. But this prohibition from the Commander of the Faithful was not an accusation of Abu Hurairah, but a support of a theory 'Umar was adopting and stressing, that the Muslims during this very period should read and memorize nothing but the Qur'aan so that it would settle in their hearts and minds. The Qur'aan is Islam's book, constitution and dictionary. Narrating about the

Messenger of Allah (PBUH) abundantly, especially in those years that followed his death (PBUH) when the Qur'aan was being compiled, caused unnecessary confusion. That is why 'Umar used to say, "Get busy with the Qur'aan; it is Allah's words. He also used to say, "Narrate a little about the Messenger of Allah but for what can be followed."

When he sent Abu Muusaa Al-Ash'ariy to Iraq, he said to him, "You are going to people where you can hear the sound of the Qur'aan in their mosques as if it were a drone of bees. Let them do what they are doing and don't occupy them with traditions. I'm your partner in this." The Qur'aan had been compiled in a warranted way so that nothing had crept into it. But 'Umar could not guarantee that some traditions were not slanted, forged, or taken as a way to tell lies about the Messenger of Allah (PBUH) and thus harm Islam.

Abu Hurairah appreciated 'Umar's point of view, but he was also sure of himself and his honesty. He did not want to conceal anything of the traditions or knowledge that he thought would be a sin to conceal. Hence, whenever he found a chance to unload the traditions he had heard or understood from his breast, he did so.

An important reason, which played a prominent role in provoking troubles around Abu Hurairah for talking about and narrating many traditions was the fact that there was another narrator in those days, who used to narrate and exaggerate about the Messenger (PBUH), and the Muslim Companions were not certain of his traditions. This narrator was Ka'b Al-Ahbaar, who was a Jew who had embraced Islam.

Once Marwaan Ibn Al-Hakam wanted to examine Abu Hurairah's ability to memorize. He invited him to sit with him and asked him to narrate about the Messenger of Allah (PBUH) while a scribe sat behind a screen and was told to write whatever Abu Hurairah said. After a year, Marwaan invited him once again and asked him to narrate the same traditions the scribe had written. Abu Hurairah had not forgotten a single word!

He used to say about himself, "No one among the Companions of the Messenger of Allah (PBUH) narrates about him more than I do, except "Abd Allah lbn 'Amr lbn Al-'Aas. He used to write, but I didn't."

Imarn Ash-Shaaf'iy (May Allah be pleased with him) said about him, "No one in his period was more capable of narrating traditions with such a memory than Abu Hurairah."

Al Bukhaariy (May Allah be pleased with him) said, "Almost eight hundred or more Companions, followers (the generation after the Companions) and people of knowledge narrated through Abu Hurairah." Thus, Abu Hurairah was a big, immortal school.

Abu Hurairah (May Allah be pleased with him) was an ever and oft-returning worshiper who used to take turns with his wife and daughter in praying the whole night. He prayed one third of the night, his wife another third, and his daughter a third. Thus, not one hour of the night passed in Abu Hurairah's house without prayers. In order to be free to accompany the Messenger of Allah (PBUH), he suffered the cruelty of hunger like nobody else. He used to talk about the times when hunger was so cruel that he would put a stone on his stomach, press his liver with his hand, and fall in the mosque while twisting that stone so that some of his friends thought that he was epileptic, but he was not.

When he embraced Islam, he had only one continuous

oppressing problem that would not let him sleep. That problem was his mother. From that day onwards she refused to embrace Islam. Not only that, she also used to hurt her son by speaking ill of the Messenger of Allah. One day she spoke to Abu Hurairah about the Messenger of Allah (PBUH) in a way that he hated. So, he left her crying and sad and went to the Messenger's mosque.

Let us listen to him narrate the rest of the story: I went to the Messenger of Allah crying and said, "O' Messenger of Allah, I used to call Umm Hurairah to Islam, and she used to refuse. Today, I called her, but she spoke to me about you in a way that I hated. Invoke Allah to guide Umm Hurairah to Islam." So the Messenger of Allah (PBUH) said, "O' Allah, guide Umm Hurairah." Then I ran out to give her the good news about the Messenger of Allah's invocation to Allah. When I arrived at the door, I found it closed, and I heard the sound of water. She called, "Stay where you are, Abu Hurairah-." Then she put on her shift and veil and she came out saying, "I bear witness that there is no god but Allah and that Muhammad is His slave and Messenger." So I hurried to the Messenger of Allah (PBUH) crying out for joy as I had cried for sadness and I said, "Here is good news, O' Messenger of Allah. Allah has answered your invocation. Allah has guided Umm Hurairah to Islam." I added, "O' Messenger of Allah, invoke Allah to make all the believers love me and my mother." He said, "O' Allah, make every believer love Your slave and his mother."

Abu Hurairah led the life of a worshiper and fighter. He did not miss a battle or a pious deed. During the caliphate of 'Umar Ibn Al-Khattaab (May Allah be pleased with him), he made him governor of Bahrain. 'Umar, as we know, used to call his rulers sternly to account. If he made one of them governor when he had two garments, on the day he ceased to govern, he should still own no more than those two garments, and it would be better to leave office with only one! But if he left office with any display of wealth, he would not escape 'Umar's reckoning, even if the source of his fortune was halaal. It was another world that 'Umar filled with wonders and miracles.

When Abu Hurairah was made governor of Bahrain, he saved some money from halaal sources. However, 'Umar knew and invited him to Al-Madiinah. Let Abu Hurairah narrate the quick conversation that took place between them: 'Umar said to me, "O' enemy of Allah and His Book, did you steal the money of Allah?" I said, "I am not the enemy of Allah or His Book. I am the enemy of their enemy. Besides, I am not the one who steals the money of Allah!" He said, "Then how did you gather 10,000?" I said, "I had a horse that had foaled repeatedly." 'Umar said, "Put it (the money) in the Bait Al-Maal (the treasury)."

Abu Hurairah gave the money to "Umar and raised his hands towards the sky saying, "O' Allah, forgive the Commander of the Faithful." After a while 'Umar called Abu Hurairah and offered him the governorship again. However, he refused and apologized. 'Umar asked why. Abu Hurairah said, "So that my honor would not be at stake, my money would not be taken, and my back would not be beaten." He added, "I'm afraid I would judge without knowledge or speak without patience."

One day, his yearning to meet Allah intensified. While his visitors were invoking Allah to cure him of his disease, he was imploring Allah saying, "O' Allah, I love to meet You, so love to meet me." In A.H. 59, he died at the age of 78: His calm body was buried in a blessed place among the reverent inhabitants of Al-Baqii.

Returning from his funeral, the people kept reciting many of the traditions that he had taught them about the noble Messenger. One of the recent Muslims asked his friends, "Why was our deceased sheikh called Abu Hurairah?" His knowing friend answered, "In the pre-Islamic time his name was 'Abd Shams. When he embraced Islam, the Messenger called him 'Abd Ar-Rahman. He used to be sympathetic towards animals. He had a cat that he used to feed, carry, clean, and shelter, and it used to accompany him as if it were his shadow. Thus, he was called Abu Hurairah, which means father of the small cat. May Allah be pleased with him."

(36)
AL-BARAA' IBN MAALIK
Allah and Paradise!

He was one of two brothers who lived for the cause of Allah and who pledged allegiance to the Messenger of Allah (PBUH) and kept their pledge in the course of time.

The first brother was Anas Ibn Maalik, the servant of the Messenger of Allah (PBUH). His mother, Umm Sulaim, took him to the Messenger at the age of ten and said, "O Messenger of Allah, this is Anas, your lad. He will serve you; invoke Allah for him." The Messenger kissed him between his eyes and invoked a blessing upon him that led his long life towards good and blessing. He said, "O Allah, let him have plenty of money and sons. Bless him and let him enter Paradise." So, he lived for 99 years, and Allah bestowed upon him plenty of sons and grandsons and provided him with a spacious garden that gave fruits twice a year!

The second of these brothers was Al-Baraa' Ibn Maalik, who led a great brave life. His motto was "Allah and Paradise!" Whoever would see him fighting in the cause of Allah would be totally amazed, for when Al-Baraa' was fighting polytheists with his sword, he was not one of those who was looking for victory — although victory then was the greatest end — but he was looking for martyrdom. His utmost hope was to be a martyr and to die on the field of a glorious battle for the sake of the truth and Islam. For this reason, he missed neither a battle nor an expedition.

One day his brothers went to visit him. He read their faces and said, "I guess you're afraid I will die in bed. No, by Allah, He will not deprive me of martyrdom." Allah made his thoughts come true, as Al-Baraa' did not die in bed, but was martyred in one of the most glorious battles of Islam.

Al-Baraa' 's bravery on the Day of Al-Yamaamah revealed the personality of this hero whom "Umar lbn Al-Khattaab forbade to ever be a leader because his boldness, courage, and search for death made it a great risk for him to lead other fighters.

On the Day of Al-Yamaamah, the Islamic armies were preparing to fight under the leadership of Khaalid. Al-Baraa' stood licking his lips while the seconds were passing away as if they were years until the leader gave his order to advance. His sharp eyes were moving quickly all over the battlefield as if searching for the most suitable place for the hero to be martyred. Yes, nothing preoccupied him in the world but this aim. With the edge of his striking sword, a great harvest of the polytheists who called for darkness and falsehood were cut down. Then at the end of the battle, the hand of a polytheist gave him a stroke that made his body fall on the ground while his soul found its way to the angels among the group of martyrs and the blessed.

Khaalid shouted, "Allahu Akbar (Allah is the Greatest)!" So the close ranks burst forth to their fate, and so did the lover of death, Al-Baraa' lbn Maalik. He started bringing down the followers of Musailamah the Liar with his sword, and they were falling like autumn leaves because of his extreme courage.

Musailamah's army was not weak or small, but was the most dangerous army of the apostasy. With its numbers, equipment, and the death-defiance of its fighters, the army posed an extremely serious challenge. They answered the Muslims' attack with such an excessively aggressive defense that they were about to gain the initiative and transform their defense into an attack. Just then, some sort of anxiety pervaded the Muslim ranks. Their leaders and orators started giving words of encouragement from their horses, and they were reminded of Allah's promise.

Al-Baraa' had a nice loud voice. His leader Khaalid called him saying, "Speak, Baraa'!" So, Baraa' shouted with very strong and meaningful words, "O people of Al-Madiinah! Today you have no Madiinah, but it's Allah and Paradise!" These words demonstrate the spirit of their speaker and reveal his characters. Yes, it is Allah and Paradise. In this situation, thoughts had to do with nothing but this. They should not even have thought of Al-Madiinah, the capital of Islam, where they had left their houses, women, and children, because if they were defeated on that day, there would not be any Madiinah to return to.

Al-Baraa' 's words spread like . . . like what? Any simile would be unfair in comparison with its true effect. Let us say only that Al-Baraa' 's words spread, and that is it.

It was a short time before the battle returned to its former advantage. The Muslims were proceeding towards a certain victory and the polytheists were failing in a shocking defeat, while Al-Baraa' was walking along with his brothers carrying the standard of Muhammad (PBUH) to its great appointment. The polytheists withdrew and fled, seeking refuge within a big garden which they entered. The Muslims' enthusiasm abated; it seemed that it was now possible to change the battle's outcome by this trick that Musailamah's followers and army had resorted to. Just then Al-Baraa' ascended a high hill and cried, "O Muslims, carry me and throw me over to them in the garden."

Did I not tell you? He was not looking for victory but martyrdom, and this plan, he thought, would be the best end of his life and the best way to die. If he was thrown into the garden, he would open its gate to the Muslims, and at the same time his body would be torn into pieces by the polytheists' swords. At the same time, also, the doors of Paradise would be preparing to receive a new glorious groom.

However, Al-Baraa' did not wait for his people to carry and throw him. He climbed the wall by himself, threw himself inside the garden, opened the gate, and the armies of Islam rushed in. But Al-Baraa''s dream did not come true: neither did the polytheists swords kill him, nor did he die as he wished.

Abu Bakr (May Allah be pleased with him) spoke the truth when he said, "Strive for death and you will live!" On that day the hero received from the polytheists' swords over eighty strikes, over eighty wounds that caused Khaalid Ibn Al-Waliid to continue supervising his nursing and care for an entire month.

All of this, however, was not what he wished. But it did not make Al-Baraa' hopeless. He waited for another battle. The Messenger of Allah (PBUH) had prophesied that his supplication to Allah would be answered. He only had to keep invoking Allah to grant him martyrdom, and he did not have to be in a hurry, for every matter there is a decree.

After Al-Baraa' was healed of the wounds of Al-Yamaamah , he rushed with the armies of Islam that went to escort the powers of darkness to their final resting place. Two evanescent empires existed: The Romans (Byzantines) and the Persians occupied with their unjust armies the countries of Allah and enslaved His servants. Al-Baraa' started fighting with his sword, and in the place of each strike was built a great wall in the building of the new world that rapidly grew under the standard of Islam like the rising sun.

In one of the Iraqi wars, the Persians in their fight resorted to every means of barbarity. They used hooks fixed on the ends of chains heated in fire and threw them from their castles so that they would hit any of the Muslims who could not avoid them. Al-Baraa and his great brother Anas lbn Maalik were assigned together with some of the Muslims to deal with one of these castles. But one of these hooks suddenly fell and caught Anas, and he could not touch the chain to save himself as it was flaming hot.

When Al-Baraa' saw the scene, he hurried towards his brother while the burning chain was taking him up the castle wall. Al-Baraa' grasped the chain with his hands and started bravely dealing with it till he broke it. Anas was saved, but when Al-Baraa' and those who were with him took a look at his hands, they did not find them in their place. All the flesh on them was gone; only their burned bones remained. And the hero spent another period of time in a slow treatment till he was healed.

Is it not time for the lover of death to reach his end? Yes, it is. Here comes the Battle of Tustur where the Muslims met the Persian armies. This was such a feast for Al-Baraa'.

The people of Al-Ahwaaz and of Persia gathered in a large army to fight the Muslims. The Commander of the Faithful 'Umar lbn Al- Khattaab wrote to Sa'd lbn Abi Waqaas in Kufa and to Abu Muusaa Al-Ash'ariy in Basra to each send an army to meet Al-Ahwaaz. He told Abu Muusaa in his message, "Make Suhail lbn 'Adiy their leader and send Al-Baraa' lbn Maalik with him."

Thus, those coming from Kufa met those coming from Basra to face Al-Ahwaaz and the Persian armies in a fierce battle. The two great brothers Anas lbn Maalik and Al-Baraa' lbn Maalik were among the believing soldiers.

The war started with dueling, and Al-Baraa' alone killed a hundred swordsmen of the Persians. Then the armies joined in battle. and the killed fell from both sides in large numbers. During the fight some of the Companions came near Al-Baraa' and said, "Remember the Messenger's words about you, Baraa': 'Perhaps there is a person with uncombed, dusty hair that people will not look at, but if he swears by Allah, He will fulfill his prayer. Among them is Al-Baraa Ibn Maalik.' O Baraa', swear by Allah, entreat Him to defeat them and render us victorious."

Hence, Al-Baraa' raised his arms towards the sky and supplicated, "O Allah, render them defeated and us victorious, and let me catch Your Prophet today." He took a long look at his brother Anas, who was fighting near him, as if saying goodbye. Then the fighting intensified and the Muslims fought as nobody in the world had done, and they were clearly victorious.

Among the martyrs of the battle was Al-Baraa', with a happy smile on his face and his right hand grasping a handful of dust soaked with his pure blood. His sword was lying beside him. It was strong, without notches, undamaged.

Finally, the traveler arrived at his home. Together with his brother martyrs, he ended the journey of a great noble age. And it will be cried out to them, "This is the Paradise which you have inherited for what you did."

(37)
UTBAH IBN GHAZWAAN
Tomorrow You'll See the Nature of the Rulers after Me

Among the foremost Muslims and the first Muhaajiruun to Abyssinia and then Al-Madiinah, among the extraordinary fighters who proved themselves brave in the cause of Allah was this towering ,bright-faced, and humble-hearted man, "Utbah lbn Ghazwaan.

He was among the first seven who embraced Islam and extended their right hands to the right hand of the Messenger of Allah (PBUH). They pledged themselves to him while challenging the Quraish with all their fortitude and power for revenge. In the first days of the mission, the days of difficulty and terror, "Utbah lbn Ghazwaan, together with his brothers, stood bravely, which turned out later to be the very provision that nourished the human conscience and made it grow in the course of time.

When the Messenger of Allah (PBUH) ordered his Companions to emigrate to Abyssinia, 'Utbah went with them, but his yearning for the Prophet (PBUH) did not allow him to settle there. Soon he hurried back to Makkah where he stayed near the Messenger until it was time for the Hijrah to Al-Madiinah. So, 'Utbah emigrated again with the Muslims.

After the Quraish started their provocations and wars, 'Utbah was always carrying his lance and bow, using them expertly and contributing with his believing brothers to the destruction of the old world, including all its idols and lies. He did not, however, put his weapons down after the noble Messenger had died, but kept fighting. His jihaad against the Persian armies was great.

The Commander of the Faithful "Umar Ibn Al-Khattaab sent him to conquer Al-Abullah and purify its land of the Persians who regarded it as a dangerous zone of action from which to launch out at the Muslim troops that would be marching across the land of the Persian Empire, trying to save the countries and slaves of Allah. While "Umar was bidding him and his army farewell, he said, "Proceed on your way until you reach the remotest Arab country and the nearest foreign country. Go, and may Allah bless you. Invite to Allah whoever answers you, and impose jizyah upon whoever refuses or else use your sword without mercy. Wear the enemy down, and fear Allah your Lord."

"Utbah advanced, heading an army that was not big until they reached Al-Abullah, where the Persians were massing one of their strongest armies. "Utbah organized his troops and stood at the front carrying his lance that never missed its target. He called out his soldiers, "Allahu Akbar (Allah is the Greatest), and Allah will fulfill His Promise," as if he were reading something invisible. It was no more than blessed patrols before Al-Abullah surrendered. Its land was purified of the Persian soldiers, its people were liberated from the tyranny that had often tormented them, and the Great Allah had fulfilled His promise.

In the same place as Al-Abullah, 'Utbah planned the city of Al Basrah, constructed it, and built its great mosque. When he wanted to leave the city and return to Al-Madiinah, escaping from the responsibilities of rule, the Commander of the Faithful ordered him to stay. 'Utbah stayed in his place leading people in prayer, instructing them in religion, judging between them with justice, and giving them the most wonderful example in asceticism, piety, and simplicity. He fiercely fought the extravagance and luxury of those who liked comforts and desires.

One day he made a speech addressing them. He said: "By Allah,

I was the seventh of the first seven with the Messenger of Allah (PBUH), eating nothing but leaves of trees until the corners of our mouths were sore. I was given a garment. I cut it into two halves and gave one half to Sa'd Ibn Maalik and I wore the other half."

'Utbah used to fear the extravagance of the world, and in order to protect his religion and the Muslims, he tried to persuade them to practice asceticism and moderation. Many people tried to turn him from his way, to arouse a sense of ruling in his soul, and draw his attention to the right of ruling, especially in those countries that were never accustomed to such type of ascetic rulers and whose people used to respect high-ranking supercilious appearances. But 'Utbah used to answer them saying: "I seek refuge in Allah from being great in your world and small in the sight of Allah." When he found people bored with his austerity he induced them to be earnest and modest saying, 'Tomorrow you'll see the rulers after me."

When it was the Hajj season, he appointed one of his brothers as successor and went to make the Hajj. When he finished, he traveled to Al-Madiinah and asked the Commander of the Faithful to discharge him from the rule. But 'Umar would not lose the reverent ascetic who fled from what the mouths of mankind watered for. He used to say to them, "You burden me with your trusts and leave me alone? No, by Allah, I'll never discharge you." And that was what he said to 'Utbah Ibn Ghazwaan.

As 'Utbah could do nothing but obey, he took his camel and rode it back to Al-Basrah. But before he mounted it he turned to the Qiblah and raised his imploring hands to heaven and invoked Almighty Allah not to return him to Al-Basrah or to government rule again. His invocation was answered, for while he was on his way to this rule, he died. His spirit was given up to its Creator. It was happy with what it had exerted and given, with its asceticism and continence, with the favor that Allah had completed upon it, and with the reward that Allah had prepared for it.

(38)
THAABIT IBN QAIS
The Speaker for the Messenger of Allah !

While Hassaan was the poet of the Messenger of Allah and Islam, Thaabit was his speaker. The words coming from his mouth were strong, comprehensive, and perfect.

In the Year of Delegations, some men of the Tamiim tribe arrived at Al-Madiinah and said to the Messenger of Allah (PBUH), "We have come to brag, so please permit our poet and speaker." The Messenger (PBUH) smiled and told them, "I permit your speaker. Let him speak."

Their speaker, 'Utaarid Ibn Haajib, stood and boasted of his people's glories.

After he had finished, the Prophet (PBUH) told Thaabit Ibn Qais, "Answer him." Thaabit stood up and said, "All praise to Allah Who created the heavens and earth, in which He controls everything, Whose throne extends over the heavens and the earth. And nothing is at all except out of His kindness. It is part of His omnipotence to make us models and selected His Messenger out of the best of His creation, among whom he is of the noblest descent and of the most sincere speech. He sent him down His book and made His creation in trust of him. And he was the best choice of Allah. Then he called on people to believe in him. The Muhaajiruun of his people and his own kinsmen believed in him. They were of the noblest descent and best deeds. Then we the Ansaar were the first to respond. We are the adherents of Allah and the ministers of His Messenger."

Thaabit witnessed the Battle of Uhud with the Messenger of

Allah (PBUH) and the battles that followed. He was incredibly willing to sacrifice himself.

In the apostasy wars, he used to be in the vanguard, holding the Ansaar standard and striking with a sword that never retreated.

In the Battle of Al-Yamaamah, which we have already mentioned more than once, Thaabit witnessed the sudden assault that the army of Musailamah the Liar launched against the Muslims at the beginning of the battle. He shouted in his loud warning voice saying, "By Allah, we did not use to fight that way with the Messenger of Allah (PBUH)!"

Then he went not far away, and returned after annointing himself and putting on his shroud. He shouted once more, "O Allah! I clear myself of what those people have done (i.e. the army of Musailamah) and I apologize to You for what they have done (i.e. the Muslims' slackness in fighting)."

Then Saalim, the servant of the Messenger of Allah (PBUH) who was holding the standard of the Muhaajiruun, joined him. Both dug a deep hole for themselves and then stood in it. They piled up the sand on themselves till it covered their hips. They stood as two gigantic mountains, with the lower body of each hurried in the sand and fixed in the bottom of the hole, while their upper bodies received the armies of paganism and infidelity.

They kept striking with their swords whoever came near them from Musailamah's army until they were martyred in their place.

The sight of them (May Allah be pleased with them) was the greatest cry that contributed to bringing the Muslims back to their positions so that they could change the army of Musailamah the Liar into trodden sand.

Thaabit Ibn Qais, who excelled as a speaker and warrior, used to be self-reproaching and to humble himself to Allah. Among the Muslims, he was extremely modest and afraid of Allah.

When this noble verse was sent down < *GOD does not love any proud and boastful one* > *(31 : 18),* Thaabit shut his house door and kept crying. It was a long time before the Messenger of Allah (PBUH) knew about him. He sent for him and asked. Thaabit said, "O Messenger of Allah! I like beautiful clothes and footwear. I am afraid to be of the arrogant." The Prophet (PBUH) laughed with content and answered, "You are not one of them. You'll live and die with blessings and enter Paradise."

And when the following words of Allah the Exalted were sent down < *O you who believe! Do not raise your voices above the Prophet's voice, and do not speak loudly to him, as you speak to one another, lest your deeds are rendered fruitless, while you are unaware* > *(49 :2),* Thaabit shut himself indoors and kept crying again. When the Messenger missed him, he asked about him and sent for him. When Thaabit came, the Prophet (PBUH) asked him the reason for his absence. Thaabit answered, "I have a loud voice and I used to raise my voice above your voice. Messenger of Allah (PBUH). My deeds are rendered fruitless then, and I'm of the people of the Fire." The Messenger of Allah (PBUH) answered, "You are not one of them. You'll live praiseworthily and be martyred, and Allah will let you into Paradise."

One incident is left in Thaabit's story about which those whose thoughts, feelings, and views are limited to their restricted, tangible, materialistic world would not feel comfortable. Inspite of this, the incident was real, and is quite easily explained to whoever uses sight and insight together.

After Thaabit had fallen martyr in battle, one of the Muslims who had not known Islam until recently passed by him and saw Thaabit's precious armor on his corpse. He thought it was his right to take it and he did.

Let the narrator of the incident narrate it himself: While one of the Muslims was asleep, Thaabit appeared to him in his dream and said to him, "I entrust you with my will, so be careful not to say it's a dream and waste it. When I fell martyr yesterday, a Muslim man passed by me and took my armor. His house is on the outskirts of the town. His horse is tall. He put his pot on the armor and above the pot put his saddle. Go to Khaalid and tell him to take it. And when you go to Al-Madiinah and meet the successor of the Messenger of Allah (PBUH) Abu Bakr, tell him I owe so- and- so. Let him pay my loan."

When the man got up, he went to Khaalid Ibn Al-Waliid and related to him his dream. So Khaalid sent someone to bring the armor, and he found it exactly as Thaabit had described it. And when the Muslims went back to Al-Madiinah, the Muslim narrated the dream to the caliph, and he fulfilled Thaabit's will. There is not in Islam a dead man's will that was fulfilled in that way after his death except that of Thaabit Ibn Qais.

Truly, man is a big mystery. < *Think not of those who are killed in the Way of Allah as dead. Nay, they are alive, with their Lord, arid they have provision* > *(3 : 169)*.

(39)
USAID IBN HUDAIR
The Hero of the Day ofAs-Saqiifah

He inherited noble characteristics, handed down from father to son. His father, Hudair Al-Kataa'ib, was a leader of Al-Aws and one of the great nobles and strong fighters of the Arabs in the pre-Islamic era.

Usaid inherited from his father his status, courage, and hospitality. Before becoming a Muslim, he was one of Al-Madiinah's leaders, a noble of the Arabs, and one of their excellent spearmen.

When Islam attracted him and he was guided to the Way of the Almighty, Worthy of All Praise, he was best honored when he took his place as one of Allah and His Messenger's Ansaar and one of the foremost believers in the great religion of Islam.

He embraced Islam.quickly, decisively, and honorably. The Messenger (PBUH) sent Mus'ab lbn 'Umair to Al-Madiinah to teach and instruct the Muslim Ansaar who had given their allegiance to the Prophet (PBUH) in the First Pledge of 'Aqabah and to call others to Allah's religion.

On that day Usaid lbn Hudair and Sa'd lbn Mu'aadh, who were leaders of their people, were discussing this stranger who had come from Makkah to denounce their religion and call to a new one unknown to them. Sa'd said to Usaid, "Go directly to this man and deter him."

So Usaid carried his spear and hurried to Mus'ab while he was a guest of As'ad lbn Zuraarah, one of the leaders of Al-Madiinah who was among the early believers in Islam. And there, where Mus'ab and As'ad lbn Zuraarah were sitting, Usaid saw a crowd of people listening carefully to the rational words with which Mus'ab lbn 'Umair was calling them to Allah. Usaid surprised them with his anger and outburst. Mus'ab said to him, "Won't you sit down and listen? If our matter pleases you, accept it, and if you hate it, we'll stop calling you to what you hate."

Usaid was an enlightened and intelligent man whom the people of Al-Madiinah called "Al Kaamil" (The Perfect), a nickname that his father used to bear before him. So, when he found Mus'ab appealing to logic and reason, he stuck his spear in the ground and said to him, "You're right, tell me what you have."

Mus'ab started reciting the Holy Qur'aan to him and explaining to him the call of the new religion, the true religion whose standard Muhammad (PBUH) was ordered to spread. Those who attended this assembly said, "By Allah, we saw Islam in Usaid's face before he spoke. We knew it because of his brilliance and easiness."

No sooner did Mus'ab finish his words than Usaid was overwhelmed and he shouted, "How good these words are! What do you do if you want to embrace this religion?" Mus'ab said, "Purify your body and clothes, and bear true witness, then pray."

Usaid's character was straight, strong, and clear. He would not hesitate a second in face of strong opposition if he knew his own way.

So Usaid got up quickly to welcome the new religion which was penetrating his heart and overwhelming his soul. He washed, purified himself, and prostrated to Allah the Lord of the Worlds in worship, announcing his embracement of Islam and abandonment of paganism.

Usaid had to go back to Sa'd Ibn Mu'aadh to give him the news of the task which had been assigned to him to deter and expel Mus'ab Ibn 'Umair. He went back to Sa'd, but as he approached Sa'd said to those around him, "Usaid's face is changed. I swear it."

Yes. He went with a challenging, angry face and came back with a face full of mercy and light.

Usaid decided to use his intelligence. He knew that Sa'd Ibn Mu'aadh was well known for his pure nature and keen determination. He knew that Islam was not far from him. He only needed to hear what he himself had heard of Allah's word, which the Messenger's envoy to them, Mus'ab Ibn 'Umair, was good at reciting and explaining. But if he said to Sa'd, I've embraced Islam; go and embrace it, the outcome would not have been ensured. He had to prompt Sa'd in a way that would push him to Mus'ab's gathering in order to see and listen. How could he do this?

As we said before, Mus'ab was a guest at As'ad Ibn Zuraarah's house. As'ad Ibn Zuraarah was Sa'd Ibn Mu'aadh's cousin. So Usaid said to Sa'd, " I was told that the Haarithah tribe went out to kill As'ad Ibn Zuraarah and they know he is your cousin."

Angry and heated, Sa'd took his spear and ran fast to where Sa'd, Mus'ab, and the Muslims with them were sitting. When he came near the gathering, he found nothing but quiet overwhelming them while Mus'ab Ibn 'Umair sat in the middle of them reciting Allah's verses humbly, and they carefully listened to him.

Just then he realized the trick that Usaid had played on him to make him go to this gathering and listen to what the envoy of Islam, Mus'ab Ibn 'Umair was saying. So, Usaid's insight into his friend's character proved to be accurate.

Sa'd had hardly heard the Qur'aan when Allah opened his heart to Islam, and soon he took his place among the first believers.

Usaid bore a strong, bright belief in his heart and mind, and his belief made him full of patience, discernment, and sound appraisal that made him a trustworthy man.

During the expedition against Bani Al-Mustaliq, 'Abd Allah Ibn Ubaiy was so furious that he said to the people of Al-Madiinah around him, " You've let them enter your town and share your money. By Allah, if you cease giving them what you have, they'll turn to another place. By Allah, if we return to Al-Madiinah indeed the more honorable will expel the meaner from there."

The venerable Companion, Zaid Ibn Arqam heard these poisoned hypocritical words, so he had to inform the Messenger of Allah (PBUH). The Messenger (PBUH) was much hurt. When he met Usaid he said, "Don't you know what your friend has said?" Usaid asked, "Which friend, O Messenger of Allah?" The Messenger of Allah (PBUH) answered, '"Abd Allah Ibn Ubaiy." Usaid said, "What did he say?" The Messenger said, "He claimed that if he returned to Al-Madiinah, the more honorable will expel the meaner from there." Then Usaid said, "By Allah, you, O Messenger of Allah, will expel him from there, by Allah's permission. By Allah, he is the meaner and you are the more honorable."

He added, "O Messenger of Allah, treat him gently. By Allah, Allah brought you to us while the people of 'Abd Allah were preparing to crown him king of Al-Madiinah He sees that Islam has deprived him of kingship."

With this calm, profound thinking, Usaid used to solve problems using his presence of mind.

On the Day of As-Saqiifah, just after the death of the Messenger of Allah (PBUH), a group of the Ansaar headed by Sa'd Ibn 'Ubaadah announced their right to succession and debated furiously. Usaid, who was a prominent Ansaar, as we know, took a positive attitude in settling the matter and his words were like the dispelling of shadows on the course of events. He stood to address the group of Ansaar: "You know that the Messenger of Allah (PBUH) was one of the Muhaajiruun. His successor, then, should be one of the Muhaajiruun. We used to be the Ansaar of the Messenger of Allah. Today we have to be the Ansaar of his successor."

And his words brought peace and safety.

Usaid Ibn Hudair (May Allah be pleased with him) spent his life as a humble worshipper, sacrificing his energy and money in the cause of goodness, and putting the advice of the Messenger of Allah (PBUH) to the Ansaars in his mind: "Be patient until you meet me in the realm of Paradise."

He was the object of honor and love by As-Siddiiq because of his religiosity and noble manners. He also had the same status in the heart of the Commander of the Faithful 'Umar and in the hearts of all the Companions.

Listening to his voice while reciting Qur'aan was one of the greatest honors that the Companions aspired to. His voice was so humble and resonant that the Messenger (PBUH) said about it that the angels came near its possessor one night to hear it.

In the month of Shaaban A.H. 20, Usaid died. The Commander of the Faithful 'Umar insisted on carrying his bier on his shoulders. Under the earth of Al-Baqii', the Companions buried the body of a great believer. They went back to Al-Madiinah remembering his virtues and repeating the noble Messenger's words about him: "What an excellent man Usaid lbn Hudair is!"

(40)
'ABD AR-RAHMAN IBN 'AWF
What Makes You Cry , Abu Mubammad?

One day while Al-Madiinah was calm, heavy dust was accumulating near it till it covered the horizon. The wind pushed these quantities of yellow dust coming from the soft sand of the desert so that they came near the gates of Al-Madiinah, blowing strongly over the streets.

People thought it was a raging storm, but soon they heard beyond the dust the noise of a great caravan. After a while, 700 heavily laden camels were crowding the streets. People were calling each other to see the festive scene and rejoicing at the provisions the caravan might be carrying.

The Mother of the Faithful 'Aa'ishah, (May Allah be pleased with her) heard about the coming caravan and asked, "What's going on in Al-Madiinah?" She was answered, "It's a caravan of 'Abd Ar Rahaman lbn 'Awf corning from Syria carrying his goods."

The Mother of the Faithful said, "But can one caravan make all this tremor?" "Yes, Mother of the Faithful. There are 700 camels."

The Mother of the Faithful nodded and looked away as if searching for the memory of a scene she had witnessed or a conversation she had heard, then she said, "I heard the Messenger of Allah (PBUH) saying, 1 saw "Abd Ar-Rahaman lbn 'Awf crawling into Paradise."

'Abd Ar-Rahman lbn 'Awf crawling into Paradise! Why does he not jump or hurry into it with the first ones to embrace Islam among the Companions of the Messenger? When some of his friends informed him of what 'Aa'ishah said, he remembered that he heard the Prophet (PBUH) say this hadith more than once in various forms.

Before unloading the camels, he hastened to 'Aa'isha's house and told her, "I call you to witness that this caravan with all its loads is in the cause of Allah Almighty." And the loads of 700 camels were distributed among the people of Al-Madiinah and the places around it in a great charity festival.

This incident alone represents the complete image of the life of 'Abd Ar-Rahaman Ibn 'Awf, Companion of the Messenger of Allah. He was very much a successful merchant and rich man. He was the wise believer who refused that his portion of this life would sweep away his portion of religion, or that his fortune would make him lag behind the caravan of belief or the reward of Paradise. He (May Allah be pleased with him) would generously sacrifice his fortune and feel satisfied.

When and how did this great man embrace Islam? He did so very early in the first hours of the mission. He had done so even before the Messenger of Allah (PBUH) entered Daar Al-Arqam's house and took it as a seat to meet his faithful Companions. He was one of the eight who were the first to embrace Islam. When Abu Bakr preached Islam to him together with 'Uthmaan Ibn 'Affaan, Az-Zubair Ibn Al-'Awaam, Talhah Ibn 'Ubaid Allah, and Sa'd Ibn Abi Waqqaas, they did not grudge or doubt the matter. On the contrary, they hastened with As-Siddiiq to the Messenger of Allah, acknowledging him as Allah's Messenger and carrying his standard.

From the time he embraced Islam till he died at 75, he was a splendid model of a great believer, which made the Prophet (PBUH) count him among the ten to whom he gave glad tidings of inheriting Paradise.This also made 'Umar (May Allah be pleased with him) count him among the six advisers whom he assigned for succession after himself. He said, "The Messenger of Allah (PBUH) died while pleased with them."

After 'Abd Ar-Rahman embraced Islam, he faced his own portion of the persecution and challenges of the Quraish. When the Prophet (PBUH) ordered his Companions to emigrate to Abyssinia, lbn 'Awf emigrated but returned to Makkah. Then he emigrated to Abyssinia in the second migration, and from there to Al-Madiinah, where he witnessed Badr, Uhud, and all the battles.

He was very lucky in his trade to an extent that aroused his amazement. He said, "If I lift up a stone, I find silver and gold under it." Trade for 'Abd Ar-Rahman lbn 'Awf (May Allah be pleased with him) was not greed or monopoly. It was not even a desire to gather money or riches. It was work and duty whose success made him enjoy them and urged him to exert more effort. He used to have an enthusiastic nature so that he found comfort in any honorable work, wherever it was. If he was not praying in the mosque or fighting a battle, he was working in his trade that was thriving so much that his caravans were arriving at Al-Madiinah from Egypt and Syria, laden with everything that the Arabian Peninsula might need in garments and food.

Evidence of his ebullient nature is his course ever since the dawn of the Muslims' Hijrah to Al-Madiinah. In those days the Messenger (PBUH) associated every two of his Companions as brothers, a Muhaajir (Emigrant) from Makkah with an Ansaar (Helper) from Al-Madiinah. This association took place in an astounding way. Each Ansaar in Al-Madiinah shared with his brother Muhaajir everything that he owned, even his bed. If he was married to two women, he would divorce one for his brother to marry!

The noble Messenger (PBUH) associated 'Abd Ar-Rahman Ibn 'Awf and Sa'd Ibn Ar-Rabii'a as brothers one day. Let us listen to the noble Companion Anas Ibn Maalik (May Allah be pleased with him) narrating to us what happened:

Sa'd said to 'Abd Ar-Rahman, "O brother. I'm the richest in Al-Madiinah. Take half of my fortune. And I have two wives. Choose the one you like better and I'll divorce her for you to marry." So 'Abd Ar-Rahman Ibn'Awf said, "Allah bless your family and money. Show me the way to the market." He went to the market, bought, sold, and gained profit.

That is how he led his life in Al-Madiinah, whether during the Messenger's lifetime (PBUH) or after his death, doing his duty towards religion or the world's work and succeeding in his trade, so much so that, as he said, if he lifted up a stone, he would find gold and silver under it!

What made his trade blessed and successful was his pursuing the halaal, and his strictly moving away from the haraam, or even the doubtful. What made it even more blessed and successful was that it was not for 'Abd Ar-Rahman alone. Allah had a bigger share in it, by which he used to strengthen the ties of his family and brothers and prepare the armies of Islam. If commerce and fortune are usually evaluated on the basis of stocks on hand and profits,'Abd Ar- Rahman Ibn 'Awfs fortune was evaluated on the basis of what was expended from it in the cause of Allah, the Lord of All the Worlds.

One day he heard the Messenger of Allah (PBUH) saying to him, "O Ibn 'Awf, you are a rich man, and you are going to crawl into Paradise. So lend to Allah in order to set your feet free." Ever since he heard this advice from the Messenger of Allah, he started lending to Allah a goodly loan. Then Allah increased it manifold to His credit in repaying.

One day, he sold some land for 40,000 dinars and distributed it all to the people of Zuhrah tribe, the Mothers of the Faithful, and the poor Muslims. Next day, he provided the Islamic armies with 500 horses, on the third day with 1,500 camels.

When he was about to die, he bequeathed 5,000 dinars in the cause of Allah and 400 dinars for each one who was still living of those who had witnessed Badr. Even 'Uthmaan lbn 'Affaan (My Allah be pleased with him) took his share of the bequeathal inspite of his riches and said, "Abd Ar-Rahman's money is halaal and pure Its food gives health and blessing."

lbn 'Awf was master of his money, not its slave. The proof of this was that he did not have trouble gathering it. He used to gather halaal money with much ease. Besides, he did not enjoy it alone, but together with his family, relatives, brethren, and all his community. He was so generous and hospitable that he used to say, "The people of Al-Madiinah are partners of lbn 'Awf in his money. He lends to a third of them, pays the debts of a third, and strengthens his ties of kinship and gives away a third."

These riches would not have made him comfortable or happy if they did not make him capable of adhering to his religion and supporting his brethren. Nevertheless, he was always apprehensive of these riches.

One day when he was fasting, he was served iftaar (the meal at sunset which breaks the fast). He had hardly seen it when he lost his appetite and cried saying, "When Mus'ab lbn 'Umair was martyred and he was better than me — he was wrapped in his garment so that if it covered his head, his feet showed, and if it covered his feet, his head showed. When Hamzah was martyred - and he was better than me — they found nothing to wrap him with except his garment. Now the world has been expanded for us, and we have been given much. I'm afraid our blessings are hastened."

One day some of his friends gathered around food in his house. Just as it was put in front of them, he wept. They asked him, "What makes you weep, O Abu Muhammad?" He answered, "The Messenger of Allah (PBUH) died when he and his family had not even satisfied their appetites with barley bread. I can't see that our latter days have shown something better."

In addition, his large fortune never brought pride on him, so much so that they said of him, "If a stranger sees him sitting among his servants, he wouldn't be able to distinguish him from the others."

If only this stranger would know a part of lbn 'Awfs fortitude and good deeds — that, for example, he was wounded on the Day of Uhud with twenty wounds, one of which left a permanent lameness in one leg, and that some of his teeth fell out on the same day, leaving a clear defect in his articulation — then the stranger would know that this tall man who had a bright face but had lost his front teeth as a result of his injury at Uhud was 'Abd Ar-Rahaman lbn 'Awf (May Allah be pleased with him).

Mankind's nature makes it a habit that riches court power; that is, the rich always like to have influence that protects their fortune, multiplies it, and satisfies the lust of pride and selfishness usually caused by riches. If we had seen 'Abd Ar-Rahman lbn'Awf with his large riches, however, we would have seen a marvelous man conquering human nature in this field and surpassing it pre-eminently.

This showed itself when 'Umar Ibn Al-Khattaab (May Allah be pleased with him) was dying. He chose six Companions of the Messenger of Allah (PBUH) for them to select from among themselves the new successor. The fingers were pointing at Ibn 'Awf. Some Companions even conversed with him about his right to win succession, but he said, "By Allah, it is better for me to put a knife in my throat and penetrate it to the other side."

Thus, the six chosen Companions had hardly held a meeting to select one of them to succeed 'Umar Al-Faaruuq (The One Who Distinguishes Truth from Falsehood), when Ibn 'Awf informed his five other brothers that he was renouncing the right given to him by 'Umar when he made him one of the six from whom the successor would be selected, and that one of them would be selected from the other five. Soon, this ascetic attitude made him the judge of the noble five. They agreed that he would select the successor among them Imam 'Aliy said, " I heard the Messenger of Allah (PBUH) describing you as honest among the people of heaven and earth." Finally, Ibn 'Awff selected 'Uthmaan Ibn 'Affaan successor, and all the rest agreed with him.

This is a real rich man in Islam. Did you see what Islam did to him, putting him above riches with all its temptations, and how it molded him in the best way? In A.H. 32 his soul ascended to its Creator. 'Aa'ishah, the Mother of the Faithful, wanted then to bestow on him a special honor, proposing as he was dying to bury him in her room near the Messenger (PBUH), Abu Bakr, and 'Umar. But as a Muslim he was so refined that he was too modest to put himself in this rank. Besides, he had made a previous promise. One day, he and 'Uthmaan Ibn Madh'uun* had promised each other that whoever died after the other would be buried near his friend.

While his soul was preparing for its new journey, his eyes were dripping tears and his tongue was stammering, I'm afraid of being held up by my friends because of what I had of abundant money." But soon, Allah's calmness overwhelmed him, and tender happiness covered his peaceful face. His ears listened closely, as if there were a sweet voice coming near them. Perhaps he was listening then to the truth of the Messenger's words (PBUH) to him, "Abd Ar-Rahman Ibn 'Awf will enter Paradise." Maybe he was listening also to Allah's promise in His book: < *Those who spend their wealth in Cause of Allah, and do not follow up their gifts with reminders of their generosity or with injury, their reward is with their Lord. On them shall be no fear, nor shall they grieve* > *(2: 262).*

---

*The biography of "Uthmaan Ibn Madh'uun is written in the earlier part of this book.

(41)
ABU JAABIR 'ABD ALLAH IBN 'AMR IBN HIRAAM
Shaded by Angels!

When the seventy Ansaar gave their allegiance to the Messenger of Allah (PBUH) in the Second Pledge of Aqabah,'Abd Allah lbn 'Amr lbn Hiraam, also known as Abu Jaabir lbn 'Abd Allah, was one of them. When the Messenger of Allah (PBUH) chose some leaders among them, 'Abd Allah lbn 'Amr was one of these leaders. The Messenger of Allah (PBUH) made him the leader of his people, the Bani Salamah. When they returned to Al-Madiinah, he sacrificed himself, his money, and his family in the service of Islam. After the Messenger's Hijrah to Al-Madiinah, Abu Jaabir found utmost enjoyment in accompanying the Prophet (PBUH) day and night.

In the Battle of Badr, he went out fighting like a hero. At Uhud he dreamed of his death before the Muslims went out to battle. He was overwhelmed by a true sense that he was not coming back, and his heart was full of joy. He called to him his son Jaabir lbn 'Abd Allah, the noble Companion, and said, "I see myself killed in this battle. Maybe I'll be the first martyr among the Muslims. By Allah, I'll leave no one that I like more than you after the Messenger of Allah (PBUH). I am in debt, so pay my debts and make your brothers your own concern."

The next morning the Muslims went out to encounter the Quraish that had come in an uproarious army to invade their peaceful city. A dreadful battle raged, at the beginning of which the Muslims achieved rapid victory. It could have been a decisive Lvictory but for the archers, whom the Messenger (PBUH) had ordered to stay at their positions and never to leave them, who were tempted by this quick victory over the Quraish.

They left their positions on the mountain and were pre-occupied with gathering the booty of the defeated army. The Quraish quickly gathered its scattered remnants when it found the Muslims' back completely exposed. They surprised them by a quick attack from behind, changing the Muslim victory into defeat.

During this bitter fight, 'Abd Allah Ibn `Amr died as a martyr. When the Muslims went to find their martyrs after the fighting had ended, Jaabir Ibn 'Abd Allah went to search for his father. He found him among the martyrs, whom the polytheists had made a dreadful display of along with other heroes. Jaabir and some of his family were crying over the martyr of Islam 'Abd Allah Ibn 'Amr Ibn Hiraam when the Messenger of Allah (PBUH) passed by. He said, "Cry over him or not, the angels are here to shade him with their wings!"

Abu Jaabir's belief was strong. His love, or even eagerness, to die in the cause of Allah was his greatest ambition. Afterward, the Messenger of Allah (PBUH) announced the great news that depicted his great fondness of martyrdom. One day he (PBUH) said to 'Abd Allah's son Jaabir, "O Jaabir, Allah has never spoken to anyone but from behind a veil, but He has spoken to me face to face. He said, 'O slave, ask Me to give you.' He said, 'O Allah, I ask You to return me to earth, to be killed again in Your cause.' Allah answered him, "I said before: They will not return to them.' He said, 'O Allah, then inform those after me of the blessings you have bestowed on us.' So exalted Allah sent down: <*Think not of those who are killed in the way of Allah as dead. Nay, they are alive, with their Lord, and they have provision. They rejoice in what Allah has bestowed upon them of His Bounty, rejoicing for the sake of those who have not joined them, but are left behind (not yet marytred) that on them no fear shall come, nor shall they grieve*>" *(3 : 169-170)*.

When the Muslims were identifying their pious martyrs after the Battle of Uhud and the family of 'Abd Allah Ibn 'Amr had identified his corpse, his wife carried him, together with her brother who was martyred also, on her camel. She began taking them back to Al-Madiinah to bury them there. Likewise did some other Muslims for their martyrs. But the crier of the Messenger of Allah (PBUH) caught up with them and announced the Messenger's order: Bury the martyrs on their battle-ground. So they all returned with their martyrs.

The Noble Prophet (PBUH) was supervising the burial of his martyred Companions who had fulfilled their promise to Allah and sacrificed their precious souls as humble offerings to Allah and His Messenger. When it was 'Abd Allah Ibn Hiraam's turn to be buried, the Messenger of Allah (PBUH) called, "Bury 'Abd Allah Ibn `Amr and 'Amr Ibn Al-Jamuuh in one grave; they were loving and sincere to each other in this world."

Now, during the moments of preparing the happy grave to receive the two noble martyrs, let us have a loving look at the second martyr, 'Amr Ibn Al-Jamuuh.

(42)
'AMR IBN AI-JAMUUH
I Want to Walk Proudly with My Lameness in Paradise !

He was related to 'Abd Allah lbn 'Amr lbn Hiraam by marriage, being the husband of his sister Hind bint 'Amr. 'Amr lbn Al-Jamuuh was one of the leaders of Al-Madiinah and one of the chiefs of the Salamah tribe. His son Mu'aadh lbn 'Amr, who was one of the seventy Ansaar of the pledge of 'Aqabah preceded him in Islam.

Mu'aadh lbn 'Amr and his friend Mu'aadh lbn Jabal * were calling the people of Al-Madiinah to Islam with the enthusiasm of bold and believing youth.

It was a custom that the nobles kept symbolic idols in their houses other than the big idols set up in places of public gathering. As a nobleman and chief, 'Amr lbn Al-Jamuuh made an idol to install in his house and called it Manaaf. His son Mu'aadh lbn 'Amr agreed with his comrade Mu'aadh lbn Jabal to make 'Amr lbn Al-Jamuuh's idol an object of ridicule. They used to enter his house at night, take the idol and throw it into a cess pit. And when 'Amr would wake up he would not find Manaaf in its place, and would keep looking for it till he found it thrown into that pit. He used to rage and say, "Woe unto you, who transgressed our gods this night!" Then he would wash and perfume it. When night came again, the two Mu'aadh, would do to the idol as they had done the previous night.

When 'Amr got weary he took his sword and put it on Manaaf's neck and said to it, "If you are a beneficial god defend yourself."

---

* His biography has already been written

When he woke up he did not find it in its place, but rather found it discarded in the same cess pit. But this time, it was not in the pit alone but was tied to a dead dog by a strong rope.

While he was angry, sorry, and surprised, some of the nobles of Al-Madiinah who had preceded him in Islam approached him. They pointed at the idol tied to the dead dog and addressed 'Amr lbn Al -Jamuuh's mind, heart and good sense, talking to him about the Most True and Most High Allah Whom there is nothing like. They talked to him about the trustworthy, faithful Muhammad who came to give, not to take, to guide, not to misguide. They talked to him about Islam that came to liberate mankind from all the shackles, revive the spirit of Allah in them, and spread His light in their hearts.

In a few moments, 'Amr discovered himself and his destiny. He purified and perfumed his clothes and body, then went, bearing his head high, to acknowledge the Seal of the Prophets (PBUH) and to take his place among the believers.

One may wonder how those nobles and leaders of their people, like "Amr lbn Al-Jamuuh could believe in helpless idols to that extent. How did their reason not restrain them? How do we render them today among the great men after their embracing Islam and sacrificing? It is easy to raise these questions nowadays, as no child would accept to set up a piece of wood in his house and worship it. But in olden days, people's hearts used to embrace such doings. Their intelligence and genius could do nothing against tradition.

For example, Athens, in the days of Pericles, Pythagoras, and Socrates, attained a dazzling intellectual progress. However, all its people, including philosophers and judges, used to believe in sculptured idols in a ridiculous way. The reason is that religious sense in those remote ages was not as developed as the intellectual progress.

'Amr lbn Al-Jamuuh dedicated his heart and life to Allah, the Lord of the Worlds. Although he was generous by nature, Islam made him more generous so that he put all his money in the service of his religion and his brethren.

The Messenger (PBUH) asked a group of the Bani Salamah tribe, the tribe of 'Amr lbn Al-Jamuuh, "Who is your chief, O Bani Salamah ?" They answered, 'Al-Jad lbn Qais, inspite of his being a miser." He (PBUH) said, "No, your chief is the white curly haired 'Amr lbn Al-Jamuuh." This testimony from the Messenger of Allah (PBUH) was a great honor to lbn Al-Jamuuh.

As'Amr lbn Al-Jamuuh dedicated his money in the cause of Allah, so he was willing to sacrifice his soul and life as well. But how? There was a severe lameness in his leg that made him invalid for participating in battle. He had four sons who were all strong Muslim men. They used to go out with the Messenger (PBUH) in expeditions, persisting in doing their duty of fighting. However, 'Amr tried to go out in the Battle of Badr. His sons implored the Prophet (PBUH) to persuade him not to go out, or even to order him if he was not persuaded. So, the Prophet (PBUH) told him that Islam exempted him from jihaad because of his severe lameness. When he began pleading, the Prophet (PBUH) ordered him to stay in Al-Madiinah.

When the Battle of Uhud came, 'Amr went to the Prophet (PBUH), imploring him to permit him. He said, "O Messenger of Allah, my sons want to prevent me from going out with you to fight. By Allah, I want to walk proudly with my lameness in Paradise." As he strongly insisted, the Prophet (PBUH) permitted him to go out. So, he took his weapon and set out to walk happily, invoking Allah in a submissive voice, "O Allah, bestow martyrdom upon me and don't return me to my family."

When the two rival forces met on the Day of Uhud, 'Amr lbn Al-Jamuuh and his four sons set out striking the polytheists with their swords. 'Amr was walking proudly in the middle of the fierce battle.

With each step his sword cut off the head of a polytheist. He strud with his right hand, then looked around at the highest part of the horizon, as if hastening the arrival of the angel who would make him die and accompany him to Paradise.

Yes, he asked his Lord for martyrdom being sure that Allah Glorified and Exalted be, He above all, would respond to him. He was very much eager to walk proudly with his lame leg in Paradise so that its people would know that Muhammad, the Messenger of Allah (PBUH), knew how to select his Companions and how to develop men.

That which he had been waiting for happened. A sword blow announced the time of the advance of a glorious martyr to the Paradise of immortality.

When the Muslims were burying their martyrs, the Messenger (PBUH) repeated his order which we have already heard elsewhere: "Put 'Abd Allah lbn 'Amr lbn Hiraam and 'Amr lbn Al-Jamuuh in one grave; they were loving and sincere to each other in this world."

The two loving friends, the two martyrs, were buried in one grave under the battlefield that received their pure souls and witnessed their extraordinary bravery.

Forty-six years after they and their companions had been buried, a violent torrent descended and covered the graveyard, because of a fountain head of water that Mu'aawiyah made. The Muslims hurried to remove the martyrs' bodies. It was a surprise, however, to find them as those who participated in removing their bodies described: "Having soft bodies and flexible limbs."

As Jaabir Ibn 'Abd Allah was still alive, he went with his family to remove the bodies of his father, 'Abd Allah Ibn 'Amr Ibn Hiraam, and his aunt's husband, 'Amr Ibn Al-Jamuuh. However, he found them in their grave as if they were sleeping. They were not changed at all: their faces even had the same smile of happiness that they had had the day they were summoned to meet Allah.

Are you surprised ? No, do not be. The great, pious, pure souls that have controlled their destinies usually leave in the bodies that once were their refuge, a kind of immunity that wards off the decomposing factors and the influence of the soil.

(43)
HABIIB IBN ZAID
A Legend of Sacrifice and Love

In the Second Pledge of 'Aqabah which has been mentioned many times, 70 men and two women of Al-Madiinah gave their allegiance to the Prophet (PBUH). Among those blessed men and women were Habiib Ibn Zaid and his father Zaid Ibn 'Aasim (May Allah be pleased with both of them). His mother was Nusaibah bint Ka'b, one of the two women who were the first to give allegiance to the Prophet (PBUH). The second woman was his maternal aunt. Thus, he was a veteran believer in whose backbone and ribs faith ran rather than blood. He lived near the Prophet (PBUH) after he emigrated to Al-Madiinah. There, he never missed an expedition in the cause of Allah or lagged behind.

One day the south of the Arab Peninsula witnessed the emergence of two presumptuous and arrogant liars who claimed prophethood and tried to drag people into the swamp of sin and disbelief. One of these impostors was called Al-Aswad Ibn Ka'b Al 'Aansiy, from San'aa'. The other was Musailamah the Liar from Al-Yamaamah. Both impostors incited people against the believers in their tribes who responded to what Allah ordained and who believed in His Prophet. They also goaded them against the Prophet's messengers whom he sent to their lands. Moreover, they even went so far as to ignite suspicion against prophethood itself and committed hideous mischief in the land, causing corruption and disbelief.

One day, the Prophet (PBUH) was surprised when a messenger arrived with a message from Musailamah in which he said, "From Musailamah Allah's Prophet to Muhammad Allah's Prophet. Peace be upon you. We are your partner in prophethood; consequently, we have half of the earth and the Quraish has the other half , but the Quraish want unjustly to have it all !"

The Prophet (PBUH) summoned one of his scribes and dictated this answer to Musailamah: "In the name of Allah, the Most Beneficient, the Most Merciful. From Muhammad the Prophet of Allah to Musailamah the Liar. Peace be upon those who followed the right path. Verily, the earth is Allah's. He gives it as a heritage to whom He will of His slaves and the blessed end is for the pious and righteous persons who fear Allah."

The Prophet's words were direct and crytal clear. They exposed the liar of the Bani Haniifah who thought that prophethood was a kingdom, so he demanded his piece of the cake, namely, half the earth and its people. The messenger carried the Prophet's answer to Musailamah, yet it only made him more mischievous and corrupt.

He went on spreading his falsehood and slander and went on abusing the believers and instigating people against them. The Prophet (PBUH) thought it best to give him one last chance, so he sent a message to convince him not to commit any more of his folly. He picked Habiib Ibn Zaid as his messenger. Habiib hastened enthusiasticly with the glorious mission the Prophet (PBUH) had entrusted him with. He hoped that Musailamah's heart would be guided to the right path and that he would be rewarded endlessly in the Hereafter.

The traveler reached his destination. Musailamah the Liar read the Prophet's message, but he was blinded by its light, which only made him more aberrant and arrogant.

Musailamah was really no more than a flagrant liar. He indeed behaved accordingly. He lacked the least manliness, sense of honor or decency of the Arabs which might have prevented him from shedding the blood of a messenger, which was highly respected and even held sacred by all Arabs.

It was as though this noble religion Islam wanted to give humanity a new lesson of greatness and herosim. Only this time, both its subject matter and its tutor were one and the same person, Habiib Ibn Zaid. Musailamah the Liar called upon people to witness one of his so-called memorable days. The messenger of the Prophet, Habiib Ibn Zaid, was brought in. It was clear from his wounds and bruises that he had been abused and tortured severely by those criminals. They thought that they could strip him of his valor so that he might appear in a state of complete humiliation and defeat before the crowd. They hoped that he would then give Musailamah the credibility he craved when he called upon him to witness to his fake prophethood before the crowd. Thus, the notorious liar would be able to make a fake miracle that would cement his prestige among those whom he deluded.

Therefore, Musailamah asked Habiib, "Do you bear witness that Muhammad is, indeed, the Messenger of Allah?" Habiib answered boldly, "Yes, I do bear witness that Muhammad is, indeed, the Messenger of Allah." Musailamah's face went white with humiliation and embarrassment yet he asked, "Do you bear witness that I am the Messenger of Allah?" Habiib scornfully replied, "Nonsense!".

The impostor Musailamah's humiliated face darkened with spiteful madness. His scheme had failed. His torture of Habiib had been futile. He was slapped so fiercely before the crowd which he himself had gathered to witness his so-called miracle. This slap was so strong that it shattered his assumed dignity once and for all. He became as violent as a wounded bull as he summoned his executioner, who rushed and stabbed Habiib's body with his sword. He slew him, cutting his body into small pieces, one by one. Habiib made no sound beside chanting stoically, "There is no god but Allah and Muhammad is His Messenger."

It was as though he wanted to celebrate his Islam until the very last moment of his life. Now, if Habiib, on that day, had tried to escape this horrible death by a pretense of his faith in Musailamah's prophethood, his faith would not have been questioned, doubted or blemished in any way. But he was a man who had witnessed the Second Pledge of Al-'Aqabah along with his father, mother, brother, and aunt, and ever since those decisive blessed moments he had carried upon his shoulders the responsibility that ensued his oath and faith to the fullest. He could not for a moment hold his life and principles as separable. Therefore, he found a rare opportunity to win his life once and for all. His life was an embodiment of his faith. It embodied his stead-fastness, greatness, heroism, sacrifice, and martyrdom for the sake of Right and Truth, the splendor of which surpassed all victories.

The Prophet received the sad news of Habiib's marytrdom with patience, for Allah's inspiration made him see the future fate of Musailamah. He could almost see his death with his own eyes. As for Nusaibah bint Ka'b, Habiib's mother, she gnashed her teeth for a long while on hearing the terrible deed, then she swore a solemn oath to avenge her son's death upon Musailamah and to thrust her sword and spear right into his wicked body.

It seemed that fate watched her anguish, patience, and courage on receiving this news and showed great admiration and sympathy for her calamity and decided all at once to stand by her until she fulfilled her oath.

After a short while, the Battle of Al-Yamaamah took place. Abu Bakr As-Siddiiq, the Prophet's caliph, organized an army to march to Al Yamama where Musailamah had already organized a huge army.

Nusaibah marched along with the Muslim army and threw herself into the battlefield armed with a sword in her right hand and a spear in her left one. She kept on shouting, "Where are you Musailamah, you enemy of Allah?"

When Musailamah was killed and his followers were like carded wool, the standards of Islam fluttered victoriously and proudly. Nusaibah's strong and brave body was strained with spear wounds . She stood there recalling the amiable face of her beloved son that seemed to linger about the place. Wherever she looked, she saw the face of her son Habiib. It was somewhere out there smiling contentedly on every victorious fluttering flag.

(44)
UBAIY IBN KA'B
Rejoice with the Knowledge, Abu Al-Mundhir

The Prophet (PBUH) asked Abu Al-Mundhir one day, "Which is the greatest verse in the Holy Qur'aan?" He answered, "Allah and His Prophet know best." The Prophet (PBUH) then repeated his question, "Which is the greatest verse in the Holy Qur'aan, Abu Al-Mundhir?" Ubaiy finally answered < *Allah! None has the right to be worshiped but He, the Ever-Living, the One Who sustains and protects all that exists . . .* > *(2 : 255)*

The Prophet's face brightened with joy as he patted Abu Al - Mundhir on the back and said, "I congratulate you for having such knowledge and insight, Abu Al-Mundhir."

Abu Al-Mundhir whom the Prophet (PBUH) congratulated for the insight that Allah had bestowed on him is Ubaiy Ibn Ka'b, the great Companion. He was one of the Ansaar, the citizens of Al-Madiinah who helped and aided the Muhaajiruun. He belonged to Al-Khazraj tribe. He witnessed the Pledge of Al-'Aqabah, the Battle of Badr, and the rest of the great events. He held a highly distiguished position among those who were the first to commit themselves to Islam.

The Commander of the Faithful 'Umar (May Allah be pleased with him.) said, "Ubaiy is the master of the Muslims."

Ubaiy Ibn Ka"b was one of the first Muslim scribes who wrote down the revelation that descended on the Prophet (PBUH) as well as messages. He was a pioneer in learning the Holy Qur'aan by heart, reciting it in a slow, pleasant tone and comprehending its content.

One day, the Holy Prophet (PBUH) said to Ubaiy Ibn Ka'b, "I was ordered to recite the Qur'aan to you." Ubaiy knew that the Prophet (PBUH) took his orders from the Spirit, therefore, he was overwhelmed with thrill and asked the Prophet (PBUH) anxiously, "You are dearer to me than my own mother and father! Please tell me, did the Spirit mention me by name?" The Prophet (PBUH) answered, "Yes, it resounded your very name and your family name in the kingdom of heaven and earth."

Now, a Muslim who was so close to the Prophet (PBUH) must indeed be a special one. Throughout the years in which Ubaiy Ibn Ka'b accompanied the Prophet (PBUH) , he tried to stay close to him so as to quench his thirst for Islam from the Prophet's inexhaustible spring. Ubaiy Ibn Ka'b adhered tenaciously to his covenant in worship, piety, and conduct. Even after the Prophet's death, he was always there to warn people against wrong-doing and remind them of their pledge, morals, and asceticism when the Prophet was alive. He used to address his companions in such impressive words saying, "We stood as one man when the Prophet was alive, but as soon as he departed we went in different directions."

He was steadfast in his adherence to piety. He resorted to asceticism to escape life's seduction and delusion. He saw that life really begins when it ends and that no matter how long a man lives in luxury surrounded by graces and blessings, he will end up emptyhanded but for his good deeds and bad deeds. Ubaiy contemplated about life and said, "Man's food is a good example of what life is all about, for no matter how much you are careful that it tastes delicious and that its ingredients are well proportioned, look what it turns to after you digest it."

Whenever Ubaiy addressed people, he was like a magnet that attracted their attention and interest. He feared no one but Allah and desired nothing of life. When Islam gained more lands and influence and he saw that Muslims flattered their rulers, he warned saying, "They are ruined and will ruin others. I don't pity them, but I pity the Muslims that they will ruin."

His extreme piety and fear of Allah made him cry whenever Allah or the Day of Judgment was mentioned. The noble Qur'aan's verses shook his heart and soul whenever he recited them or heard them recited. Yet a certain verse made him incredibly sad: < *He has the power to send torment on you from above or from under your feet, or to cover you with confusion in party strife, and make you to taste the violence of one another* > *(6:65).*

The thing that Ubaiy most dreaded was that one day the Islamic nation would suffer turmoil and violence at the hands of its own sons. He always asked Allah's safety and protection. He won it by Allah's mercy and grace and met Allah as a true believer who felt completely secure and rewarded.

(45)
SA'D IBN MU'AADH
Rejoice, Abu 'Amr!

He committed himself to Islam at the age of 31 and won marytrdom at 37. This seven years lapse was a tough one in which Sa'd lbn Mu'aadh (May Allah be pleased with him) exerted all his enegry in the service of Allah and His Messenger (PBUH).

Look ! Do you see that handsome, gallant, tall man with a radiant face? He is the one.

He ran quickly to As'ad lbn Zuraarah to see this man who came from Makkah, Mus'ab lbn'Umair, whom Muhammad (PBUH) had sent to Al-Madiinah to call people to commit themselves to Islam and monotheism. He was going there to drive this stranger out of Al-Madiinah along with his religion ! But no sooner had he approached Mus`ab's assembly at the house of his nephew, As'ad lbn Zuraarah, than his heart was revived by a sweet pacifying breeze. No sooner had he reached those men who gathered there, taken his place among them and listened intently to Mus`ab's words than Allah guided him to the right path that illuminated his heart and soul. In one of the incredible miracles of fate, the leader of the Ansaar put aside his spear and shook hands with Mus'ab as a sign of his allegiance to the Prophet (PBUH).

A new sun shone on Al-Madiinah as soon as Sa'd lbn Mu'aadh committed himself to Islam. It would encompass many hearts that would revolve in the sphere of Islam later on. Sa'd committed himself to Islam and withstood the hardships that ensued with much heroism and greatness. When the Prophet (PBUH) emigrated to Al-Madiinah, the houses of Bani Al-

Ashhal—Sa'd's tribe —welcomed the Muhaajiruun, and their money was utterly at their disposal without arrogance, abuse, or limitation.

When the Battle of Badr was about to take place, the Prophet (PBUH) gathered his Companions, both Ansaar and Muhaajiruun, to consult them on the preparations for war. His amiable face turned towards the Ansaar and he addressed them saying, "I want to know your opinion about what should be done concerning the imminent battle."

Sa'd lbn Mu'aadh stood up and said "O Prophet of Allah, we firmly believe in you, and we witness that what descends on you is the truth. We swore a solemn oath and gave you the allegiance, so go ahead with whatever you want, and we shall stand by your side. We swear by Allah Who has sent you with the truth that if you reach the sea and cross it, we will cross it hand in hand with you. No man will lag or stay behind. We are absolutely ready to go to war against our enemy tomorrow for we are given to terrible warfare and we are sincere in our desire to meet Allah. I hope that Allah will make us do what will make you proud of us. So go on with whatever is in your mind. Allah bless you."

Sa'd's words made the Prophets' face brighten with satisfaction and happiness as he addressed the Muslims and said, "Rejoice, for Allah promised me one of the two parties of the enemy (either the army or the caravan). By Allah I can almost see with my own eyes where each one of the enemy will be killed."

In the Battle of Uhud, the Muslims lost control and dispersed. as they were taken by surprise by the army of disbelievers. Everything was hectic, yet Sa'd lbn Mu'aadh stood there as if pinned to the ground next to the Prophet (PBUH). He defended him courageously as a noble warrior should do.

The Battle of Al-Khandaq came as a suitable opportunity for Sa'd to show his admirable manliness and amazing valor. The Khandaq Battle came as a clear sign for the shrewd and deceitful schemes with which Muslims were being ruthlessly haunted by an enemy who had no consideration whatsoever for justice or covenant. For while the Prophet (PBUH) and his Companions were living in Al-Madiinah in peace, reminding one another to worship and obey Allah, hoping that the Quraish would refrain from their hostility, a group of Jewish leaders stealthily headed for Makkah to instigate the Quraish against the Prophet (PBUH). The Jews pledged to help the Quraish if they decided to raid Al- Madiinah. They made an agreement with the disbelievers and even laid down the battle plan. Moreover, on their way home they incited Bani Ghatfaan — one of the biggest Arab tribes — and made an agreement with its leaders to join forces with the Quraish army.

The war plan was ready and everyone knew his role. The Quraish and Ghatfaan were to attack Al-Madiinah with an enormous army, whereas the Jews were to sabotage Al-Madiinah simultaneously with the attack.

When the Prophet (PBUH) found out the treacherous scheme, he resorted to counterplot. First, he ordered his Companions to dig a trench around Al-Madiinah to hold back the attackers. Second, he sent Sa'd Ibn Mu'aadh and Sa'd Ibn 'Ubaadah to Ka'b Ibn Asad, the leader of Bani Quraidhah, to learn exactly where they stood concerning the imminent war. At that time, mutual agreements and treaties were already signed between the Prophet (PBUH) and the Jews of Bani Quraidhah. The two messengers of the Prophet met with the Jewish leader, yet to their surprise he denied the agreement by saying, "We did not sign any agreement or treaty with Muhammad."

It was hard for the Prophet to expose the people of Al-Madiinah to such a deadly invasion and exhausting siege; therefore, the only answer was to neutralize Ghatfaan so that the attacking army would lose half of its men and strength. He began to negotiate with the Ghatfaan leaders so that they would forsake the Quraish in exchange for one third of Al-Madiinah's crops. The leaders of Ghatfaan accepted this agreement, and both parties were to sign it shortly.

The Prophet (PBUH) could not go any further without consulting his Companions. He valued Sa'd Ibn Mu'aadh and Sa'd Ibn 'Ubaadah's opinion, for they were the leaders of Al-Madiinah and had the right to have a say in any decision that affected it.

The Prophet (PBUH) told them about his negotiations and that he had resorted to this compensation lest Al-Madiinah and its inhabitants be exposed to this dangerous attack and horrible siege. Both Sa'ds asked the Prophet (PBUH), "Is it a matter of choice or is it an inspiration from Allah?" The Prophet (PBUH) answered, "It is actually a matter that I chose for you. By Allah, I only do this because I can clearly see that the Arabs joined forces to strike you as one man so I want to curb their strength." Sa'd Ibn Mu'aadh had the intuition that their fate as men and as believers was being subtly tested so he said, "O Messenger of Allah, when we and those Jews were disbelievers and polytheists, they did not even dream of eating a date from our land unless we gave it to them out of generosity, hospitality, or for trade purposes. So how is it, after Allah has guided us to Islam and made us honored by it and by you, that we give them our money? By Allah, we can do without this agreement, and we will give them nothing but warfare until Allah settles our dispute." The Prophet (PBUH) at once changed his mind and notified Ghatfaan's leaders that his Companions rejected the proposed agreement and that he approved and supported their opinion.

A few days later Al-Madiinah witnessed a horrible siege. It was, in fact, a siege which it brought upon itself rather than was forced upon it due to the trench that was dug as a protection and safely procedure. The Muslims were prepared for war. Sa'd lbn Mu'aadh marched around with his sword and spear and recited lines of poetry that mean, "I waited anxiously for the battle to start. How beautiful death seems when the time is the right time."

In one of the rounds of war, Sard's arm was showered with the arrows of one of the disbelievers, and blood gushed severely from his wounds. He received first aid assistance to stop the bleeding, then the Prophet (PBUH) ordered him carried to the mosque where a tent was put up so that he would be near the Prophet while he was nursed. The Muslims carried their great hero into the Prophet's mosque and Sa'd looked up to the sky and said, "O Allah our Lord, if the war against the Quraish is to last any longer, please do let me live a little while longer to fight against them, for I like nothing better than fighting those people who hurt Your Prophet, disbelieved him, and even drove him to emigrate. But if the war has already ended, please make my wounds pave my way to martyrdom. I implore You, dear Allah, not to let me die until I avenge myself upon Bani Quraidhah!"

Allah will stand by you, Sa'd lbn Mu'aadh! For who could say such a thing in such a situation but you ? Allah did fulfil his suplication. His injury caused his death a month later, but he did not die until he had taken his revenge on the Jews of Bani Quraidhah. After the Quraish became desperate in their attempt to vanquish Al-Madiinah and their soldiers were gripped by panic, they took their arms and equipment and returned to Makkah ashamed and disappointed.

The Prophet (PBUH) believed that Al-Madiinah had been compromised by the deceit and treachery of the Jews for too long. They left the Muslims in the lurch whenever they chose, a thing that the Prophet could no longer accept. Therefore, he ordered his Companions to march towards Bani Quraidhah, and there the Muslims besieged them for 25 days. When the Jews were certain that there was no escape from the Muslims, they pleaded with the Prophet (PBUH) to let Sa'd Ibn Mu'aadh, their ally in pagan times, decide what would become of them.

The Prophet (PBUH) sent his Companions to bring Sa'd from his tent at the mosque. He came carried on a camel and he looked so pale and sick. The Prophet (PBUH) addressed him, "Sa'd, decide what should be done to Bani Quraidhah." Sa'd remembered their treachery and deceit in general and in the Battle of Al Khandaq in particular, when Al-Madiinah had come too close to its ruin, and said, "I say kill their warriors, capture their children, and distribute their money." Thus Sa'd did not die until he had taken his revenge.

Sard's wounds became worse every day. One day, the Prophet (PBUH) visited Sa'd and found him on the verge of death, so he put his head on his blessed lap and called upon Allah, "O Allah, Our Lord, Sa'd has striven hard in the way of Allah. He believed in Your Prophet and did his very best. So please do accept his soul with goodly acceptance." The words of the Prophet (PBUH) fell like coolness and safety on the departing noble soul. He strove to open his eyes, hoping that the last face he saw would be the Prophet's and said, "Peace be upon you. Prophet. I do witness that you are indeed the Messenger of Allah."

The Prophet (PBUH) took a farewell look of Sa'd's face and said, "Rejoice, Abu 'Amr." Abu Sa'iid Al-Khudriy (May Allah be pleased with him) said, "I was one of those who dug Sa'd's grave, and each time we dug out a layer of sand, we smelled musk. This went on until we reached his burial niche." Sa'd's death was a tragic loss for the Muslims. Their only consolation was when they heard the Prophet (PBUH) say, "The throne-of the Most Beneficient shook when Sa'd !bn Mu'aadh died."

(46)
SA'D IBN 'UBAADAH
The Carrier of the Ansaar Standard

Sa'd lbn Mu'aadh is hardly ever mentioned without Sa'd lbn 'Ubaadah. Both were leaders of Al-Madiinah. Sa'd lbn Mu'aadh was the leader of Al-Aws tribe and Sa'd lbn 'Ubaadah of Al-Khazraj. Again, both were foremost in Islamic faith. They witnessed the Pledge of Al-'Aqabah and lived next to the Prophet (PBUH) as obedient and sincere believers and soldiers.

Sa'd lbn 'Ubaadah held a special position among the Ansaar as he had his share of the abuse and torture Muslims were subjected to at the hands of the Quraish in Makkah! It was only natural that the Quraish would torture those who lived in Makkah, but to torture a man from Al-Madiinah was rather exceptional. 'Ubaadah was not an ordinary man; he was a distinguished and influential leader. This was a privilege that was enjoyed only by Sa'd lbn 'Ubaadah.

After the Pledge of Al-'Aqabah allegiance was concluded in secret and the Ansaar were getting ready to travel, the Quraish found out about the allegiance the Ansaar had given to the Prophet (PBUH). Their agreement with the Prophet (PBUH) allowed him to emigrate with his Companions to Al-Madiinah to flee the power of polytheism and darkness and seek sanctuary and support there.

At that point, the Quraish lost self-control, so they went on hunting those who pledged the Prophet. The disbelievers captured Sa'd lbn 'Ubaadah, tied his hands to his neck with his saddle girths, and dragged him back to Makkah, where they beat and tortured him!

How could this happen to Sa'd Ibn'Ubaadah? He was the leader of Al-Madiinah who always helped anyone of the Quraish who needed help, protected their trade, and was hospitable to them whenever they visited Al-Madiinah. Those who captured and abused him surely did not know who he was. But even if they had known, would it have made any difference? They were the ones who tortured the elite of Makkah when they committed themselves to Islam, were they not? In those days, the Quraish were absolutely mad. They watched Ignorance collapse under the pressure of Truth, so the only thing that they could do was to avenge themselves ruthlessly and heedlessly.

As we have already said, Sa'd Ibn 'Ubaadah was surrounded by disbelievers who battered and tortured him. Now, let us hear the story as told by Sa'd himself: By Allah, I was in such a terrible state in their mercy, when I saw a group of people from the Quraish approaching me. Among them there was this white man who looked as bright as daylight, so I said to myself. Well if there is someone among those people left with the least sense of compassion and mercy, then it must be this man. Unfortunately, as he came close to me, he raised his fist and punched me severely, so I said to myself that none of them is kind-hearted enough to come to my rescue. And there I was a prey in their hands as they dragged me when a man hurried to me and scolded me saying, "Fie on you! Doesn't anyone of the Quraish owe you a favor of good neighborliness?" I answered, "Yes, of course, I used to help Jubair Ibn Muta'm's traders and stand by them against those of my people who were unjust to them. I also gave aid to Al-Haarith Ibn Harb Ibn Umaiyah." Then the man urged me to shout their names and say they owe me the right of good neighborliness so I did. Then the man rushed to them and told them, "A man from Al-Khazraj is being beaten in the valley and he is calling out your names and saying that you owe him the right of good neighborliness." They asked him who I was, and as soon as he told them, they told him that everything I said was true and rushed to rescue me.

Sa'd left Makkah after this premature assault which made him realize the extent of brutality and savageness the Quraish were willing to exercise against unarmed people who called for good, truth, and peace. This assault sharpened his will, and he decided to do his utmost to help the Prophet (PBUH) and his Companions.

The Prophet (PBUH) emigrated to Al-Madiinah just after the Hijrah of his Companions. There, Sa'd put his fortune at the disposal of the Muhaajiruun. Sa'd was generous by nature and heredity, being the son of 'Ubaadah Ibn Dulaim Ibn Haarithah, who was famous for his generosity in pagan times. Sa'd's generosity turned into a sign of his deep-rooted and solid faith.

Narrators commented upon his generosity and said, "The Prophet's houses were always full of food sent by Sa`d." They also said that a man from the Ansaar used to invite one, two, or even three Muhaajiruun over for meals, whereas Sa'd Ibn 'Ubaadah used to invite over 80 of Muhaajiruun.

Solely for this, Sa'd always implored Allah to bestow him with more of His good provision and used to invoke, "O Allah, little provision does not suffice me to be righteous or to act righteously." Therefore, it was justifiable for the Prophet (PBUH) to supplicate saying, "O Lord, bring Your blessings and mercy on the family of Sa'd Ibn 'Ubaadah."

Sa'd directed not only his fortune to the service of Islam, the straight and right religion, but also his energy and skills. He was a skilled marksman. He showed singular spirit of self-sacrifice during the battles under the Prophet's command (PBUH). Ibn 'Abbaas said about him (May Allah be pleased with them both), "The Prophet (PBUH) used only two standards each time he was at war: the Muhaajiruun's flag with 'Aliy Ibn Abiy Taalib and the Ansaar's flag with Sa'd Ibn 'Ubaadah.

It seemed that his characteristic strictness was part of his strong personality. He was stern in upholding what was right or what he believed to be his right. If he was convinced about a certain matter, he would rise to make it known in public in an unwavering outspokenness and uncompromising firmness. This strictness, or should we say this extremism, was the reason behind many of his viewpoints which were called into question.

For instance, on the Day of the Conquest of Makkah, the Prophet (PBUH) assigned him to lead an army battalion. Hardly had he reached the outskirts of Makkah, the sacred town, when he shouted, "Today is the day of fierce battle. Today is the day of transgression." 'Umar Ibn Al-Khattaab heard his threat and hurried to the Prophet (PBUH) and said, " Messenger of Allah, listen to what Sa'd just said. . . He should not be entrusted with the command of the battalion that will attack the Quraish." The Prophet (PBUH) gave his assent and ordered 'Umar to catch up with him and take his place in the command.

It seems that when Sa'd saw Makkah in a state of surrender and helplessness, he saw flashbacks of the abuse and torture that the believers and he himself had suffered at one time at the hands of disbelievers. He recalled all the wars they had waged against the Muslims who called for monotheism just because they believed that there is no god but Allah. His stern nature made him rejoice at the Quraish's calamity and vow revenge.

This sternness or extremism that was characteristic of Sa'd made him take his famous attitude on the Day of As-Saqiifah. After the Prophet (PBUH) died, a group of the Ansaar met Sa'd at Bani Saa'adah's shaded meeting place to tell him that the Prophet's caliph must be one of the Ansaar, as the caliphate was an honor in this world and in the next; therefore they craved to win that honor. But the Prophet (PBUH) had already chosen his caliph when he asked Abu Bakr to take his place as Imam (prayer leader) while he was sick. His Companions saw this and other special qualities enjoyed by Abu Bakr — for instance, he was the second of the two in the cave — as a sign for his right to the caliphate.

On the one hand, 'Umar Ibn Al-Khattaab, along with his companions, took the side of Abu Bakr and held fast to their opinion. On the other hand, Sa'd Ibn 'Ubaadah, along with his companions, took the other side and held fast to it. This angered many of the Prophet's Companions who held Ibn 'Ubaadah responsible for such a dispute.

However, Sa'd Ibn 'Ubaadah was only being himself when he held fast to his viewpoint, for as we have already said, he always held tenaciously to his convictions and insisted on being outspoken and precise concerning exactly where he stood. This feature came out clearly at the Battle of Hunain before the Prophet himself. When the Muslims were victorious in battle, the Prophet (PBUH) always distributed the spoils of war among all the Muslims, yet on that particular day, he took special care of those whose hearts Allah had joined, namely, the elite who had committed themselves to Islam a short time before, so as to help them discipline themselves by this privilege. He did not give anything to the Muslims in whom Islam was deeply rooted, as he thought that their Islam sufficed them. He gave to the warriors who were in need. The Prophet's mere bounty was an honor most people competed for. The war booty became an important source of revenue on which the Muslims lived. Therefore, the Ansaar bitterly wondered what made the Prophet deprive them of the booty.

Hassan Ibn Thaabit, the poet of the Ansaar, recited lines of poetry that mean: Go to the Prophet and say you are the best among all human beings. Why should you invite Sulaim tribe to take a share of war spoils although they are mere Muhaajiruun while you deprived the Ansaar who gave shelter, support and help to Muhaajiruun. Allah called them the Ansaar because they believed in and supported the religion of guidance in the time of fierce struggle and war. They rushed to strive in the way of Allah and endured difficulties and hardships without getting weary or losing faith.

In those lines, the poet of the Prophet and the Ansaar expressed quite eloquently the embarrassment and disappointment the Ansaar felt when the Prophet gave his Companions the spoils of war and did not give them anything.

The leader of the Ansaar, Sa'd Ibn 'Ubaadah, realized the dilemma they were in, as he heard people talk about it secretly. This did not appeal to him, so urged by his candor, he went immediately to the Prophet (PBUH) and said, "O Messenger of Allah, this group of the Ansaar are displeased with what you did with the spoils of war. You have distributed war booty among your people and were most generous to the Arab tribes, but you did not give the Ansaar anything."

Thus, the frank man got it off his chest and gave the Prophet a candid account of the situation. The Prophet (PBUH) asked him, "What is your opinion about it?" Sa'd answered with the same bluntness, "I have the same viewpoint as my people." Then the Prophet (PBUH) asked him to gather the Ansaar. We must narrate the story to its very end as it is irresistably fascinating.

When the Prophet (PBUH) came where the Ansaar gathered, he looked at their disgruntled faces, and his smile brightened with gratitude and appreciation. Then he said, "O Ansaar, I heard that an incident that happened recently made you feel ill at ease. Now, didn't I find you ignorant and guided you to the way of Allah. Didn't I find you poor and Allah enriched you of His bounty? And didn't I find you enemies and Allah joined your hearts together?"

They answered, "Indeed, Allah and His Prophet are far more generous and better."

The Prophet then said, "Don't you have anything to say?"

They answered, "There is nothing to be said but that Allah and His Prophet have the grace and bounty."

The Prophet (PBUH) then said, "By Allah, you could have justly said. We believed in you at a time when all called you a liar. We supported you at a time when you were frustrated. We gave you our money at a time when you were poor and we even sheltered you at a time when you were homeless. O Ansaar, are you upset for a thing so trivial and worldly that I gave to some people so as to join their hearts to Islam and left you out of it, believing that your Islam sufficed you? Is it not enough for you that the rest of the people will go home with a sheep or a camel, whereas you will return accompanied by the Prophet's love and appreciation? By Allah, if I were not one of the Muhaajiruun I would rather be one of the Ansaar, and if people moved in different ways, I would choose the way taken by the Ansaar. Allah, do have mercy on the Ansaar, their children, and their children's children."

By the time the Prophet (PBUH) concluded his words, their beards were wet with tears, for the words of the great Prophet filled their hearts with tranquility and enriched their souls. All of them including Sa'd cried out, "It is enough for us to have the Prophet's love as our reward."

In the first days of 'Umar's caliphate, Sa'd went to the Commander of the Faithful and said with his extreme candor, "By Allah, we prefer your companion Abu Bakr over you. By Allah, I cannot stand to live near you." "Umar calmly answered, "Anyone who hates his company should seek a better one elsewhere." Sa'd said, "I will indeed seek better company somewhere else."

Sa'd words to 'Umar were not an expression of hate or spite, for the man who was satisfied with the Prophet's love as his reward cannot possibly deny loyality to such a man as 'Umar, whom the Prophet (PBUH) had always cherished and honored. It was just that Sa'd Ibn'Ubaadah did not want to wait around for some event to come up and result in an inevitable dispute between him and the Commander of the Faithful 'Umar Ibn Al-Khattaab, a thing he did not want or accept. Sa'd was one of the Companions whom the Qur'aan described as "merciful among themselves." He traveled to Syria. Shortly after he had settled in the Hauran plateau, he died and went back to the Lord the Most Merciful.

(47)
USAAMAH IBN ZAID
The Beloved Son of the Beloved

'Umar lbn Al-Khattaab, Commander of the Faithful, sat down to distribute money from the treasury among the Muslims.

It was 'Abd Allah Ibn 'Umar's turn, and 'Umar gave him his share. Then it was the turn of Usaamah lbn Zaid. 'Umar gave him double of what he gave his son 'Abd Allah. As 'Umar gave people according to their merit and endeavor, 'Abd Allah lbn 'Umar was afraid that his position was not as highly acknowledged as he desired, to be one of the closest to Allah through his obedience, endeavor, piety, and asceticism.

Therefore, he asked his father, "You preferred Usaamah, although I experienced with the Messenger of Allah what he did not." 'Umar answered, 'Usaamah was more beloved by the Prophet (PBUH) than you were, and his father was more beloved by the Prophet (PBUH) than your father was."

Who was it, together with his father that was so close to the Prophet's heart and love? It was a high position which Ibn 'Umar did not reach, nor did his father, 'Umar himself.

Who was it? It was Usaamah lbn Zaid who has been called among the Prophet's Companions "The Beloved Son of the Beloved".

His father was Zaid lbn Haarithah*, the Prophet's servant, who preferred the Prophet (PBUH) over own his father, mother and

---

* His biography has previously been mentioned.

kin. He was with him when the Prophet (PBUH) stood in front of a large group of Companions saying, "I let you bear witness that Zaid is my son, inheriting from me and I inheriting from him."

His name remained Zaid Ibn Muhammad until the practice of child adoption was abolished by the Qur'aan. Usaamah is his son. His mother was Umm Aiman, the Prophet's servant and nurse maid.

Usaamah's physical appearance made him appear a good-for-nothing. Historians and narrators described him as being dark-skinned and snub-nosed. By these two words, not more, did history summarize Usaamah's physical appearance. However, since when did Islam ever care about a person's physical characteristics? Was it not the Prophet (PBUH) who said, "Maybe a Muslim's hair is unkempt and his feet covered with dust and his clothes are not neat, but, if he swore by Allah he would fulfill his oath?"

Therefore, let us set his appearance aside. Leave his dark skin and snub nose alone; nothing of that sort has weight in Islam. Let us instead take stock of his loyalty. How was his devotion? How was his virtue? How was his honesty? How was his piety? How great was his soul? On account of the qualities of his soul, he reached a worthiness that made him eligible to receive the Prophet's infinite love and acknowledgement: "Usaamah Ibn Zaid is the most beloved to me and I wish him to be one of the virtuous. I recommend you to treat him well."

Usaamah (May Allah be pleased with him) had all the great characteristics which enabled him to be so close to the Prophet's heart and beloved in his eyes. He was the son of two generous Muslims belonging to the first converts to Islam who, at the same time, were the closest and most loyal to the Messenger of Allah (PBUH).

As one of the true sons of Islam, he was nurtured from his first days by Islam's pure nature without experiencing the murkiness of the pagan period. Despite his young and tender age, he was a firm believer and a staunch Muslim fulfilling all the duties of his faith with deep loyalty and an unbreakable will. With great intellect and humility, limits to his devotion to Allah and His Prophet (PBUH) could not be found.

Furthermore, he represented the victims of all kinds of discrimination who were saved by Islam. How could this dark-skinned, snub-nosed fellow attract the heart of the Prophet (PBUH) and Muslims to such an elevated rank! This could only be possible when Islam corrected human norms and values dealing with discrimination against people: *<Surely the most honorable of you in the sight of Allah is the most pious of you > (49 : 13).*

On the day of the Conquest of Makkah, the Prophet's Companion who was riding behind him on horseback was that dark-skinned, snub-nosed Usaamah Ibn Zaid. Among the most victorious days of Islam was the day of the Conquest of Makkah. On that day, on the Prophet's right and left were Bilaal and Usaamah, two dark-skinned men; however Allah's word which they carried in their pure, virtuous hearts made them deserving of all kinds of merit and elevated position.

Usaamah had not yet reached the age of 20 when the Prophet (PBUH) ordered him to be head of an army which had among its soldiers Abu Bakr and 'Umar. A growl spread around among a group of Muslims who were distressed by this matter and who found it too much for a youth such as Usaamah Ibn Zaid to command an army which included a large number of Muhaajiruun and elderly Ansaar. Their whispers reached the Messenger of Allah (PBUH), so he ascended the pulpit, thanked and praised Allah and then said, "Some people criticized Usaamah's army command; they criticized his father's command before him. His father deserved to be the commander as well as Usaamah. He is the most beloved to me next to his father, and I hope he is among the virtuous ones. I request you to treat him well."

The Prophet (PBUH) died before the army set off towards its destination; however the Prophet had left his wise testament to his Companions: "Fulfill Usaamah's commission. Fulfil Usaamah's commission."

Despite the new circumstances created by the Prophet's death, Abu Bakr As-Siddiiq, the first caliph, insisted upon fulfilling the Prophet's testament. Usaamah's army set off to its destination; the caliph only requested Usaamah to allow "Umar to stay behind to be with him in Al-Madiinah.

At the same time, the Roman (Byzantine) emperor heard the news of the Prophet's death and that an army headed by Usaamah Ibn Zaid was attacking the borders of Syria. He could not hide his astonishment and wonder about the strength of the Muslims, whose plans and potential were not affected by the Prophet's death. Consequently, the Romans abstained from utilizing the Syrian borders as a leaping point upon Islam's center in the Arabian Peninsula, and thereby their power began to shrink.

Usaamah's army returned safely without any casualties so that the Muslims said, " We've never seen a safer army than Usaamah's."

It was by the Prophet (PBUH) himself that Usaamah had been

taught the lesson of his life, a very wise lesson. Usaamah lived according to its wisdom from the Prophet's death until he himself left our world during thc latter phase of Mu'aawiyah's caliphate.

Two years before the Prophet's death, Usaamah was sent by the Prophet (PBUH) to lead a detachment which was meeting some polytheists attacking Islam and its followers. It was the first time for Usaamah to be appointed head of a detachment. He accomplished his duty successfully and victoriously. News of his victory preceded his arrival and the Prophet (PBUH) was indeed glad.

Let us leave the rest of the story to be narrated by Usaamah himself: When I reached the Prophet (PBUH) the proclamation of good news had already reached him. The Prophet's face beamed jubilantly. He asked me to sit closer to him and said, "Tell me." I went on telling and narrating. I mentioned to him that at one point the polytheists were defeated and I could reach a man, at whom I pointed my spear. The man said, "There is no god but Allah. Nevertheless I pierced and killed him with my lance. The Prophet's attitude changed. He said, "Woe unto you! How dare you do that when he said, There is no god but Allah. Woe unto you! How dare you do that when he said. There is no god but Allah." He continued saying that to such an extent that I wished to rid myself of all my deeds and embrace Islam afresh on that day. No, by Allah, I will never fight anyone saying. There is no god but Allah, after what I have heard from the Prophet (PBUH).

Usaamah was guided by the wisdom of this lesson throughout his life. What a wise lesson! A lesson revealing the Prophet's humanity, his justice, the eminence of his principles, the greatness of his faith and manners. Despite the fact that it was a polytheist warrior who had been killed by Usaamah, the killing was much regretted by the Prophet (PBUH).

At the same moment this warrior said, "There is no god but Allah," he was holding a sword in his right hand, a sword upon which pieces of Muslim flesh were still hanging. He said it to save his soul or to give himself another chance to change his direction or resume fighting.

Nevertheless, because he said it, his blood became inviolate and his life secure and safe at the same moment and for the same reason, whatever his intention or his inward desire may have been. Usaamah understood the lesson fully. If the Prophet (PBUH) forbids the killing of a man in such a situation for the reason that he said, "There is no god but Allah," what about the true believers and true Muslims? Therefore, Usaamah held a neutral position during the period of the civil strife between Imam 'Aliy with his followers on one hand and Mu`aawiyah on the other.

He loved 'Aliy very much and could see the truth on his side. But after having been blamed by the Prophet (PBUH) for the murder of a polytheist who said, "There is no god but Allah," how could he ever kill a Muslim believing in Allah and His Prophets? Therefore, he sent a message to 'Ally saying, "If you were in a lion's jaw, I would love to enter it with you. But I've never seen a situation like this before."

He kept within doors during the whole period of the fighting and war. When some of his companions came to argue with him over his decision, he simply said, "I will never fight anyone saying. There is no god but Allah."

Once, one cited him the verse < *And continue fighting them until there is no more persecution and GOD'S Religion prevails* > *(2:193)*. He replied," Those are the polytheists and we fought them until there wasn't any persecution and Allah's religion prevailed."

In A.H. 54 Usaamah longed to meet with Allah. On that day the gates of Paradise opened to receive one of the most reverent and pious believers.

(48)
'ABD AR- RAHMAN IBN ABI BAKR
A Hero to the End!

He was a clear image and reflection of Arab chivalry in its depth. His father was As-Siddiiq, the first convert, an incomparable believer, one of two who were in the cave. Despite all that, his son 'Abd Ar-Rahman stuck persistently and firmly to the pagan religion of his clan and to the idols of the Quraish.

At the Battle of Badr, he fought on the side of the Quraish. During the Battle of Uhud he was in the forefront of the spearmen recruited by the Quraish to combat the Muslims.

Before any fight there was a traditional dueling round (single combat), "Abd Ar-Rahman stood out asking the Muslims whom they were going to choose to fight with him. His father, Abu Bakr As-siddiiq (May Allah be pleased with him) rushed out to combat his son. However, the Prophet (PBUH) held him back, hindering him from doing so.

Any true Arab is primarily characterized by his loyalty to his conviction. Being convinced with a faith or an idea means being enslaved by such conviction; there is no way to rid him self of it, unless a new conviction fills his mind and soul without deceit or falsification.

Despite 'Abd Ar-Rahman's respect for his father, his trust in his father's rationality, and. the greatness of his manners and soul, despite all that, his loyalty to his conviction proved to be superior. His father's conversion to Islam did not tempt him to change his conviction. He remained unchanged, carrying out the responsibilities of his faith and conviction, defending the idols of the Quraish and fighting under their standard, the way brave warriors do.

As for the noble and powerful men of that type, truth prevails eventually, no matter how long it takes. Their noble essence, the light of their sincerity is soon going to guide them, uniting them with guidance and blessing.

The clock of fate struck to announce a new birth for "Abd Ar-Rahman. Light of guidance lit up sweeping away all murkiness, darkness, and devices inherited from pagan days. He soon could visualize Allah, the One and Only, in all surrounding creatures and things. It was here that guidance deepened its roots within his soul, it was here, he became a Muslim.

Without delay he set off towards the Prophet (PBUH). He became one who returns ever to the religion of truth. Abu Bakr's face beamed with happiness and delight seeing his son swearing the oath of allegiance to the Prophet (PBUH).

He had been a true polytheist, but now he was a true Muslim. No greed directed his steps, no fear pushed him, just a rational, rightly-guided conviction blessed by Allah's guidance and success. Soon he started to replace previous deeds with doing the best, striving in the cause of Allah, His Prophet and the faithful.

During the whole period of the Prophet (PBUH) and the era of caliphs who succeeded him, 'Abd Ar-Rahaman never missed a battle nor refrained from taking part in any jihaad. His endeavor and striving on the Day of Al-Yamaamah will never be forgotten. His firm resistance and bravery played a great role in achieving victory against the apostate army of Musailamah. It was he, `Abd Ar-Rahman, who killed Muhkam Ibn At-Tufail, Musailamah's schemer and the main guard of the castle inside which, the apostate army took refuge.

As soon as Muhkam fell down from the hard stroke of 'Abd Ar-Rahman, all those around him scattered, leaving a wide entrance open so the Muslim warriors could hasten inside.

Under the standard of Islam 'Abd Ar-Rahman's habits became more bright and shining. He was loyal to his conviction, completely determined to carry out and follow what was right and true, refusing all kinds of flattery and servility. All these manners were the essence of his personality as well as his whole life. He never abandoned his principles even when tempted by a desire or influenced by a fear.

Even on that terrible day, when Mu'aawiyah decided to force the pledge to Yaziid by the sword. On that day, a message was sent to Marwaan, the governor of Al-Madiinah. It included the oath of allegiance, which was to be read aloud in the mosque so that all the Muslims would hear it. Marwaan did what was ordered. When he finished reading it, 'Abd Ar-Rahman Ibn Abi Bakr turned the atmosphere of silence and depression which covered the mosque into one of loud opposition and firm resistance saying, "By Allah, it's not the welfare of Muhammad's nation that you are seeking. On the contrary, you want to turn it into a Heraclian rule. When Heraclius dies another follows."

"Abd Ar-Rahman could clearly see the dangers awaiting Islam if Mu'aawiyah was to carry out his desire. He could see how the transfer of power within Islam was changing from one based on national consultation by which the nation chooses its leader, to one of autocracy, by which emperors are imposed upon the people, one after the other.

'Abd Ar-Rahman had hardly finished these firm and loud resisting words when a group of Muslims hurried to support him. Leading them were Al-Hussain lbn 'Aliy, `Abd Allah lbn Az-Zubair and 'Abd Allah lbn 'Umar.

However for some compelling reason which occurred later on, they all were forced to hold a position of silence towards this pledge of allegiance which Mu'aawiyah decided to take by force of sword. But 'Abd Ar-Rahman continued to resist loudly. Mu'aawiyah sent him someone with 100,000 dirhams, hoping to please him.

lbn As-Siddiiq threw the money and said frankly to Mu'aawiyah's messenger, "Go back to him and tell him, it's not 'Abd Ar-Rahman who is going to buy his life by losing his faith." As soon as he heard the news that Mu'aawiyah had set off towards Al-Madiinah, he left it heading to Makkah.

Allâh wanted to save him the temptation of such a situation and its bad results. He had hardly reached the borders of Makkah when his soul submitted itself to Allah's appeal. Men carried the body and buried it in Makkah, which had witnessed his pagan past but also witnessed his conversion to Islam, the conversion of an honest, free, and brave man.

(49)
'ABD ALLAH IBN 'AMR IBN AL-AAS
The Submissive Returner to Allah !

The submissive, repentant, ever returning worshiper whom we are going to talk about is 'Abd Allah lbn 'Amr lbn Al-'Aas. Just as his father was famous for his rationality and cunning tricks, so was he famous for his highly elevated position among worshipers and hermits. His whole life was devoted to worship. Days and nights were not enough for his acts of worship.

He embraced Islam before his father. Since the day he swore the oath of allegiance, his heart shone like sunlight by means of Allah's light and the light of obedience.

He devoted himself to reciting and understanding the Glorious Qur'aan, so that when it was completely revealed he would have learned it all by heart. He did not recite it merely by power of a retentive memory, reproducing a book learned by heart, but rather he lived according to its laws, filled his heart with its magnificence, was its obedient servant and responded to its appeals. He then dedicated himself to its reading and recitation as well as understanding it, walking most delightfully in its mellow orchards, pleased with a joyful soul, happy with its holy verses, with eyes crying in anxiety and fear due to the effect of its verses.

'Abd Allah was created to be a worshiping saint. Nothing whatsoever could distract him from what he was created for and guided to. If the army of Islam waged jihaad against the polytheists who had been attacking Islam, he could always be found insistent in the front rows, aspiring to die as a martyr. It was the aspiration of a loving soul and the insistence of a lover.

When the war was over, where was he to be found?

There in the great mosque or the small mosque beside his house, fasting in the daytime, praying at night. His tongue did not know any worldly talk no matter how legitimate it was. His tongue did not know anything but invoking of Allah, the reciting the Qur'aan, praising Allah, and asking Him His forgiveness and remission of sins.

It is worthwhile to know how deep his worship and asceticism was. The Prophet(PBUH) found himself once forced to interfere in order to limit 'Abd Allah's extremism in worship.

Therefore, the moral which can be abstracted from 'Abd Allah's life is twofold. It demonstrates how excessively the human soul can be filled with an extraordinary ability to reach utmost degrees of devotion, worship, and virtue. On the other hand, it demonstrates Islam's concern to maintain a middle course and moderation, even when perfection is aspired to, lest the human soul should lose its zeal and aspiration and in order to maintain a healthy and safe body.

It reached the Prophet that 'Abd Allah spent his life in a uniform manner. If there was no battle to join, then it was non-stop worshiping, fasting, praying, and reciting the Qur'aan.

The Prophet (PBUH) sent for him, appeals to him to be moderate. The Prophet (PBUH) said, "Is it true what I heard, that you fast every day without eating (without breaking your fasting by one or two days) and that you pray all night without sleeping? It's enough to fast just three days every month." 'Abd Allah said, "I can bear more than that "' The Prophet (PBUH) said, "It's enough to fast two days each week." 'Abd Allah said, "I can bear more than that." The Prophet (PBUH) said, "Then, why don't you fast the best fasting of all, Daawud's (David's) fast; he fasted one day and ate on the other."

The Prophet(PBUH) continued asking him, "I've been informed that you recite the whole Qur'aan in one night. I'm afraid when you get older you will feel bored reciting it. Recite it once each month. Recite it once every ten days. Recite it once every three days." Then he said, "I fast and eat. I pray and sleep. I marry women. Whoever abstains from following my path, indeed, is not of me."

'Abd Allah lived long and when he got older and weaker he always remembered the Prophet's advice saying, "If only I had accepted the Prophet's advice."

It is not easy to find a believer of that sort engaged in a war fought by two Muslim parties against each other. How was it possible that his feet carried him from Al-Madiinah to As-Siffiin where he joined Mu'aawiyah's army in the battle against Imam 'Aliy? The more we contemplate 'Abd Allah's position, the more we will find it worthy of your respect and honor.

We saw how 'Abd Allah was engaged in worship in a way, which truly endangered his life. His father was always concerned about this matter. Therefore, he often complained to the Prophet (PBUH). On that particular instance when the Prophet (PBUH) asked 'Abd Allah to be moderate in worship, clearly suggesting suitable intervals, 'Abd Allah's father `Amr was present. The Prophet (PBUH) put 'Abd Allah's hand into his father's saying, "Do as I ordered you and obey your father."

Although 'Abd Allah was obedient to his father due to his faith and belief, the Prophet's order to him in such a way and on such an occasion had a very special impact on him. 'Abd Allah lived his whole life always remembering this short statement, "Do as I ordered you and obey you father."

Days and years passed. Mu'aawiyah in Syria refused to swear the oath of allegiance to 'Aliy. 'Aliy refused to submit to an illegal rebellion. War broke out between the two Muslim parties. The Battle of Al-Jamal passed, and now it was the turn of As-Siffiin.

'Amr lbn Al-'Aas had chosen to fight on Mu'aawiyah's side. Knowing how much people trusted and acknowledged his son's faith, he found it very beneficial for Mu'aawiyah's party to convince him to join and engage in the war. In addition, 'Amr was always optimistic whenever he had 'Abd Allah beside him in times of war. He could not forget his striving and endeavor in the conquest of Syria and on the Day of Yarmuuk.

When he intended to set out towards Siffiin, he appealed to his son to join saying, "O' 'Abd Allah, get ready, you're going to fight with us." 'Abd Allah replied, "How? The Prophet (PBUH) has entrusted me never to hold a sword to a Muslim's neck." By means of his cunning tricks, `Amr tried to convince his son that they just intended to kill 'Uthmaan's murderers and to take revenge.

Then he surprised his son with the following words, "O' 'Abd Allah, do you remember the last thing the Prophet committed you to, when he put your hand over mine saying. Obey your father? I order you now to join us and fight with us."

'Abd Allah went obediently but with the deep intention to neither carry a sword nor kill a Muslim. But how was that going to be possible? For the time being, he was just joining his father, but when the fight starts let Allah do as He wills.

It was a hard and fierce battle. Historians argue and differ among themselves, whether 'Abd Allah joined the battle from the very beginning or not. We think that he joined it from the very beginning, because the battle had hardly begun when something happened which forced 'Abd Allah to stand openly and clearly against the whole war and against Mu'aawiyah.

'Ammaar Ibn Yaasir, who was well respected by the Companions, was fighting on the side of Imam "Aliy. Once in the far remote past the Prophet (PBUH) had foreseen 'Ammaar's murder. This was in the days, when the Prophet (PBUH) and the Companions were building their mosque at Al-Madiinah after the Hijrah. The rocks were extremely big and even the strongest ones could not carry more than one at a time. However, `Ammaar was so cheerful and glad that he went on carrying two rocks at a time. The Prophet (PBUH) looked at him with tearful eyes saying, "Woe upon the son of Sumaiyah. He is going to be killed by the unjust party." All the Companions who took part in the building heard the prophecy and remembered it well. 'Abd Allah Ibn 'Amr was one of those who heard it.

At the beginning of the battle between 'Aliy and Mu`aawiyah's parties, 'Ammaar ascended a hill shouting, "Today is the day that we are going to meet Muhammad and his Companions." A group of Mu'aawiyah's party committed themselves to killing "Ammaar, so they pierced him with a lance, whereby he fell as a martyr.

The news of 'Ammaar's death spread rapidly. 'Abd Allah stood up agitatedly and said, "Is it true that 'Ammaar has been killed? Did you do it? That means you are the unjust party! You are the mislead warriors!" Like a portent he burst into the army, discouraging the fighters, shouting loudly, "You are the unjust party as long as it's you who killed 'Ammaar. The Prophet

(PBUH) foresaw his murder by the unjust party some 27 years ago."

'Abd Allah's words soon reached Mu'aawiyah, who sent for 'Amr and his son. He said to 'Amr, "Can't you stop your mad man?" 'Abd Allah said, "I'm not mad, but I heard the Prophet (PBUH) once saying to 'Ammaar, 'You will be killed by the unjust party." 'Mu'aawiyah continued asking, "Why, then, did you join our party?" 'Abd Allah said, "Because the Prophet (PBUH) asked me to obey my father and I obeyed him in joining you, but I didn't fight."

While they were arguing, someone entered asking Mu'aawiyah to permit the entrance of 'Ammaar's murderer. At that moment 'Abd Allah shouted, "Let him in and announce the 'good news' he is in hell." Hereby Mu'aawiyah lost his temper despite his calmness and mildness. He shouted to 'Amr, "Can't you hear what he is saying?"

'Abd Allah continued to ensure Mu'aawiyah that what he was saying was the truth and that the murderers were no more than unjust tyrants. Then he turned to his father and said, "Had it not been for the Prophet's order to obey you, I would not have gone out with you." While inspecting their army, Mu'aawiyah and "Amr were astonished and terrified to hear all the people talking about the Prophet's prophecy to 'Ammaar, You are going to be killed by the unjust party.

'Amr and Mu'aawiyah were afraid that this mere grumble was soon going to turn into a revolt against Mu'aawiyah. They thought together till they found a cunning trick. They spread the following words among the people: "Yes, the Prophet (PBUH) said to 'Ammaar on that day. "You'll be killed by the unjust party" The Prophet's prophecy is true. 'Ammaar has been killed. But who killed him? The true murderers are those who asked him to go out to fight."

In the midst of such confusion and turmoil, any logic could easily be spread. In this way Mu'aawiyah's and 'Amr's logic prevailed. The battle continued. 'Abd Allah went back to his mosque and to his worship.

He lived a life filled with nothing else than worship and adoration. Nevertheless, the mere act of going out to the battlefield always remained a reason for worry. He never remembered this act without weeping and saying, "What did I have to do with As-Siffiin?" Why did I bother myself with the killing of Muslims?"

One day, while sitting with some companions in the Prophet's mosque, Al-Hussain Ibn 'Aliy (May Allah be pleased with him) passed by and they greeted each other. When Al-Hussain went away 'Abd Allah said to those sitting with him, "Would you like to know the human being most beloved to the angels? It's the one who just passed by, Al-Uussain Ibn `Aliy. He has not talked to me since the Day of As-Siffiin. I would like him to talk to me more than I desire all the blessings of this world."

He decided with Abu Sa'iid Al-Khudriy to visit Al-Hussain. There, at Al-Hussain's house the meeting of these two great men took place. 'Abd Allah began to talk. When he mentioned As-Sifflin, Al-Hussain asked him scolding, "You, did you join the fight on Mu'aawiyah's side?" 'Abd Allah said, "One day `Amr Ibn Al-'Aas complained to the Prophet (PBUH) saying, 'Abd Allah fasts the whole day and prays all night.' Then the Prophet said to me, 'O' 'Abd Allah, pray and sleep, fast and eat. Obey you father.' When it was the day of As-Siffiin, my father swore by Allah that I had to go out with him. I went out, but, by Allah, I didn't pierce with a lance, I didn't fight with a sword and I didn't shoot any arrows."

At the age of 72, while praying in his mosque, asking for Allah's forgiveness, praising Allah gratefully, he was invited to join the eternal voyage. Filled with a longing aspiration he responded. His soul left the world joyfully to join his brethren who had preceded him. The announcer of good news proclaimed from Heaven, < *"O' soul at peace, return to your Lord, well pleased and well pleasing. Enter you among My servants, and enter into My Paradise!"> (89:27-30).*

(50)
ABU SUFYAAN IBN AL HAARITH
From Darkness to Light !

Here is another Abu Sufyaan, a different one than Abu Sufyaan Ibn Harb. His story is one of being guided after straying from the path of truth, a story of love after hatred, happiness after suffering. It is the story of Allah's infinite mercy and how it opened the gates to someone seeking Allah's refuge after a long journey full of hardship and suffering.

Can you imagine, Ibn Al-Haarith spent 20 years in a continuous fight against Islam! Twenty years from the beginning of the revelation until the day of the Conquest. During this whole period Abu Sufyaan was encouraging the Quraish and their allies, attacking the Prophet (PBUH) by means of satires, never absent when a battle or fight was fought. His three brothers, Nawfal, Rabii'ah, and 'Abd Allah, converted to Islam before him.

The Abu Sufyaan, about whom we are talking, was the cousin of the Prophet (PBUH), as he was the son of Al-Haarith Ibn 'Abd Al-Muttalib. Furthermore, he was the foster brother of the Prophet (PBUH), having been suckled for a few days by Haliimah Al-Sa'diyah, the Prophet's wet-nurse.

One day, destiny called him to meet his happy fate. He called his son Ja'far and said to his men that they were both going to travel. "Where to, Ibn Al-Haarith? What is your destination?" "To the Messenger of Allah (PBUH) to submit ourselves to Allah, Lord of the Worlds."

With a repenting heart he began to ride his horse. At a place called Al-Abuwaa', he could see a great army approaching. Soon he realized that it was the Prophet (PBUH) moving forward to enter Makkah. He began to search for a way out. The Messenger of Allah (PBUH) had allowed the Companions to shed Abu Sufyaan's blood because of his long continuous fight against Islam, a fight in which he used his sword as well as his tongue.

If anyone in the approaching army saw him, he would no doubt take revenge. Therefore Abu Sufyaan had to find a clever way which would enable him to meet the Messenger of Allah (PBUH) first before any Muslim could see him. He disguised himself, hiding all his features, then took his son and walked a while until he could clearly see the Prophet (PBUH), who at that moment was approaching amidst a large number of the Companions.

Suddenly, Abu Sufyaan threw himself between the Prophet's hands, removing his disguise. As soon as the Prophet (PBUH) recognized him, he turned his face. Abu Sufyaan turned and approached him from another direction, in vain; the Prophet turned his face again. Abu Sufyaan and his son Ja'far both shouted, " We bear witness that there is no god but Allah. We bear witness that Muhammad is the Messenger of Allah." They came nearer saying, "O'Prophet, no reproach!" The Prophet (PBUH) replied, "No reproach shall be upon you, Abu Sufyaan." Then the Prophet (PBUH) handed him over to 'Aliy lbn Abi Taalib and said to him, "Teach your cousin ablution, the Sunnah and take him away right now." 'Aliy took him and soon returned. The Prophet (PBUH) told 'Aliy, "Tell people that the Prophet (PBUH) is pleased with Abu Sufyaan, so be pleased with him."

It was nothing more than a moment which Allah blessed in order to close a period of suffering, misery, hardship, and error while opening the gates of infinite mercy. He nearly converted to Islam when, during the Battle of Badr, while fighting on the side of the Quraish, he saw something that confused his mind.

During that battle Abu Lahab stayed behind, sending Al-'Aas Ibn Hishaam in his place. Abu Lahab was waiting eagerly to hear the news when the shocking defeat was announced. He was sitting near the well of Zamzam in the middle of a group of the Quraish, when a horseman approached. It was Abu Sufyaan Ibn Al-Haarith. Abu Lahab did not give him a chance to rest, but asked him immediately, "Come nearer, my cousin. You have the latest news! How was it?" Abu Sufyaan Ibn Al-Haarith said, "By Allah, we had hardly begun fighting when it was as if we offered them our bodies, let them do with us whatever they wanted, let them fight us as they pleased, took us prisoners as they liked. I swear, by Allah, I do not blame the Quraish, as we met white men riding piebald horses filling the space between heaven and earth. Nothing is like to them, nothing could stop them."

Abu Sufyaan surely meant that angels were fighting on the Prophet's side. Why is it then that Abu Sufyaan did not submit himself to Allah, at that time after having seen what he first described?

Doubt paves the way to certainty. The more obstinate and opinionated his doubt, the firmer and more persistent his conviction. Finally, it was the day of guidance and certainty, the day of his conversion as previously mentioned.

From the very beginning, from the first moments after his conversion, he began to strive and to worship as if entering a race with time, hoping to erase all traces of his past to compensate for what he had missed during that time.

He took part in all the battles after the Day of the Conquest. On the Day of Hunain, a very dangerous trap was prepared by the polytheists, who attacked the Muslims so fiercely that a great deal of Muslim warriors lost their reason and retreated, but the Prophet (PBUH) stood firm appealing, "O'people. I'm the Prophet, it's not a lie. I'm the son of 'Abd Al-Muttalib."

During those fearful moments, a small group, not losing their reason, continued fighting. Among them was Abu Sufyaan and his son Ja'far. Abu Sufyaan was holding the bridle of the Prophet's horse, but when he saw what happened, he felt deeply that his chance had finally come, the chance of dying as a martyr in the cause of Allah, between the Prophet's hands.

He held the horse's bridle with one hand while cutting the throats of the polytheists with the other. The Muslims regrouped around the Prophet (PBUH) and Allah blessed them with victory. Although the fight was over, when the Prophet (PBUH) looked around he could see a faithful believer still holding his horse's bridle. It was Abu Sufyaan, who had not left his place since the battle began. The Prophet (PBUH) glanced and asked, "Who is it? My brother Abu Sufyaan Ibn Al-Haarith?"

Immediately after hearing the word "brother" Abu Sufyaan's heart was filled with joy and dignity. He knelt down and kissed the Prophet's feet, crying. His poetic sensibility was so much moved that he began to describe his joy and happiness because Allah had blessed him with so much bravery and success.

Abu Sufyaan turned to worship and adore Allah very persistently. It was after the Prophet's death when his soul longed for its meeting with the Prophet. He had desired for a long time to die soon, to the extent that people saw him digging out his grave at Al-Baqii, a grave which he prepared and arranged in a very nice way. When people expressed their astonishment he just said. "I'm preparing my grave."

Three days later he was lying at home, when his relatives began to cry and weep. When he opened his eyes, he said in complete tranquility, "Don't cry. I didn't commit a single sin since I converted to Islam."

Before his head fell upon his chest he said his last farewell to the world.

(51)
'UMRAAN IBN HUSAIN
The Angels' Resemblance

It was in the year of Khaibar that he turned to the Prophet (PBUH), swearing to him the oath of allegiance. Since the moment he put his right hand into the Prophet's right hand, his hand became subject to respect. He promised himself to use it only in good and virtuous deeds, an attitude displaying how much sensitivity this person enjoyed.

'Umraan was a clear image of honesty, humility, piety, and devotion to Allah. Although he was blessed with a great deal of divine success and guidance, he never stopped weeping and saying, "I wish I were ashes dispersed by the wind."

God-fearing men of this type did not fear Allah because of their sins. They rarely committed sins, since the day of their conversion to Islam. The more they got acquainted with Allah's greatness, majesty, and sublimity, the more they recognized their inability to truly thank and worship Allah and the more God-fearing they became, no matter how much they prayed, praised Allah or submitted themselves to Him.

Once the Prophet's Companions asked him, "O' Prophet of Allah, why when we are sitting with you do we feel calmness and tenderness in our hearts as an ascetic, seeing the Hereafter as if it were before us, but when we leave you to meet our wives, children, and our worldly affairs, we deny ourselves?" The Prophet (PBUH) responded, "By Allah, if you adhered strictly to your first state, the angels would have shaken your hands clearly. So it is natural for there to be a worshiping time followed by business."

When 'Umraan heard this Prophetic saying (hadith), his longing desire was moved; therefore, he promised himself never to abstain from striving to reach such a great goal, even if it cost him his whole life. He was never convinced to live dividing his time one-hour for leisure and one hour for worship. He wanted instead his life to be a long chain of intimate prayer and total devotion towards the Lord of the Worlds.

During the caliphate of "Umar lbn Al-Khattaab, he was sent to Basra, to teach its inhabitants jurisprudence. He settled there and soon people turned to him to seek his blessing and the guiding light of his religiosity. Al-Hasan Al-Basriy and lbn Siiriin said, "No one of the Prophet's companions who entered Basra can be considered better than "Umraan lbn Husain.

'Umraan refused to occupy himself with anything but worship. He spent his whole time doing nothing but adoring Allah until it seemed as if he belonged to another world other than the one in which he lived among his people and walked on its ground. Yes, it is true. He became like an angel living among angels, listening to, talking to, and shaking hands with them.

When the great uprising between the parties of 'Aliy and Mu'aawiyah took place, he did not just hold a neutral position, but appealed to people to abstain from joining the fight, adhering to the cause of peace. He went on saying, "I would prefer to be a shepherd on top of a mountain till I die rather than shoot an arrow at anyone in either party, right or wrong." Any Muslim he met, he advised saying, "Keep to your mosque. If it is broken into forcefully, then keep indoors. If the doors are broken into forcefully by someone who aims at taking your life and wealth, then fight him."

'Umraan lbn Husain's faith reached a very high level. For 30 years he suffered from severe disease. However, he never showed any sign of discontent nor did he grumble. Instead he adored and worshiped Allah persistently, all through his life. When his visitors came to encourage him, he always replied, "The dearest things to my heart are those dearest to Allah."

When he felt that death was approaching, he said to his family and kin, "When you finish burying me, slaughter and feed the people."

Truly, they should slaughter and feed the people. The death of someone like 'Umraan should be considered a great and glorious wedding festival, wherein his soul is being wedded to a Paradise as wide as earth, heaven prepared for the pious.

(52)
SALAMAH IBN AL-AKWA
The Infantry Hero

His son Iyaas summarized all his virtues in just one sentence: "My father never lied." To be described by this singular virtue makes a person eligible for a highly elevated position among the pious and virtuous. Salamah lbn Al-Akwa` achieved such a position, one which he deserved. Salamah was one of the rare Arab spearmen, but he was also famous for his courage, generosity, and charitable deeds. He sincerely submitted himself to Islam; then it was Islam that molded his personality according to its system.

Salamah was one of those, who attended the Pledge of Radwaan. In A.H. 6, the Prophet (PBUH) and his Companions aimed at visiting the Sacred House in Makkah, but the Quraish hindered them from doing so.

The Prophet (PBUH) sent 'Uthmaan lbn 'Affaan to tell them that he came as a visitor, not as a fighter. While they awaited 'Uthmaan's return, a rumor spread that the Quraish had killed him. The Prophet (PBUH) sat under a shady tree to take the Companion's oath of allegiance, one by one. They gave him their word to be ready to die.

Salamah reported: I swore the oath of allegiance in front of the Prophet to be ready to die. Then I stepped aside. When the crowd of people nearly ended, the Prophet (PBUH) said, "O' Salamah, aren't you going to swear your oath of allegiance?" I said, "I've already done that." He said, "Again." I swore the oath again.

Salamah had redeemed his oath long before that day. He

redeemed it since the day he admitted that there is no god but Allah and Muhammad is His Messenger. He said, "I joined the Prophet (PBUH) in seven battles and joined Zaid Ibn Haarithah in nine battles."

He was one of the most skillful warriors as an infantryman and one of the best to shoot arrows and throw spears. His tactics were similar to present day guerilla warfare: if an enemy approached, he retreated waiting for him to move backwards or to take a rest, in order to attack him by surprise. In this way he was able to chase alone the force led by 'Uyainah Ibn Hisn Al-Fizaarii which raided the environs of Al-Madiinah in the Dhii Qarad Raid. Totally alone, he followed their traces, then continued fighting and pushing them away from Al- Madiinah until the Prophet (PBUH) reached him with a great number of Companions. On that day the Prophet (PBUH) said to the Companions, "Our best infantryman is Salamah Ibn Al-Akwa`.

Salamah never knew deep sorrow and anxiety except when his brother 'Aamir Ibn Al-Akwa died during the Battle of Al-Khaibar.

'Aamir was the one singing in front of the Muslim army:

Had it not been for You
We would not have been guided,
Nor prayed nor given charity.
Bless us with tranquility,
And let us be strong and firm-hearted
when meeting our enemies.

In that battle 'Aamir wanted to strike a polytheist with his sword. However, his sword bent and its edge injured him fatally. Some Muslims said, "Poor 'Aamır, he has been deprived of martyrdom." Salamah's anxiety was severe because he thought, like others, that his brother, who had killed himself accidently, was deprived of the recompense of jihaad and the reward of martyrdom. But soon the Prophet (PBUH) put things in their right order when Salamah went to him saying. “O’ Messenger of Allah, is it true that by dying in this way ‘Aamir has been deprived of the reward of all his previous deeds?” The Messenger (PBUH) answered, “He has been killed as a mujaahid. He is to be granted two rewards. He is right now swimming in the rivers of Paradise.”

Salamah was very generous. However, he was more so when asked to give something for the sake of Allah. If someone had asked him to give away his life for the sake of Allah, he would not have hesitated to do so. People knew this attitude of his, so when anyone needed something, he just asked him for the sake of Allah. He always said, “If someone would not give for the sake of Allah, for whose sake then would he give?”

On the day of ‘Uthmaan’s murder (May Allah be pleased with him) the great mujaahid realized that the gates of sedition had been opened. How could it be possible for him who had fought among his brethren all his life to turn into a warrior against his brethren? It was not his right to use his fighting skill, which had been praised by the Prophet (PBUH), against believers and Muslims.

It was therefore more proper that he carry his belongings and leave Al-Madiinah for a place called Ar-Rabzah, the same place to which Abu Dhar chose to emigrate and settle.

Salamah spent the rest of his life at Ar-Rabzah. In A.H. 74 his burning desire took him to Al-Madiinah, where he spent one or two days as a visitor, and on the third day he died. It was as if the dear, moist earth of Al-Madiinah appealed to him to offer his body a cool, safe shelter, as it had previously offered all the blessed Companions and pious and virtuous martyrs.

(53)
'ABD ALLAH IBN AZ-ZUBAIR
What a Man! What a Martyr!

A blessed child in his mother's womb was he, when his mother passed over the burning desert sand leaving Makkah for Al-Madiinah on her emigration route. While still unborn, 'Abd Allah was to emigrate with the Muhaajiruun. His mother Asmaa' (May Allah be pleased with her) had hardly reached Qubaa', when she began to suffer labor pains.

'Abd Allah, the first child to be born after the Hijrah, was carried to the Prophet's house in Al-Madiinah. There the Prophet (PBUH) kissed him, then chewed a date and rubbed it on the newborn's gums (a Sunnah called *tahniik*). Thus the Prophet's saliva was the first thing to enter "Abd Allah's belly.

Muslims gathered, carried the newborn baby and went round with him through the streets of Al Madiinah applauding and shouting "Allahu Akbar"(Allah is the Greatest).

When the Prophet (PBUH) and the Muslims settled in Al-Madiinah, the Jews there, bearing deep spite against the Muslims, were subdued. They spread the rumor that their priests had made the Muslims infertile by means of their witchcraft and Al-Madiinah was not going to witness the birth of Muslim babies. When 'Abd Allah came out from the unseen, he was an irrefutable proof from Allah that the Jews' claims were mere lies and deceptive tricks.

'Abd Allah did not reach the age of majority during the Prophet's lifetime. However, his intimate contact with the Prophet (PBUH) during childhood granted him the basic materials of manliness and taught him the principles of life, principles which would be the subject of people's admiration and talk, as will be mentioned later.

The little child's character developed rapidly. He displayed extraordinary energy, intellect, and firmness. His youth was full of chastity, purity, worship, and heroism beyond imagination. As days went by his manners did not change. He was a man sure of his path, walking his way with strong will and firm belief.

He did not exceed the age of 27, during the conquests of Africa, Spain, and Constantinpole, when he proved to be one of the great heroes. That happened, in particular, during the Battle of Ifriiqiyah (Tunisia) when 20,000 Muslim soldiers confronted an army of 120,000.

The battle was in progress and the Muslims encountered a real danger. 'Abd Allah took a look at the enemy's army and soon realized the source of their strength. It was the leader, the Berber king, who effectively encouraged his soldiers, pushing them towards death. 'Abd Allah knew that the battle's outcome depended primarily on the death of their stubborn leader. But how was he going to reach him? He had first to pass through a great and fiercely fighting army. However, 'Abd Allah's courage and bravery were not ever subject to question. He called his companions and said, "Protect my back, attack with me." Like a flying arrow he forced his way towards the leader, bursting through fighting warriors. When he reached him, he struck him dead. Immediately the leader fell down motionless. Then he turned towards those who surrounded their king and leader, killing them all. "Allahu Akbar" was then to be heard.

The Muslims soon saw their standard lifted on the same spot where the Berber leader had commanded his soldiers. They realized that victory had almost been achieved. They strengthened their force and soon everything was over in favor of the Muslims. The leader of the Muslim army, 'Abd Allah Ibn Abi Sarh was told about the great role 'Abd Allah Ibn Az-Zubair had played. He rewarded him with the honor of personally carrying the news of victory to Al-Madiinah and to the Caliph 'Uthmaan lbn 'Affaan.

Nevertheless, his miraculous and extraordinary heroism in fighting came second to his heroism in the sphere of worship. His family, his youth, his position and its eminence, his wealth, his strength, nothing of that sort could hinder "Abd Allah from being an admirable God-fearing worshiper, fasting all day long while praying all night.

'Umar lbn 'Abd Al-'Aziiz once asked lbn Abi Mul^ikah to describe 'Abd Allah, so he said, "By Allah, I've never see a soul similar to his. When he began his prayer, he left everything behind. He bowed down and prostrated for such a long period that birds stood on his back considering him a wall or a gown thrown away. Once a projectile passed between his beard and chest while praying. By Allah, he did not feel it nor was he shaken by it. He did not stop his recitation nor hurry his bowing."

Similar to legends, the truthful information about 'Abd Allah's worship was transmitted by history. His fasting, his prayer, his pilgrimage, his noble soul, his continuous fear of Allah, his close relation to Allah, his being a devoted worshiper and a fasting fighter throughout his life were all in him like inter woven threads.

Although there was some kind of disagreement between 'Abd Allah lbn Az-Zubair and lbn 'Abbaas, the latter described 'Abd

Allah in the following words: "He was a reciter of the Qur'aan, a follower of the Sunnah, submissive to Allah, a God-fearing faster, son of the Prophet's disciple. His mother was As-Siddiiq's daughter, his aunt 'Aa'ishah, the Prophet's wife; his rank can only be ignored by the blind."

The strength of high mountains did not equal 'Abd Allah's firmness and assiduity. Sincere, noble, strong, he was always ready to sacrifice his life for his clarity and straightforwardness.

During his dispute and wars with Bani Umaiyah (the Ommiads), Al-Husain Ibn Numair, the leader of the army sent by Yaziid to suppress Ibn Az-Zubair's revolt, went to visit 'Abd Allah Ibn Az-Zubair in Makkah after the news reached there that Yaziid had died. Al-Husain offered 'Abd Allah to go with him to Syria where he would use his power to force people to swear the oath of allegiance to Ibn Az-Zubair. However, Ibn Az-Zubair refused this golden chance because he was totally convinced of the necessity to take revenge on the Syrian army for the terrible crimes committed while marching on the Prophet's Madiinah to satisfy the Ommiads' greed.

We may differ with 'Ábd Allah, wishing he would have preferred peace and forgiveness by responding to a rare chance offered by Al-Husain, Yaziid's leader. Nevertheless, the man's position in favor of his conviction and faith, rejecting lies and tricks, deserves respect and admiration.

Al-Hajaaj attacked with his army, besieging him and his followers. At that time, among 'Abd Allah's warriors was a group of very skillful Abyssinian spearmen and warriors. 'Abd Allah heard them talking about the late Caliph "Uthmaan (May Allah be pleased with him). Their conversation lacked all forms of justice and fairness. 'Abd Allah reprimanded them severely saying, "By Allah, I don't like to defeat my enemy with the help of someone hating 'Uthmaan." He sent them away at a very critical time in which he needed help so desperately, like a drowning man seeking hope.

His sincerity and honesty in faith and principles made him indifferent to the loss of 200 of his most skillful spearmen, the faith of whom he could no longer trust. All that despite the fierce decisive battle, which stood in front of him, the outcome of which could have been different if those spearmen had remained.

His resistance against Mu'aawiyah and Yaziid was an extraordinary legend of bravery. He considered Yaziid lbn Mu'aawiyah lbn Abi Sufyaan the most unqualified person to rule the Muslim community. That was true. Yaziid was totally corrupt. He did not possess one single virtue which would forgive his crimes and evils which have been narrated by history.

How was it possible for lbn Az-Zubair to swear the oath of allegiance to him? He strongly refused to do so while Mu'aawiyah was alive and more so when Yaziid became caliph. Yaziid sent someone to threaten him. He, however, said, "I'm not going to swear the oath of allegiance to a drunkard."

lbn Az-Zubair became Commander of the Faithful with Holy Makkah as his capital, extending his rule over Hejaz, Yemen, Basra, Kufa, Khurasan, and Syria except Damascus. The inhabitants of all these provinces swore the oath of allegiance to him. But the Ommiads were not satisfied. Restless, they waged continuous wars, most of which ended in their defeat. Nothing changed until "Abd Al-Maalik lbn Marwaan ordered one of the most harsh, criminal, cruel, and merciless human beings to attack 'Abd Allah in Makkah. This was Al-Hajaaj Ath-

Thaqafiy, who was described by 'Umar Ibn Abd Al-'Aziiz: "If all nations were to weigh together their sins, and we came with Al Hajaaj only, the balance would sway to our part."

Al-Hajaaj personally led his army to invade Makkah, Ibn Az-Zubair's capital. He besieged it nearly six months, preventing the provision of water and food to force people to abandon 'Abd Allah. Under the severe pressure of hunger, a large number of fighters surrendered and 'Abd Allah found himself almost alone. Although chances to save his life and soul were still available, he decided to carry out his responsibilities to the very end. He went on fighting with legendary courage, although he was 70 years old at that time.

We will only grasp the full image of that situation if we listen to the conversation which took place between 'Abd Allah and his mother, the great and noble Asmaa' Bint Abu Bakr, a short while before his death.

He went to her presenting the whole situation and what seemed to be his destiny. Asmaa' told him, " My son, you know yourself better than anyone else. If you know that you are adhering to the truth and calling to it, then be patient till you die for its sake and don't let the boys of Bani Umaiyah reach your neck. But if life in this world has been your main concern, then you're a wretched son, destroying yourself and those killed on your side."

'Abd Allah said, "By Allah, mother, I've never sought life in this world, nor did I submit myself to it. I've never ruled with injustice, treated anyone unfairly, or betrayed anyone."

His mother Asmaa' said, "I hope I will receive good consolation if you precede me to Paradise or I precede you. May Allah have mercy for your long prayers at night, your fasting during hot days and your reverent treatment of me and your father. Allah, I've handed over my son to Your fate; I will be pleased with Your destiny. Reward me for sacrificing my son as You reward thankful and patient believers."

They embraced each other and exchanged a farewell look. After one hour of fierce, unparalleled battle, the martyr received a deadly stroke. Al-Hajaaj, cruel, cunning, and deceiving as he was, insisted. on crucifying the lifeless body.

'Abd Allah's mother, who was on that day 97 years old, went to see her crucified son. Like a high towering mountain, his mother stood in front of him when Al-Hajaaj approached with shame and humiliation and said, "O' Mother, the Commander of the Faithful 'Abd Al-Maalik Ibn Marwaan has recommended me to treat you well. Do you need anything?"

She shouted, "I'm not your mother. I'm the mother of that one crucified on the cross. I don't need you. But I'm going to tell you a hadiith which I heard from the Prophet (PBUH). He said, 'He will emerge from Thaqiif, a liar and a vicious one.' We have already seen the liar and the vicious one. I don't think he's anyone else but you."

'Abd Allah Ibn 'Umar approached to console her and asked Allah to grant her patience. She replied, "What hinders me from being patient? Wasn't the head of Yahyaa (John) Ibn Zakariyaa granted to an Israelite harlot?"

How great she was, daughter of As-Siddiiq! Are there more eloquent words to be directed at those who cut 'Abd Allah's head off his body before crucifying him?

If 'Abd Allah's head had been handed over as a present to Al-

Hajaaj and 'Abd Al-Maalik, the head of a great Prophet (PBUH), Yahyaa Ibn Zakariya had been granted to Salome, a miserable Israelite harlot. What a magnificent comparison! What truthful words!

Having suckled the milk of such an extraordinary mother, could 'Abd Allah possibly have lived a different life, a life not reaching such great levels of success, virtue, and heroism?

May peace be upon 'Abd Allah.
May peace be upon Asmaa'
May peace be upon them among the eternally living martyrs.
May peace be upon them among the most reverent and pious.

(54)
'ABD ALLAH IBN 'ABBAAS
The Scholar of This Nation!

lbn 'Abbaas was similar to lbn Az-Zubair in that both experienced the Prophetic era while still children. The Prophet (PBUH) died before lbn `Abbaas had reached manhood. He had also been granted, while still very young, all the basic materials of manliness and the principles of life by the Prophet (PBUH), who liked him most, praised him, and taught him pure wisdom.

Due to his firm belief, gentleness, good character, and the richness of his knowledge, he was able to occupy a very high rank among the men around the Prophet (PBUH).

He was the son of Al-'Abbaas lbn 'Abd Al-Muttalib lbn Haashim, the Prophet's uncle. His epithet was "The Nation's Scholar" He deserved the title and position due to his vast knowledge, the enlightenment of his mind, and his versatility.

lbn 'Abbaas came to knowledge at a very early age, a knowledge which increased as days went by. That is because the Prophet (PBUH) was always drawing 'Abd Allah close to him, patting his shoulders and asking Aliah, "O' Allah, bless him with the full knowledge of the religion and interpretation of the Holy Qur'aan."

The Prophet (PBUH) repeated the same prayer for his cousin 'Abd Allah in various situations. In this way 'Abd Allah lbn 'Abbaas realized that he had been created to acquire knowledge, and his intellectual capabilities inclined strongly in that direction. Although his age did not exceed 13 when the Prophet (PBUH) died, he had not spent his childhood in vain. He had attended the Prophet's assemblies and learned his words by heart. When the Prophet (PBUH) died, he was eager to learn from the Companions what he had failed to hear or learn from the Prophet (PBUH) himself. He turned into a continuous question mark. Whenever he heard that someone had acquired wisdom or learned a hadiith by heart, he hurried to learn it from him. His bright ambitious mind forced him to examine all that came to his ears. He was not just concerned with gathering information, but with examining it and its sources. He once said about himself, "If I wanted to know something about an issue I would ask 30 Companions."

He drew a picture demonstrating his concern to reach truth and knowledge: When the Prophet (PBUH) died, I said to one of the Ansaar youth, "Let's go to the Prophet's Companions to ask them, as they are still numerous." He said, "O' lbn 'Abbaas, how strange you really are' Do you think that people are in need of you while the great Companions are still among them?" The young man dropped the matter, whereas I turned to ask the Prophet's Companions. Whenever I was informed that someone had related a hadiith, I would go to him in the afternoon while he was napping. I put my gown as a pillow under my head in front of his door. The wind scattered the dust over me. When he finished his nap and came out and saw me, he said, "O' Prophet's cousin, what is it that brought you here? Why didn't you send for me?" Then I would say, "No, it's you who deserves to be visited." Then I would ask him about the hadiith and learn from him.

In this way our young man went on asking and asking and asking, then examining the answers and discussing them with a curious mind. Every day his wisdom and knowledge developed until he achieved, while still a youth, the wisdom, patience, and eloquence of the elderly, so much so that the Commander of the Faithful 'Umar (May Allah be pleased with him) was eager to consult with him in every great issue. He called him, "The young leader of the elderly". Ibn 'Abbaas was once asked, "How could you acquire all that knowledge?" He answered, "By means of a questioning tongue and a reasoning mind." Through his continuously inquiring tongue, his ever detecting mind, and, moreover, his humility and gentleness, lbn `Abbaas was to become the nation's scholar.

Sa'd lbn Abi Waqqaas described him in the following words: I've never seen one with such presence of mind nor more intellectual and milder than lbn 'Abbaas. I've seen 'Umar (May Allah be pleased with him), although surrounded by those who attended Badr, inviting him to discuss difficult problems. Whenever lbn 'Abbaas spoke out his viewpoint, Umar always stuck to it.

'Ubaid Allah lbn `Utbah once said "I've never seen anyone more knowledgeable in the Prophet's hadiith than lbn 'Abbaas. Neither did I see anyone more knowledgeable during Abu Bakr, 'Umar or 'Uthmaan's caliphates than him; or more accurate in what he says in terms of jurisprudence or more knowledgeable in terms of poems, the Arabic language, Qur'aanic interpretation or religious matters. He divided his time, each day teaching one subject or another, jurisprudence, Qur'aanic interpretation, invasions, poems, and history, each one a different day. I've never seen a scholar listening to him without submitting himself completely to him, nor asking without being impressed by his vast and rich knowledge."

lbn 'Abbaas, who was appointed governor of Basra during the caliphate of 'Aliy lbn Abi Taalib (May Allah be pleased with him), was once described by a Muslim in the following words: He stuck to three matters, and gave up three. He dazzled men's hearts whenever he talked. He was a good listener whenever he was spoken to. He chose the easier of two matters whenever he was opposed. He gave up hypocrisy. He gave up the companionship of wicked people. He gave up all that is excusable.

His diverse culture and vast, comprehensive knowledge were admirable. He was the skillful, shrewd authority in every field of knowledge: Qur'aanic interpretation, jurisprudence, history, Arabic language and literature. Therefore, he was recourse for the seeker after truth. People traveled to him in-groups from all parts of the Islamic world in order to listen to him and to learn from him.

A Companion who was contemporary with him narrated: I've seen one of lbn 'Abbaas's scholastic assemblies. If the whole tribe of the Quraish had been proud, it would have been enough for their pride. I've seen people gathering in front of his door until the whole path had become so crowded that no one could enter or exit.

I entered, informing him that a great number of people were sitting in front of his door. He asked me to prepare his water for ablution, which he performed, then sat down and said, "Go out to them and invite those interested in Qur'aanic interpretation."

I went out and let them in. They entered, filling the house. They didn't ask about anything without being answered in a satisfactory manner. Then he said to them, "Don't forget your brethren." They went out to allow others to enter. Then he said, "Go out and invite those interested in jurisprudence."

I went out and let them in. They entered, filling the house. They didn't ask about anything without being satisfactorily answered. Then he said, "Don't forget your brethren." They went out to allow others to enter. Then he said, "Go out and invite those interested in religious duties."

I went out and let them in. They entered, filling the house. They didn't ask about anything without being satisfactorily answered. Then he said, "Don't forget your brethren." They went out to allow others to enter.

Then he said, "Go out and invite those interested in the Arabic language and literature." I went out and let them in. They entered, filling the house. They didn't ask about anything without being satisfactorily answered.

Ibn 'Abbaas had not only a sharp memory but an extraordinary one, and extreme brilliance and intelligence. His arguments were as clear, bright, and cheerful as sunlight. He would not let his opponent leave until he was not only convinced but, in addition, completely satisfied and pleased with the magnificence of his logic and brilliance of his speech.

In spite of his rich knowledge and effective argument, he never considered his discussion and conversation a battle of intellects in which he could be proud of his vast knowledge and victory over his opponents. On the contrary he considered it a straightforward path to visualize and realize truth.

For a long time his fair and sharp logic had been a source of alarm to the Khawaarij. Once Imam 'Aliy (May Allah be pleased with him) sent him to a large group of the Khawaarij. "They had a wonderful discussion, in which he was in control of the talk, arguing in a very admirable way. The following is an extract of that long conversation:

Ibn 'Abbaas asked them, "What do you have against "Aliy?"

They said, "We are discontented with three matters. First, he let men judge in Allah's religion, whereas Allah said, < . . . *surely judging is only for GOD* > *(6:57)*.

"Second, he is a murderer. However, he didn't take any captives or war booty. If they had been disbelievers, then their wealth would have been permissible, and if they had been Muslims, then their murder would have been prohibited.

"Third, during the arbitration, he agreed to give up the title 'Commander of the Faithful' in response to his enemies. If he isn't Commander of the Faithful, then he must be Commander of the Disbelievers."

Ibn 'Abbaas began to refute their claims. "As for letting men judge in Allah's religion, what's wrong with that? Allah said, < *O you who believe! Do not kill animals of the hunt while you are on the Pilgrimage, and whoever of you kills it intentionally, he shall make recompense the equal of what he has killed from the cattle, which shall be judged by two just men among you* > *(5: 95)*. Tell me, by Allah, is letting men judge in sparing the Muslim blood not worthier than letting them judge in the case of compensating a killed rabbit that is worth a quarter of a dirham?"

Their leaders stammered in speech under the pressure of that sarcastic but decisive logic. Then he continued his talk. "As for your claim that he is a murderer who didn't take prisoners or war booty, did you expect him to take 'Aa'ishah, the Prophet's wife and Mother of the Faithful, a prisoner and her belongings as booty?" At that moment their faces went blank out of shame and they tried to cover them with their hands.

Ibn 'Abbaas went on to the third claim. "As for your claim that he agreed to give up the title 'Commander of the Faithful' to give arbitration a chance, let me tell you what the Prophet (PBUH) did on the Day of Hudaibiyah. While he was dictating the agreement between him and the Quraish, he said to the scribe, 'Write, This is what the Messenger of Allah agreed upon.' The representative of the Quraish said, 'By Allah, if we believed that you were the Messenger of Allah, we wouldn't have hindered you from entering the Sacred House or fought against you.' The Prophet (PBUH) then said, "Then write. This is what Muhaammad Ibn 'Abd Allah has agreed upon. By Allah, I'm the Messenger of Allah even if you deny that. Write whatever you like.' "

The discussion between Ibn 'Abbaas and the Khawaarij went on in such a miraculous, magnificent way. The discussion had hardly ended when some 20,000 of the Khawaarij announced their conviction in what was said and announced the end of their opposition to 'Aliy's Imamate.

Ibn 'Abbaas not only possessed a great fortune of knowledge but also a greater fortune of manners of knowledge and the knowledgeable. He was a great figure in his generosity. He spent his wealth abundantly for the people's sake with the same willingness with which he shared his knowledge. His contemporaries said, " We've never seen a house more filled with food, drinks, fruits, and knowledge than Ibn 'Abbaas's house."

He possessed a pure soul that never carried any spite. He never tired of wishing all the good for people, those whom he knew and those whom he did not. He said about him-self, "Whenever I recited a verse, I wished that all people had acquired the knowledge I've acquired. Whenever I heard about a just ruler ruling fairly, I was filled with delight and prayed for him, although I did not need him. Whenever I heard about rain falling on Muslim land, I was filled with delight although I did not own any livestock grazing on that land."

He was a devoted repenting worshiper, praying at night and often fasting. No one could miss the stream of tears on his cheek. That is because he cried so much whenever he prayed or recited the Qur'aan. Whenever he read a scolding or threatening verse, or the mention of death and resurrection, his wail and laments grew louder and louder.

In addition, he was honest, brave, and eloquent. He had his own viewpoint and opinions about the dispute between Imam 'Aliy and Mu`aawiyah, which proved his capacity for stratagem.

He preferred peace to war, kindness to violence, logic to compulsion.

When Al-Hussain (May Allah be pleased with him) intended to go to Iraq to fight Ziyaad and Yaziid, Ibn 'Abbaas did everything he could to prevent him. Afterwards, he was informed about his martyrdom. He felt deep grief and kept indoors.

Whenever a dispute between two Muslims arose, he could always be seen carrying the banner of peace, forgiveness, and tenderness.

It is true that he himself was involved in the battle between 'Aliy and Mu'aawiyah when he fought on 'Aliy's side. But he did that because, at the beginning, the war represented a necessary eradication of a movement, which was causing a terrible split within the Islamic community, threatening the unity of the faith and of the believers.

As long as he lived he filled the whole world with knowledge and wisdom, spreading among people his scent of piety.

When he reached the age of 71, he was invited to meet Allah. The city of Al-Taa'if witnessed a great scene for a believer who had been promised Paradise. While his body settled safely in its grave, the horizon was shaken by the echo of the truthful divine promise: < *"O soul at peace. Return to your Lord, well pleased and well pleasing. Enter you among My servants. And enter into My Paradise!"* > *(89:27-30).*

(55)
'ABBAAD IBN BISHR
With Him Was the Light of Allah!

When Mus'ab Ibn 'Umair went to Al-Madiinah, appointed by the Messenger of Allah (PBUH) to teach the Ansaar—who had given their oath of allegiance to the Messenger in Islam—and to lead them in prayer,'Abbaad Ibn Bishr was one of the devoted whose hearts Allah opened to good. So Mus`ab approached the assembly, and 'Abbaad listened to him and stretched out his right hand to give his oath of allegiance to Islam. From that day on, he took his place among the Ansaar with whom Allah is pleased and they with Him.

The Prophet (PBUH) emigrated to Al-Madiinah after the believers of Makkah had preceded him there. Then began the military campaigns in which the forces of good and light clashed with the forces of darkness and evil. In each of these battles, 'Abbaad Ibn Bishr was in the front ranks fighting heroically in the cause of Allah, completely consumed and dedicated with heart and soul in a dazzling, overwhelming way. Perhaps the event, which we now narrate, will disclose something of the heroism of this great believer.

After the Messenger of Allah and the believers had finished the military campaign of Dhaat-Ar-Riqaa', they stopped over at a place to spend the night and the Messenger chose guards from the Companions to take turns. Among them, were 'Ammaar Ibn Yaasir and 'Abbaad Ibn Bishr on one watch.

'Abbaad saw that his companion 'Ammaar was exhausted, so he demanded that he sleep the first part of the night and he would stand guard so his companion could take some rest. He could resume guard after he awoke.

'Abbaad saw that the place around him was safe, so he thought, why not fill up his time with prayer, so that he would be rewarded both for praying and standing guard. So he stood praying.

While he was standing reciting a surah from the Qur'aan after Al-Faatihah, an arrow passed through his shoulder, so he pulled it out and continued his prayer. Then the attacker shot a second arrow in the darkness of the night, so he pulled it out, also, and completed his recitation. Then he bowed and prostrated. Weakness and pain had dissipated his strength, so he extended his right hand, while prostrating, to his companion sleeping near him and continued to shake him until he woke up. Then he sat up from his prostration and recited the Tashahhud (i.e. the last part of his prayer) and completed his prayer.

'Ammaar awoke at the weary, trembling voice of his words, "Stand guard in my place. I am wounded!" 'Ammaar jumped up yelling noisily and quickly frightened away the attackers, so they ran away. Then he turned to 'Abbaad and said to him, "Glory be to Allah! Why didn't you awaken me when you were first hit?"

'Abbaad replied, "In my prayer I was reciting verses from the Qur'aan that filled my soul with such awe that I didn't want to interrupt it nor cut it short. By Allah, I swear, because I did not want to lose a single word which the Messenger of Allah ordered me to preserve, I would have preferred death more than interrupting those verses which I was reciting."

'Abbaad was extremely devoted and strong in his love of Allah, His Messenger, and His religion, and this devotion lasted throughout his life. Since he heard the Prophet (PBUH) saying to the Ansaar, "You are my people. You are the people who protect. There is no nation which has come like you before." . . . We say, since 'Abbaad heard these words from his Prophet (PBUH), teacher, and guide to Allah, he spent generously of his wealth and gave his spirit and life in the way of Allah and His Messenger. In the areas of sacrifice and even death, he constantly put them first, and even in a seizure of booty and spoils of war. In places of hardship and struggle, his companions searched for him until they found him.

He was always a worshiper—worship completely absorbed him; brave—bravery and heroism engrossed him; generous—generosity engaged him. He was a strong believer. He pledged his life to the cause of faith. The Companions of the Messenger knew all of this of him. The Mother of the Faithful 'Aa'ishah (May Allah be pleased with her) said: "There are three from among the Ansaar who are not surpassed in virtue by anyone: S"ad Ibn Mu'aadh, Usaid Ibn Hudair and 'Abbaad Ibn Bishr."

The first Muslims knew "Abbaad as a man in whom was light from Allah. His radiant, clear vision guided to areas of goodness and certainty without searching or difficulty.

His brothers believed in his light to the extent that they attributed to him the picture of perception and discipline. They agreed that once 'Abbaad was walking in the darkness and there emanated from him a light that lit the way for him. In the apostasy wars, after the death of the Messenger (PBUH), 'Abbaad carried his responsibility with incomparable death-defying courage.

On the battlefield of Al-Yamaamah, where the Muslims faced the most cruel and skillful army under the leadership of Musailamah, the Liar, 'Abbaad perceived a danger threatening to Islam. His willingness to sacrifice and his vigor constituted sufficient importance, such that it gave him his faith and raised him to the level of his aspiration and ability to perceive danger, making him one willing to sacrifice and give up everything for his faith, not desiring anything other than death and martyrdom.

A day before the beginning of the Battle of Al-Yamaamah he saw in his sleep a vision that did not remain long enough to be clear: above the land of the great destructive battle which the Muslims went through...So let an honorable companion, Abu Sa'iid Al-Khudriy, tell us the story of the vision which 'Abbaad saw, his explanation of it, and his amazing attitude in fighting which ended in martyrdom.

Abu Sa'iid reported:'Abbaad Ibn Bishr said to me, "O' Abu Sa'iid, I saw last night as if the sky had opened up for me. Then it closed and covered over me. Indeed, I see it, if Allah wills, to mean martyrdom." I said to him."Good. I swear by Allah, you did indeed see it." On the Day of Al-Yamaamah, I looked at him and indeed saw him shouting to the Ansaar, "Use your swords forcefully and be distinguished among the people!" So 400 men came quickly to him, all of them from among the Ansaar people, until they stopped at the gate of the garden. They fought violently, and 'Abbaad Ibn Bishr was martyred. I saw on his face much beating and I did not know him except by a mark, that was on his body.

Thus was 'Abbaad raised to the level of his duties as a believer from among the Ansaars. He gave the oath of allegiance to his Messenger, dedicating his life to Allah and death in His cause.

When he saw the destructive battle turning in favor of the enemy, he remembered the words of the Messenger to his people, the Ansaar: "You are my people. I can not be defeated through you. There has not come and people like you before." This sound filled his heart and soul and penetrated his consciousness, until it was as if the Messenger of Allah was now standing before him repeating these words of his.

'Abbaad felt that the whole responsibility of the battle was placed completely on the shoulders of the Ansaar, on the shoulders of those about whom the Messenger of Allah had said, "There has not come any people like you before." And on the shoulders of no one else, besides them.

Then and there, 'Abbaad went up on a hill and shouted, "O' people of the Ansaar! Carry your sword in a valiant way, and be honored and distinguished among the people!"

When 400 of them answered his call, he led them and Abu Dajaanah and Al-Baraa' Ibn Maalik to the garden of death, where the army of Musailamah had fortified itself for protection. The hero fought a worthy fight as a man, as a believer, and as an Ansaar.

On that glorious day, 'Abbaad attained martyrdom. The vision, which he saw in his dream the day before, came true. Did he not see the sky open until, when he entered it from that opening, it returned and folded on him and closed?

He interpreted it as meaning that his spirit would ascend in the coming battle to its Creator. The vision was true and the interpretation of it was true. And the doors of heaven were opened to welcome to happiness the spirit of 'Abbaad Ibn Bishr, the man who had with him a light from Allah.

(56)
SUHAIL IBN AMR
From Liberation to Martyrdom

When he was captured into the hands of the Muslims in the Battle of Badr, 'Umar lbn Al-Khattaab approached the Messenger of Allah (PBUH) and said, "O' Messenger of Allah, let me extract the teeth of Suhail lbn 'Amr until no speaker stands against you after today."

The great Messenger responded, "No, 'Umar. I do not treat anyone harshly so Allah will not harm me, even though I am a Prophet." Then 'Umar came nearer to him and the Prophet said, "Perhaps Suhail will take a stand tomorrow that will make you happy."

So the prophecy of the Messenger came true. The greatest orator of the Quraish, Suhail lbn 'Amr, changed into a brilliant and dazzling speaker of Islam. This polytheist who was always against Islam changed into an obedient believer. His eyes never stopped crying out of fear of Allah. One of the senior chiefs of the Quraish and a leader of its army, changed into a very hard fighter in the path of Islam, a fighter who vowed to himself to be persistent and to persevere in courage, self-control, and fighting until he died on that path, so that perhaps Allah would forgive his previous sins.

So who was that obstinate polytheist? He was Suhail lbn "Amr, one of the prominent leaders of the Quraish, and one of its wise men and people of intelligence and discernment. He was the one whom the Quraish appointed to convince the Messenger to change his mind and refrain from entering Makkah in the year of Hudaibiyah. At the end of A.H. 6, the Messenger and his Companions went out to Makkah to visit the Sacred House and to perform 'Umrah. They did not want war and they were not prepared to fight.

The Quraish knew they were on their way to Makkah, so they went out to block the way and stop them from achieving their objective. The situation became critical and hearts became tense. The Messenger said to his Companions, "The Quraish do not call me today to a plan but ask me instead about the bonds of kinship. So I gave them to them."

The Quraish began to send their messengers and representatives to the Prophet, so he informed all of them that he did not come to fight but to visit the Sacred House and glorify its sacredness. Each time one of their representatives returned, they sent another after him more vigorous and unyielding and stronger in persuasion, until they chose 'Urwah lbn Mas'uud Ath-Thaqafiy. He was among the strongest and cleverest of them. The Quraish thought that 'Urwah would be able to convince the Messenger to go back; however, he quickly came back to them saying, "O' people of Quraish, indeed I went to the Persian emperor in his kingdom and Caesar in his kingdom and the Negus in his kingdom, but, by Allah, I swear I never saw a king whose people magnify him as the Companions of Muhammad magnify him. I saw around him a people that shall never surrender to evil. So, what will you do and what is your opinion?"

At that time the Quraish believed that there was no way for their attempts to succeed, so they decided to resort to negotiation and reconciliation. They chose for this task the most suitable of their chiefs. He was Suhail Ibn 'Amr.

The Muslims saw Suhail coming towards them and recognized him and realized that the Quraish preferred the way of peace making and mutual understanding when at last they sent Suhail.

Suhail sat in front of the Messenger, and a long dialogue took place ending with a peace treaty. Suhail attempted to gain much for the Quraish. The tolerant leniency, noble-mindedness, and excellent manner in which the Messenger managed the negotiations and peace making helped him in achieving that.

Days passed until A.H.8 came. The Messenger and the Muslims went out for the conquest of Makkah after the Quraish had violated its treaty with the Messenger of Allah. The Muhaajiruun returned to their homes, which earlier they had been expelled from by force. They returned and with them the Ansaar, who had taken care of them in their city and preferred them over themselves.

With its flags fluttering victoriously in the sky, Makkah opened all of its gates and the polytheists were stopped in bewilderment. What would be their destiny and fate today, since they were the ones who had done wrong to the Muslims previously by killing them, burning them, torturing them, and starving them? The merciful Prophet (PBUH) did not want to leave them for long under the pressure of these debilitating feelings. He received them and turned to them in a good and noble manner and said to them with his merciful voice flowing tenderly and lovingly, "O' people of Quraish, what do you think I will do with you?"

At that time the enemy of Islam in the past, Suhail lbn 'Amr, stepped forward and answered, "We think you will treat us well, O' noble brother and son of a noble brother."

A smile formed from light appeared on the lips of the Beloved of Allah and he called to them, "Go, you are free, liberated." These words did not come from the victorious, triumphant Messenger except to change human beings with living feelings by melting them to obedience, humility, and repentance. At the same moment, this situation, filled with nobility and glory, stimulated all of Suhail Ibn 'Amr's feelings, so he surrendered to Allah, the Lord of the Worlds. His Islam, at that time, was not the surrender of a defeated man, resigned to fate. It was, as his future shall reveal in what follows, the surrender of a man overwhelmed and fascinated by the majesty of Muhammad and the grandeur of the religion that Muhammad demonstrated in his conduct in conformity with its teachings and instructions. These teachings, as he saw them, conveyed extraordinary benevolence, friendship, and devotion.

Those who announced their Islam on the Day of the Conquest of Makkah were designated with the name "At-Tulaqaa"or those who were transferred by the forgiveness of the Prophet from polytheism to Islam when he said to them, "Go, you are free."

Consequently, some persons from among those Tulaqaa' (or those who were liberated) were raised by their sincerity to a far distant horizon of sacrifice, worship, and purity which placed them in the first rank of the Prophet's righteous and devoted Companions. Among these was Suhail Ibn 'Amr.

Islam molded and fashioned him afresh and refined all of his original skills and gifts and, what is more, increased them and placed all of them at the service of truth, goodness, and faith. They described him in these words: "The kind, generous, outstanding one. The one who performs prayer much and fasts and gives in charity, and reads the Qur'aan and cries out of fear of Allah."

That was the greatness of Suhail. For in spite of the fact that he accepted Islam on the Day of the Conquest of Makkah, and not before that, we see him truthfully affirming his Islam and its certainty, to the extent that he excelled in it with distinction, exerting himself with all his heart. He was transformed into a worshiper, self-denying and abstentious, and into one who sacrifices and strives in the path of Allah and Islam.

When the Messenger was transported to the company of the Most High, the news soon reached Makkah. Suhail at that time was residing there, and the Muslims were overwhelmed by agitation and perplexity, just as the Muslims were in Al-Madiinah. However, the confusion of Al-Madiinah was dissipated by Abu Bakr at that time by his decisive words: "Whoever worships Muhammad, know that Muhammad is dead; and whoever worships Allah, indeed Allah is living and never dies."

So we were amazed when we saw Suhail holding the same position in Makkah as Abu Bakr in Al-Madiinah. He gathered all of the Muslims there, and he stood dazzling them with his salubrious words, informing them that Muhammad was truly the Messenger of Allah and that he did not die until he had executed his trust and conveyed the message and that the duty of the believers towards this message was to assiduously devote all their efforts to it in pursuance of his methodology and approach.

On account of Suhail's position and his rightly directly words and strong faith, he warded off the discord and civil strife which almost extirpated and uprooted the faith of the people of Makkah when the news of the death of the Messenger reached them.

Did not he, the Messenger, say to 'Umar on the day 'Umar asked the Prophet (PBUH) for permission to pull out the two teeth of Suhail when he was taken prisoner at Badr, "Leave them, perhaps they will make you happy one day."

So on the day when the news of the position of Suhail in Makkah and his dazzling speech which made the faith firm in the

Muslims' hearts reached the Muslims in Al-Madiinah, 'Umar Ibn Al-Khattaab remembered the prophecy of his Messenger and laughed a long time, for the day had come in which Islam benefited from the two teeth of Suhail which 'Umar had wanted to crush and tear out.

When Suhail accepted Islam on the Day of the Conquest of Makkah and after he had tasted the sweetness of faith, he imposed on himself a vow he summed up in these words: By Allah, I do not leave situations and battles with the polytheists except I support the Muslims equally and no wealth I spent with the polytheists but I spend an equal amount with the Muslims. Perhaps my support of the Muslims will be followed by an ever-greater support. I stood a long time with the polytheists in front of their idols, so let us now stand for a long time with the believers in the presence of Allah, the One and Only.

Thus, he started praying and praying and fasting and praying. He would not let a chance pass him by which would sharpen his spirit and make him close to his Lord Most High but that he took from it a sufficient portion.Thus in his past he stood with the polytheists in situations of oppression and war against Islam. So, now let him take his place in the Muslim army, fighting bravely to extinguish, with the battalion of truth, the fire of the Persian king who used to worship idols and false gods other than Allah, and fighting to burn the destinies of the peoples who participated in this false worship. So, let him fight also to destroy with the battalion of truth the darkness of Rome and its injustice and spread the word of monotheism and the fear of Allah to every place.

Thus, he went out with the Muslim army to Syria participating in its wars. On the Day of Yarmuuk, the Muslims courageously plunged into battle, encountering harm, violence, and danger.

Suhail Ibn 'Amr was almost flying out of joy when he found on this crucial day the rich opportunity to make the effort, from his soul, to annihilate the sins and mistakes of jaahiliyah before accepting Islam.

He used to love his house in Makkah greatly, so much so that it made him forget himself. Nevertheless, he refused to return to it after the Muslim victory over Syria, and so he said, "I heard the Messenger of Allah saying, 'The rank and position of one of you who spends one hour in the cause of Allah is better for him than his work throughout his life.' Therefore, I will strive in the path of Allah until death, and I shall not return to Makkah."

And Suhail died true to his vow and continued to strive for the remainder of his life committed to his religion until the appointed time of his demise. So his soul flew quickly to the Mercy of Allah and His pleasure.

(57)
ABU MUUSAA AL-ASH'ARIY
Sincerity and Let Be What Will Be

When the Commander of the Faithful 'Umar Ibn Al-Khattaab sent him to Basra to become its commander and governor, he gathered its inhabitants and spoke to them saying, "Indeed the Commander of the Faithful 'Umar sent me to you to instruct you in the Book of your Lord and the traditions of your Prophet and to purify your ways for you."

The people were overcome with astonishment and surprise at what he said when they came to understand that one of the incumbent duties of the commander and governor was to show them how to become people of culture and education and to give them understanding of their religion. Also among his obligations was the purifying of their ways, and that was something new for them—one could even say exciting and remarkable.

So, who was this ruler about whom such good is said: "No horseman ever came to Basra who was better for its people than him"? Indeed, he was "Abd Allah Ibn Qais, nicknamed Abu Muusaa Al-Ash'ariy..

He departed his country and homeland of Yemen for Makkah immediately upon hearing of the appearance of a Messenger there who was calling to monotheism and inviting to Allah with clear vision and ordering noble morals. In Makkah, he sat in the presence of the Messenger of Allah (PBUH) and received from him guidance and certainty. He then returned to his country carrying the word of Allah. Afterwards, he returned to the Messenger (PBUH) immediately after the victory over Khaibar.

His arrival coincided with the arrival of Ja'far Ibn Abi Taalib, returning with his companions from Abyssinia, so the Messenger gave all of them a share of the booty.

On this occasion, Abu Muusaa did not come alone, but with approximately 50 men from the people of Yemen, including his two brothers Abu Ruhm and Abu Burdah, to whom the Messenger (PBUH) taught Islam.The Messenger (PBUH) named this delegation and its people the Ash'ariyiin. The Messenger (PBUH) described them as the people with the most delicate feelings and kind, gentle hearts. That which is most often mentioned about them as the highest example of his Companions is as follows: "If they exhausted their food in a military campaign or their food became diminished, they would gather what they possessed in one garment and divide it among themselves equally. So they are from me and I from them."

From that day, Abu Muusaa took his permanent and high place among the Muslims and believers who were destined to be the Companions of the Messenger of Allah and his pupils, and to become the carriers of Islam to the world in every age and time.

Abu Muusaa was a wonderful combination of extraordinary attributes. He was a bold and daring fighter, a firm combatant when he was forced to fight, while at the same time he was peaceful, good, and gentle to the most extreme degree of goodness and kindness. He was a scholar who possessed comprehension, sound judgment, and judicious discrimination. He was intelligent, and his understanding excelled in the most complicated, abstruse and obscure issues which radiated in legal decisions and judgments, until it was said of him, "The judges of this nation are four: 'Umar, 'Aliy, Abu Muusaa and Zaid Ibn Thaabit."

In addition to that, he possessed an innocent nature. Whoever attempted to deceive him in matters of Allah was himself deceived. He possessed great loyalty and responsibility and great trust of the people. If we wanted to choose a fact of his life as a slogan, it would be this expression: "Sincerity, and let be what will be" In the sphere of jihaad, Al-Ash'ariy carried his responsibility in such a glorious and heroic manner that it made the Messenger of Allah (PBUH) call him, "Master of horsemen, Abu Muusaa." He shows us a picture of his life as a fighter, when he says, "We went out with the Messenger of Allah on a military campaign and our feet were full of holes and my feet were also full of holes until I lost my toe nails and we wrapped our feet with rags."

An enemy in battle did not provoke his goodness and the peace of his real conviction and innermost thoughts. He was in such a posture that he saw matters in complete clarity and he decided them with decisive willpower and determination. It happened that while the Muslims were conquering the kingdom of Persia, Al-Ash'ariy came down with his army upon the people of Isfahan, who agreed to pay him the jizyah so he made a peace settlement with them.

However, it seems that they were not truthful in their agreement. They only wanted to make themselves ready for the opportunity to prepare a treacherous attack. Nevertheless, in the time of need, the cleverness of Abu Muusaa was not oblivious to their secret plan. He perceived and saw through their scheme and the evil plans they were contriving, so when they began their attack, the leader was not taken by surprise. Therefore, the war overwhelmed them, and the first half of the day was not over before he gained a decisive victory.

In the battles in which the Muslims engaged against Imperial Persia, the performance of Abu Muusaa (May Allah be pleased with him) was outstanding, and his fighting for the cause of Allah was noble.

In the Battle of Tustar particularly, in which Hurmuzan withdrew with his army to fortify his position and gathered massive armies, Abu Muusaa was the hero. On that day, the Commander of the Faithful 'Umar supplied him with a massive number of Muslims, at the head of which were "Ammaar Ibn Yaasir, Al-Baraa' Ibn Maalik and Anas Ibn Maalik and Maja'ah Al-Bakriy and Salamah Ibn Rajaa'. The two armies—the Muslims under the command of Abu Muusaa and the Persians under the command of Hurmuzan—met in the battle, which was one of the fiercest in ruthlessness and violence. The Persians withdrew inside the fortified city of Tustar and the Muslims besieged it for many days until Abu Muusaa employed his skill and intelligence and sent 200 cavalrymen with a Persian agent. Abu Muusaa instructed him to enter the fort in order to open the gate of the city in front of the advanced guard, which he chose for the mission. The gates had hardly opened when the soldiers of the advance guard charged on the fortified citadel until Abu Muusaa swooped down with his army in a massive attack.

He captured this important fortified position in only hours, and the Persian leader surrendered, after which Abu Muusaa sent them to Al-Madiinah to learn the Commander of the Faithful's judgment.

However, this fighter of great prowess did not leave the field of battle until he changed to a persistent worshiper with much weeping, and was mild-tempered, peaceable, and gentle-hearted as a sparrow. He recited the Qur'aan with such a voice that made the inner heart of the one who listened to it tremble that the Messenger (PBUH) said about him, "Abu Muusaa was given a musical voice like the musical instruments of the people of

Dawuud." Every time 'Umar saw him he called him to recite to him from the Book of Allah saying to him, "Make us aspire to our Lord, O' Abu Muusaa."

Also, Abu Muusaa did not participate in fighting except against the army of the polytheists or armies fighting against the religion, wanting to extinguish the light of Allah. Whenever there was a fight between Muslims, he indeed ran away from it and never had any role in it. This position of his was clear in the dispute between 'Aliy and Mu'aawiyah and in the war which ignited between the Muslims, as we shall see.

Perhaps this point, from the account which follows, will bring us to an understanding of the most famous position of his life, and that is his position in the arbitration between Imam 'Aliy and Mu'aawiyah. This position is often taken as evidence of the immoderation in Abu Muusaa's good nature or his extraordinary naivete, which made tricking him quite easy. However, the situation, as we shall see, in spite of what hastiness or error there might have been, reveals the greatness of his soul, the greatness of his faith in the truth and in people.

Indeed, the view of Abu Muusaa in the case of arbitration can be summarized by the fact that he saw the Muslims killing one another and each party fanatically clinging to its Imam (ruler). As he saw it, the situation between the combatants had reached a critical state that was impossible of resolve and placed the destiny of the Muslim nation on the edge of an abyss. In his opinion, the situation had reached a stage of deterioration. It was exemplified in the change of the whole situation, which thus required starting over again.

The civil war, at that point, revolved around two parties of the Muslims disputing over the person of the ruler. Some desired

Imam 'Aliy to relinquish the caliphate temporarily and Mu'aawiyah to renounce it, so that the entire matter could be referred again to the Muslims. Then, they could choose, by way of consultation, the caliph they wanted. This was how Abu Muusaa argued the case and this was the way he saw its resolution.

It is correct that Imam 'Aliy was soundly sworn in as caliph and correct that every illegal rebellion should not be allowed to achieve its aim of overturning the legal right. However, the issues in the dispute between the Imam and Mu'aawiyah and between the peoples of Iraq and Syria had, in the view of Abu Muusaa, reached a state which imposed a new kind of thinking and resolution. For the insurgency of Mu'aawiyah was not considered just a revolt alone, and the rebellion of the people of Syria was not considered just an insurrection alone, and the entire difference was not considered just a difference in opinion nor a matter of choice. All these things developed into a harmful civil war in which thousands were killed on both sides and continued to threaten Islam and Muslims with the worst ramifications and consequences. So removal of the causes of the dispute and war and stepping aside of both parties was in the thinking of Abu Muusaa, the starting point on the road to salvation.

The view of Imam 'Aliy, when he accepted the principle of arbitration, was that 'Abd Allah Ibn Abbaas or someone from among his companions would represent his front in arbitration, but a large party of those with power in his group and army imposed on him Abu Muusaa Al-Ash'ariy. The reason for their choice of Abu Muusaa was that he had never participated in the dispute between 'Aliy and Mu'aawiyah since the dispute began, but had separated himself from both parties after giving up all hope of encouraging the two of them to a common understanding and peace. So he withdrew from the fight between them. He had, from this respect, the most right of all the people to arbitrate.

There was nothing in the religion of Abu Muusaa nor in his sincerity and truthfulness that made the Imam suspicious. Nevertheless, he did realize, the intentions of the other side and the degree of their dependency on maneuvers, deception, and trickery, and that Abu Muusaa, inspite of his understanding and knowledge, hated deception and maneuvers and loved to deal with people on the basis of truth and not his wits. Therefore, Imam 'Aliy was afraid Abu Muusaa would be deceived by the others and that the arbitration would be turned into maneuvers by one side, which would make matters worst.

The arbitration between the two parties began, with Abu Muusaa Al-Ash'ariy representing the party of Imam "Aliy and "Amr lbn Al-'Aas representing the party of Mu'aawiyah. It is true that "Amr lbn Al-"Aas depended on his sharp wits and his broad cunning in carrying the banner for Mu'aawiyah.

The meeting between the two men, Al-Ash'ariy and 'Amr, began with a proposal presented by Abu Muusaa. It was for the two arbitrators to agree on the nomination of 'Abd Allah lbn 'Umar, declaring him the Caliph of the Muslims because he enjoyed a broad consensus in respect to his love, admiration, and distinction. 'Amr lbn Al-'Aas saw in this orientation and direction of Abu Muusaa a great opportunity, so he took advantage of it.

The content of the proposal by Abu Muusaa did not consider a conditional link with the party which he represented, which was the party of Imam 'Aliy. That meant, also, that Abu Muusaa was ready to give support and backing for caliph to others from among the Prophet's Companions, the proof for that point being his suggestion of `Abd Allah lbn 'Umar

Thus, 'Amr found, by his shrewdness and wits, a wide entrance for the achievement of his goal. So he therefore suggested Mu'aawiyah. Then he suggested his own son 'Abd Allah, who possessed a great position among the Messenger's Companions. The intelligence of Abu Muusaa was not less than the wits of 'Amr. When he saw 'Amr adopting the principle of nomination as a rule for the discussion of arbitration, he boldly confronted 'Amr, saying that the choice of caliph was the right of all Muslims and that Allah had made their affair one of consultation between themselves, so it was incumbent to leave them alone entirely to the right of choice.

We shall now see how 'Amr exploited this lofty principle for the interest of Mu'aawiyah. However, before that, let us listen to the historical dialogue which took place between Abu Muusaa and `Amr Ibn Al-'Aas at the beginning of their meeting. We transmit it on the authority of the book Al-Akhbaar At-Tawaal by Abu Hunaifah Ad-Daiyanuuriy;

Abu Muusaa: O' 'Amr, do you desire in this matter the good of the nation and the pleasure of Allah?`Amr: And what is it?
Abu Muusaa: That we appoint 'Abd Allah Ibn 'Umar, for indeed he never involved himself in the war.
'Amr-: And where are you with respect to Mu'aawiyah?
Abu Muusaa: Mu'aawiyah does not deserve it nor is he worthy of it.
Amr: Do you not know that 'Uthmaan was unjustly killed?

Abu Muusaa: Yes.
Amr: So indeed Mu'aawiyah is guardian (walii) of the blood of "Uthmaan and his house is in the Quraish, as you know. So the people said. Why not assume responsibility for the matter since it has no precedents. In that you have no excuse. You say, I indeed found him the guardian of 'Uthmaan's blood and Allah Most High says, *<And whoever is killed (intentionally with*

h*ostility and oppression and not by mistake). We have given his heir (walii) the authority* > (17: 33).

The brother of Umm Habiibah, the wife of the Prophet (PBUH) has this and he is one of his Companions.

Abu Muusaa: Fear Allah, O' 'Amr! As for what you mentioned concerning the nobility of Mu'aawiyah, if worthiness for the caliphite were based on nobility, the one with the most right to it among the people would be Abrahah lbn As-Sabbaah, for indeed he is one of the sons in the line of the kings of Yemen, who ruled the east cf the earth and its west. Furthermore, how does the nobility of Mu'aawiyah compare with that of 'Aliy lbn Abi Taalib? As for your talk that Mu'aawiyah was the guardian of 'Uthmaan's blood, his son 'Amr lbn 'Uthmaan is more 'Uthmaan's guardian than he. But if you acceded to me, we would revive the practice of 'Umar lbn Al-Khattaab and his son 'Abd Allah.

'Amr: What prevents you from my son 'Abd Allah, with his merit and goodness and his previous Hijrah and his companionship ?

Abu Muusaa: Indeed your son is a truthful man, but you have completely immersed him into these wars. We have made it (i.e. the caliphate) for a good man and the son of a good man. 'Abd Allah lbn 'Umar.

'Amr: "O' Abu Muusaa, no man is suitable for this affair unless he has two molars. He eats with one and he feeds (others) with the other.

Abu Muusaa: Woe to you, O' 'Amr! Indeed, the Muslims have entrusted the matter to us, after they have fought with one another by force of arms and swords. Do not hurt them with spears! Do not turn them back to civil war and discord.

'Amr: So what do you see?

Abu Muusaa: I see that we should depose the two men, 'Aliy and Mu'aawiyah. .Then make consultation between the Muslims. They will choose for themselves who they want.

'Amr: I am pleased with this view. So indeed the goodness of the heart is in it. This argument completely changes the form, which we are accustomed to see.

This argument completely changes the form which we are accustomed to see every time we mention the incident of arbitration. Indeed, in these arguments, Abu Muusaa was not of a neglectful mind, but very active. On the contrary, in this dialogue, his intelligence was more active than the intellect of 'Amr Ibn Al-'Aas, who was famous for his wit and shrewdness. So when 'Amr wanted to propose the caliphate of Mu'aawiyah based on genealogy in the Quraish and guardianship of the blood of 'Uthmaan, the refutation of Abu Muusaa came sharply and brilliantly as the edge of a sword.

"If the caliphate were based on nobility, then Abrahah Ibn As-Sabbaah, who is from a line of kings, is more worthy of guardianship than Mu'aawiyah. And if the caliphate were based on guardianship of the blood of 'Uthmaan and defense of his right, then Ibn 'Uthmaan is more worthy of this guardianship than Mu'aawiyah."

After this dialogue, the responsibility for what followed was assumed by 'Amr Ibn Al-'Aas alone.

So, Abu Muusaa was exonerated from guilt by referring the

matter back to the nation to give their word and choose their caliph. 'Amr agreed and adhered to this view. It did not come to his mind that 'Amr was going to threaten Islam and the Muslims with an evil disaster, and that he would resort to maneuvers whatever may be his conviction about Mu'aawiyah. Ibn 'Abbaas warned him when he returned to them and informed them about the maneuvers of 'Amr and said to him, "By Allah I fear that 'Amr will trick you, so if the two of you agree on something, let him come forward before you to speak. Then you speak after him."

However, Abu Muusaa saw the situation on a more lofty and sublime level than the maneuvers of 'Amr. From then on, he had no doubt or suspicion of the commitment of 'Amr with regards to what they had agreed on. They gathered the following day, Abu Muusaa representing the side of Imam 'Aliy and 'Amr Ibn Al-'Aas representing the side of Mu'aawiyah. Abu Muusaa invited 'Amr to speak first, but 'Amr refused and said to him, "I am not going to precede you when you are more virtuous than I, and emigrated before me, and are older than me."

Abu Muusaa advanced first and greeted the waiting crowd from both parties and said, "O' people, indeed, in this matter concerning which Allah has gathered together this nation and to put its affair in proper order, we do not see anything better than the deposition of the two men, "Aliy and Mu'aawiyah and to call for consultation among the people to choose for themselves whom they like. Therefore, I depose 'Aliy and Mu'aawiyah. So take upon yourselves as guardians whom you love."

Now, the turn of 'Amr Ibn Al-'Aas came to announce the deposition of Mu'aawiyah, just as Abu Muusaa had deposed 'Aliy in fulfillment of the confirmed, established agreement of the previous day.

'Amr ascended the pulpit and said, "O' people, indeed, Abu Muusaa has said what you heard and deposed his companion Indeed, I depose his companion just as he deposed him and confirm my companion Mu'aawiyah. He is indeed, the guardian of the Commander of the Faithful 'Uthmaan and the guardian of his blood and the one having the most right to his dignified position."

Abu Muusaa did not conceive as possible this sudden happening, and he reprimanded 'Amr severely with angry and furious words.

He returned again to his seclusion and made his way swiftly to Makkah, in the vicinity of the House of Allah and spent there the remainder of his days.

Abu Muusaa (May Allah be pleased with him) had a position of trust and love with the Messenger and a position of trust with his Companions and successors. In his life the Prophet gave him, along with Mu'aadh lbn Jabal, the govemorship over Yemen. After the death of the Messenger, he returned to Al-Madiinah to carry his responsibility in the great holy war, which the Muslim armies engaged in against Persia and Rome.

In the period of "Umar the Commander of the Faithful, Abu Muusaa was governor of Basra, and Caliph "Uthmaan put him in charge of Kufa. He was one of the people of the Qur'aan, those who memorized it, understood it, and acted on it. Some of his radiant words about the Qur'aan were " Follow the Qur'aan and do not desire that the Qur'aan should follow you."He was of the people of persistent worshi, and on the very days which almost caused the breath of people to pass away, he would yearn to fast and say, "Perhaps the thirst of the midday heat will be intercession for us on the Day of Judgment."

On that humid day, his appointed time of death came to him and covered his countenance with a radiance which is for those who hope for the mercy of Allah and a good reward. And the words, which he was always repeating during his faithful life, his tongue went on repeating while he was in the departing moments of death: "O' Allah, You are peace and from You is peace."

(58)
AT-TUFAIL IBN 'AMR AD-DAWSIY
The Rightly Guided Nature

In the land of Daws, he grew up in a noble, respected family. He was gifted with poetry, and his fame and excellence spread among the tribes. During the season of 'Ukaadh, when Arab poets came from all directions and the people gathered and assembled to show off their poetry, At-Tufail used to take his place in the forefront.

He used to frequent Makkah at times other than "Ukaadh. Once he visited Makkah when the Messenger had just started declaring his mission and the Quraish feared that At-Tufail would meet him and convert to Islam and then put his poetic gift at the service of Islam. That would be a curse upon the Quraish and their idols. On account of this, they circled around him and prepared for him a hospitality that included every kind of joy, comfort, and ease. Then they went on to warn him about meeting the Messenger of Allah. They said to him, "He has charming speech like magic and he makes division between a man and his son, and a man and his brother, and a man and his wife. I fear for you and your people from him. So do not talk to him nor listen to any talk from him."

Let us listen to At-Tufail himself telling the remainder of the story: So by Allah, they were still insisting on my not listening to anything from him and not meeting him. And when I went over to the Ka'bah, I filled my ears with cotton so as not to hear anything he had to say when he spoke. There I found him standing praying at the Ka'bah, so I stood close to him. Allah refused nothing but He made me hear some portion of what he was reading. I heard a fine speech, and I said to myself, "Oh, may I lose my mother! Indeed I am an intelligent poet. I would not fail to recognize the good from the ugly. What is it that hinders me from listening to the man and what he says? If that which he brings is good, I should accept it, and if it is bad . . ."

I stayed until Muhammad departed to his house. I followed him until he entered his house, so I entered behind him and said to him, "O' Muhammad, verily your people have told me such-and-such about you. By Allah, they kept making me afraid of you until I blocked my ears with cotton in order not to hear your words. But Allah willed that I hear, so I heard a fine speech. Set forth to me your message."

So the Messenger presented to me Islam and recited to me from the Qur'aan. By Allah, I had never heard a speech better than it, nor a matter more just than it. So, I surrendered and bore witness to the truth.

I said, "O'Messenger of Allah, indeed I am a person of credibility among my people and I am returning to them to invite them to Islam, so call on Allah to make a sign for me that will be a help for me in that which I call them to." He said, "O' Allah, make for him a sign. "Allah has spoken appreciatively in His book < *Those who listen to the speech and follow the best part of it* > *(39:18).*

We have met one of those great people and he is, indeed, a true picture of the image of the rightly guided nature. No sooner had he heard it, than he accepted the message of some of the blessed guiding verses which Allah had revealed to the heart of His Messenger until all his hearing was opened and all his heart, until he stretched out his right hand to swear the oath of allegiance. Not only that, but he immediately took upon himself the responsibility of inviting his people and kin to this religion of truth and the straight path.

For this reason, as soon as he reached his country and house in the land of Daws, he confronted his father about that which was in his heart concerning the principles of faith and perseverance. He called his father to Islam after speaking to him about the Messenger who calls to Allah. He spoke to him about his greatness, about his purity and honesty, and his father became a Muslim immediately. Then he went to his mother, and she became a Muslim. Then to his wife, and she became a Muslim. When he was sure that Islam had swept over his household, he moved on to his tribe and to all the inhabitants of Daws. However, no one from among them accepted Islam except Abu Hurairah (May Allah be pleased with him).

They went on disappointing him and turning away from him until he ran out of patience with them, so he rode his beast, cutting through the desert, returning to the Messenger of Allah to complain to him and to take more and more of his teachings. When he arrived in Makkah, he hastened to the house of the Messenger, driven by his yearning to see him. He said to the Prophet (PBUH), "O' Messenger of Allah, indeed adultery and usury have beaten me in our fight over Daws. So, call on Allah to destroy Daws." Suddenly, At-Tufail was baffled when he saw the Messenger (PBUH) raise his hands to the sky while saying, "O' Allah, guide Daws and bring them to Islam as Muslims." Then he turned to At-Tufail and said to him, "Return to your people, call them and be lenient with them."

This scene filled the soul of At-Tufail with awe and filled his spirit with peace. He thanked Allah with the deepest praise for making this human merciful Messenger his teacher and instructor, and for making Islam his religion and his joy. He returned to his land and people, and there he went on calling to

Islam gradually and leniently, just as the Messenger had advised him.

During the period he spent among his people, the Messenger emigrated to Al-Madiinah and the battles of Badr, "Uhud and Khandaq took place. While the Messenger of Allah was in Khaibar, after Allah had given the Muslims victory over it, a full procession including 80 families from Daws approached the Messenger saying, "There is no god but Allah and Allah is the Greatest." They sat before him giving the oath of allegiance one after the other.

When this lavish spectacle of theirs and their blessed oath was over, At-Tufail lbn 'Amr sat alone by himself reiterating his memories and contemplating his steps along the way. He remembered the day he came to the Messenger asking him to raise his hands to the sky saying, "O' Allah, destroy Daws." Yet, the Prophet supplicated and humbly prayed to Allah on that day with another prayer, which aroused his amazement. "O' Allah, guide Daws and bring them to Islam as Muslims." And Allah had guided Daws and brought them as Muslims. And here they were, 80 families of them, consisting of the majority of its inhabitants, taking their place in the pure ranks behind the trustworthy Messenger of Allah.

At-Tufail continued his work with the believing community, and on the day of the Conquest of Makkah, he entered it with tens of thousands of Muslims. They never withdrew in pride and strength but with their foreheads bowed in adoration, glorifying and thanking Allah, Who rewarded them with victory and a clear help.

At-Tufail saw the Messenger of Allah destroying the idols of the Ka'bah and purifying it with his own hands from the impurity which had lingered for so long. Immediately afterwards, he remembered an idol belonging to 'Amr Ibn Humamah. Whenever he stayed over as his guest, he used to show it to him, so he became fearful in its presence and pleaded to it. Now the opportunity had come for At-Tufail to erase the sin of those days from his soul. He approached the Messenger, requesting permission to go burn the idol of Humamah called "The Two Palms", and the Prophet (PBUH) gave him permission.

At-Tufail went over and lit the fire on it and every time the flame went down, he stoked it again to a blazing fire. All the while he said,

O Idol of Two Palms,
I am not one of your worshipers.
Our origin is older than your origin.
I have filled fire in your heart.

Thus did At-Tufail live with the Prophet (PBUH), praying behind him, learning from him, and fighting with him. The Prophet (PBUH) was transported to the most exalted horizon. However, At-Tufail saw that his responsibility as a Muslim, did not end with the death of the Messenger, but rather it was about to start. Therefore, no sooner had the apostasy wars erupted than At-Tufail prepared for them and embarked courageously on their hardships and terrors with a yearning for martyrdom. He participated in the apostasy wars, battle after battle.

In the Battle of Al-Yamaamah, he went out with the Muslims accompanied by his son "Amr Ibn At-Tufail. At the beginning of the battle he advised his son to fight the army of Musailamah the Liar, like one who desires death and martyrdom.

He told him that he felt he would die in this battle, and thus his sword carried him. He plunged into the fight in a glorious performance. He did not defend his life with his sword but he defended his sword with his life. So, when he died his body fell down, but the sword remained sharp and intact so that another hand whose owner had not yet fallen could strike with it.

In the battle, At-Tufạil Ad-Dawsiy was martyred. His body fell down under the flurry of stabs and strikes while he was waving to his son, who was unable to see him, amidst the crowd. He was waving to him as if he were calling him to follow and join him. And he did actually follow him, but after a while. In the Battle of Yarmuuk in Syria, "Amr lbn At-Tufail went out to fight and died as a martyr. At the time his spirit was coming out of his breast, he extended his right hand and opened his palm as if he would shake the hand of someone else. And who knows? Perhaps at that time he was shaking the spirit of his father.

(59)
'AMR IBN AL -`AAS
Liberator of Egypt from Rome !

There were three from the Quraish who used to trouble the Messenger of Allah (PBUH) with the fierceness of their resistance to his call and their torture of his Companions.

The Messenger called them and pleaded to his glorious Lord to inflict them with His punishment, and while he was calling and inviting, he received the revelation of these noble verses: < *The matter is not in your hands, whether GOD turns to them or chastises them, for surely they are evildoers* > *(3: 128).*

The Messenger's understanding of the verse was that he was to stop calling Allah to punish them and to leave their affair to Allah alone. Either they would continue their wrongdoing and His punishment would be inflicted upon them, or He would accept their repentance.

They repented, so His mercy reached them. 'Amr Ibn Al-'Aas was one of these three. Allah had chosen for them the path of repentance and mercy, so He guided them to Islam. He transformed 'Amr Ibn Al-'Aas into a Muslim fighter and into one of the brave leaders of Islam.

In spite of some of 'Amr's positions, his point of view of which we cannot be convinced of, he played a role as a glorious Companion. He sacrificed and gave generously; he was a defender and combatant, and our eyes and our hearts shall continue to open on his countenance, especially here in Egypt. Those who see in Islam, a glorious valuable religion and see in its Messenger, a merciful gift and a blessed gift. Those who see the truthful Messenger who called to Allah according to clear vision and inspired life abundantly with its sensible conduct, forthrightness and devout piety. Those who carry this faith shall continue with enhanced allegiance to look to the man whom fate made the cause—for whatever reason—for the introduction of Islam to Egypt and the guidance of Egypt to Islam. So, blessed is the gift and blessed is the gift giver.That is he, 'Amr lbn Al-'Aas. The historians were accustomed to describing 'Amr as the conqueror of Egypt. However, I see in this description, an underestimation and an overestimation. Perhaps a more truthful description of 'Amr would be that which we call him, "Liberator of Egypt". For Islam did not conquer the country with the modern understanding of conquering, but it liberated it from the hegemony of two imperial powers, two modes of worship of two countries, and the worst punishment, the imperial power of Persia and the imperial power of Rome.

Egypt, in particular, on the day the advanced guard of Islam appeared, had been plundered by the Romans, and its inhabitants were resisting without result. When the shouts of believing armies reverberated over the frontiers of their country, "Allah Akbaar! (Allah is the Greatest)" they hastened all together, in a glorious crowd, toward the coming dawn and embraced it, finding in it liberation from Caesar and from Rome.

So, 'Amr and his men did not conquer Egypt but opened the way for Egypt to attach its destiny to the truth, tie its fate to justice, and find itself and its reality in the light of the words of Allah and the principles of Islam. He was careful to separate the inhabitants of Egypt and its Copts away from the army and keep the fighting restricted between himself and the Romans who occupied the land and robbed the wealth of its people.

On account of that, we find him talking to the Christian leaders of that day and their high priest. He said to them, "Indeed Allah sent Muhammad with the truth and ordered him to teach it. The Prophet carried out his mission, and he died after leaving us on that path, the clear straight path. Among the things he ordered us to do was to be responsible to the people, so we call you to Islam. Whoever responds, is of us. He has what we have and he has the same rights and obligations as we do. And whoever does not respond to Islam, we enforce on him the payment of jizyah and we offer to him defense and protection. Our Prophet informed us, that Egypt would open for us and advised us to be good to its people, saying, 'Egypt will be opened to you after me, so you are advised to treat its Copts well, for indeed, they have a covenant of protection and kinship relations,' so if you answer to what we call you to, you will have protection and security."

No sooner had 'Amr finished his words, than some of the priests and rabbis shouted, saying, "Indeed the kinship of which your Prophet advised you is a remote kinship relationship, the like of which cannot be reached except by the prophets." This was a good start for the hoped-for understanding between 'Amr and the Copts of Egypt, in spite of what the Roman leader had tried to do to frustrate it.

'Amr Ibn As-'Aas was not among the earliest ones to embrace Islam. He embraced Islam with Khaalid Ibn Al-Waliid, just shortly before the Conquest of Makkah. It is surprising that his Islam began at the hands of An-Najaashiy in Abyssinia, and that is because An-Najaashiy knew 'Amr and respected him because of his several visits to Abyssinia and abundant gifts which he used to carry to An-Najaashiy. In his final visit to that country, mention was made of the Prophet who was calling to monotheism and to the nobility of morals in the Arabian Peninsula. The Abyssinian ruler asked 'Amr, "How could you not believe in him and follow him, when he is truly a Messenger from Allah?" 'Amr then asked An-Najaashiy, "Is he thus?" An Najaashiy answered, "Yes, so obey me, O' 'Amr, and follow him, for indeed by Allah, he is on the path of truth and he will surpass those who stood against him!"

'Amr traveled, taking the sea route, immediately returning to his country and turning his face in the direction of Al-Madiinah to surrender to Allah, Lord of the Worlds.

On the road leading to Al-Madiinah, he met Khaalid Ibn Al-Waliid coming from Makkah, going also to the Messenger to swear allegiance to Islam. No sooner did the Messenger see the two of them coming than his face beamed with joy and he said to his Companions, "Makkah has gifted you with its most noble leaders." Khaliid approached and swore allegiance. Then 'Amr approached and said, "Indeed, I swear allegiance to you provided that you ask Allah to forgive me my previous sins." So the Messenger answered him saying, "O' 'Amr, swear allegiance, for indeed Islam disregards whatever preceded it."

'Amr swore allegiance and placed his wits and bravery at the service of his new religion. When the Messenger passed on to Allah, Most Exalted, 'Amr was appointed ruler over Oman and during the caliphate of 'Umar he performed his famous deeds in the Syrian wars and then in the liberation of Egypt from the rule of Rome.

Oh, if only 'Amr Ibn Al-'Aas could have resisted the love of commanding and rule in his soul, then he would have greatly overcome some of the positions which this love entangled him in. Yet, 'Amr's love for the authority of ruling, to a certain extent, was a direct expression of his nature, which was filled with talent. Moreover, his external appearance, his way of walking and conversing, indicated that he was created for commanding, to the extent, that it has been related that the Commander of the Faithful 'Umar Ibn Al-Khattaab saw 'Amr once approaching, so he smiled at the way he was walking and said, "It should not be for Abu 'Abd Allah to walk on the earth except as a commander."

The truth also is that Abu 'Abd Allah did not forget the right. Even when dangerous events overwhelmed the Muslims, 'Amr dealt with these events in a commanding manner, as one who possesses intelligence, wits, and a capability which made him self-confident and proud of his excellence. Moreover, he possessed such a portion of honesty that it made 'Umar Ibn Al-Khattaab—even though he was strict in choosing his governor—choose 'Amr as governor over Palestine and Jordan, then over Egypt, throughout the life of 'Umar. This, even though, the Commander of the Faithful knew that 'Amr had exceeded a certain limit in the opulence of his life style, while the Commander of the Faithful demanded from his governors to set an example by staying always at the level or at least close to the general level of the people.

Even though the caliph knew about the abundance of 'Amr's wealth, he did not remove him but sent Muhammad Ibn Maslamah to him and ordered 'Amr to split with him, all of his wealth and possessions. So, he left him one half of it and carried the other half to the treasury in Al-Madiinah. However, if the Commander of the Faithful had known that 'Amr's love for wealth would lead him to carelessness in his responsibility, it is conceivable that his reasonable conscience would not have allowed him to stay in power for even one moment.

'Amr (May Allah be pleased with him) was sharp-witted with strong intuitive understanding and deep vision, so much so that whenever the Commander of the Faithful saw a person incapable of artifice, he clapped his palms in astonishment and said, "Glory be to Allah! Indeed, the Creator of this and the Creator of 'Amr Ibn Al-Aas is one God!"

'Amr was also very daring and unhesitant. He used to combine his daring with his wits in some instances so that he would be thought to be cowardly or hesitant. However, it was the capacity to trick which 'Amr perfected with great skill to get himself out of a destructive crisis.

The Commander of the Faithful 'Umar knew these talents of his and appreciated their true value. For that reason, when he sent him to Syria, before his going to Egypt, it was said to the Commander of the Faithful, "At the head of the armies of Rome in Syria is Artubun, a shrewd and brave leader and a prince." 'Umar's response was, "We have buried at Artubun of Rome, Artubun of the Arabs, so let us see how the matter unfolds."Matters unfolded in a massive victory for the Artubun of the Arabs, their dangerous, sly old fox, 'Amr Ibn Al-'Aas, over the Artubun of Rome, who left his army to defeat and fled to Egypt. 'Amr would catch him shortly thereafter to raise the standard of Islam above its secure lands.

What are the situations in which the intelligence and wits of 'Amr excelled? We do not count among them his position with Abu Muusaa Al-Ash'ariy in the incident of arbitration when the two of them agreed to depose 'Aliy and Mu'aawiyah to refer the matter back to consultation between the Muslims. Abu Muusaa implemented the agreement and 'Amr relented from carrying out his part of the agreement.

If we want to witness a picture of his wits and the skill of his intuitive insight, we find it in his position with respect to the commander of the Citadel of Babylon (near present day Cairo) during his war with Rome in Egypt, and, in another historical narration, in the battle we shall mention which took place in Yarmuuk with Artubun of Rome.

When Artubun and the commander invited 'Amr to talk, they gave an order to some of their men to throw a rock at him immediately upon his departure from the Citadel and to prepare everything so that the killing of 'Amr would be an inevitable matter.

'Amr met the commander, not suspecting anything from him, and their meeting ended. While 'Amr was on his way out of the Citadel, he glimpsed over the walls something suspicious that aroused in him a strong sense of danger, and immediately he behaved in an outstanding manner. He returned back to the commander of the Citadel, in safe, secure, slow steps, with confident, happy feelings, as if nothing had scared him at all or had aroused his suspicion. He met the commander and said to him, "An idea came across my mind I wanted you to know. I have with me, where my companions are camped, a group from among the first Companions of the Messenger to enter into Islam. The Commander of the Faithful would not decide anything without consulting them and would not send an army unless he put them at the head of its fighters and soldiers. I will bring them to you so that they hear from you that which I heard, so they will become as clear in the matter as I am."

The Roman commander realized that 'Amr, by his naivete, had granted him the opportunity of a lifetime. Therefore, he thought. Let us agree with him, and when he returns with this number of Muslim commanders and the best of their men and their leaders, we will deliver the coup de grace and finish off all of them at once, instead of finishing off 'Amr alone.

Secretly he gave his order to put off the plan that was devised to assassinate 'Amr, and he saw 'Amr off cordially and shook his hand with enthusiasm and fervor. 'Amr smiled the most intelligent of Arab smiles as he was leaving the Citadel:

In the morning "Amr returned to the Citadel at the head of an army, mounted on his horse that whinnied in a loud burst of laughter, behaving proudly and haughtily and making fun. Yes, for it, too, knew a lot of things about the shrewdness of its owner.

In A.H. 43, death caught up with 'Amr Ibn Al-'Aas in Egypt, where he was ruling. He recaptured his life in the moments of departure, saying, "In the first part of my life I was a disbeliever, and I was one of the fiercest people against the Messenger of Allah, so if I had died on that day, the fire would have been my fate. Then, I swore allegiance to the Messenger of Allah, and there was no person dearer to me than he was and more glorious in my eyes than he. If I wanted to describe him, I could not, because I was not able to fill my eyes with him on account of being in awe of him. If I had died back then, I would have wished to be of the inhabitants of Paradise. Then after that I was tested with command and with material things. I do not know if they were for me or against me."

Then he raised his sight to the sky in awe, calling upon his Lord, the Merciful, the Magnificent, saying, "O'Allah, I am not innocent, so forgive me. I am not mighty, so help me. And if Your mercy does not come to me, I will surely be of those destroyed."

And he continued in his yearning and his prayers until his spirit ascended to Allah and his last words were, "There is no god but Allah."

Under the ground of Egypt, which 'Amr acquainted with the

path of Islam, where his corpse was finally placed, and above its hard earth, his seat is still standing throughout the centuries. Here, he used to teach, judge, and rule, beneath the ceiling of his ancient mosque, the Mosque of 'Amr, the first mosque in Egypt, in which the name of Allah, the One and Only is mentioned and declared between its walls and from its pulpit, the words of Allah and the principles of Islam.

(60)
SAALIM MAWLAA ABI HUDHAIFAH
Blessed Be the Carrier of the Qur'aan

The Messenger of Allah(PBUH) advised his Companions one day, "Take the Qur'aan from four people: 'Abd Allah lbn Mas'uud, Saalim Mawlaa Abi Hudhaifah, Ubai lbn Ka'b and Mu'aadh lbn Jabal."

We have met before with lbn Mas'uud and Ubai and Mu'aadh. So, who was this fourth Companion whom the Messenger made as an authority for the teaching of the Qur'aan and a source of reference?

Verily, he was Saalim Mawlaa Abi Hudhaifah. He was a kind servant. Islam was exalted on account of him until it made him a son of one of the great Muslims who, before his Islam, was honored to be one of the most noble of the Quraish and one of their leaders. When Islam cancelled the practice of adoption, he became a brother, a friend, a protector of those whom he had adopted. Such was the glorious Companion, Abu Hudhaifah lbn 'Utbah. By the grace of Allah and His favor upon Saalim, he reached an elevated lofty position, which his spiritual virtues, along with his behavior and his piety, had prepared him for.

Saalim Mawlaa Abi Hudhaifah was known by that name because he had been a slave and emancipated. He believed in Allah and His Messenger early, and took his place among the first generation. Abu Hudhaifah lbn 'Utbah became Muslim at an early age and hastened to Islam, leaving his father, 'Utbah lbn Rabiiah, swallowing his anger and his concerns which disturbed the purity of his life, due to the Islam of his son, who was noble among his people. His father had been preparing him for leadership among the Quraish.

Abu Hudhaifah adopted Saalim and emancipated him, and he became known as Saalim lbn Abi Hudhaifah. Both of them continuously worshiped their Lord in awe and fear and were extremely patient under the hardship of the Quraish and their schemes.

One day, verses of the Qur'aan were revealed which outlawed the practice of adoption and every adopted person returned to carrying the name of his real father who had begotten him. So, Zaid lbn Haarithah, for example, whom the Prophet had adopted and who had been known among the Muslims as Zaid lbn Muhammad, returned to carrying the name of his father, Haarithah and became Zaid lbn Haarithah. But Saalim's father was not known to him, so Abu Hudhaifah became his guardian and he was called Saalim Mawlaa Abi Hudhaifah.

Perhaps when it cancelled the practice of adoption Islam wanted to say to the Muslims, Do not take kinship nor relationship, nor the bond by which you affirm your brotherhood as greater and stronger than Islam itself and the religious faith by which you are really made brothers. The early Muslims understood this very well. So, nothing was more loved to any one of them after Allah and His Messenger than their brethren in faith and in Islam.

We have seen how the Ansaar welcomed their brethren, the Muhaajiruun. They shared with them their wealth, their homes, and all they owned. This is what we saw happening between Abu Hudhaifah, the noble of the Quraish, and Saalim, who was an emancipated slave and did not know his father.

They remained more than brothers up to the last moment of

their lives, even until death: they died together, spirit with spirit and body close to body. This is the unique, incomparable greatness of Islam, but this is only one of its greatness and its superiority.

Saalim believed with a sincere faith and took his path to Allah by adopting the behavior of the devout and pious. Neither his genealogy nor his position in society had any consideration for him. He was elevated by his piety and sincerity to the highest degree of the new society, which Islam came to establish and caused to rise on a new, great and just foundation-a foundation summarized in the following glorious verse < *Surely, the most honourable of you in the sight of GOD is the most pious of you* > *(49:13)* and in the noble hadiiths: "Arabs have no superiority over non-Arabs except in piety" and "The son of a white woman has no superiority over the son of a black woman except in piety."

In this new, rightly-guided society, Abu Hudhaifah, who was only a slave yesterday, found for himself honor to be in charge, to have power and to govern. Moreover, he found honor for his family, to marry Saalim to his niece Faatimah Bint Al-Waliid lbn 'Utbah. And in this new, rightly-guided society, which destroyed the unjust class structure and outlawed false distinctions and privileges, Saalim found himself always in the first rank on account of his truthfulness, faith, and bravery.

Yes, he became an Imam for the Muhaajiruun of Makkah to Al-Madiinah during their prayer in the Qubaa' Mosque. There is proof in the Book of Allah, when the Prophet ordered the Muslims to learn from him. There were with him men of goodness and excellence, which made the Messenger say to him, "Praise be to Allah, Who made in my nation the like of you." His Muslim brothers called him Saalim from among the Righteous."

Indeed, the story of Saalim is like the story of Bilaal and the story of many tens of slaves and the poor from whom Islam shook off the factors of servitude and weakness and made them Imams and commanders in a society of guidance, reason, integrity of conduct, and frankness.

Saalim was a receiver of all the rightly guided virtues of Islam. These virtues accumulated in him and around him, and his truthful, deep faith arranged them in proper order in the most beautiful disposition. Among his most prominent virtues was his overt, public frankness about what he perceived as the truth. Indeed, he did not keep silent when he perceived something, which he felt it was his duty to speak about. He did not betray life by maintaining silence when mistakes were made.

After Makkah was liberated by the Muslims, the Messenger of Allạh (PBUH) sent some detachments to villages and tribes around Makkah to inform them that whenever he sent someone to them, they were coming only as callers to the Faith, so not to harm them or kill them.

At the head of one of these companies was Khaalid lbn Al-Waliid. When Khaalid reached his destination, some incident led him to use the sword and shed blood. When the Prophet (PBUH) heard the news of these events, he apologized to his Lord a long time saying, "O' Allah, indeed I absolve myself from all that Khaalid has done."

The Commander of the Faithful 'Umar ever remained to recollect and assess him saying, "In the sword of Khaalid, indeed, is a heavy burden."

Saalim Mawlaa Abi Hudhaifah accompanied Khaalid on this expedition, along with other Companions. As soon as Saalim saw the actions of Khaalid, he confronted him with a sharp objection and went on enumerating to him the mistakes he had committed. Khaalid, the leader, the great hero in both jaahiliyah and Islam, listened the first time, defended himself the second time, and became more forceful in speech the third time while Saalim, holding on to his point of view, spoke without fear or evasion or circumvention in speech. Saalim at that time did not look at Khaalid as a nobleman from among the nobles of Makkah, while he was one who only yesterday was a slave. No, Islam had created equality between them. He did not look at him as a leader, venerating his errors, but as a partner in duty and responsibility. Moreover, his opposition to Khaalid did not originate from a selfish purpose or interest; it was advice, consecrated by Islam, which was his right. What he heard all the time from his Prophet was a foundation and essence of the entire religion when he said, "Religion is sincere advice. Religion is sincere advice. Religion is sincere advice."

When the action of Khaalid reached the Messenger (PBUH), he asked, "Did anyone stand up to him?" He did not delay to question, and he was not alarmed. His anger was pacified when they said to him, "Yes, Saalim critically examined him and opposed him."

Saalim lived with his Messenger (PBUH) and the believers. He did not stay behind from any battle, nor refrain from performing any worship, and his brotherliness with Abu Hudhaifah increased daily with mutual self-sacrifice and solidarity.

The Messsenger (PBUH) passed away to the Most Exalted Guardian and the caliphate of Abu Bakr was confronted with the conspiracies of the apostates. Then the Day of Al-Yamaamah came and it was a terrible war. Islam had not gone through anything like it. The Muslims went out to fight and Saalim and his brother Abu Hudhaifah went out to fight in the cause of Allah. At the start of the battle, the Muslims did not withstand the attack. However, each believer there felt that the battle was his own and the responsibility was his own. Khaalid Ibn Al-Waliid gathered them together again and reorganized the army with astonishing skill and genius.

The brothers Abu Hudhaifah and Saalim embraced and pledged martyrdom in the cause of the religion of truth, which gave them the happiness of this world and the next. They threw themselves into the vast, terrible sea of battle. Abu Hudhaifah was calling, "O' people of the Qur'aan, decorate the Qur'aan with your actions," and his sword was like a violent hurricane in the army of Musailamah the Liar. And Saalim was shouting, "What a bad carrier of the Qur'aan I would be if the Muslims were attacked through me." Drive into a trap, O' Saalim, but yes, you are our best carrier of the Qur'aan.

And Saalim's sword was forceful on the necks of the apostates who embarked upon celebrating the jaahiliyah of the Quraish and extinguishing the light of Islam. The swords of apostasy fell upon his right hand and cut it off, while he was carrying with it the standard of the Muhaajiruun after its bearer, Zaid Ibn Al-Khattaab, had fallen. When his right hand was cut off, he picked up the standard with his left and kept on waving it high while shouting the following noble Qur'aanic verses: < *And how many of the Prophets have fought, and with them large troops of godly people? But they never lost heart when adversity befell them in GOD'S cause, nor did they weaken, nor did they fail. And GOD loves those who show fortitude*> *(3:146)*

Is not that the most magnificent slogan? That is the one he chose on the day of death.

A group of apostates circled around him, so the hero fell, but his spirit kept on repeating in his purified body, until the battle ended with the killing of Musailamah the Liar, the defeat of his army, and the triumph of the Muslim army.

When the Muslims were examining their sacrificed and martyrs, they found Saalim in the last agony of death. He asked them, "What has Abu Hudhaifah done?" They said, "He died a martyr." He said, "Lay me next to him." They said, "He is next to you, O' Saalim." He had died a martyr in the same place.

He smiled his last smile and did not speak again. He and his companion had realized what they desired. Together they had become Muslims. Together they had lived and together they had died as martyrs.

Oh, the magnificence of fortune and beauty of destiny! And he went to Allah, that great believer about whom 'Umar lbn Al-Khattaab said while he was dying, "If Saalim were alive, I would have given him the command after me."

FAREWELL

Now, while we bid farewell to the graceful company of the Companions of Muhammad, the Messenger of Allah (May peace and blessings be upon him and upon them all), we may ask ourselves, have we given the matter what it deserves? Have we taken into account all such great men?

The answer is. No. We have been honored by their greatness through a close examination and have followed a blessed number of them during some bright moments, but we were not fortunate to accompany all of them.

Indeed, the sixty men introduced in this book, stand for many thousands of others of their glorious brethren who saw the Messenger (PBUH), lived during his time, believed in him, and struggled with him. In the lives of these sixty righteous men we perceive the images of all the Companions. We see their faith, their steadfastness, their heroism, their sacrifices, and the loyalty. We see the effort they exerted and the victory they achieved. We also see the role they played in liberating all humanity from the paganism of conscience and the loss of destiny!

These sixty men, then, are a superb and magnificent example the significance of which we welcome and contemplate. We see in this example, the heroes and soldiers of the greatest epoch of human struggle in general and of religious struggle in particular. It was an epoch when the ancient world was destroyed by the new force of truth, which came to announce the oneness of Allah and the unity of creation. There were no idols or images in the new era, no worshiped emperors or czars. There is only One God, Who is Allah, while all people are as equal as the teeth of a comb.

I desire not to repeat what I have already written about the causes that induced that amazing faith which filled the hearts of these men.

Muhammad (PBUH) with his truth, steadfastness, purity, and eminence could not but reflect faith of a rare quality on the people around him. It was the faith of people who had known him well and had seen him in all his perfection and grace, saw his humanity and his devotion to Allah, saw his loftiness and modesty, saw all his superb qualities and his simplicity, saw him in his strength and his compassion.

They saw him and perceived the nobility of his motives and his undeviating and straight method. Therefore, doubt did not prevent them at all from believing in him. They did not even make use of their right to ask him for a miracle to ascertain his prophethood and his mission.

Every nation has asked its prophet for a miracle in order to believe in him, except Muhammad's Companions, the men round the Messenger. They never said, "Show us a miracle as proof of your truthfulness." This was because Muhammad himself was the miracle! Seeking another miracle outside of him, his personality, and his principles would have been a kind of naivete such intelligent people could not be involved in, especially after their hearts had been filled with the guidance of Allah and their perceptions had been illuminated with His light.

Indeed, the faith of that first generation of Muslims bestowed upon the whole of humanity — with its different religions, different ages and races—a great trust that revived its youth and its determination. After all, they were human beings. They lived during certain circumstances. They appeared unable to do what they actually did afterwards. Collectively they had not yet achieved all the necessary characteristics to form a society. They were scattered, discordant, fighting tribes led by inflexible narrow-minded individuality. As a political power, they had not achieved anything that could be mentioned. As an economic power, they were the poorest of people. In number, they were less than other peoples.

What happened, then, to make these minorities the constructors of a new world, having wonderful features? Was it due to the power of weapons and the plenitude of armies? But Alexander before them and Genghis Khan after them had plenty of weapons and a great number of soldiers. Where is Alexander today? Where is Genghis Khan? What is left of them and their waves of armies or their astounding victories? What is left of all that, in the conscience of life and the conscience of mankind? Nothing.

Therefore, materialistic power in all its aspects was not the reason that turned the Companions of the Messenger (PBUH) into what we have seen. It was but faith: faith in truth and in what is good. Above that, faith in the Lord of truth and good. This is the true lesson, which was given and is still being given to all man-kind by Muhammad, the Messenger of Allah, (May Allah be pleased with him and his Companions).

When people devote their lives to the cause of truth and benefaction, surely darkness turns into light, chaos turns into order, weakness turns into strength, property becomes protected, humiliation becomes greatness, ignorance becomes knowledge, privation becomes plenitude, and all thorns become flowers. That was what the Messenger (PBUH) and his Companions did, and that was what all the messengers and their companions of believers had done before. And it is the lesson they left us to learn from.

Since truthfulness and benefaction were the quintessence of

the role of the Messenger (PBUH) and his Companions, and since true, pure, and brave faith was their means and principle, we saw them bequeathing the best heritage to humanity. They filled the human conscience with vigor, illumination, and integrity of behavior.

Today, most of the radios of the world openly broadcast verses from the Glorious Qur'aan which was to the Messenger (PBUH) and his Companions, the guide and the light. Most of the radios of the world, even the states that have another religion and the states that have no religions, most of them start their program with verses from the Qur'aan in their broadcasts in Arabic. In all the spots of the earth, among Muslims and Christians, among Jews, Hindus, and Buddhists, and in the territories of states that have no religion, the lofty minarets are erected to repeat from their top the same words reverberated through the voice of the muezzin of the Messenger (PBUH) 1400 years ago!

Allah is the Greatest, Allah is the Greatest.
I bear witness that there is no god but Allah
I bear witness that Muhammad is the Messenger of Allah
Come to the Prayer.
Come to success

Every where on earth, the Qur'aan of that religion is recited, every where on earth the mosques are filled, and every where on earth its principles are announced.

What power has given Islam such eternity? It is the same power we witnessed before that gave this religion and its men a superb and extraordinary power to change the world and to change the people, values, and destinies in it. It is the power of faith in truth and benefaction. Above all, it is the belief in the Lord of truth and benefaction, in the Messenger, and in all other messengers who came before and devoted their lives to truth and benefaction, who gave everything and took nothing for themselves.

There remains one word to be said in this conclusion. It is a question that inevitably occurs to the mind after witnessing such illuminating scenes such as we beheld in these 60 men of the Messenger's Companions. The question is, "How could dispute and disagreement ruin the strong ties between the rightly guided brothers, and how could the civil war that broke out between 'Aliy's supporters and those of Mu'aawiyah — some incidents of which we have witnessed throughout this book — overcome their splendid brotherhood?"

In order to give an answer to this question, we have to go back to the virtue of faith in these Companions, and then to other historical factors as well. Indeed, their true, clear, and decisive faith had made them follow the same path. To them, truth had but one face, which they recognized and followed. It did not have multiple and assumed faces to let some waver among them according to their dispositions and interests. While the Messenger (PBUH) was living among them, guidance to what is true and right — a matter in which people differed — was an easy matter. Revelation or the Messenger, or both of them, usually clarified every obscure or unintelligible matter.

When the Messenger (PBUH) passed away, they never differed in what had been clarified and explained by Allah's revelation or through Muhammad's interpretation. However, when 'Uthmaan (May Allah be pleased with him) was killed, his murder had been preceded and accompanied with pernicious commotion which shook all Islamic nations at that time. As a consequence of that terrible occurrence, the dispute widened. It was inevitable for each of the Companions according to his attitude to choose one of the multiple views.

Their way of choosing, like their way of believing, was characterized by clarity and decisiveness. There was no hesitation or hypocrisy. Those who were convinced of Imam 'Aliy's point of view, chose his side, and those convinced that the two parties were wrong chose a third side in which they urged the two disputing parties to renounce their differences. When the die was cast, they chose to be neutral and abandoned the dispute.

The above concerns the Companions, the early believers in Islam who lived at the time of the Messenger (PBUH) and fought with him the forces of polytheism and darkness. However, these Companions did not represent by themselves the "center of gravity " in the Islamic state at the time of the dispute, between 'Aliy and Mu'aawiyah. This is because the state at that time had expanded tremendously, and a new power emerged and started to take part in the events and direct them. The best evidence for this is that the conspiracy to claim the life of Caliph 'Uthmaan and the agents assigned to carry it out came from outside Al-Madiinah, rather from outside the whole Arab Peninsula. They came from some distant Islamic countries.

This new power played a role, which the first Companions could not repel. The role was serious and effective in turning the dispute between 'Aliy and Mu'aawiyah into warfare. This reached the extent that the people of Syria siding with Mu'aawiyah and the people of Iraq siding with 'Aliy, became the real protagonists in that war. Even in the final analysis, the war was not between two Islamic camps as much as it was between two regional ones: the Syrians on one side and Iraqis on the other!

There was a third force which should not be ignored, an evil force which lay waiting for Islam since sovereignty was taken from its hand and leveled to the dust. That was the power represented in the remains of Persia and some few who continued to perpetuate their schemes against Islam through their many agents who infiltrated Islam, pretending to embrace it. Some of them were able to cause a lot of damage and destruction in the ranks of Muslims, which the two defeated empires could not do.

This is a rapid look at the circumstances of that critical situation which the Companions and Islam as a whole passed through. However, we should not ignore another fact, which is that each of the leaders of the two fighting camps did not think at all that the matter would develop to that terrible degree. Imam 'Aliy and his followers saw their advance towards Syria as merely a scare tactic and thought that Mu'aawiyah would soon awaken to realize the power of the state and would respect and obey it.

On the other hand, Mu'aawiyah and his followers believed that Imam 'Aliy was merely testing their strength and their readiness. If he found they were strong and well equipped, he would seek a reconciliation through another means. Yet, the matter developed in a strange and unusual way. This sudden and strange development discloses the hidden forces working in each camp to turn the dispute into warfare.

Let us now end our talk about this war with this incident. Az-Zubair (May Allah be pleased with him) was fighting in the ranks of Mu'aawiyah, but at the end of the battle he realized his mistake in joining the war, and so he withdrew. However, some fighters followed him and stabbed him to death while he was praying. The killer robbed Az-Zubair of his sword and ran to Imam 'Aliy, desiring to tell him the good news of the murder of Az-Zubair and to lay in his hands the sword he had used in fighting with Mu'aawiyah against 'Aliy. He came to the Imam's door asking for permission. When 'Aliy learned of the matter he shouted a command to dismiss the killer, saying, "Give the good tidings to the killer of Ibn Sufiyah that he will be cast in hell-fire." By Ibn Sufiyah, he meant Az-Zubair (May Allah be pleased with him). He ordered further to have Az-Zubair's sword taken from the killer and brought to him.

When 'Aliy saw the sword, he kept kissing it. He was crying and saying, "A sword whose owner had so many times removed the distress from the Messenger of Allah."

This remarkable and great scene bestows upon the above mentioned disagreement and its painful development much calmness and tranquility. It fills us with much understanding and appreciation when we remember it.

Now we bid farewell to those men with whom we lived a happy and blissful time on the pages of this book. We thank Allah for His blessings, hoping to have more blessing, compassion, and good health from Almighty Allah.

With awe and reverence, we say to our eminent teacher, the last of the Messengers, "May peace and the mercy of Allah and His blessings be upon you. May Allah grant you the best reward for the teachings you gave and for your guidance." And with a renewed, overflowing yearning, we say to his blessed Companions, "Righteous men, farewell!"

But, when were they really absent from our lives to bid them farewell? Let our greeting to them, be "Peace". Peace we extended at the beginning with awe and reverence, and peace is extended at the end with awe and reverence.

GLOSSARY

aadhaan the call to prayer, called from the minaret five times daily

Ansaar Helpers. The Muslims who were resident of Al-Madiinah and helped those who emigrated from Makkah

Al-Arqam the house of Al-Arqam which was used as a meeting place by to earliest Muslims in Makkah

Dhuhr the. noon prayer, one of the five daily prayers

Duha an optional prayer, one of the five daily prayers

Al-Faatihah the opening surah of the Qur'aan, recited in each raka'h of prayers

Fa jr the dawn prayer, one of the five daily prayers

Fatwah anglicized plural used in text) Islamic legal opinion based on the Qur'aan and hadiiths

Fiqh Islamic jurisprudence

fitnah sedition, disorder, trial, affliction, temptation

hadiith anglicized plural used here) a saying or action of the Prophet Muhammad (PBUH), the sum of them being the second basis of Islamic law after the Qur'aan

Hajj pilgrimage to Makkah

halaal lawful according to Islamic law

haraam unlawful according to Islamic law

Al-Hijrah emigration. The first two Hijrahs were those of the Companions to Abyssinia. The Hijrah from which the Islamic calendar begins was that of Muhammad (PBUH) and his Companions from Makkah to Al-Madiinah.

Al-Hijr a spot next to the Ka'bah

Ijtihaad Islamic legal opinion based on anaylsis and analogy

Imam leader; prayer leader

Jaahiliyah the Period of Ignorance, i.e. paganism, before the revelation of the Qur'aan

Jibriil the Angel Gabriel

Jihaad fighting or struggle in the cause of Allah

Jizyah a tax paid by non-Muslims living under a Muslim government

Ka`bah the cube-shaped in Makkah which Muslims circumambulate during the Hajj rituals. It was first built by Prophet lbraahiim (Abraham)

Khawaarij an early splinter group within Islam. Originally supporters of Imarn "Aliy, they broke away from him when he agreed to arbitration in his dispute with Mu'aawiyah

Muhaajiruun (sing-Muhaajir) Emigrants. The Muslims who emigrated from Makkah to AI-Madiinah

mujaahid one who fights or struggles in the cause of Allah

PBUH Peace be upon him

Quraish the ruling tribe of Makkah, to which the Prophet (PBUH) belonged

rak'ah (anglicized plural used in text) a unit of prayer consisting of a series of motions: standing, bowing, prostrating, sitting and prostrating again.

sunnah a practice of the Prophet Muhammad (PBUH) which is imitated by Muslims

surah/surat a chapter of the Qur'aan

urnmah nation; leader

"Umrah minor pilgrimage to Makkah

Printed in India